Wide Area Network Performance and Optimization

Data Communications and Networks Series

Consulting Editor: Dr C. Smythe, University of Sheffield

Selected titles in the Data Communications and Network Series

Wide Area Network Performance and Optimization:

Practical Strategies for Success

Robert Lloyd-Evans

ADDISON-WESLEY

Harlow, England • Reading, Massachusetts • Menlo Park, California
New York • Don Mills, Ontario • Amsterdam • Bonn • Sydney • Singapore
Tokyo • Madrid • San Juan • Milan • Mexico City • Seoul • Taipei

© Addison Wesley Longman Ltd 1996

Addison Wesley Longman
Edinburgh Gate
Harlow
Essex
CM20 2JE
England.

Cover designed by op den Brouw Design and Illustration, Reading
and printed by The Riverside Printing Co. (Reading) Ltd
Typeset by Meridian Colour Repro Limited, Pangbourne-on-Thames, Berkshire
Printed and bound by T.J. Press Ltd., Padstow, Cornwall.

First printed 1996

ISBN 0-201-42270-0

British Library Cataloguing-in-Publication Data
A catalogue record for this book is available from the British Library.

Library of Congress Cataloguing-in-Publication Data applied for

Preface

The intended readership for this work is network professionals who are responsible for the design, implementation and operation of real data communications networks, rather than for the academic community. As most such potential readers have little inclination nor need for mathematics, only a minimum is included here, and most of that is relegated to an appendix. The book assumes that these readers already have a moderate knowledge of data communications protocols, but need a better understanding of the performance-related aspects. As a result, it concentrates on issues such as timers, flow control and overheads for the various protocols with suggestions on how to optimize them. There is no magic formula for arriving at the best performance of a network; instead there is usually a trade-off between several different aspects of performance.

Organization

This book starts with introductory and relatively historical material in the first three chapters. Chapter 4 covers multiplexer networks, which have relatively limited options for performance enhancements, before going on to the much more tunable packet switch technologies. Chapter 5 on X.25 also acts as an introduction to many of the common features of flow control in packet switch networks in general. Chapter 6 deals with a wide range of packet switch protocols from the point of view of functionality associated with OSI data link, network and transport layers. Unlike X.25, many of these protocols possess intrinsic routing algorithms, and these are described along with bridging in Chapter 7. Optimization features relevant to common applications are presented in Chapter 8. Chapter 9 covers the basic performance aspects of cell relay technologies which need to be considered in addition to those of any other protocol running on top over the network. Chapter 10 is concerned with other modern technologies, more from the point of view of showing what they can achieve than with actual optimization in some cases.

Chapter 11 switches to aspects of network management of performance and the types of design tool on the market; as such it is largely independent of the previous chapters. Chapter 12 describes the general features of public networks, basic tariffing principles and some of the distinctions between private and public networks, while Chapter 13 is a brief summary of the main principles discussed earlier.

Chapter 14 is an appendix that contains slightly more mathematical parts that are likely to be needed by designers of large networks but not by network engineers or operators.

Acknowledgements

The author wishes to thank D. Higgins and other colleagues at Racal–Datacom for useful suggestions and discussions, and Access Network Systems for constructive review comments.

Contents

11   Network Management and Analysis   237

12   Public Network Issues   259

Trademark notice

AppleTalk, AppleShare, Macintosh are trademarks of Apple Computer, Inc.

DEC, DNA (Digital Network Architecture), DECnet, Polycentre are trademarks of Digital Equipment Corporation.

Open View, Netperf, Perfview, Performance Collection Software are trademarks of the Hewlett-Packard Company.

NetWare is a trademark of Novell, Inc.

Network File System (NFS) is a trademark of Sun Microsystems, Inc.

VINES is a trademark of Banyan Systems, Inc.

UNIX is a trademark of Novell Inc.

Patrol is a trademark of BMC.

Sentry is a trademark of Tivoli.

Netsolve is a trademark of Quintessential.

Autonet is a trademark of Network Design and Analysis.

BT Kilo/MegaStream is a trademark of British Telecom plc.

ACP is a trademark of Telematics.

TP4000 is a trademark of Sprint.

Ecotool is a trademark of Compuware.

Quartz and Modline are trademarks of Simulog.

IBM, Netview, Systems Application Architecture (SAA), Systems Network Architecture (SAN), Snapshot, Systems Monitor/6000 are trademarks of International Business Machines Corporation.

Netmaker XA, Netool are trademarks of Make Systems.

COMNET III is a trademark of CACI.

BONES, BONES_DESIGNER, PLANnet are trademarks of the Alta Group.

WorkBench is a trademark of SES.

OPNET is a trademark of MIL3.

Optivity Network Designer is a trademark of Bay Networks.

1

Introduction

1.1 Scope

The aim of this book is to provide a comprehensive guide to the practical aspects of optimizing the performance of wide area networks. Much of the performance potential is fixed by the initial network design, so a significant portion of the text is devoted to understanding what technologies and bandwidths are required in order to support a given type of application. Once a network is installed, the major task is to tune it to support an evolving range of traffic profiles throughout its life cycle until a major redesign becomes essential. This book examines the parameters that can be adjusted for each of the major data communication protocols, showing what effect each has, and how to obtain the desired results.

Performance itself is not a uniquely defined entity. There are many different measures, for example throughput, call set-up time and response time, not all of which can normally be simultaneously optimized. This book shows how each can be optimized separately, and how they impact on each other.

A wide range of data communication protocols is now in existence, and this volume covers everything from telex up to ATM.

1.2 History

Prior to the advent of computers, the only data communications protocol in widespread existence was telex. The throughput of this protocol was determined by the requirement to support the maximum rate at which a typist could normally work, typically about seven characters a second. Using the 5-bit ITA-2 alphabet with parity protection this could be supported at 50 baud. Apart from an automatic exchange of answerbacks for authentication, telex is not interactive, so does not require any complex flow control procedures.

The introduction of interactive sessions between teletype terminal users and computers led to the appearance of asynchronous echoplex applications. In these, error correction is provided by echoing back from the host of the character entered, so that it can be re-entered if wrong. This simple mechanism works well for low-cost terminals directly connected to the host, but suffers from many performance problems when used across a wide area network. In this it is typical of many other protocols and applications that have been developed for use in a local environment, then subsequently employed in the wide area as an enterprise has expanded its networks.

Online data entry to computers led to the appearance of more sophisticated protocols with higher throughputs and flow control to support batch entry as well as having the ability to share expensive communication lines between several devices. Most of the early protocols were character oriented, either synchronous or asynchronous (some both), and specific to a single computer manufacturer. Synchronous examples of this are IBM and other vendors' BSC with DEC's DDCMP supporting both asynchronous and synchronous, while asynchronous protocols were favoured by many companies such as DEC themselves, Burroughs, Honeywell and Sperry. The use of a larger alphabet based on seven or eight bits plus control characters allows for much greater flow control and error recovery than telex, as well as for more sophisticated messages.

The other character-based protocols have more sophisticated error correction plus some form of polling to enable them to share costly resources, such as host ports and leased lines. Sharing of resources inevitably leads to some loss of performance, so the ability to minimize this adverse effect is a major essential, both for the design of a network and for a networking protocol.

As individual characters are unable to carry information that identifies them as belonging to one specific user, the only way that such protocols are able to share a single line is by means of polling or contention. The next advance in wide area protocols was the use of packet switched synchronous bit streams, such as SDLC and X.25, to allow segments of data to be uniqely identified as belonging to a specific user, thereby enabling many users to share a single line without the performance degradation that goes with polling mechanisms. Degradation still occurs, but the use of queuing instead of polling allows a higher line utilization plus full duplex operation.

All these early protocols are connection oriented inasmuch as they appear to the user like a single line to the destination. Within the local area, the availability of high-capacity cable with low error rates allowed the development of simpler connectionless protocols such as Ethernet and Token Ring. This high bandwidth has meant that until very recently performance was not an issue on local area networks (LANs); any equipment could be added, subject to a few simple rules, and the system would work. However, this readily available bandwidth has also allowed the development of user-friendly applications, such as image and object linking and embedding, that take full advantage of it. As a result, performance limitations are beginning to become significant on LANs themselves, and are critical issues when such applications are used across a wide area network (WAN), where high costs inevitably lead to only the bare minimum of bandwidth being provided.

Further performance issues arise from the need to support multimedia applications on a network. This has led to the appearance of techniques and protocols that are able to handle both constant and variable bit rate applications simultaneously at high quality. The most notable example of this is Asynchronous Transfer Mode (ATM) which is rapidly becoming established as the preferred protocol for high bandwidth applications.

1.3   Types of network

A wide range of data communications network types exists today. In addition to physical differences, these networks can also be public, private or hybrid in nature with vastly differing performance and control characteristics.

The earliest data networks consisted entirely of either private leased or public dial-up analog circuits. Such networks are characterized by high error rates and low performance, so are rapidly being phased out in more advanced countries, although advances in modem technology have provided them with a much longer life than was envisaged a few years ago. In many countries, however, analog lines seem likely to remain the main carrier of communications for a good many years to come, so making their optimization a matter of continuing importance. Even in the more advanced countries dial-up circuits will remain important for isolated users.

The main forms of communications technology associated with these analog networks are modems, packet switches and statistical multiplexers in the wide area, with local connectivity being provided by cluster controllers, front-end processors and PADs. This technology usually requires a high degree of planning and configuration effort, with relatively complex upgrades required to meet changes in requirements.

Digital circuits have been a fast expanding component of wide area networks. Initially most of these were based on copper circuits, but most modern lines are based on optical fibre. Use of digital lines has led to much lower error rates and higher capacity. Data transmitted across analog links shows typical error rates of about 1 in 10^5, whereas digital circuits vary from about 1 in 10^6 for metallic circuits down to 1 in 10^{11} for the best optical fibres. Data rates for digital circuits vary from a few kilobits per second up to many gigabits per second, so allowing vastly higher throughputs. Dial-up circuits have also increased in throughput, with modem links replaced by ISDN basic and primary rate services as well as pure data switched 56/64. The relatively low cost of optical fibre bandwidth also makes it realistic to run applications across a network that would be prohibitively expensive, as well as slow, on the older analog circuits. Another vital feature of digital circuitry has been the enabling of voice–data integration.

The appearance of digital circuits in the WANs has also been accompanied by the gradual replacement of local PADs and cluster controllers with LANs based on structured cabling systems that are much easier to maintain. Until the appearance of very high bandwidth multimedia and client–server applications, performance was very rarely a significant issue on the LANs themselves, where servers tended to be the only bottlenecks. Low-cost bandwidth on LANs favoured the development of connectionless broadcast protocols instead of the more sophisticated connection-oriented WAN protocols. When used across a WAN these are inherently inefficient, and one of the main performance tuning requirements for LAN interconnection is the minimization of such traffic. A further problem of the early LAN operating systems, such as Netware, is the absence of the windowing features used on WANs to ensure good throughput. This leads users of early versions of Netware to experience major throughput problems over a WAN, particularly where X.25 is used.

Digital networks support a wider range of technologies than the analog varieties. Packet switches, cluster controllers, and so on can still be used, but the main additions are pulse code modulated (PCM) multiplexers for voice, terminal adaptors (TAs) for ISDN access, plus hubs, routers and bridges for the LANs. Most digital networks are currently based on a plesiochronous digital hierarchy with standards varying from country to country in which high bandwidth circuits have to be broken down into constituent 2 Mbps or 1.544 Mbps parts every time that any drop and insert operation has to be performed owing to the slightly variable bit rates inherent in the plesiochronous scheme (see Chapter 4). These networks are beginning to be replaced or at least overlaid by internationally standardized synchronous digital hierarchy (SDH) networks with improved manageability and no need for this unscrambling.

The digital technology is quickly expanding to extend LAN concepts over wider areas via the IEEE 802.6 MAN (metropolitan area network), and towards the widespread use of cell relay instead of packet switching. All of this poses new challenges in network performance optimization as applications also expand to take advantage of the increased bandwidth.

The other major network component consists of microwave and satellite links. This type of network is extremely important in remote areas, where leased lines are unavailable. The satellite links are the source of major performance problems due to the long propagation delay associated with transmission to and from satellites in geostationary orbits 22 400 miles above the earth. This requires greater buffering capability than terrestrial communications, but often has the advantage of allowing relatively easy increases in the allocated bandwidth. The other main equipment type required for this is a microwave antenna, usually called a VSAT (very small aperture transmitter) in the case of satellite links.

1.4   Communications architectures

The main computer manufacturers realized at an early stage that the use of layered communications architectures allowed programmers to be isolated from the details of network operation, thereby greatly simplifying the evolution of both networks and applications. The main architectures are IBM's SNA and DEC's DNA (Decnet), each of which has gone through a number of phases, and the later OSI (Open Systems Interconnection) model. This book covers performance issues for all three of these architectures, but in the following general discussion, the OSI protocol stack is used as a paradigm.

In later sections of this book, performance issues are subdivided according to the layer of the OSI protocol stack with which they are associated. These layers are shown in Figure 1.1.

When an application transmits data, the latter is passed down the protocol stack acquiring new headers at each stage except the last. The network performance is heavily influenced both by the sizes of these headers, and by the protocol associated with each layer. The application and presentation layers do not directly contribute to any protocol delays, but each of the subsequent layers does.

Layer	Name
7	Application
6	Presentation
5	Session
4	Transport
3	Network
2	Data link
1	Physical

Figure 1.1   OSI protocol stack.

The session layer can contribute to network delays through the use of synchronization points. These are of two types: major and minor, of which the first must be acknowledged before any more data is sent. This wait for an acknowledgement can lead to a reduction in throughput.

The transport layer contains flow control in some of its classes, notably class 4, intended to prevent congestion of the end-point devices, such as printers. The windows and acknowledgements can be a major restriction on throughput in some networks, even in the absence of any end-device congestion.

The network layer is a major source of network delays due to its end-to-end window-based flow control mechanism intended to prevent network congestion.

Similar flow control principles also apply to the data link layer, but they are less significant as a source of delays.

Finally, at the physical level there are the obvious delays due to the finite propagation rate of the basic signals, together with the finite time required to put the bits of information constituting the message onto a transmission medium. In addition to the delays caused by the propagation medium, this layer also includes the processing delays due to such devices as modems and multiplexers.

Other protocol stacks, such as SNA, contain similar functions, but are distributed differently between layers. The protocol stack for SNA is shown in Figure 1.2.

Layer	Name
7	Transaction
6	Function management
5	Data flow control
4	Transmission control
3	Path control
2	Data link control
1	Physical control

Figure 1.2   SNA protocol stack.

Layers 1, 2 and 6 perform very similar roles to those of OSI, but corresponding functions in 3, 4 and 5 are intermixed, while OSI's application layer 7 is much less developed than SNA.

1.5   Basic delay parameters

Many features of protocol tuning require sophisticated tools, such as monitors and modelling tools, but there are a number of basic, easily understood fundamentals that determine many of the delays and bottlenecks. These are the propagation delay of an electrical signal resulting from the finite velocity of light, the bit rate of a transmission line and the switching delay in a packet switch or router. They are treated in outline below.

1.5.1   Propagation delay

The velocity of light is about 300 000 kilometres per second, so on short links the delays are unimportant but for intercontinental or satellite links they are of major significance. Most satellites used for communications are in geostationary orbit at a height of about 36 000 kilometres and this leads to a delay of about 270 milliseconds for an intercontinental hop via satellite. In the case of terrestrial cable connections, the propagation velocity is slightly less than that in empty space, so that the delay is about 1 ms for every 200 kilometres. This is illustrated in Figure 1.3.

1.5.2   Delay due to bit rate

It takes a finite amount of time to put a specified quantity of digital data onto a transmission line that depends on the data volume and the speed of the line. Figure 1.4

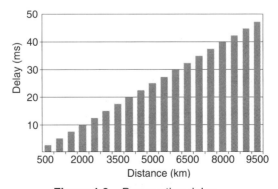

Figure 1.3   Propagation delay.

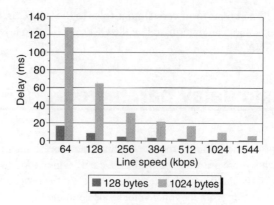

Figure 1.4   Transmission delay.

shows what sort of delay can be expected for several of the main data types over a typical range of WAN speeds.

1.5.3   Packet switching delay

The time taken to switch a packet depends on the processing rate and the internal switch architecture in a variable manner, but tends to be slightly greater than the reciprocal of the packet processing rate. Figure 1.5 shows this minimum delay for a range of typical switching/routing rates. This graph only gives a very rough order of magnitude as there are other effects, such as internal queuing and polling, that depend on the architecture of the switch.

Later chapters describe the more intricate features of the delays and their significance for performance tuning for a range of protocols.

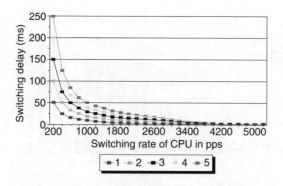

Figure 1.5   Switching delay and CPU number.

2

Requirements Analysis

2.1   Introduction

This chapter examines the nature of requirements analysis that must be performed before a network can be successfully specified or designed. The basic topics to consider are connectivity, protocol support, traffic estimates and performance criteria. Of these, it is only the last two that are considered in detail in this book as connectivity and protocol requirements need little explanation.

2.2   Performance measures

As mentioned in Chapter 1, there are many different measures of performance that are applicable to a network.

2.2.1   Call set-up time

Before any data can be transmitted in any connection-oriented network service (CONS), it is necessary to first establish the call or session. On the other hand, for a connectionless network service (CLNS) this not required. Examples of CONS are X.25 and SNA, while IP (ex-TCP) and ISO 8473 are examples of CLNS protocols. CONS are normally preferred on the wide area and by service providers who have to give a guarantee to deliver data, while CLNS are used on reliable media such as LANs.

For a few applications, such as credit card checks, the set-up time is the most important performance measure. The set-up time consists of both the physical layer establishment, such as modem dialling over the PSTN, and contributions from layers 2 up to 6 in the OSI protocol stack. Where modems are involved, they are normally the biggest single component in this, although for SNA on some devices, such as low-end AS/400s, the higher-level session establishment is also slow.

2.2.2   Response time

The most basic performance measure for data transfer is the network response time. This is clearly the time required for a user to receive a response to a message, but, even this has several modes of definition. First of all it is necessary to distinguish between the (one-way) network transit time and the roundtrip (two-way) response time. Of these, the roundtrip delay is usually the more important for interactive applications, whereas the former may be more relevant to batch operations. There are then four further modes of defining each of these in terms of which part of the message is used, whether first or last element. These four are: First-In Last-Out (FILO), First-In First-Out (FIFO), Last-In Last-Out (LILO) and Last-In First-Out (LIFO). It can make a big difference as to which of these methods is used, so statements of requirements and evaluations of responses to invitations to tender need to take this into account.

FILO is the most pessimistic of these definitions, and is applicable to screen-based applications where no data is transmitted until a screen is completed and no return data displayed until a complete screenful has been received by the terminal. In a one-way transaction it applies to the case in which a host does not start to process information until the complete transaction has been received.

FIFO is similar to FILO, except that the terminal starts to display return data as soon as it arrives. A roundtrip may sometimes consist of a FILO leg into the host, followed by a FIFO return.

LILO applies to the situation where data is transmitted as it is generated, but only displayed or processed once the complete transaction has been received.

LIFO is the most optimistic version of the response time, so is liable to be quoted by network vendors unless there is a clear reason for not doing so. It applies to situations where transaction data is both transmitted and processed as it is generated. A common example of a LIFO process is one in which a user terminal and a host computer use an asynchronous protocol to communicate across a packet switch network via PADs. The user types characters into the terminal, which sends them to a PAD which in turn forwards them as a packet only on receipt of a packet forwarding character, such as a carriage return; this packet then goes to the host PAD which disassembles it and sends asynchronous data into the host.

The differences between these measures are illustrated in Figure 2.1 for the network transit time of the PAD example.

Suppose that 128 bytes of data are transmitted from the terminal to the host, and that the central PAD–PAD link adds 9 bytes of overhead. Furthermore, assume that the network is lightly loaded so that there are no measurable queuing delays, and that there are no significant propagation delays. The transit time then includes contributions common to all four definitions of 17 ms for the central PAD–PAD link and say 5 ms for each PAD, plus a variable part. The variable part depends on either a single character or 128 characters, according to mode, being transmitted on the PAD to host/terminal links. Assuming two stop bits per character this leads to the transit times shown in Table 2.1. The very large difference in response time is immediately apparent.

Figure 2.1   Network transit time via PADs.

Table 2.1   Queuing disciplines.

Model	Transit time (ms)
FILO	227
FIFO	165
LILO	105
LIFO	43

If a roundtrip is considered for a response to appear on the originating terminal, then these figures would be doubled for the case of another 128 byte return message.

It is also important to distinguish between the average response time and some characteristic worst acceptable case. Measures which are often used for the worst case type scenario are the 90th, 95th or 99th percentile response times. These are the values within which respectively 9 /10, 19/20 or 99/100 transaction response times fall. The 95th percentile is often regarded as the most psychologically appropriate measure to choose, since there is a tendency for the worst out of 20 transaction times to be remembered and quoted as typical of the network, whereas the worst of 100 transactions will usually be regarded as a freak.

2.2.3   Jitter

There are some cases where it is not the response time itself that is the criticial factor in determining quality, but rather its variability. This is known as jitter. The area in which this is most important is in multimedia applications. A variable delay can have the effect of making it sound as if a speaker is stuttering, clearly not what you want to happen if you are broadcasting a videoclip of a peptalk by the company president. Some figures are quoted for the acceptable magnitude of jitter in Table 2.2.

2.2.4   Skew

Another feature of the response time that is sometimes important in multimedia applications is the difference in delay for different parts of the application; this is known as skew. The main example of this is the skew between voice and image in video applications, where the two parts of the message can get noticeably out of synchronization with each other due to skew. A distinction is sometimes drawn between fine skew, which refers to aspects to which the user is especially sensitive, and coarse skew for less sensitive aspects. Lip synchronization is the typical example of fine skew, while general background sound effects are governed by coarse skew criteria.

2.2.5   Throughput

For file transfers or other large transactions, the most important measure of perfor-mance is likely to be throughput. This is defined as the quantity of error-free data that is transmitted per unit time. As such, the definition automatically excludes any data that has to be retransmitted for any reason. This is usually defined for a specific connection or transaction, but in some cases it is the total throughput potential of a network that is of importance rather than some specialized part. This aspect of per-formance may be limited either by the capacity of the underlying transmission medium or by the processor capacity in the network. Different optimization tech-niques are applicable to the two cases, achieving one at the expense of the other in many cases.

2.2.6   Residual error rate

In a few specialized instances the most important measure of performance may be the quality of the information that is transmitted rather than the quantity. It is some-times possible to reduce the residual error rate at the expense of throughput and response time. It is desirable for large corporate or public networks to use routing protocols that enable routes to be selected which optimize the performance measure that is of greatest importance to each specific user.

ITU-T X.140 and X.213 give detailed definitions of these in relation to OSI network services.

2.2.7   Cost

Financial constraints may dictate that the only really important performance parameter of a network is its ability to carry the maximum amount of traffic for a given financial cost. This means that it is desirable for large networks to have a routing protocol that enables traffic to be selectively carried on minimum tariff routes.

2.2.8   Security

Like residual error rate and cost, it is desirable to be able to select routes on the basis of the degree of security that they provide.

2.3 Traffic volumes

Traffic volumes are often the biggest source of errors in initial network design, as it is extremely hard to estimate what use will be made of a new network apart from the effects of existing applications. In addition to the volume of actual user data, it is often necessary to know the structure of the individual transactions so that protocol overheads and packet processor loads can be reliably estimated. Pilot studies are one way of obtaining reasonably accurate information on new applications, but actual levels can be distorted by operators feeling that they too are under test.

Often new network operations are related to business functions for which market forecasts have already been prepared. In such cases the projected business transactions have to be translated into network transactions. The transactions can then be subdivided into data, voice and video applications, each with their own estimation procedures.

2.3.1 Data estimation

Business transactions need to be broken down into message pairs consisting of a message and its immediate response. This may be an interactive process, or else be essentially a one-way process consisting of a file transfer and an acknowledgement.

Protocol overheads can lead to drastic modifications to estimates based solely on actual user data. As each segment of user data moves down the protocol stack, it acquires a new header, and in extreme cases this overhead can exceed the useful data volume. Packet or frame processing load is almost entirely concerned with work performed on these headers rather than the user data so, except in the case of multiplexer systems, this structure has to be known.

An extreme example of this would be the case of user data sent either from an intelligent synchronous terminal or from a dumb asynchronous terminal across a bridged Ethernet network. In the synchronous case, up to 1500 bytes of user data plus TCP/IP headers could be sent in a single frame whereas, for the asynchronous version, each character of data would be placed in a single Ethernet frame by a terminal server, leading to 1500 frames each containing 1 user character, 40 TCP/IP header characters and 21 bytes of Ethernet header and padding. It would obviously be essential in this case to know which mode of operation was being used.

The choice of protocol stack is determined to a large degree by the types of computer in use, for example SNA/SAA for IBM mainframes. Off-the-shelf applications normally specify the main options to be used within such a stack so that the precise overheads can be estimated using details on the specific protocols, such as those given in later chapters of this book.

In the case of LAN interconnect, broadcasts are a major additional consideration, occasionally swamping the real traffic unless tuned. The designer has to estimate the likely levels based on an understanding of the protocol and topology, then delete unnecessary components. This optimization can make a significant difference on low-speed WANs.

2.3.2   Voice estimation

Voice is likely to be a component of many modern multimedia applications. The traffic level is determined by the number of digital voice channels to be carried, their duration and the degree of compression.

2.3.3   Video estimation

Video traffic needs to be divided into two parts, still and moving, as they require different optimization techniques. In each case the image quality and resolution have a very large impact on the final traffic level, with colour obviously having a much higher bandwidth requirement than black and white. For still images the information needed is the number of pictures to send, the degree of colour and the resolution required. For moving pictures the duration of the films, number of frames per second, degree of colour and resolution are needed.

In most cases the traffic will require to be heavily compressed before it can be sent cost-effectively across the network, so it is essential to know what techniques are available for this purpose and to base traffic estimates on them. These options are outlined in Table 2.2 and discussed in more detail in Chapter 8 of this book.

2.3.4   Typical traffic requirements

Table 2.2 gives typical throughputs, with values in bits per second. Most applications will not achieve the values quoted for hardware components, so these are included only to show potential and the extent to which the network may act as a bottleneck.

For the multimedia applications, the coarse skew limit is about 150 milliseconds, while fine skew must be less than 20 milliseconds for audio advance over image or less than 120 milliseconds for image advance. The reason for the difference between skew values for audio or image advance is simply that people are accustomed to image advance in everyday life. The low velocity of sound, about 300 metre/s, means that any scene 10 metres from an observer will automatically have a skew of about 33 milliseconds due to the delay in hearing the sound.

Table 2.2 Performance requirements.

Traffic type	Throughput	Response time (ms)	Jitter (ms)
Interactive teletype (async)	50 bps	< 150	
Interactive teletype (X.25)	500 bps	< 150	
Interactive teletype (TCP/IP)	2000 bps	< 150	
Interactive teletype (LAT)	200 bps	< 150	
Form filling	10 kbps	1000	
Page printer (30 page/min)	120 kbps		
PC tape backup	1 Mbps		
PC disk backup	3 Mbps		
PC raid disk backup	5 Mbps		
A4 page b/w image (uncompressed)	15 Mbps		1000
A4 page b/w image (200 dpi JPEG compressed)	512 kbps		1000
A4 page colour image (uncompressed)	90 Mbps		1000
A4 page colour image (200 dpi JPEG)	3 Mbps		1000
2 sides of cheque image (uncompressed)	2.5 Mbps		1000
2 sides of cheque image (JPEG compressed)	80 kbps		1000
Digital voice (2 bit RELP)	2400 bps		
Digital voice (8 bit CELP)	7200 bps		
Digital voice G.721 ADPCM	32 kbps		
Digital FM radio quality voice	132 kbps		
Digital stereo CD voice	384 kbps		
DVI video (15 frame/s, 128×120 pels, 8-bit colour)	288 kbps		
H261 video (15 frame/s, 128×120 pels)	64 kbps		
H261 video (15 frame/s, 256×240 pels)	384 kbps		
H261 video (30 frame/s, 256×240 pels)	2000 kbps		
Grey scale video server	384 kbps		
VHS VCR quality video server	1100 kbps		
Broadcast quality video server (MPEG)	4000 kbps		
HDTV (compressed, 30 frame/s, 24 bit colour)	100 Mbps		
HDTV(uncompressed)	800 Mbps		
CD-drive (PC – MPC1)	1.2 Mbps		
CD-drive (PC – MPC2)	2.4 Mbps		
CD-drive (PC – high speed)	8 Mbps		

2.4   Reliability

Another important measure of network performance is reliability. This itself can be split into several independent components.

2.4.1   Network availability

This factor is the percentage of time for which the network is available to the user, taking account of hardware and software faults, but not congestion. It is defined in ITU-T X.137 by the formula:

Availability = MTBSO/ (MTBSO + MTTSR)

where MTBSO denotes mean time between service outages, and MTTSR denotes mean time to service restoral. Typical values range from 99% to 99.99%. In the UK analog lines tend to have an availability of 99.6 to 99.7% with significant regional variations, while 64K KiloStreams are around 99.8 to 99.9%. Varying sensitivity of different applications to bursts of errors means that the availability of a circuit is not a unique fixed number; in some cases it is the proportion of error-free seconds that matters, while for others it is only complete outages that are significant.

Networking hardware is usually more reliable than the lines, with availability exceeding 99.95% in most cases, but depending on the callout time in the maintenance contract.

Network availability of 99.9 to 99.95% is normally most cheaply provided through the use of dial backup; via PSTN for analog circuits or ISDN for digital. Higher values require multiple permanent circuits.

When dual homing is used to obtain high levels of resilience it is sometimes advisable to obtain circuits to a site from two independent suppliers, since otherwise common failure modes are apt to exist, for example termination on the same multiplexer in the carrier's exchange.

2.4.2   Circuit availability

The fact that a network is fully operational at some time does not guarantee that a user will be able to obtain a circuit, since except in non-blocking systems, there may be no spare capacity at the time. Different connection probability standards are specified for public circuit and packet switch networks in ITU-T recommendations X.130 and X.136. Typical circuit availabilities are in the region of 99.9%.

2.4.3 Rerouting time

Most networks have the ability to reroute round failed components, but the time required to do this varies widely according to network and protocol, thereby giving widely differing qualities of service to users. The time taken can vary from a few milliseconds up to several minutes. Optimum performance on a network depends on adjusting timers where possible to take account of this factor. Unintelligent table-driven routing algorithms are often much faster than complex intelligent systems, while in the LAN interconnection arena, OSPF is much faster than RIP. These differences will be handled in later chapters in relation to categories of equipment and protocol.

Long rerouting times may be unacceptable for some applications, such as air traffic control when passing an aircraft from one controller to another, but in many data services can be fully compensated by adjusting the timers, so these requirements need to be specified.

3

Analog Links

3.1   Introduction

The earliest data communications networks consisted of analog links, and in most parts of the world such links still constitute the most common means of access. Data communications are intrinsically digital in essence, so in order to transmit data across an analog link it is necessary to first modulate, then demodulate the signals; this is done by a pair of modems.

Analog lines themselves were originally primarily intended for telephones, and have characteristics optimized for voice communications. Where analog lines are specifically intended for data, they are modified by conditioning to reduce problems such as dispersion and echo.

Analog line quality is frequently defined in terms of certain overall standards, the CCITT/ITU-T M.Series recommendations, rather than by arbitrary combinations of quality features, such as detailed noise levels. These recommended line categories are listed in Table 3.1.

The differing characteristics of the analog lines lead to different classes of modem. Modem types are further specified by the bit rate that they support, whether they can support synchronous or asynchronous data, full or half-duplex transmission and single or multipoint operation.

Modems are usually described in terms of the ITU-T standards or, in the case of old American modems, by the Bell standards.

Some vendors provide modems to the standards listed in Table 3.2 that are able to carry asynchronous data as well as synchronous, even though only the latter is specified in the ITU-T recommendation. This is normally done by adding software to synchronize asynchronous data before transmission in accordance with ITU-T recommendation V.14.

In addition to the normal data modems listed above, there is also the V.17 standard that is specifically for fax with a bit rate of 14 400 bps.

Additional information on the early standards can be found in Black (1988).

Table 3.1   Analog line quality.

Recommendation	Features
M.1020	Intended for high-quality data circuits. No equalizers needed for modems
M.1025	Intended for high-speed data circuits. Modems must have equalizers
M.1040	Basic voice circuit

Table 3.2   Modem standards.

Standard	Bit rate	Line type	Full/half duplex	Synchronous or asynchronous
V.21	300		Full	Either
V.22	1200		Full	Either
V.22 bis	2400		Full	Either
V.23	1200, 75/1200		Half	Either
V.26	2400		Full	Synchronous
V.26 bis	2400		Half	Synchronous
V.26 ter	2400		Either	Either
V.27	4800		Either	Synchronous
V.27 bis	4800		Either	Synchronous
V.27 ter	4800		Half	Synchronous
V.29	9600		Either	Synchronous
V.32	9600		Full	Synchronous
V.32 bis	14400		Full	Synchronous
V.33	14400		Full	Synchronous
V.34	28800		Full	Synchronous

3.2   Modem delays

Implementation of some of these standards, particularly those for the higher line speeds, involve considerable processing that leads to significant delays. These delays are partially defined by the ITU-T recommendations, and are associated with the correction of particular quality problems.

3.2.1   Equalization

When data is transmitted across an analog line it is essential to be able to distinguish between the individual symbols, but in practice there is always some intersymbol interference (ISI) due primarily to the fact that the analog signal consists of various frequencies that suffer differing delays and attenuation as they cross the link. Circuits that are intended to carry data are normally conditioned by the circuit provider to reduce this problem, the degree of conditioning varying according to the M.Series recommendation, but it is not eliminated. On an unconditioned telephone circuit the dispersion of a pulse is roughly 10 ms, so at a baud rate of B transitions/s it is necessary to equalize the differential delays at B/100 points. Typically B is 1200 or 2400, although the bit rate may be higher, so equalization at 12 or 24 control points is required. This number is even higher for the more sensitive high bit rate protocols. The usual way of performing this equalization is by means of a transversal digital filter, sometimes also referred to as a tapped delay line. The signal is tapped at each of the control points and multiplied by a weighting coefficient to obtain the equalized signal (see Figure 3.1).

These coefficients are initially established at the start of the call by the modem training procedure, which consists of several transmissions of set bit streams defined by the ITU-T standards. For some of the lower speeds, a fixed set of coefficients is all that is required, but most of the faster standards require automatic equalization in which these coefficients are constantly adjusted. This leads to a modem propagation delay both on transmission and reception to take account of the tapped delay line and the associated processing. This processing load is increased further by the need to eliminate harmonic effects on the equalization, which is done by a binary scrambler. The type of equalization performed, and the characteristic delays, are quoted in Table 3.3.

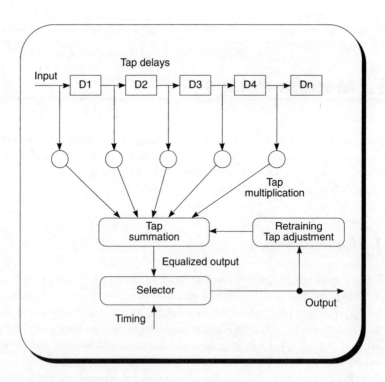

Figure 3.1   Equaliser delays.

Table 3.3   Modem performance parameters.

Standard	Bit rate	Equalizer	RTS/CTS	DCD on	DCD off
V.21	300	–	20–50	≤20	20–80
V.22 (const carrier)	1200	Fixed	≤2	105–205	10–24
V.22 (switch carrier)	1200	Fixed	210–275	105–205	10–24
V.22 bis	2400	Fixed/adaptive	3–5		40–65
V.23	1200, 75/1200	–	20–40 ex Prot	10–20	5–15
V.26	2400	–	25–45 MP, 65–100 PP		
V.26 bis	2400	Fixed	65–100 Echo Pr 200–275 ex Pr	5–15	5–15
V.26 ter	2400	Fixed/adaptive	≤2(const carr)	5–15	5–15
V.27	4800	Manual	17–20, 30–70	10–16	
V.27 bis	4800	Adaptive	25 @ 4800 67 @ 2400		5–15
V.27 ter	4800	Adaptive	50 ex talk Pr. 215 + talk Pr		5–15
V.27 ter	2400	Adaptive	67 ex talk Pr 215 + talk Pr.		5–15
V.29 (const carrier)	9600	Adaptive	10–20	5–25	21–39
V.29 (switch carrier)	9600	Adaptive	253	5–25	21–39
V.32	9600		≤2		
V.32 bis	14 400		≤2		
V.33	14 400	Adaptive		15–35	30–50
V.34	28 800		≤2		
V.34 bis	33 600				

3.2.2 Adaptive echo cancellation

Another source of distortion of the signal is the echo that results from changes in the transmission medium, most notably any points in voice grade networks where 4-wire to 2-wire conversion takes place. Correction of this problem for modems such as V.26 ter and V.32 which support 2-wire PSTN operation is again by means of a transversal filter with associated delays analogous to those for the equalizers.

3.2.3   RTS/CTS turnaround time

Where polled protocols are used there is a turnaround time before a modem can switch from receiving to sending data. This is associated with CCITT circuits 105 and 106, known in Europe as RTS and CTS, but in the USA as CA and CB. The delay is largely defined by the modem standards so as to take account of the propagation delays described above. Often polled protocols are used over multipoint circuits, and manufacturers usually provide a choice of RTS/CTS delays to take account of the different roles, that is, master or slave, that the modems play in the circuit.

Half-duplex protocols over 2-wire circuits suffer considerable delays due to RTS/CTS turnaround time, but if 4-wire circuits are available this can be avoided by use of constant carrier.

3.2.4   Call set-up delay

In a few applications, such as credit card checking, calls may be extremely short and too infrequent to justify a leased line, so that the call set-up delay is more important than the data propagation delay. This set-up delay consists of the dialling time plus the initial training time.

The largest factor in the dialling time is the choice between pulse dialling and tone dialling. Pulse dialling tends to take about 10 seconds, while DTMF needs only 2–3 seconds. This is determined by the characteristics of the telephone network used; old exchanges often only support pulse dialling.

3.2.5   Modem performance parameters

Many of the modem performance parameters are largely set by international standards, and these are listed in Table 3.3 for V.Series modems.

Training time

Even more important in determining call set-up time is the initial training time for the modem, which is related to the parameters in Table 3.3. Typical values in practice are about 10 seconds for V.22 bis, 10–15 for V.32 and 15–20 for V.32 bis. Early experience with V.34 indicates a much lower value of 5–12 seconds, in line with one of the design aims of the recommendation.

Propagation delay

Once the call has been established there is a data propagation delay through a pair of modems that is related to the above parameters and the processing time associated with scramblers and equalization. The minimum time is roughly equal to typical uncorrected pulse dispersion of about 10 ms, and becomes larger for the more complex processing needed for the high-speed standards. Thus a delay of 10 ms is typical for V.22 bis, 20–30 ms for V.29, 30–40 for V.33 and 40–60 for V.FAST, the precursor to V.34 as well as for V.34 itself. The very long delays for the high-speed modems make them relatively poor for short bursts of data, especially echoplex. Some of these modems have configuration options enabling the user to reduce the complexity of the processing in these cases in order to cut delays at the expense of a higher error rate. For a short burst of data the probability of retransmission due to an error remains low due to the short length, but for file transfers the high-quality option should be used. Delay is also greater than the filter delay if error correction and compression are used, so for interactive traffic with short message lengths performance is best with these features disabled if integrity is not vital.

Both cellular radio and ISDN are much better in this respect, particularly the latter which is described in Chapter 5.

3.3   Data compression

Significant improvements can be made to throughput, particularly for asynchronous protocols, by the use of data compression. The main standards used are the proprietary MNP (Microcom Network Protocol) series and the CCITT recommendation V.42 bis. The typical degrees of compression and the main features of each are listed in Table 3.4.

Values of compression factors vary greatly according to the type of data transmitted, and the figures in Table 3.4 are for long text messages. For short interactive strings, there is little to choose between MNP 5, MNP 7 and V.42 bis. The V.42 bis standard also contains an option for MNP 4. Many asynchronous modems allow the DTE port speed to be set at up to four times the link speed, that is, 57.6 kbps for V.32

Table 3.4 MNP compression standards.

Standard	Compression	Features
MNP 3	1.08	Start/stop bits eliminated
MNP 4	1.2	Adaptive packet assembly
MNP 5	1.6	Run length encoding
MNP 6	1.6	As MNP 5, but supports V.29 also
MNP 7	1.8	Hoffman enhanced compression
MNP 8	1.8	As MNP 7, but supports V.29 also
MNP 9	1.8	As MNP 7, but supports V.32 also
V.42 bis	2	Lempel-Ziv algorithm

bis and up to 115.2 kbps for V.34. It is clear from the table of typical compression factors that the maximum reduction of four will rarely be attained, but for asynchronous data this is not a problem as the modem can use XON/XOFF flow control to slow down the DTE when necessary. For synchronous data ports, flow control is more of a problem as it can only be reliably done if the level 2 protocol is supported and terminated by the modem. For many DTEs it is also not possible to benefit from these speeds because of a limited maximum speed of 19.2 or 38.4 kbps on their own data ports. The port speed supportable on a PC depends on the UART chipset, and is often limited to 38.4 kbps; without a hardware upgrade the solution is to use compression in the communications software package instead of in the modem. Serial boards are available for PCs offering port speeds up to 230.4 kbps, which allows the full potential of data compression to be used.

Some modems can offer a higher degree of compression by using a larger dictionary size in the Lempel-Ziv algorithm. This is beneficial for file transfers, but has a slight downside through increasing the processing delay, making it potentially detrimental to interactive traffic as regards response time.

3.3.1   V.34 issues

V.34 is a much more complex standard than most of the others and raises a number of performance issues. Firstly, the standard requires three mandatory baud rates, 2400, 3000 and 3200, together with another three optional baud rates, namely 2743, 2800 and 3429. The bit rate is obtained by multiplying the baud rate by the number of bits per symbol, for example the normal maximum rate of 28 800 bps results from 9 bits per symbol with baud rate of 3200, while a few manufacturers offer a peak bit rate of 33 600 bps based on the 3429 option.

The higher the baud and bit rates, the more susceptible the modem is to noise in general. Noise problems are reduced by two optional techniques. The first is precoding, which is a form of equalization, and the second is using the higher members of the three permitted numbers of states for trellis-encoding forward error correction (see Section 3.4). These three options are 16, 32 and 64, with few modems offering 64 because of the heavier processing load, although it should give the best results on a noisy line.

V.34 is an improvement over earlier standards as it defines a method of falling back to lower data rates if transmission deteriorates, and of stepping back up when conditions improve. This is accomplished in steps of 2400 bps, and V.34 modems with a nominal speed of 28 800 bps will often be found running at a step or two below this, so throughput will not always be as high as expected. For M.1020 lines 28.8 kbps should always be achieved, and the same for a high proportion of M.1025 circuits, but M.1040 and international circuits may easily fall back as far as 14.4 kbps.

Two other advantages of V.34 are non-linear encoding to cut interference from pulse code modulation on trunks with analog to digital conversion, and the ability to transmit and receive at different rates.

One issue specific to satellite link users is that Satcom uses ADPCM which is unable to support more than 3000 baud, making it incompatible with the normal 3200 rate for V.34. In this case either the mandatory 2400 rate should be used or the optional 2743 and 2800. Thus highest throughput for such links needs a modem that supports the 2743/2800 options.

In order to obtain the full benefit of the numerous options, they have to be supported at both ends of a link. For corporate networks this is easy to ensure, but for users who dial up public networks, it is worth trying to ascertain what options are in use on the modem at the other end. Slight implementation differences mean that performance on poor lines is usually worse with modems from different manufacturers than when they are the same.

3.4   Error correction

Throughput of correct user data is also affected by the occurrence of errors during transmission, and by the delays incurred in correcting them. Error correction is not always necessary if quality is not an issue, and a typical uncorrected error rate of 1 in 100 000 will be adequate for many textfile transfers. A lower error rate than this can normally only be obtained by the use of error correction. There are two main methods, forward and backward error correction, of which the former is incorporated in the later modem standards, such as V.32 and V.33, while the latter is inherent in most synchronous protocols, and is also employed by the V.42 and MNP standards for asynchronous data.

Forward error correction is achieved by the use of trellis-coding algorithms, whereby an additional bit is created for each four bits, or two extra for V.34. The current bit pattern created is dependent on the previous bit pattern, and numerous patterns are not valid at all. Together these enable the receiving modem to guess the next state and correct minor errors by replacing an invalid pattern by the nearest valid pattern. Potentially this can reduce the error rate by a factor of a 100 or even occasionally 1000 without recourse to retransmission. Unfortunately, the line quality has to be very good to start with, else the technique can be counterproductive, except in the case of V.34. For example, a four-wire leased circuit that gives a bit error rate of 1 in 1000 to 1 in 10 000 with V.29 modems will frequently not train up at all for V.33 modems when data is transmitted. If the V.29 error rate is 1 in 1 000 000, however, then it will be less than one hundredth of that with V.33 modems. For synchronous data link protocols, this reduction in error rate allows a greater frame size and higher throughput, with additional error correction by the intrinsic retransmissions of the protocol.

V.34 is able to withstand about 6 dB more of noise than V.32 bis and should be able to operate over most M.1040 circuits unlike the other high-speed standards, although frequently at reduced speeds.

The alternative ARQ methods are of two types, selective retransmission and Go-Back N. Of these, the former gives the better performance as only the single erroneous frame is retransmitted, whereas the latter requires all subsequently received frames to be retransmitted as well as the erroneous frame until its corrected version arrives. Selective retransmission is rarely used in practice because it requires much more memory on the modems as well as the intelligence to resequence the frames. For synchronous protocols this retransmission is intrinsic to the protocol, but for asynchronous protocols it is added by the modems' synchronization technique. This synchronization is based on HDLC both for MNP and V.42 standards. MNP uses the LAPB subset of HDLC (similar to X.25 level 2 – see Chapter 5), while V.42 uses LAPM (similar to LAPD for ISDN) that contains XIDs that can be used for parameter exchange at link set up as well as a TEST command.

In each case asynchronous characters are stripped of their start/stop bits and blocked together into frames complete with header and CRC error check field. Throughput is improved by removal of the start/stop bits, but reduced by the frame overheads, the extra modem processing delay and the potential delay in forwarding the frame due to waiting for the appropriate frame forwarding condition to occur. Frames are subject to the flow control of a windowing mechanism (see Chapter 1), so unless the window is sufficiently large, throughput will be impeded.

In the case of LAPM for V.42 the parameters that can be set to adjust the performance are as shown in Table 3.5. In this table T401 is recommended to be set according to the following formula:

$$T401 \geqslant Ta + Tb + Tc + Td + Te + Tf$$

where: Ta is the propagation delay in transmitting the frame,

Tb is the time needed by the remote DCE to process and acknowledge the frame,

Tc is the maximum time for the remote DCE to complete transmission of already queued frames,

Td is the time needed to transmit the acknowledging frame,

Te is the propagation delay for the acknowledgement,

Tf is the processing time for the received acknowledgement.

A typical lower limit for T401 for a 14 400 bps terrestrial line would be about 500 ms. Allowance for a maximum window size, required on satellite links, of maximal size frames would increase this to 1500 ms for 128 byte frames, increased by a factor of two for each doubling of the frame size.

Table 3.5   LAPM parameters.

Parameter	Symbol	Default
Acknowledgement timer	T401	(Rec. formula)
Maximum retransmissions	N400	ND (>1)
Maximum octets in frame	N401	128
Window size	k	15

3.4.1   Comparison of ARQ techniques

Early half-duplex protocols used a Stop and Wait version of ARQ, which gives very poor performance especially on satellite links, but most modern ARQ techniques use either the GO-BACK N or Selective Reject (SREJ), with a few hybrids also. Some modems offer the user a choice of SREJ or GO-BACK N, so it is worth examining the practical differences in more detail.

GO-BACK N drops all frames after the erroneous frame in addition to it, so in the worst case will drop K frames where K is the link level window size. Assuming that transmission is part of a file transfer or other large transaction, data will continue to be transmitted until either a reject or a link level timeout occurs; in many cases this will be before the full window has been transmitted, the main exception to this being on satellite links. In the case of a reject on a terrestrial link, the reject frame is much shorter than most data frames, so there will only be time for either one or two frames to be transmitted by the sender before it receives this. For protocols such as LAPM that use retransmission on timeout, the number of frames to retransmit will normally be at least three up to the window size, because of the need to set a timer that does not lead to retransmissions due to congestion, thereby worsening that situation. The volume of traffic that is produced per frame by the GO-BACK N type of ARQ is

$$V = P_c * (L + OHD) + (1 - P_c) * (L + OHD) * N$$

where P_c is the probability that the frame is correctly received, L is the data length, OHD the protocol overhead and N the average number of frames retransmitted per erroneous frame.

In the case of Selective Reject, there is the extra memory and processing requirement that is needed to retain all frames subsequent to the error and re-sequence them, but also another disadvantage inasmuch as only a single SREJ can be outstanding at any one time unless the protocol has a special positive acknowledgement for each SREJ. Protocols with SREJ usually use another alternative, which is to issue an ordinary REJ for any further errors until the correction requested by the SREJ has been received. The volume of traffic transmitted in this case is just

$$V = P_c * (L + OHD) + (1 - P_c) * (L + OHD) * A$$

where A is the number of times that the retransmission has to be carried out, which is normally just once, giving

$$V = (L + OHD)$$

Figure 3.2 compares GO-BACK N with SREJ for the case of a 9600 bps line with 256 byte message block and a BER of 10^{-5}. The case of SREJ with REJ for immediate subsequent errors gives slightly more traffic than the ideal SREJ case.

At error rates of more than about 1 in 10 000, SREJ will give noticeably better throughput, particularly for large frames, but when the error rate is less, then there is little advantage in SREJ, while its use may limit frame and window sizes if memory is short.

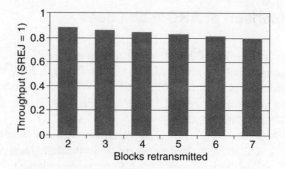

Figure 3.2   Effect of GO-BACK N on throughput.

It is important to note that neither ARQ techniques nor FEC can correct all errors, so that there is always a residual error rate due to some errors passing undetected where multiple errors occur. This proportion depends on the error detection method used, and is discussed further in the appendix. More detailed analysis is given in Hal[92].

3.5   Response time and throughput

This section considers how the parameters described above affect response time and throughput on analog links in practice. There are two basic types of application to consider: file transfers and polled protocols. The simpler of these is the file transfer, which also can be considered as part of the other, so it will be considered first.

3.5.1   Non-polled file transfers

The transit time for a block of data of size M bytes over a single modem link of bit rate S bps on a FILO basis is given by

$$T = (M \times b/S) + Dt + Dr + P$$

where

b is the number of bits per character,
Dt is the transmitter delay of the modem,
Dr is the receiver delay of the modem,
P is the propagation delay of the signal.

The propagation delay, P, is about 1 ms per 100 miles for terrestrial links, and about 270 ms for a geostationary satellite link. A graph of typical delays is shown in Figure 3.3 for different bit rates and block sizes, all assuming a link of much less than 100 miles so that P can be ignored.

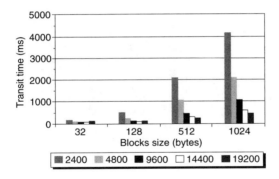

Figure 3.3   Modem link transit time.

For very short blocks of data, particularly the case of single echoplex characters, it is evident that increasing the line speed may also increase the transit time due to the greater modem delays incurred. Indeed, in extreme cases of high-speed modems, these modem delays may exceed 150 ms, rendering them useless for this special case of echoplex, where the roundtrip time has to be less than that to prevent irritating the user. Manufacturers of such modems recognize this potential problem, and sometimes provide several quality options for receiver equalization/cancellation delays. A short delay may be given for short block sizes where the probability of an error in the block is low, and a high value for long blocks with a greater error probability.

The throughput of the link depends on the transit time, window size for acknowledgements and the error rate on the line (assuming that error correction is provided). The throughput of the link is defined as the net number of characters transmitted per unit time after deducting retransmissions due to errors, and is given by the following formula.

$$\text{Throughput} = B \times S \times (EC - 1)/((B + OHD) \times EC \times (1 + S \times ISD/8k))$$

where:

EC is the number of blocks sent per error cycle, that is, the number of blocks up to and including one that contains an error,

OHD is the level 2 protocol overhead,

ISD is an intersequence delay(in seconds) between sending blocks of data if the window size is too small to allow continuous transmission of blocks,

k is the window size.

EC is related to the bit error rate (BER) and the block size by:

$$EC = 1/(1-(1-BER)^{8 \times (B+OHD)})$$

In the case of the V.42 defaults, the block size B is 128 bytes, OHD is 6, k is 15 and there is no intersequence delay due to the modems (but other higher-level protocols may cause one; see later chapters). For a typical BER of 1 in 100 000, this leads to an EC of about 92 and a throughput at 14 400 bps of 13 600 bps. Figure 3.4 shows the effect of the bit error rate on throughput. Figure 3.5 shows the effect of varying the block size B, while keeping the other factors constant.

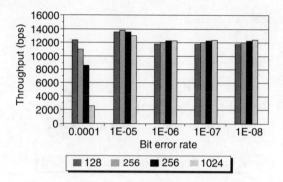

Figure 3.4   Error rate and throughput.

Another potential factor is the effect of reducing the window size significantly. It is unlikely that this would be done in either V.42 or MNP protocol, but it is quite likely to occur indirectly as a result of a higher-level protocol. For example, the default window size in X.25 is only 2 at level 3, while many PC file transfers require a block acknowledgement for every 512 byte disk read. These can cause an intersequence delay and considerable reduction of throughput. This is shown in Figure 3.6 for a 64 kbps line.

In particular, the large propagation delays of some high-speed modems will lead to low line utilizations unless the block size is large. The usual rule of thumb for setting the window size to be large enough for continuous transmission is

$$K = S * T/(B + OHD)$$

where T is the roundtrip time required to receive an acknowledgement for the block of data.

Data compression can lead to a significant increase in throughput, but its effectiveness depends both on the nature of the data, and on the block and window sizes. V.42 bis gives a compression factor of about 1.5 for application file object

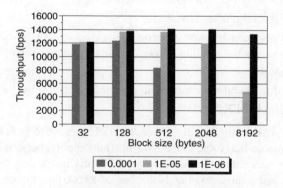

Figure 3.5   Effect of error rate.

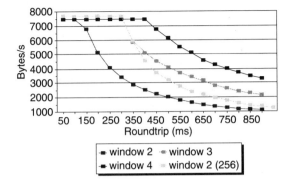

Figure 3.6   Throughput of 64K line.

code and about 2.3 for a typical textfile, but rising to about 10 in the extreme case of E-MAILS that contain large numbers of spaces. Provided that the window sizes of all protocols are large enough to ensure that there is no intersequence delay, this compression will increase throughput by the corresponding factor. If these windows are not large enough for this, then the additional processing delay of a few milliseconds per block in each modem will increase the ISD and reduce this benefit, especially for short blocks.

3.6   Polled protocols

When several devices share a line, either via a single cluster controller or via multipoint operation, the throughput achievable drops considerably as compared to the direct case examined above. The main factor is the polling protocol used, but the modem also contributes an extra factor due to its RTS/CTS turnaround time. The sources of the delays and the manner of optimizing them can be determined by consideration of the data flows involved. Two cases are considered here, the first a half-duplex protocol with priority to output over input, for example most BSC applications, and the second a full-duplex mode, such as some SDLC operations.

3.6.1   Half-duplex operation

There are three basic scenarios:

(1) poll with negative response,

(2) poll with input,

(3) select with output.

The associated dataflows are shown diagrammatically in Figure 3.7 for BSC.

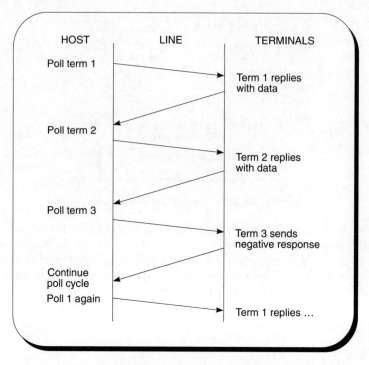

Figure 3.7 Half-duplex polling.

It is apparent that the main sources of delays additional to the actual messages are the overhead characters of the protocol and the RTS/CTS time of the
modem, with the latter featuring once in the negative poll, but twice in (2) and (3).
For distances of less than 100 miles, the propagation delay of less than 1 ms can be
ignored. Figure 3.8 shows the effect on throughput of various RTS/CTS delays for
transmission of a 256 byte message at 9600 bps.

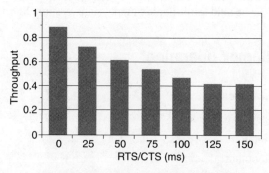

Figure 3.8 Effect of RTS/CTS delay.

A number of simple observations can be made:

(1) Line speed is very important for long messages, but for short messages, the longer RTS/CTS delays associated with the faster modems greatly reduce this benefit.

(2) For a given total line loading, the number of multidropped devices only has a small effect on response time as the transit time of a typical 6 byte poll/select is very short.

(3) The biggest effect is just the average message length.

One important factor that is not shown on these graphs is the effect of inactive devices. Whenever a device fails to respond, the host has to wait for a timeout before polling the next device. With typical timeouts of one to two seconds, a few inactive devices can have a disastrous effect on performance for the remainder, so it is essential to configure infrequent subsequent polls of devices found to be inactive.

3.6.2 Full duplex

Again there are three scenarios as in the half-duplex case, the main difference as compared to half-duplex being the drop in RTS/CTS components. This means that increasing the line speed is more beneficial for short full-duplex messages than for half-duplex.

3.7 Cellular radio

A special case of analog networks is provided by the use of cellular radio for data networks, particularly for mobile data networks. The main effects to consider are the different protocols that have to be used, and the different transmission speeds available. Where an analog mobile telephone network is used for both voice and data, shortage of bandwidth means that data transmission speeds are normally limited to only 2400–4800 bps, whereas for pure data networks speeds of up to 9600 or 19 200 bps are available. The other differences are in the initial signalling and the need for the protocols to handle varying error rates and handover effects. When a mobile user moves from one cell to another, most cellular systems operate on a break before make principle, such that carrier is lost for about 100–300 ms. Another problem is multipath fading lasting for several seconds and producing very high bit error rates.

3.7.1 Call set up

One significant advantage of cellular radio for very short transactions, such as point of sale or credit checking, is the reduction in call set-up time. Cellular radio does not require the long training sequences needed over copper circuits, so call establishment time drops from a typical 10–15 seconds to about 3, which can be vital to satisfaction when a customer is standing at a checkout desk as well as reducing slightly the number of such points required by the reduction in total service time.

3.7.2 MNP 10

Any degree of mobility in the network is likely to lead to variability in line quality, so that the optimum values for such parameters as block size and line speed keeps changing. In addition, fading of the signal may lead to loss of carrier for more than the maximum 1 to 1.5 seconds that can be accepted by most modems. The simplest standard that takes account of these issues is the proprietary MNP 10 standard, which is becoming fairly widely supported. This will automatically reduce the block size when the error rate is high and increase it when low to optimize throughput, while tolerating loss of carrier for up to five seconds. Similarly it will vary the line speed and V.series protocol. The line is initially set up at 1200 bps using V.22, then negotiated upwards in stages to the highest effective speed and standard that the modems are able to use satisfactorily.

In practice two main problems arise: the first is that the error rate may become too high for even these techniques, while the second is that the range of parameters in the AT command set of PC communications packages may be inadequate to permit satisfactory operation even where theoretically possible. This means the the MNP 10 mobile user must ensure that the communications package in use is intended for use with cellular networks, and still be prepared to park in an area of good reception if problems occur.

3.7.3 Cellular data link control (CDLC)

In the case of fully mobile networks, where the user is likely to be in a rapidly moving vehicle, more drastic correction for variability of quality is required. Signal quality varies very rapidly, particularly in urban areas, due to buildings and other obstructions acting as waveguides or reflectors. In addition, there are the breaks in the signal due to cell handover between base stations and (on mixed voice/data networks) voice signalling. These factors lead to bit error rates as high as 1 in 50, so mobile network operators have had to develop their own protocols to deal with this; one such example is Vodafone's CDLC protocol. This is a derivative of HDLC that has been enhanced by the addition of synchronization fields, forward error correction, bit interleaving and selective retransmission instead of the usual GO-BACK N approach. At high BER there is also a high chance of corruption of the HDLC flag delimiters, so CDLC replaces this by a 6 byte synchronization field containing a length indicator that is more error-proof. The frame also contains 2 bytes of addess/control data and a 2 byte checksum, so giving a total overhead of 10 bytes, while the user data field can be up to 63 bytes. Forward error correction is provided by one of two methods, BCH or RS, depending on the error rate. When BCH is used, about 50% of data transmitted is for error protection, whereas with RS the overhead is only a few per cent. Bit interleaving has to be employed to enable FEC to work, as otherwise groups of consecutive bit errors would often occur leading to retransmissions, whereas interleaving distributes the errors enough for FEC to correct most of them. Most of the time (around 80% of the time) RS is adequate, so user data throughput is around 2000 bps, while for the remainder BCH has to be used with throughput dropping to 1000–1200 bps on a nominal 2400 bps service.

Other sophisticated proprietary cellular data transfer protocols are Motorola's Enhanced Cellular Control (ECC) and AT&T's Enhanced Throughput Cellular (ETC). ETC has roughly similar features to MNP 10, but starts at the highest possible speed, dropping to the most effective level and using LAPM instead of MNP 4 for error correction.

Pure data networks, such as Ardis and RAM, offer higher transmission speeds than the voice/data networks. Each uses its own proprietary protocols to handle the sorts of effects mentioned above, with network access provided by dedicated interface units.

A penalty of sophisticated error control techniques, such as bit interleaving, is that modem propagation delays are very high, so timers should allow for about 200 ms extra on top of the expected transmission times.

4

Digital Circuit Switch Networks

4.1   Introduction

This chapter discusses the performance issues of pure circuit switch networks. Such networks are much simpler than packet switch networks and have little need for optimization. The main issues are concerned with priorities for different types of traffic in the few occasions where there is any form of contention for bandwidth, plus optimization of packetized data that passes through such a network. The other significant factor is the use of compression and other techniques to minimize bandwidth requirements.

4.2   Multiplexers

The main form of networking equipment used on such networks is a multiplexer. There are three main types of these – frequency division, time division and statistical of which the first is now largely confined to use in analog environments, such as cable TV, as in data networks it has mainly been supplanted by the other two, which are faster and more efficient.

4.2.1   Time division multiplexers

These are now the most important type of multiplexer, and often handle both voice and data. Where voice is supported it must first be converted into digital form, thereafter it is treated as data; the standards for this are outlined later in this chapter. Incoming traffic is assigned onto trunk channels on a regular time basis.

Bits, bytes or blocks of incoming data are interleaved to form frames on the trunk circuit according to either proprietary or open standards, with interworking between multiplexers only possible where they adhere to precisely the same standard. In the simplest case where no preprocessing such as voice digitization is required, the delay due to the multiplexer consists of a latency caused by the need to buffer a certain amount of data before anything is transmitted, plus a delay due to cross-channel switching if the multiplexer switches trunk circuits as well as providing trunk access. If voice is digitized, then this type of traffic experiences an additional delay. The latency varies with the multiplexer and the type of interleaving used. Most multiplexers use byte interleaving, as data from terminals is character-based, while the commonly supported PCM (pulse code modulation) voice algorithm is based on 8 bit samples. The slowest multiplexers tend to have a buffering delay of one trunk frame size, 193 bits for T1 or 256 for E1, and access traffic can be delayed by this quantity divided by the speed of the access circuit, that is, around 20 ms for a

9600 bps circuit or 3 ms for a 64 kbps circuit, but many have very much shorter delays of under 1 ms. These delays are normally fixed for the particular multiplexer and not tunable in the field. These delays are too small to be noticed by users, and only become significant when other sources of smallish delays are present.

It is essential to remember that the multiplexers require a certain amount of bandwidth for their own management, so the aggregate access channel speed must always be slightly less than the trunk bandwidth. Usually this overhead is a few thousand bits per second, but on low-speed access multiplexers this is still a critical design consideration, and may be tunable. Typical percentage management overheads are in the range 2–10%.

If access circuits are only lightly used, then this inefficient use of bandwidth carries over to the potentially expensive trunk circuits, leading to the development of statistical multiplexers to overcome the problem.

TDMs are available for a very wide range of circuit speeds, ranging from analog trunks at 9.6 kbps up to fibre-optic multiplexers with trunks running at 155 Mbps over fibre-optic links. The latter can provide a low-cost reliable alternative to ATM where individual circuit utilizations are all high.

4.2.2 Statistical multiplexers

Instead of assigning incoming traffic to dedicated timeslots, the statistical multiplexer takes bursts of data from each active circuit and puts them into proprietary frames with some form of channel identifier and error checkfield. These frames are then buffered and transmitted seqentially down the trunk circuit, and so long as the frame overhead is kept small, the trunk throughput is increased. Statistical multiplexers are used mainly for asynchronous data, and cannot support voice at all. Some statistical multiplexers also use data compression on the trunk, thereby increasing throughput by a further factor of between 1.5 for synchronous protocols and from about 2 to as much as 10 for some asynchronous traffic. The penalty of this increase in efficiency and line utilization is increased latency due to the packetizing effort and the queuing delay before transmission. The multiplexer scans the buffers of each access circuit in an overall cycle time Tc (which includes queuing), packetizes trunk data in a processing time Tp, then transmits a trunk frame in Tt, so that the overall delay is:

$$T = Tc + Tp + Tt = OHD/(S-A) + Tp + B/S$$

where:

OHD is the frame overhead in bits,

S is the trunk bit rate,

A is the total average arrival rate of data on the access circuits,

B is the total frame size in bits.

Some typical values are 24 bits for OHD, 480 bits for the frame size and 10 ms for the processing time Tp, so for a 64 kbps trunk with traffic arriving at say 32 kpbs on the access circuits, this delay T is

$$T = 0.75 + 10 + 7.5 = 18.25 \text{ ms}$$

In addition, there will be a second processing delay Tp at the remote end before onwards transmission. The delay is relatively constant until the access rate becomes comparable to the trunk speed, as is shown in Figures 4.1, 4.2 and 4.3.

It is apparent that choice of a trunk protocol with low frame overhead is the key to minimizing delay as the load approaches the trunk capacity. Data compression increases the effective trunk speed pro rata by the compression factor.

Another important feature of statistical multiplexers is that because they create multi-user trunk frames, they are able to give interactive traffic a much lower queuing delay in the presence of file transfers than is the case in the packet switched networks discussed in the next chapter.

Most statistical multiplexer trunk protocols also support error correction by means of an ARQ GO-BACK N approach, so net throughput is reduced by errors in the same way as for modems as described in the previous chapter.

When a statistical multiplexer is used to support both asynchronous and synchronous data then further performance problems can occur. The typical problem is that when synchronous block mode data is sent at the same time as asynchronous, timeouts are liable to occur in the middle of the blocks. This forces the multiplexer to have to be able to understand the protocols and recognize the blocks, or else to insert idle characters recognizable by the host into the blocks.

One form of synchronous statistical multiplexer that has been appearing recently is a combination of a time division multiplexer with statistical mixing of synchronous data frames from multiple access circuits into a single frame relay channel on the trunk.

This differs from the asynchronous case inasmuch as complete data frames are taken from each access circuit, then encapsulated in frame relay headers if not already native frame relay protocol and transmitted down the frame relay channel on

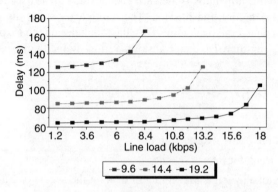

Figure 4.1 Statistical multiplexer delay.

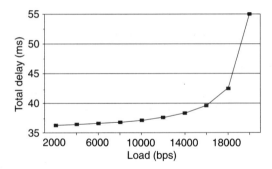

Figure 4.2   Load at 19.2 Kbps.

the trunk. The delays in this case consist of a queuing time Tq, a processing time Tp (to add frame relay headers if necessary) and a transmission time Tt. Unlike the asynchronous case, the frame size is very variable, depending entirely on the access traffic, so that small frames associated with interactive traffic can be queued behind very large frames for file transfers. The queuing delay Tq is given roughly by the M/M/1 or M/G/1 models of analytic queuing theory (see Chapter 14) so the average delay is given by:

$$T = Tq + Tp + Tt = Tt \times (U/(1 - U) + Tp + Tt = B/S \times (1/(1 - U)) + Tp$$

where the simpler M/M/1 model is quoted,

B is again the frame size,

S is the bandwidth reserved on the TDM trunk for frame relay,

U is the utilization of the frame relay channel.

What the average delay curve fails to show is the horrendous delay that can occur for frames that get queued behind the worst case 16 Mbps Token Ring frame size of 17 992 bytes; for that the delay would be the frame transmission time, which could be more than a second.

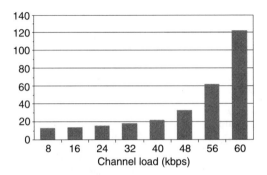

Figure 4.3   Load at 64 Kbps.

4.3   Digital voice

This section is concerned with the throughput and response time issues associated with digital voice. There are a number of different approaches to digitizing voice, depending on circumstances, of which pulse code modulation (PCM) is the most important.

4.3.1   PCM voice

The bandwidth requirements for PCM voice arise from the application of Nyquist's theorem and the quality of voice required. Nyquist's theorem states that the sampling rate required for digitizing voice is at least twice the frequency range of the sound to be encoded. For the normal situation of telephone traffic from a PABX, the audio frequency range is from 300 to 3400 Hz, so a sampling rate of at least 6800 per second is required with 8000 as the recommended standard. Quality of voice also depends on the number of bits per sample, with eight as the standard for PCM. This gives 64 000 bps as the bandwidth of a PCM voice channel, leading to 23 channels in a T1 trunk and 32 on an E1 trunk. Framing of PABX digital interfaces is defined by the CCITT G.704 recommendation, which describes how the timeslots are interleaved into 256 bit frames for E1 or 192 for T1, while G.707 and G.708 describe framing for higher speed trunks. For the case of E1 and T1 there is a dedicated timeslot (#16) for the common channel signalling between the PABXs, with framing control in timeslot 0. This means that only 30 out of the 32 timeslots are available for user traffic. Most manufacturers also modify the use of timeslot 0 so that it also (or sometimes instead) carries their own proprietary management traffic; in addition the proprietary implementation may allow part of the slot to be used for user traffic.

Unless the number of network hops exceeds six or thereabouts, there is normally no need for the full PCM voice quality, so most multiplexers offer compression facilities according to any one of a number of standards.

4.3.2   Adaptive differential pulse code modulation (ADPCM)

The main standard for compressed digitial voice is ADPCM. This is defined in recommendation G.721–726, and offers three different quality options corresponding to bandwidths of 32, 24 and 16 kbps. The choice between these is made on the grounds of the number of network hops, the type of traffic and the additional delays incurred in compression. Quality of compression is largely defined by the algorithm, but delay depends on the implementation and can vary markedly between multiplexer types. The delay incurred varies from a minimum of about 0.2 ms up to a maximum of about

5 ms according to type, and this can affect the number of hops acceptable at 32 kbps, while at the lower speeds the distortion involved in compression/decompression cycles is the limiting factor. In addition to the distortion and delay due to the multiplexers, there is also a contribution from the PBX, usually of the order of 3 dB loss and around 0.5 ms delay. Types of call that may need to be distinguished are fax traffic and break-in/out from the PSTN. The reason for this is that fax traffic is adversely affected by compression, so that throughput drops; typically 32 kbps ADPCM causes 9600 or 14 400 bps Group 3 fax to fall back to 4800 or 7200 bps, 24 kbps causes fallback to 2400 or 4800 bps and 16 kbps to 2400 or less. Traffic entering the network from the PSTN may already have suffered compression and distortion at an earlier stage in its journey, so cannot be subjected to as many network hops as native traffic. Only multiplexers with the ability to read the common channel signalling are able to distinguish these types.

The subjective loss of quality associated with 32 kbps ADPCM is 3 to 4 quantization distortion units (QDU). The maximum recommended level is around 15, so about four such hops can be tolerated, although many networks restrict it to two.

4.3.3   Digitization of analog voice

Often a multiplexer may be required to support a few analog voice channels rather than a G.704 digital PABX interface. It can do this either by using the ADPCM standards for digitization, or by several others, notably the linear predictive techniques, CELP and RELP. These use a much lower amount of bandwidth per call than ADPCM, but the voice quality is also slightly lower. The bandwidth required depends on the number of bits required to encode a voice sample, which for CELP determines the range of codes that can be used. At 9.6 kbps the subjective distortion associated with a single CELP hop is about 17 QDU, which is the maximum acceptable for most purposes. Lower speeds per channel of 6.4 and 4.8 kbps are also fairly widely available, but of minimal quality. This makes this type of quantization suitable for situations where a user dials up a central organization, but not for onwards networking. Multihop CELP is unacceptable to most people and sometimes unintelligible. The usual reason for using CELP or other low bit rate algorithms is to provide cost-effective transport of several voice channels over a 56 or 64 kbps circuit along with some data.

Some implementations of CELP are rather slow, introducing delays of the order of 100 ms, so echo cancellers and echo suppressors are usually necessary.

4.3.4   Network synchronization

Apart from ensuring adequate bandwidth, the main design criterion for multiplexer networks is maintaining synchronization. Most contemporary multiplexer networks are based on the plesiochronous digital hierarchy (PDH), in which high-speed trunks have to be de-multiplexed to E1 or T1 constituent channels whenever any cross-connection is needed. At the E1 or T1 level the plesiochronous system is able to accommodate a small amount of slippage between different interconnected networks, but uses a rigid clocking scheme within the component networks. Private networks normally take their clocking from ports connected to public networks, for example BT Kilo/MegaStream or Mercury in the UK, with the most accurate clock. A clocking table lists the clock sources in a descending order of reliability, so that for every possible failure mode it should be possible to maintain synchronization within individual network fragments. Loss of synchronization leads to the dropping of frames and retransmission of data.

Clocks are graded according to their accuracy, expressed as a stratum level. Stratum levels range from 1 to 5, with level 1 corresponding to one slippage per day being the best. The highest grade available, that is, lowest stratum level, should be given top priority. This is normally potentially derived from GPS satellites carrying Caesium clocks, but small private TDM networks have to use lower-grade derived clocks often taken from T1/E1 interfaces of PABXs, such as DASS2 in the UK. These are usually propagated through the network by means of 2 Mbps trunks.

Some problems arise with mixtures of the traditional PDH hierarchy and the newer SDH/SONET. The latter make use of variable pointers for the position of channels within a high-speed container (see Chapter 10), and this can introduce significant jitter into PDH. This may require modifications to SDH/SONET clocking.

4.3.5   Resilience

Where financially possible, most networks provide alternative routes in the event of either trunk or node failure, but some reduction in quality normally also occurs. The biggest issue is to find the necessary bandwidth. Usually the design is carried out so as to be able to handle the loss of any one trunk (sometimes a group of trunks) or any one node at a time. Many multiplexers support a priority system of reassigning bandwidth, so that important circuits are guaranteed to continue in failure modes but lesser traffic may be dropped. On some multiplexers this is extended to priority bumping, whereby in severe failure modes the important traffic may displace low priority circuits that were unaffected by the actual failure itself. An alternative that avoids this is to dial up extra trunk bandwidth using ISDN or switched 56 services to provide a temporary replacement. In all strategies a key element from the point of view of network optimization is the time taken to perform these rerouting operations.

There are several important delays involved. The first is simply the time taken to decide that a failure has taken place. In order to prevent rerouting when there is merely a burst of errors on the trunk, a threshold of poor performance is normally set, which is liable to be several seconds, before a trunk is regarded as out of order. There is then a rerouting delay. In the case of multiplexers whose routing algorithm is defined by a preconfigured routing table, this process is fairly quick, taking a few seconds also, as does dialling up extra bandwidth where that technique is used.

However, in the case of intelligent routing multiplexers that collectively calculate their response without external tables, this process can be very slow, possibly as long as several minutes in major failures. This factor often limits the maximum number of multiplexers that can be used in a single network. Where such multiplexers are used, it is necessary to check the timers on all circuits carried in order to see whether timeouts or session loss will occur during rerouting. In many cases, particularly SNA, it will be necessary to extend the timers and/or the retry counter to prevent loss of service. The aim is to ensure that routes are always backed up before the individual link protocols detect the failure and take their circuits down. Some of these scenarios are considered in more detail for individual protocols in later chapters of this book.

4.3.6   Bandwidth managers

Some multiplexers are designed to make optimum use of scarce bandwidth by transferring temporarily unused bandwidth from the circuits to which it is normally allocated to others with a greater temporary need; such devices tend to be referred to as bandwidth managers, although there is no well-defined class.

There are several approaches to this requirement, all of which depend on the ability to monitor some or all of the traffic and react intelligently. At the data level, bandwidth adaption depends on monitoring the flow in a channel either within the multiplexer or via an external device, usually the latter since the former is not compatible with basic circuit switch operation. Typically an attached device, such as a router, passes an uprated clocking signal to the multiplexer on exceeding some buffer threshold, thereby causing the multiplexer to expand the circuit bandwidth either at the expense of lower priority channels or through a pool of unassigned bandwidth.

The main scenario is to transfer bandwidth from voice to data. In order to provide a reasonable grade of voice service over the network, it is necessary to allocate more bandwidth than is required on average so as to handle transient peaks.

Voice traffic is measured in terms of Erlangs in Europe and Call Century Seconds (CCS) in the USA. The number of Erlangs is equal to the average number of simultaneous calls in progress, while one CCS is equal to 100 call-seconds per hour; this means that one Erlang is equal to 36 CCS.

Bandwidth allocation is done on the basis of Erlang tables which show how many voice channels are required to support an average number of simultaneous calls subject to a call blocking probability not exceeding some threshold, such as 1 in 50.

Table 4.1 shows that allowing for statistical fluctuations is exceptionally wasteful when a reasonable quality of service has to be offered with a small average load. From the table it is apparent that the number of channels allocated to voice often has to be three times that which is required on average, leading to a lot of bandwidth and revenue wastage. Bandwidth managers usually reallocate this spare

Table 4.1   Erlang-B channel numbers.

Average	1 in 50	1 in 100
1	3.9	4.5
2	5.9	6.4
3	7.6	8.2
4	9.1	9.8
5	10.6	11.4
6	12.0	12.8
7	13.4	14.2
8	14.7	15.6
9	16.1	17.1
10	17.4	18.6
11	18.5	19.9
12	19.7	21.1
13	20.9	22.5
14	22.0	23.8
15	23.2	25.0
16	24.3	26.2
17	25.5	27.4
18	26.6	28.6
19	27.7	29.7
20	28.8	30.8
21	30.0	32.0
22	30.9	33.1
23	32.0	34.3
24	33.1	35.5
25	34.3	36.7
26	35.4	37.8
27	36.4	38.9
28	37.5	40.0
29	38.6	41.2
30	39.7	42.4

bandwidth to the data channels whenever possible, but, in order to do so, they have to be able to read the voice signalling protocol. For PABX interfaces the signalling will usually be one of DPNSS, QSIG, Q.931 or CCS #7, and the multiplexer has to know which. On access multiplexers, the voice will more often be analog, in which case individual ports will carry their own signalling using E&M, AC13 , AC15, and so on (see the glossary for signalling systems). The data channel that benefits from this spare bandwidth will normally be a packet or frame channel in which the frames can easily be associated with specific ports. Voice calls typically last for a few minutes, so the data channel will show significant fluctuations in bandwidth on this time scale, with contraction or expansion in terms of units equal to the bandwidth occupied by a single call, for example 64 kbps for PCM voice or 4.8 to 9.6 kbps for CELP voice. The extra bandwidth leads to a significant improvement in file transfer times if the multiplexer trunk is the main bottleneck, but can cause problems with timers. For protocols that use fixed timers, such as HDLC and SDLC, the timers must be set in accordance with the response time appropriate to the minimum bandwidth, else retransmissions will occur with the possibility of avalanche decay if the trunk is already congested. Likewise the network has to be sized at the design phase so that the minimum guaranteed data bandwidth gives an adequate grade of service. Certain protocols, such as TCP/IP and DECNET V, automatically redetermine their retransmission timeouts in the light of the latest transit time for receipt of acknowledgements. There is a danger with these that the sudden change of bandwidth will lead to a timeout and retransmission. This will not happen at all for circuits with port speed small compared to the minimum data channel bandwidth, but may occur for bursts of data on relatively high-speed ports when the common data channel loading is over 70 to 80%. This retransmission danger is reduced if compressed voice is used, as the percentage change in bandwidth caused by the start up of an extra voice call is proportionately less, so that the best data quality occurs with the maximum degree of voice compression. Where the same CPU is responsible for both voice call set up and frame relay processing, there will be an additional source of data delay due to the voice activity that will further degrade quality of service.

When voice compression is used, it is desirable that the multiplexer should be able to recognize fax calls and avoid applying compression to them. If ADPCM compression to 32 kbps is applied to fax at 14.4 or 9.6 kbps, then this traffic tends to drop back to 12 or 7.2 kbps respectively, while 24/16 kbps compression tends to reduce 9.6 kbps fax to 4.8/2.4 kbps respectively. Recognition of fax traffic normally requires a PABX to be able to distinguish the type and include this information in the call set-up packet for the relevant signalling protocol.

The large statistical fluctuations associated with low Erlang levels also make these low bit rate voice compression techniques very important for leased line voice services to small offices. One Erlang of voice traffic requires four voice channels to give a 1 in 50 calling blocking probability, so the ability to provide four such channels within 28.8 kbps of a 64K circuit shared with data provides immense financial benefit. The only disadvantage is that the large level of distortion means that just one, or very occasionally two, such hops can be used before quality becomes unacceptable.

4.3.7   Packetized voice

An alternative method of providing extra bandwidth for data is the use of packetized voice. This is potentially more effective than the bandwidth management technique above, as it is able to utilize the periods of silence within a voice call as well as the unutilized channels. About two thirds of a voice call consists of silences in at least one direction, so this improvement is potentially quite significant. The standard for this is ITU-T G.764.

The main issue in this case is to maintain voice quality, as any interruption to voice of more than a few milliseconds will be detected by a listener. This requires that voice packets be given a higher pre-emptive priority than data and, where contention for bandwidth occurs, that the maximum quantity of data which a voice packet has to queue behind is never more than this period. This in turn limits the absolute maximum size of data packet that can be used to around 250 bytes per Mbps of bandwidth, with much lower values preferable to take account of multiple voice and data packets being queued at all but very low utilizations. This means, for example, that typical 1500 byte Ethernet MTUs must be fragmented before reaching such a trunk, thereby imposing a heavy load on packet switching equipment and creating very large protocol overheads.

At heavy utilization, the trunk must be capable of supporting one packet per active voice call plus data packets, giving about 80% utilization of the spare bandwidth simultaneously queued, that is, the order of 20–30 packets for instantaneous congestion on a 2 Mbps trunk so bringing the acceptable packet size down to 10–20 bytes, where headers become ludicrously large proportionately. Reducing the size still further permits even sub-64 kbps circuits to be used in this way. Worst voice quality occurs when most of the traffic is voice, since prioritization ceases to apply.

G.764 has some features to overcome these factors for T1/E1 and Nx64K lines. Firstly it collects samples over 16 ms periods that can be configured to have from 1 to 8 bits per sample, putting these into 128 bit blocks. The number of blocks per 16 ms is then equal to the number of bits per sample. These are transmitted as unnumbered frames of from 10 to 490 bytes each over PVCs. Congestion control is provided by the ability to drop up to three blocks if delays are building up. In addition, variable delay is reduced by a 'build-out delay' at the destination end of up to 199 ms. G.764 does not explicitly consider performance, but some implementations can also reduce the number of bits per sample during congested periods.

A common problem experienced with packetized voice is the clipping of calls, where some information is lost, mainly at the start of bursts of speech after pauses. When this happens to data it necessitates retransmission.

When carried to its logical conclusion of very small packets, the most effective way to do this type of thing is ATM using higher speeds and larger cells, which is described in Chapter 9 of this book.

4.4   Mobile digital networks

Nowadays many digital networks contain mobile elements as well as static. The main standards for mobile digital data services are the American USDC (US Digital Communications), Japanese JDC, European GSM (Global Service Mobile) and

DECT (Digital European Cordless Telecommunications) standards, of which the last is restricted to an office environment rather than a WAN. From a performance perspective, the main feature is the throughput that can be expected. For GSM this is restricted by shortage of bandwidth to 9.6 kbps and for USDC to 8 kbps, while for the local DECT it can go up to several hundred kbps. As with the analog mobile services, there are potential quality issues associated with the handover from one base station to another, leading to retransmissions, but the general error rate is very much lower than for the analog cases. Another improvement is a great reduction in the number of calls that get completely lost.

4.5   ISDN

The standards for Integrated Services Digtal Networks (ISDN) make use of the packet/frame protocol standards defined in ITU I.441, Q.931, Q.921 and related standards for call control, but the individual B-channels can be used for any digital form of voice or data traffic. I.441 is the overall definition of services, with Q.931 describing the packet level call set-up facilities and Q.921 giving the link-level features. These standards describe several modes of operation, defining B, D, and H-channels. The B-channels are each 64 kbps and used for voice or data, three H-channels give 384, 1536 or 1920 kbps that is intended primarily for videoconferencing and the 16/64 kbps D-channel primarily for signalling. Basic rate ISDN has 2 B-channels and a 16 kbps D-channel, while primary rate has 30 B-channels and a 64 kbps D-channel.

From a performance point of view the significance of ISDN is that in many countries it is the only source of either digital or high-speed dial-up capacity. The actual dial-up time is much less than for most analog lines, with a typical time to bring up a B-channel of 0.5 to 2 seconds, that is, a tenth of that for modems. This is important for credit card or point of sale applications, where the dial-up time is a major source of cost through the added holding time for processor ports and checkout staff. International ISDN set-up times are longer, reaching about 20 seconds in the worst cases.

The H-channels, where supported, provide homogeneous bandwidth, but in general different B-channels to the same destination point are routed separately across the ISDN, and so are liable to arrive with differing delays. This means that a user who wants $N*64$ kbps requires an inverse multiplexer at each end of the ISDN link to aggregate the N B-channels into a homogeneous uniform delay circuit. The only exception to this is those ISDN networks which have an option to guarantee routing of B-channels by the same physical route, for example Mercury in the UK, or protocols that perform their own resequencing, such as OSI TP4.

There is no official standard for inverse ISDN multiplexers, but most vendors have agreed a proprietary set of standards known as bonding to allow interoperability of their products. This standard has been adopted by both ANSI and ISO. There are four components of this, whose main features are illustrated in Table 4.2.

The standard allows for the inverse muxing of up to 63 channels, that is, to 4.032 Mbps. Two different maximum delay options are provided, one for terrestrial networks and the other for satellite systems, so the appropriate type of inverse multiplexer must be used.

Bonding is beneficial for file transfers, but may sometimes be detrimental to interactive response times due to the buffering delay. This delay is sometimes referred to as injected delay and tends to be in the range 2 to 100 ms, depending on implementation, so it is worth finding out the likely delay for any individual terminal adaptor or mux offering bonding. A short packet taking the faster of two paths can easily get 30 ms ahead of a preceding large packet taking the slow route, and the buffering has to compensate for this. Another potential problem is the lack of an error recovery mechanism; this is not necessary for intrinsically multilink protocols like SNA transmission groups, X.25 multilink or MP but may affect other protocols. A forthcoming ITU-T standard will address this.

Access to ISDN is provided either by native ISDN capability (ISDN TE1) or via a terminal adaptor (TA), in each case having a physical attachment to the network at the NT1 (plug in the wall). Development of ISDN cards for PCs has been held up by the delay in arriving at a general ISDN Application Program Interface, so many PCs need to make use of a terminal adaptor for ISDN access. These normally provide rate adaption according to the V.110 standard so that a single low speed, for example 19.2 kbps port, is bitstuffed up to the 64 kbps B-channel bandwidth; thus the data rate is still 19.2 kbps, and the TA does not provide any data compression. V.110 allows data rates up to 64 kbps for synchronous traffic, but only 19.2 kbps for asynchronous, although the most common chip set used extends this to 38.4 kbps and some to 57.6 kbps. Data compression becomes applicable only for DTE ports that operate above 64 kbps, when a compressor preprocessor in the TA would be beneficial. The best solution is to have the compression included in the file transfer program rather than the TA itself. There is an alternative standard to V.110, called V.120, that supports higher asynchronous speeds and is more able to use data compression within the TA. Relatively few early TAs use this, but where the end device has an asynchronous port faster than 38.4 kbps, this is the standard to go for. Speeds of 115.2 and 230.4 kbps are quite widely supported. A further advantage of V.120 over V.110 is the ability to support different asynchronous port speeds on the two ends of a link.

Table 4.2   BONDING standards.

Standard	Features
0	Initial parameter exchange, then delay equalization by customer equipment
1	Negotiation and compensation fixed at set up, full b/width
2	In-band monitor and control via BERT test, only 63K/channel, packet networks only
3	Monitor and control with 64K per channel, voice or data

Internal ISDN cards are also able to support 64 kbps B-channel bit rates for asynchronous data since they avoid use of the usual comm ports on a PC.

Basic rate ISDN supports an S-Bus with up to eight devices on it that can contend for the two B-channels. Incoming access to the correct S-Bus member is controlled by the use of either subaddressing or multiple subscriber number supplementary functions. Erlang-B calculations can be used to decide how many devices to put on the S-Bus up to eight.

Basic rate ISDN uses the same types of copper circuit as analog PSTN links, so is exposed to the same sources of error as the latter. The digital signalling is less sensitive, so error rates are lower, often in the range 10^{-5} to 10^{-7}, with a good deal of variation of quality; long lines to the local exchange tending to be worst. These error rates allow packets of the order of 500 bytes without significant retransmissions in most cases.

5

X.25 Networks

5.1 Introduction

5.2 X.25 parameters

5.3 X.25 call set up

5.4 Interpretation of manufacturers'
performance figures

5.5 X.25 PADs

5.6 PADs for polled protocols

5.7 Performance optimization

5.8 Level 2 timers

5.9 General X.25 network design

5.1 Introduction

One of the most widespread packet switch network varieties is X.25. The standard is extremely stable, having been first defined in 1976, then upgraded in 1980, 84 and 88. X.25 itself is an access protocol defined by the CCITT, and does not contain any recommendations for the mechanism to use for routing. This leads to the existence of many different subtypes which are distinguished by the routing protocol and algorithms. X.25 has a reputation in some quarters as being very slow, but this need not be the case. Early X.25 networks were slow because of the low-speed analog links and low-power switches when the standard began, but modern digital networks with link speeds up to 10 Mbps can give very high performance.

X.25 is arguably the best protocol to use for dumb terminals and error-prone lines, such as modem links and satellite links, owing to its complex error checking, but for optical fibre networks and intelligent terminals it is very clumsy.

This chapter commences with the X.25 parameters that influence performance, then considers the influence of the routing protocol before treating other protocols that are often associated with X.25 networks. Only those aspects of X.25 which are relevant to performance are considered.

5.2 X.25 parameters

5.2.1 Basic definitions

The X.25 recommendation covers both levels 2 and 3, data link and network, in the OSI model. X.25 calls are connection-oriented and defined on an end-end basis by a level 3 virtual circuit that maps onto local logical channels on the individual links. Four types of X.25 call are supported; permanent virtual circuits (PVC), switched virtual circuits (SVC), fast select call and fast select with immediate clear. Originally datagrams were supported, but they were replaced in the 1984 version by fast select. From a performance perspective, the importance of the different call types is the set-up/clear-down time and the amount of network resource required.

The level 2 frames must conform to either HDLC LAPB or LAP, although LAP is almost obsolete now. Data link frames belong to three categories: information frames (I-frame) and supervisory frames (S-frame) or unnumbered frames (U-frames). Each I- or S-frame contains 6 bytes of overhead for basic mod 8 operation or 7 for the optional mod 128, comprising two 8 bit flags, a 16 bit frame check sequence, an 8 bit control field for mod 8 or 16 bit for mod 128 and an 8 bit address field. Flow control is provided by means of sequence numbers in the control field, with acknowledgements either by means of separate level 2 RRs (receive ready) and

RNR (not ready) or by piggybacking the ready response into the control field of a returning I-frame via its sequence numbers. Tuning of this functionality is a major factor in optimizing X.25 performance. U-frames control the link state and consist of the two flags plus an 8 bit control field. From 1984 onwards the X.25 recommendation has contained an option for multilink operation (analogous to SNA transmission groups) as well as the mandatory single link style, but although this offers performance benefits it is rarely implemented.

The LAPB system parameters that affect performance are the frame size, the frame window size, the maximum number of outstanding I-frames, the timers T1 and T2 and the maximum number of transmission attempts, N2, and the choice of either single link (SLP) or multilink protocol (MLP). LAP has an analogous set of parameters, but no MLP option. Normally the frame window size is set at a default of 7 for basic operation or between 15 and 127 for extended operation over satellite links. Use of a value of 7 for terrestrial operations ensures that data can flow continuously at the data link level provided that there is sufficient traffic at level 3.

At the network level, packets belong to any of six categories: call set up/ clear, data and interrupt, flow control and reset, restart, diagnostic and registration. Of these, it is essentially the first three categories that are of interest in network optimization.

5.3   X.25 call set up

Once the link has been brought up at level 2, the level 3 call can be established. This is done by the transmission of a call request packet by the originating DTE, followed by a call accept from the remote DTE. This initial exchange can be used to negotiate the parameters that control the subsequent data throughput of the connection. The structure of the call request and accept are shown in Figure 5.1, with the facilities field used for the optional parameters.

The parameters that influence performance are listed below.

5.3.1   Level 3 performance parameters

Fast select

This facility enables short calls to be performed more efficiently. If not more than 128 bytes of data needs to be sent in either direction, then it can be included in the original fast select call request issued by the originating DTE, subject to the proviso that the destination DTE supports the optional fast select acceptance feature. There

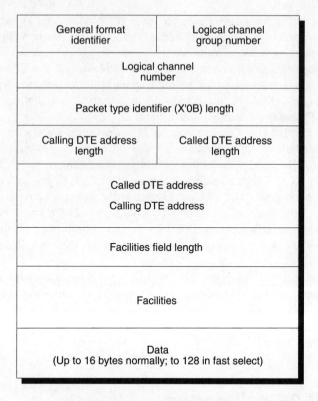

Figure 5.1　X.25 Call request.

are two classes of fast select, restricted and unrestricted. The restricted case requires a clear indication, including up to 128 bytes of data, to be sent in response to the original call request. In the unrestricted case, the response can either be a call accept with up to 128 bytes of data, to which the originator responds with a clear indication including up to 128 bytes more of data, or else a clear indication as in the restricted case. These options are defined by bits 7 and 8 in the facilities field of the initial fast select call request. These options cut the port holding time of short calls, as well as possibly reducing the call charge on a public network.

Packet size

Packet size can have a major influence on the throughput and response time. It can either be configured as a static parameter on the X.25 ports of the DTE and DCE, or else be negotiated on a per call basis when this option is supported by DCE and DTE. In the negotiable case, bits 4, 3, 2 and 1 of the first octet of the facilities field are used to define a value in the range 16 to 4096 in multiples of two, and the corresponding bits of octet two for the reverse direction. The call accept then returns the negotiated values analogously. The default is normally 128, although networks can optionally support other values of the default. This default is suited to the high bit error rates of analog lines plus the need to avoid excessive degradation of interactive response times by file transfers over low-speed lines. In typical modern X.25 networks where many of the lines are digital with speeds of 56/64 kbps a value of 256 may be better, particularly for the file transfers.

5.3.2   Window size

Window sizes in the range 1 to 7 are similarly either statically configured for the X.25 ports, or else negotiated on a per call basis using bits 7 to 1 of the first and second octets of the facilities field for the two directions. The default is normally 2, although networks can optionally support other values of the default.

Larger window sizes are beneficial when the D-bit is set, but require more memory, so reduce the number of virtual circuits that can be simultaneously supported.

Window sizes need to be especially large (greater than 7 in general) for satellite networks, for which level 3 sequence numbering modulo 128 is required. See Chapter 10 for satellite issues in general.

D-bit

This bit is set in the general format identifier of the call request to indicate whether acknowledgements are to be local (D-bit = 0) or end to end (D-bit = 1). If the D-bit is set, then throughput will normally be reduced unless the window size is increased from the default of 2.

Understanding of the implications of the D-bit in X.25 is also the basis for understanding end-to-end delays in general, for example OSI transport level 4 or TCP.

When the D-bit is set, the source destination can only transmit a number of packets equal to the window size before it has to stop and wait for an acknowledgement from the destination DTE. Unless the window is very large, this will cause a significant interruption to transmission and hence poor response time and low throughput. This is particularly important on large public networks.

M-bit

This bit is set in data packets to show that they belong to a larger unit, normally an OSI level 4 TPDU. Some networks also use this to fragment DTE packets within the general packet switch network to obtain better performance, then reassemble them before transmission to the destination DTE. When large packets from LAN protocols are encapsulated in X.25 it is more efficient to break the original packets down by using the X.25 M-bit than to first fragment the LAN packet, as LAN protocols have much larger headers than X.25 (see Chapter 6 for LAN headers).

Flow control parameter negotiation

This must be subscribed to in order to allow the negotiation of packet and window size.

Throughput class negotiation

An optional throughput class can be supported either by static port configuration or by call request negotiation. This optional parameter can range from 75 bps to 19 200 bps in multiples of two, in addition to options of 48 000 and 64 000 bps. Where this is supported, the DCE should set up the virtual connection over the network by a route which will be compatible with the configured or negotiated throughput class. This can only be achieved for the higher rates if appropriate choices of D-bit, packet size and window size have been made. Most systems do not have the intelligence to correlate these parameters, and throughput class tends to be a bit academic. In practice, users need to negotiate with the network administrator to have ports and routes configured statically in such a way as to meet their requirements.

Transit delay selection and indication

Where response time is the critical factor, a DTE can request a maximum transit delay if this optional feature is supported. Values from 0 to 65 534 ms can be specified in this field. Most packet switch networks do not have sufficient intelligence to support this, and negotiation with the network administrator is required instead.

Registration packet

Negotiation with the network administration can in principle be automated using the registration facility, but this is rarely, if ever, supported.

Priority

Annex G of X.25 includes features to support OSI network service quality of service parameters, which include traffic priority in addition to minimum throughput class and transit delay. Three values are specified: target, available and selected. The allowed range of priorities is from 0 to 254. A DCE can then maintain different queues for each supported priority level. This should normally be used to give interactive sessions priority over file transfers, and is fairly widely supported.

5.3.3 X.25 flow control

The way in which X.25 controls the flow of traffic is the key to setting the optimum values of these parameters. There are two main scenarios to consider: the first in which the D-bit is not set, and the second in which it is. In the first case, all acknowledgements are local, and the typical windowing aspects of flow control are shown in Figure 5.2.

This example illustrates the case of a window size of 2, the usual default. The X.25 source only has to wait for the first of the level 3 RRs to arrive back from the first switch before it can commence transmitting the third packet. If the RR was piggybacked onto a very long data packet, then there may be a slight gap in transmission when using window size 2, so it is often better to use 3 or 4 to obtain uninterrupted flow.

In the second case, all level 3 acknowledgements are end to end. This means that there are liable to be long gaps in file transfers while the source waits for an acknowledgement unless the level 3 window is quite large. This is shown in Figure 5.3.

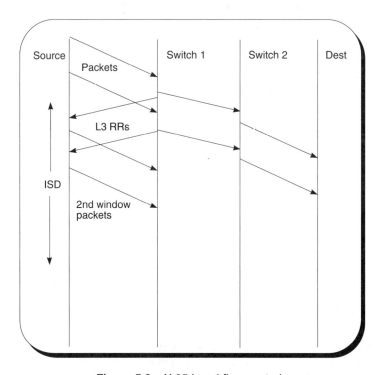

Figure 5.2   X.25 Local flow control.

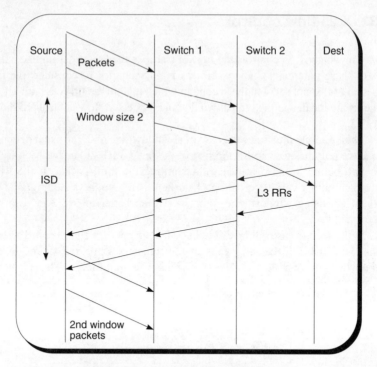

Figure 5.3 X.25 End-End flow control.

This example illustrates the case of a window size of 2, the usual default. The X.25 source has to wait for a significant period, the intersequence delay (ISD), after completion of transmission of the first window before it can commence the second. Level 3 RRs are sometimes piggybacked onto large packets, so the ISD varies as a result of the consequent variable transmission time.

Data packets

Flow control of data is based on send/receive sequence numbers for both levels 2 and 3 in conjunction with the configured window sizes. The packet structure is shown in Figure 5.4.

Setting an L2 or L3 receive sequence number to N(R) acknowledges all frames/packets respectively up to and including N(R) – 1. Figure 5.4 shows modulo 8 sequence numbers, but modulo 128 can be defined instead by changing flags for L2 or L3 as appropriate in the header and using extended 7 bit fields.

Acknowledgements can either be piggybacked on data frames or packets using these sequence numbers or else sent in dedicated RRs at level 2 or 3 that do not contain data. Response time is faster with the dedicated RRs due to their lower transmission time, but packet processing efficiency is much higher when piggy-

Start flag						
Address (DTE/DCE)						
0	L2 send SEQ.NO		P/F	L2 receive SEQ.NO		
Q-bit	D-bit	0	1	Logical group		
Logical channel number						
L3 receive SEQ.NO		M-bit	L3 send SEQ.NO		0	
Data						
CRC						
End flag						

Figure 5.4   X.25 Data packet.

backing occurs. This will take place if there is a frame already queued and awaiting transmission in the opposite direction. Without tweaking of timers, the proportion of acknowledgements that are piggybacked is very roughly equal to the line utilization as a percentage, either in total for level 2 or for the specific virtual circuit in the case of level 3. Level 3 piggybacking is thus negligible normally except for multi-user VCs that use up most of the bandwidth.

X.25 overheads

Overheads associated with X.25 include the supervisory frames, such as call requests, clears and confirms, plus the acknowledgements if not piggybacked, the headers and bit stuffing.

For long duration calls using packets of average length in the region of 100 bytes, the bandwidth overhead is about 15%. This drops to about 10% or less if larger packets can be used consistently.

5.3.4   X.25 routing

Routing of packets does not form part of the X.25 recommendation, which is purely an access protocol. As a result, there are a large number of different methods, with significant associated performance factors.

The basic essentials are to have some method of determining the best route to follow, and to avoid closed routing loops where the packet passes through a node more than once. Choice of route is usually based on tables held in each node together with up-to-date link state tables, although a few systems use dynamic pathfinder packets. Link state tables are maintained by means of triggered updates based on proprietary alarms sent by nodes when failures are detected.

Routing of the actual packets within the networks is normally based on following a virtual circuit established in the initial call set up using the proprietary routing algorithm. There is frequently also a proprietary trunking protocol, which leads to modified headers and a different degree of link processing on the trunks as compared to native X.25; as a consequence X.25 switches from different vendors can only interwork at the access level and not on trunks.

The simplest (from an X.25 viewpoint) way of avoiding closed routing loops is to include routing information in the call user data field of the call request that enables nodes to see where the request has already been to in the network. A more popular technique is to use a trunk protocol based on the X.75 international gateway recommendation with the advantage over X.25 derivatives that it is easier to support reconnection over alternative paths without loss of service in the event of a failure. Some other devices use a statistical multiplexer trunk protocol that offers better performance for interactive traffic in the presence of file transfers due to the use of multi-user packets on the trunks. Some switches offer a configurable choice of trunk protocol for each trunk.

5.4   Interpretation of manufacturers' performance figures

Any network manager purchasing X.25 equipment needs to be able to interpret vendors' switch performance claims accurately, but this is not always straight-forward. Figures are naturally quoted for optimal conditions, but these optima can differ drastically from the real case in ways that differ from one type of switch to another.

Most of the work performed by a packet switch is on the packet headers rather than any data content, so protocol overhead packets and frames, in particular levels 2 and 3 RRs, impose a major processing load on the switch. As a result, performance figures are usually quoted under the ideal circumstance in which almost all RRs at both levels 2 and 3 are piggybacked onto actual user data packets by means of updating the frame and packet sequence numbers. For this to be possible there has to be another packet waiting to be transmitted in the reverse direction to carry the acknowledgement. Both experience and elementary queuing theory show that for level 2 this is not normally true until about 50–60% trunk loading, while at level 3 it is very rarely true at all. Where processor loading is a network limiting factor some tuning of parameters can improve this, but the normal consequence is that the real-life performance of the packet switch will be about one third to half the optimum quoted. The next factor is that performance also varies according to whether the traffic is (a) trunk–trunk, (b) X.25–trunk or (c) X.25–X.25. For the switches using slightly modified X.25 as trunk protocol, there is little difference between these, but for many others there is a vast difference with case (a) being up to eight times as powerful as case (c), while (b) is intermediate. An example of extreme difference is the Sprint TP4000 range, while the Telematics ACP range has very little difference between trunk and X.25 access processing. Vendors automatically take account of such factors when designing a turnkey network, but network managers need to ascertain what these factors amount to for each possible trunk protocol.

5.5 X.25 PADs

X.25 networks often cater for other access protocols by means of a PAD (packet assembler disassembler) that converts their data into X.25. Potentially, there are as many such PAD functions as there are other data communications protocols, but this chapter only considers a few of the main ones.

5.5.1 Asynchronous PADS

The most important PAD type is asynchronous or triple X, which is based on the three recommendations X.3, X.28 and X.29. From a performance point of view some factors are the same as for X.25 itself, for example the packet and window sizes, but the main new factor is the forwarding criterion and its relation to the processing load on the PAD. The processing load consists of two main components, (a) the work done to create the packet header and (b) the character analysis on packet assembly and disassembly, with assembly the much more laborious.

Where a PAD also functions as a switch, an upper bound to the character throughput is given by the product of the packet switching rate and the packet size, but achievable throughput is usually less than this due to the character processing. Recommendation X.3 includes packet forwarding criteria: data forwarding characters as specified by parameter 3 in the PAD configuration tables and an idle timer that is specified similarly by parameter 4. Many PADs also allow the proprietary addition of forwarding on receipt of a fixed number of characters, for example 128 or 256.

Processing effort is much less if forwarding is based on either an idle timer or a fixed number of characters, rather than on recognition of special characters. This difference can be a factor of about three where multiple choices of forwarding character have to be detected as compared to the idle case. Character throughput for disassembly is close to the upper bound quoted above.

Where the attached device is a dumb terminal it may be necessary to provide character echo, either globally from the application or locally via the PAD. This can be set by X.3 parameter 2 of the PAD, with overall network performance much better in the local case which relies on X.25 error correction instead of the old echoplex technique.

X.28 specifies the PAD control commands while X.29 defines the procedures for exchange of control information between one PAD and another packet mode DTE or PAD; neither of these has much significance for performance. The only exception to this is the use of the X.29 reselect feature. This enables any call to be sent to an alternative address, usually a security gateway instead of the ultimate destination, before the final address is reselected. This increases the call set-up time because of the initial checks, and in some cases the security gateway may be the limiting factor on network capacity.

5.6   PADs for polled protocols

There are many PADs for such protocols. The common feature with performance implications is that the PADs respond to the polls rather than sending them across the network; this avoids timeout problems for the polls, but can impose a heavy load on the PAD. Such PADs are divided into terminal PADs (TPADs, sometimes called forward PADs) and host PADs (HPADs, sometimes also called reverse PADs). In extreme cases an HPAD can be overloaded when there is no data traffic on the network, but have a light and acceptable load when there is such traffic. The reason for this paradox is that the host may be polling as fast as possible on each of its multipoint circuits imposing an overload on a low-powered HPAD, but when it has a large message to send polling is interrupted and the PAD performs the much lighter load of buffering and forwarding the data. This will normally only happen if the host-polling rate is unnecessarily fast, so both host and PAD performance can be improved by reducing this rate on the host, either explicitly or implicitly by a pause parameter, without degradation of the network performance. In principle, the same situation could occur with the TPAD, but because it is the PAD that performs the polling in this instance, it will automatically slow its rate as overload is approached; again it can also be configured for a lower maximum rate.

5.7   Performance optimization

The first thing that must be appreciated in optimizing X.25 performance is that there are different facets of performance that have different and even mutually incompatible optimization techniques. The first thing to do is to identify what are the most critical aspects of performance that have to be improved. Typical scenarios are as follows:

(1) The network has plenty of capacity on both switches and links, but response time is too long on short transactions.

(2) As (1), but the throughput is not high enough on certain routes.

(3) Most of the network is adequate, but a critical link that cannot be upgraded quickly is overloaded at peak times.

(4) Response time, line loadings and throughput are all adequate, but some switches are fully loaded at peak times, so preventing new applications from being added to the network.

(5) Combinations of all of these.

Case (1)

Scenario (1) can be approached in several ways. Firstly, if the transaction uses a multihop route across the network, then for a message size of over about 64 bytes, it is possible that using a smaller packet size, so that two or three would be needed for the message, would improve the response. In the case of long transactions with uninterrupted flow this would only produce a small gain at the start of the message. The reason for this is that in X.25 a packet must be fully received by a node before it is onward transmitted. As a result, there is a delay at each node equal to the transmission time over the preceding link of the whole message, before any processing is done by the node. Splitting the packet down into smaller units reduces this by almost a half or two thirds, but at the expense of higher network loadings and more switch delays. For this to work, the switch packet processing time needs to be significantly smaller than the message transmission time over the adjacent links; some examples are shown below.

Another factor in this scenario is the influence of other traffic. Giving the short transactions a higher level of priority than larger ones with bigger packets will mean that their packets will be put onto the transmission queue by the node ahead of (or at least preferentially) the others, so improving the response time for this class at the expense of the rest. This effect may not be large enough, and a more drastic version of this that is available on a few switches is to use the option of a statistical multiplexer multi-user packet trunk protocol. In this case the short transaction is mixed with characters from the longer ones, so that they do not have to wait for the completion of transmission of a large packet before being transmitted themselves.

Case (2)

Scenario (2) typically applies to the case where a file transfer has to be completed in a tight timescale. The main factors in this case are obtaining the optimum packet and window sizes, taking into account the error rate on the lines. The window size has to be made large enough at both levels 2 and 3 to ensure that there are no interruptions to data flow due to intersequence delays waiting for X.25 acknowledgements to arrive.

The basic formula for the minimum window size for uninterrupted flow is:

$$K = \frac{S * T}{L}$$

where S is the line speed, T the roundtrip delay before an acknowledgement is received and processed, and L is the packet or frame length. For local acknowledgements over terrestrial links a value of 3 to 4 is usually the minimum for 128 byte frames, but more for very short frames. In the case of geostationary satellite links, the large propagation delay entails much larger values, and this special case is discussed more fully under satellite networks. For end–end packet acknowledgements over multihop routes larger windows are needed, usually from 4 to 7, but possibly larger on very large networks with trunks little faster than the access links.

If the packet switch network does not support large packet or window sizes, then the only step is to ensure that the D-bit is not set. This means that acknowledgements are all done locally without waiting for any remote response, and can in extreme cases raise throughput from about 5000 bps to 40 000 bps on a 64 kbps X.25 access link into the network. Where large packet and window sizes are available, the D-bit can be set for end–end acknowledgements with their greater integrity. There is no point in making the packet size larger than the size of a disk read; often 512 bytes for a PC, plus high-level headers, and high error rates will reduce throughput more with a large packet size. On networks containing some analog links, where the BER is about 1 in 100 000, the optimum packet size for file transfer is usually 256 bytes, but rising to 512 bytes for digital networks with their lower BERs. Specific effects associated with other protocols, such as NetWare, are given in later chapters.

Case (3)

In scenario (3), where a link is overloaded it is assumed that, wherever possible, traffic has already been diverted from this critical link. In this event the key X.25 feature is to try to reduce the protocol overheads to a minimum, although the scope for this is limited. Each data packet has 9 bytes of level 2, 3 overhead including flags plus a few more bytes due to bit stuffing. Increasing the packet size for large transactions will reduce the number of packets, and hence reduce the line loading by a few per cent. The main effect, however, would be achieved by using data compression, either between modems if it is an analog link, or in the file transfer application.

Case (4)

In scenario (4), the objective is to reduce the processing load on the packet switches. The first task is to identify the cause of the overload by examining the switch statistics.

Call set up imposes a much heavier load than individual packet switching, and in some cases this may be the prime factor. In a few networks replacing SVCs by PVCs would reduce the switch loading due to call requests at critical times, although this is not often appropriate. Sending call accounting records to a network management system is one significant source of call set ups if SVCs are used that can be changed to PVCs, whereas dial-up calls such as credit card transactions have to be handled by fast select SVCs, unless a combination of ISDN and X.25 link spoofing is used.

The main method of load reduction is to increase the packet size if the message sizes are large enough for this to have any effect and the bit error rate low enough for not more than 1–2% of packets to require retransmission due to errors. On multihop routes an undesirable side effect of increasing packet size is likely to be an increase in network response time due to the need to receive frames fully at each node before onwards transmission.

If the links are not very heavily loaded, then the packet switches will be generating individual level 2 RRs for most of the data frames, which takes almost half as much processing as for a single level 3 packet. The proportion of frames acknowledged in this way can be reduced by extending the level 2 timer T2 and by increasing the outstanding acknowledgement threshold. In the extreme case of 10% loaded links, an increase of T2 to about half a second plus Ackthresh of 7 would reduce a 100% peak switch load to 70–80%.

If T2 is increased it is essential to check that the level 2 window size remains adequate to allow uninterrupted flow, else throughput will drop. In the extreme case of a value of T2 of 100 ms on a 2 Mbps trunk, almost 200 128 byte frames could be transmitted before T2 permitted an acknowledgement to be sent, so the effect is potentially quite drastic and also emphasizes that T2 must be related to the link speed and frame size.

Another variation on scenario (4) is that the CPU load is quite acceptable, but that the X.25 device is running out of memory. Often the best solution to this is to upgrade the memory, but where this is impractical the alternative may to be reduce the frame, packet and window sizes to reduce the number of logical channels configured on each link (and hence the maximum number of simultaneous calls over it).

Case (5)

Scenario (5) is usually grounds for upgrading the network as a whole, but some stopgap improvements can be made by the above techniques. The switch and load reduction techniques in (3) and (4) are mutually compatible, but are incompatible with the response time optimization of (1). Throughput optimization may be compatible with (3) and (4), but this is not always the case.

5.8   Level 2 timers

Part of the optimization process is the choice of values for the level 2 timers. Before a specific choice can be made, it is necessary to decide what are the most important quality of service features for the network. For example, as shown in the previous section, the criteria for maximum possible switch throughput are different to those for other optima, such as file transfer time or resilience. This section treats each parameter, and how it should be optimized for different purposes.

5.8.1   T1 retransmission timer

This is the timeout for retransmitting a frame that has not been acknowledged. The X.25 recommendation itself gives some general rules to follow in setting this. These are that T1 need not be the same for both ends of the link and should be greater than the maximum time between the transmission of any frame, whether a data frame, supervisory command or SAM and so on, and the frame returned as answer. This can be expressed as an inequality:

$$T1 > 2*P + T2 + Tt(1) + Tt(2) + Tp$$

where:

> P is the propagation delay over the link due to the finite signal propagation speed,
>
> $T2$ is the permitted switch delay before acknowledgement,
>
> $Tt(1)$ is the time to transmit the initial frame over the link,
>
> $Tt(2)$ is the time taken to transmit the answering frame and
>
> Tp is the remote frame processing time including any queuing due to processor congestion.

If the frame size in the two directions of the link differ radically, then different values of $T1$ for the two ends may be desirable. To avoid any unnecessary retransmissions, the values of Tt and Tp must be the greatest of any of the frame types expected on the network; usually this will be the time for the largest I-frame. Many X.25 DTEs and DCEs have defaults of one to three seconds, possibly dependent on link speed, that are adequate if neither large data frames nor multihop satellite links occur. DTE or DCE frame processing times, Tp, are usually of the order of the reciprocal of the frame processing rate for a single frame, and in congested conditions there may be about 10 frames queued ahead, so a value of the order of 10 times the reciprocal processing rate is reasonable for Tp. For a low-powered DTE or DCE with a processing rate of 20 frames/s this would give Tp of half a second, dropping to 50 ms at 200 frames/s. In congested conditions, unnecessary retransmissions only make matters worse, so it is reasonable to allow for about six (link window size minus one) frames to be queued on the link ahead of the answer frame, each of the average frame size. For 128 byte frames on a 9.6 kbps link, $Tt(1)$ and $Tt(2)$ would each be about 800 ms each on this basis, while $T2$ often has a default of 250 ms, so $T1$ has to be greater than about 2.7 seconds for these conditions. Suppose, that the frame size is increased to 1024 bytes; this increases Tt to about 6.5 seconds, so $T1$ has to go up to about 14 seconds. Conversely, if the link speed is increased to 256 kbps, the Tt for the 1024 byte frames comes down to about 200 ms, so $T1$ need only be about 1 second.

If it is known that the network is only to be operated at very light loads, then $T1$ can be reduced by a factor of 2 or 3 from these values, since there will be no heavy congestion. The advantage of a short value of $T1$ is in handling retransmissions due to bit errors on the link, as the longer $T1$ is, the greater the degradation of throughput due to errors. This is the choice to make for time critical file transfers across lightly loaded analog lines, and may entail reducing the defaults.

5.8.2   Retransmission counter N2

After $N2$ retransmissions without acknowledgement, the link is reset and higher-level sessions possibly taken down (dependent on protocol). In some networks it may be desirable to do this very quickly, to enable users to be reconnected by alternative routes with minimum downtime, whereas on other networks link failure may force the higher-level session to be taken down with considerable delay or difficulty in re-establishing it. The first of these two cases requires the total time $T1 * N2$ to be short, while the latter requires it to be comparatively long. Once $T1$ has been selected, then $N2$ can be determined by the requirement $N2 = Ts/T1$ where Ts is the maximum time for which the session inactivity is to be tolerated. The usual default of $N2$ is 10, and most X.25 devices support a range from 1 to at least 15. If $T1$ has been set to a long value, such as 10 seconds for large frames over slow congested links, then it will usually be desirable to reduce $N2$ to 3 or 4 to prevent keeping an ineffectual link up for too long. For high performance systems with $T1$ under 1 second, it may be a good idea to increase $N2$ to prevent over-sensitivity to bursts of errors resulting from impulse noise, and so on. As with $T1$, $N2$ need not be the same at both ends of the link.

5.8.3   Acknowledgement timer T2

This is the time between a switch receiving a frame and issuing an acknowledgement. Many X.25 implementations either use a fixed default, such as 250 ms, or else merely acknowledge as soon as possible, so it is not always possible to adjust this parameter. The reason for changing it is to increase the proportion of level 2 frames that are piggybacked, and so reduce the load on a congested X.25 switch. It is usually necessary also to increase the outstanding acknowledgement parameter at the same time. The occasion to increase $T2$ is when there are a large number of lightly loaded links on the switch, and the aim is to ensure that whenever a frame has to be acknowledged, there is a frame queued in the opposite direction onto which it can be piggybacked. If frames are being transmitted at a rate of F per second, then $T2$ needs to be at least equal to Tp plus $1/F$. A 9600 bps line at 10% utilization will often only be carrying 1 to 2 frames per second, so will need a value of 0.5 to 1 second for $T2$, whereas for a 10% loaded 2 Mbps link, $T2$ need only be about 50 ms.

5.8.4   Idle timers T3 and T4

X.25 specifies a link state idle timer T3 on whose expiry the DCE should assume the link is non-operational and re-establish the link. This must be greater than $T1$, but inactivity may be due to lack of network traffic, so a further timer T4, defined by ISO 8878, is often implemented whereby an RR is sent instead to test the link if it appears inactive. In this case $T3$ is several times as long as $T4$.

5.9   General X.25 network design

Adjustment of X.25 parameters cannot completely compensate for an inadequate underlying network design. Detailed knowledge of likely traffic flows if required before a reliable design can be proposed, with the principles of traffic analysis as described in Chapter 2, failing which all that can be said is that the design has a specified capacity subject to many plausible assumptions that have to be stated. Traffic is often specified as a peak hour rate in packets per second, bits per second and call set up/clears per second. Manufacturers packet throughputs and call set-up rates are usually quoted on an either/or basis, so the loads due to the two functions have to be estimated as fractions of the relevant figures, then added. In some cases of multiple processor models, only one CPU may be used for one of these tasks, so separate calculations need to be done for each CPU; there may also be some degradation of performance due to save/restore type of operations when switching between the two functions.

5.9.1   Loadings

To ensure an adequate quality of service these traffic levels have to be related to congestion controls, timers and transient traffic peaks in order to decide what peak hour loading is acceptable on the network components. Frequently this is done by means of rules of thumb, such as 70–80% peak hour processor loads and 50–60% link loads. The rationale for these particular figures comes from experience and the typical existence of 20 to 200 statistically independent virtual circuits over a trunk. The higher processor load comes from the greater statistical averaging resulting from the larger number of virtual circuits handled by it as compared to a single link, and to the more uniform processing time within the CPU, as well as the need to cater for single link failures when considering the lines. Where most of the traffic on a net-work component is coming from a very small number of sources, such as a few routers or file servers, then more allowance has to be made for simultaneous transient traffic peaks from the different sources. Part of this allowance is to increase the value of the retransmission timers T1 to prevent a transient overload condition being turned into an avalanche decay by a flood of retransmissions. Small level 3 windows help to minimize avalanche decay, but have an adverse effect on normal throughput.

One exception to the use of statistical rules for sizing comes in situations such as emergency services where allowance must be made for all end-point devices to be fully utilized simultaneously within a region.

Another factor is to look at the worst case in terms of the sizes and durations of traffic bursts that can be expected for ordinary file transfers. Simple statistical approaches to traffic arrivals breakdown in this case because it is sequences of packets, rather than individuals, that are sent at random times. This particular feature is more important for frame relay than for X.25 and will be dealt with at more length in the next chapter.

5.9.2   Packet and window sizes

This is selected as part of an iterative process in the network design on the basis of the expected bit error rate and the response time requirements. The window segment size in bytes for file transfers should be the lesser of $S*T/8$ and about 1% of the reciprocal of the bit error rate, where S is the access speed and T the expected roundtrip time for acknowledgement (FILO). With the D-bit set this is end–end, but otherwise just for the first link.

T depends on the choice of packet size, particularly for multihop routes with trunk lines of comparable speed to the access lines. Routes with many such hops or important interactive traffic favour small packets and a large window, K, whereas a single slow hop without interactive requirements favours a large packet size and smaller K. Long packet switching times compared to line transmission times also favour large packets. If packet switching time is small compared to link transmission time, then fragmentation into 128 byte packets will give the best FILO response time in many instances, but a high processor loading.

For single digital links or analog links with forward error correcting modems, the typical BER is 1 in 10^6 so the upper bound to the segment size is about 10 000 bytes, dropping as the number of links increases. The theoretical optimum packet size for this BER is about 512 bytes over a single link. With 64K links in and out of a 2-hop 256K backbone, typical single packet FILO end–end roundtrip times at about 50% loading including host response time would be about 90 ms for 128 byte packets or about 500 ms for 1024. This would give segment sizes of about 700 bytes and 3000 bytes respectively. In the absence of interactive traffic and with a maximum K of only 7, the best combination would be 1024 byte packets and window, K, of 3 as regards long file transfers and switch CPU loadings provided sufficient switch memory were available for buffering, 128 bytes and window 4 for shortish transactions where response time is important. If the D-bit was not set, the response time would drop to about 30 ms and 150 ms (assuming acknowledgements are not piggybacked on data packets), so that a window, K, of 3 would do in each case. This would reduce buffer memory problems, and the choice of packet size would be 512–1024 bytes unless there was interactive traffic with low response time needs.

On poor analog lines with BER of 1 in 10^4 and access speed 14.4 kbps and two 19.2 kbps trunk hops, the error rate would limit the window size to about 128 bytes, so the traditional X.25 defaults of 128 byte packets and window size 2 would have to be used, leading to very slow file transfers with acknowledgement waits if the D-bit were set as well as quite a few retransmissions. The best solution would be to use local acknowledgements only in this case, or to reduce the packet size to 64 bytes otherwise.

5.9.3 X.25 and compression

A few X.25 devices provide data compression as an option. This can either be used across a single link with both header and payload compression, or across a complete network using payload compression only. The main value of this is for file transfers over slow links to give both bandwidth and response time reductions, but for inter-active applications the compression/decompression time may negate the reduction in transmission time. Payload compression is particularly useful for file transfers over the D-channel of ISDN networks.

6

Other Packet Switch Networks

6.1   Introduction

This chapter considers other packet switch networks from the point of view of their data link, network level and transport level features, other than routing. Routing itself is treated in the next chapter as a separate subject, as many of the packet switch protocols described here can be carried by other networks using their routing methods.

X.25 networks were dealt with at length in the previous chapter because of their widespread availability and the fact that they are more complex to tune than some other types, which only exhibit subsets of the issues. The most numerous category of corporate network is probably SNA, and this is the next one to be considered.

6.2   SNA networks

The earliest parts of SNA predated X.25, with the HDLC link protocol derived from IBM's SDLC, but SNA was very slow to encompass peer–peer networking. One of the main issues in SNA performance is optimization of polled multidrop environments; however, this was treated at some length in the chapter on analog networks so this aspect is only briefly reconsidered in relation to digital networks. This antiquated feature of SNA is leading to its gradual evolution to support more efficient link layers, such as Token Ring and frame relay, as well as issues such as support over TCP/IP in router networks via data link switching.

6.2.1   SNA layers

SNA has a layered architecture that predates the OSI model, achieving broadly similar functionality with a different distribution of features between the layers. This architecture is shown in Figure 6.1. The functions of these layers are listed below.

Layer	Function
7	Transaction services
6	Presentation services
5	Data flow control
4	Transmission control
3	Path control
2	Data link control
1	Physical control

Figure 6.1   SNA protocol stack.

6.2.2   Transaction services

This consists of programs such as SNADS (SNA Distribution Services), DIA (Document Interchange Architecture) and DCA (Document Content Architecture) as well as network services such as Configuration Service.

6.2.3   Presentation services

This is responsible for LU–LU communication protocols and covers data mapping, data editing and function control.

6.2.4   Data flow control

This layer provides the session flow control. This is done by assigning sequence numbers, correlating responses and requests, grouping related requests into chains and related chains into brackets, and coordinating session send and receive modes.

6.2.5   Transmission control

Transmission control is responsible for processing session set-up and clear-down commands, sequence number checking and handling session level pacing.

6.2.6   Path control

Path control routes the messages through the network and monitors data traffic. These functions include virtual route pacing, message sequencing on multi-link connections and priorities on virtual routes.

6.2.7   Data link control

This supports transmission of messages across individual links, link level flow control and transmission error recovery. The exact procedures depend on the type of link, which may be either SDLC, frame relay, X.25 or Token Ring LLC. X.25 has two variants, QLLC (Qualified Link Level Control) and ELLC (Enhanced Link Level Control), of which the latter is only used where it is important to keep sessions up during relatively long link failures.

Presentation services combine many of the features of the OSI presentation layer with some of those of the OSI application level, while data flow control is concerned with similar synchronization issues to OSI's session level. Transmission control and path control share roughly the routing and flow control features of the OSI network and transport levels, but with a different subdivision.

6.3   Protocol overheads

The first performance factor to consider for SNA is the size of the protocol overheads, both in terms of header sizes and in terms of supervisory packets. As data is passed down the protocol stack from the application to the physical layer a new header is liable to be added. For SNA the magnitude of this overhead depends on the LU (logical unit) type and the degree of segmentation used in the network. Of these, the former is fixed for the device type, for example LU type 2 for 3270 and LU type 7 for 5250, so the tunable part concerns buffer sizes and segmentation issues. The first header always inserted is the request header (RH) which is added to the request unit (RU) by the transmission layer to form the basic information unit (BIU). There may already be a header, the function management header (FMH), which is added by the function management layer; if so its presence is indicated by a bit in the RH. The usage and magnitude of the FMH is shown in Tables 6.1 and 6.2.

Table 6.1   Function management header types.

FMH type	Size (bytes)
1	10+
2	4+
3	4+
4	13+
5	9++
6	8+
7	7
8	Variable
9	Not defined
10	6
11	Not defined
12	10

Within Table 6.1 a plus sign indicates that the header is larger than the minimum quoted due to the addition of a variable number of parameters; the actual length is given by the first byte of the FMH. The LU types that can use these headers are shown in Table 6.2.

6.3.1   LU usage of FMH headers

Table 6.2   Function management header usage.

LU type	FMH types
0	Arbitary
1	1,2,3
2	None
3	None
4	1, 2, 3 .
6.1	4, 5, 6, 7, 8, 10
6.2	5, 7, 12
7	None

The common legacy SNA types, 3270 and 5250, do not use FMH headers. The increasingly important LU 6.2 uses FMH 5 with RUs for conversation allocation, FMH7 for any error report RUs and FMH12 for security during LU–LU verification. The request header (RH) always consists of 3 bytes.

Path control then adds a transmission header (TH) to form the path information unit (PIU). The data link control may then segment (or sometimes block) this into basic transmission units (BTU), to which are added link headers and trailers to form the basic link units (BLU) that are actually transmitted over the link. This process of adding headers is shown sequentially in Figure 6.2. The sizes of the transmission headers and their LU usage is shown in Table 6.3.

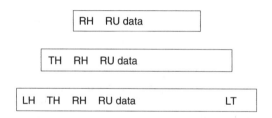

Figure 6.2   SNA data headers.

6.3.2 Transmission headers

Table 6.3 SNA transmission headers.

FID type	Size (bytes)	Users
0	10	SubArea–SubArea (non-SNA)
1	10	SubArea–SubArea (no explicit/virtual routes)
2	6	LU types 2, 3, 6.2
3	2	LU types 4, 7
4	26	SubArea–SubArea (with explicit/virtual routes)
F	26	SubArea–SubArea (with transmission groups)

6.3.3 Segmentation and blocking

Once the sizes of the headers are known, the best strategy for blocking or segmentation to optimize network performance can be ascertained. The main criteria are to select buffer sizes such that the message fits neatly into BLUs without small fragments left over, and that the BLU size should be compatible with the error rate on the link. If the link is to be carried across another network, such as X.25 or IP, then the SDLC or LLC2 headers must be allowed for also in relation to the ultimate carrier I-frames. A number of parameters can be adjusted that affect performance. The first of these is the maximum length of a request/response unit. Each type of device has a range of permissible values, and the size to be used is negotiated at session establishment. Maximum efficiency occurs if the RU size is equal to or a multiple of the frame size minus the SNA and line protocol headers, since this avoids fragments. The header size is 3 for RH, 6 for FID2 TH, 6 for SDLC or LLC2, 9 for X.25 QLLC (Qualified Link Level Control) and 15 for X.25 ELLC (Enhanced Link Level Control). Allowable values range from 241 up to 16384 on some systems. The optimum RU size may exceed the frame size, in which case transmission control segments the RU and the above calculation has to be modified to take account of the RH only being in the first segment.

Optimum frame size depends on the medium. For WAN links using SDLC or X.25 the optimum is much less than for the more reliable Token Rings – usually 256 or 512 bytes as compared to 1977 – with the smaller value for multihop networks.

Flow control at the session and virtual route levels is performed by the appropriate pacing, which is a sliding window credit system. Session level pacing applies to specific LU–LU sessions, and can occur as either two stages involving the host also, or one stage for LUs only. Vpacing operates between the host's VTAM and NCP, and pacing between NCP and the LU. Pacing is the number of PIUs that can be sent to an LU before waiting for a pacing response from the LU. The initial pacing parameter is usually set equal to the maximum number of SNA frames that can be sent without waiting for an acknowledgement. Vpacing is usually set at a value one or two greater than pacing to ensure that the network is not held up by the host on the output side. Virtual route pacing applies to multiple sessions over a single virtual route, and handles network congestion for peak traffic levels. The pacing window is automatically decreased if congestion is detected and increased when it clears. This is much better than the situation in X.25 where window sizes do not adjust in relation to congestion.

A further enhancement to pacing on modern equipment is the option for dynamic pacing instead of the fixed version described above. In the fixed case, buffer memory is reserved for the full window, possibly leading to restrictions on the number of sessions that can be supported where memory is strictly limited. Dynamic pacing increases the pacing window when memory permits and reduces it if a large number of sessions need to be supported. The size of this window is not critical for interactive traffic, but is for file transfers. In this case values of at least 8 are likely to be needed for optimum throughput on the WAN.

At the link level, flow control is done by SDLC/LLC2 or X.25 windows except that, with X.25 ELLC, ISO TP4 style functionality has been inserted at level 2 within the I-frames. ELLC has its own timers and retries, LT1 and LN2, which can be used to keep a session up for very long periods after a link failure; this is for use where re-establishing lost sessions is a major problem, for example with bottom of the range AS/400.

SDLC uses windows and acknowledgements modulo 8 for normal operation or mod 128 for satellite links. The arguments for large window and frame sizes for SDLC are similar to those for X.25 given in the previous chapter. For a direct SDLC link 512 bytes (= 521 bytes SNA frame) is best for error rates around 1 in 1 000 000 provided that the end-device can support it. The window size should be sufficiently large to allow a complete pacing set of frames to be transmitted without interruption provided that the bit error rate is low enough not to cause many retransmissions. As SDLC uses a Go-Back N algorithm, an error in one frame of the window will cause the retransmission of any subsequent correct frames also (see Chapter 5). If a multi-hop route across an X.25 network is used instead, then 256 is better because of the delays associated with fully receiving a frame before onwards transmission.

Token Ring LLC2 uses similar parameters to SDLC and X.25 but with different values. The retransmission timer (TRNRSPTMR for AS/400) is determined by the frame size and number of rings to be traversed. In a pure local environment with the maximum SNA frame (MAXFRAME) of 1994 bytes, the delay in seconds should be roughly equal to the number of rings traversed (4 Mbps), but reduced pro rata if the frame size is less. If a WAN link is introduced between the rings, then allowance has also to be made for the maximum number of outstanding frames permitted to be received before an acknowledgement(TRNACKFRQ) at the link speed; however, the frame size would also need to be reduced to allow for line errors. Parameter values also depend on the type of equipment involved, particularly as regards TRNACKFRQ. This has to be related to the maximum number of frames that can be transmitted to a station before waiting for an acknowledgement (TRN-MAXOUT). This ranges from 1 to 127, with 2 the default for communicating with PCs, and depends on the processing ability of the destination station; some NetBIOS stations expect an acknowledgement for every frame. Smaller frame sizes or more powerful stations allow larger values. TRNACKFRQ should be equal to or less than TRNMAXOUT to prevent unnecessary retransmissions from taking place.

Token Ring also has an acknowledgement timer (TRNACKTMR), analogous to X.25's T2, that determines how long a station can delay before sending an acknowledgement. This must be less than the retransmission time by at least the worst case time taken to transmit an acknowledgement, otherwise unnecessary retransmissions will take place. Relatively large values minimize network load and reduce station processing; this is mainly of importance in congested systems with low-speed remote bridges, otherwise a very short value should be used for optimum throughput, especially if every frame has to be acknowledged.

6.3.4   Choice of LU type and protocol

Quite a lot of modern devices, such as PS/2 with Comms Manager, allow a choice of LU type, especially LU 2 and LU 6.2. Of these, the latter will usually give much better performance for large file transfers, since it avoids the need for individual transaction ACKs inherent in the old data entry LU type 2. It also allows a larger maximum amount of data, 64K instead of 32K, which improves performance over satellite links in particular (see Chapter 10).

Many IBM devices, such as cluster controllers, allow the user a choice of connectivity mode, such as SDLC, BSC, X.25 or Token Ring. In many cases it is obvious that where applicable Token Ring will give the best performance and BSC the worst, but there are other situations where the variability of detailed configuration options may make the choice unexpected. One such case is the use of screen-based applications with the AS/400 over either X.25 or SDLC. Normally the additional encapsulation overheads associated with X.25 QLLC or ELLC make X.25 slightly slower than SDLC, but in some cases the response time is heavily influenced by the time taken by the AS/400 to receive a packet containing the SNA transmission header, rather than a complete RU. A case in point is a stock check card-swipe system that sends information back to the AS/400 as screenfuls of data. On receiving the TH, the AS/400 sends a 'release' back to the screen enabling it to recommence gathering information while continuing to transmit the buffered data. X.25 permits a smaller packet size (128 bytes without the M-bit set) than SDLC (256) on some systems, so the 'release' is sent earlier in the X.25 case, thereby allowing the card-swipe operator to work more efficiently.

Another major protocol choice is often between using APPC/APPN and TCP/IP. In this case it appears that APPC normally gives better throughput than TCP/IP. The reason for this is that many TCP/IP implementations are rather inflexible, allowing the user to set a window size (in bytes) but not the frame size, whereas APPC has the normal SNA pacing and frame size features that allow it to optimize its traffic flow.

6.4   DECnet

Since its inception DECnet has gone through several phases, of which the most recent is Phase V. This section concentrates on Phase IV, while Phase V is an implementation of the OSI connectionless network stack and is treated under OSI. The overall protocol stack of Phase IV is shown in Figure 6.3.

The main packet switch features of DNA are governed by layers 2, 3 and 4, whose functions are close to those of the OSI model. The end communication layer is responsible for managing communications on a connection-oriented basis using DEC's Network Services Protocol (NSP). In addition to connection control, NSP supports data segmentation, error control and flow control. On connection establishment the receiver sends a count of the number of segments that it can accept. NSP uses both positive and negative acknowledgements, and retransmits data on timeout if it is not acknowledged by the remote NSP.

The routing layer is divisible into a control sublayer and initialization sublayer, of which the former handles the routing (see Chapter 7) and congestion control.

The data link layer covers three distinct scenarios, DDCMP, Ethernet and X.25, which have widely differing characteristics and so are treated separately below.

6.4.1   DDCMP

Digital Data Carrier Message Protocol (DDCMP) is the oldest DEC link layer protocol, somewhat analogous to BSC, but with sliding windows, acknowledgements and piggybacking analogous to the later bit-oriented protocols. DDCMP is used in DECnet IV in several different modes; synchronous or asynchronous, point or multipoint. The main form of relevance in current networks is full-duplex synchronous point-to-point configuration to provide wide area links between Ethernets. There are

Layer	Function
7	Network management
6	Network application
5	Session control
4	End communication
3	Routing
2	Data link
1	Physical link

Figure 6.3   DECNet protocol stack.

seven types of DDCMP message, comprising a variable length data message and six types of control message, for example Acknowledgement, each of which is 8 bytes long. A typical DDCMP data message block has also got 8 bytes of control information whose structure is shown below with sizes in bits:

SOH	LOW ADDR.	HIGH ADDR.	FLAGS	RESP (RECV. NUM)	SEQ. NUM (SEND)	ADDR	HEADER CRC
8	8	6	2	8	8	8	16

Flags indicate following SYN characters and Select respectively, where select is used on half-duplex and multipoint lines for the last data message in a transmission.

The parameters that can be tuned are somewhat analogous to those in other point-to-point link level protocols. The maximum size message that a node can forward or receive is set through the buffer size parameter, with high values providing lower node processor levels, but a higher probability of retransmission due to errors; the default is 576 bytes (also the maximum for some routers), with a minimum of 192 bytes. The low values, such as 192 and 256 bytes are only applicable to error-prone analog lines, particularly dial-up, or multihop paths. Where a node receives a message longer than its buffer size, it will drop the message, hence the buffer size should be the same throughout the network. The receive buffers parameter lies in the range 1–32, and determines how many buffers are allocated to a line. This depends on the buffer size and throughput, typically ranging from about 4 for 56 kbps lines with default buffers up to about 10 for fractional T1 lines. A retransmit time is configured for the line based on the speed, buffer size and receive buffers parameters according to the formula:

$$\text{Retransmit timer} = 2.5 * 8 * \text{Buffer size} * \text{Receive buffer/Line speed}$$

where the timer is in milliseconds, the buffer size in bytes and the line speed in kbps. This allows for the maximum permitted congestion in each direction with a small additional safety margin. The window for transmission of data over the line is set via the transmit quota. The default is 3000 bytes, corresponding to about five buffers, with at least 6000 used for satellite links.

Individual logical links over the data link also have their own parameters that are used by NSP. The most important of these for tuning the network are the delay weight and factor and pipeline quota. NSP calculates roundtrip times and uses the delay parameters to control its sensitivity to changes in the observed value. Low delay weight permits rapid change. Normally these parameters are left at their defaults, but unusual situations, such as links through a bandwidth manager as described in Chapter 3, may require changes. Pipeline quota effectively determines the logical link window size before an acknowledgement is required as the ratio of the quota to the buffer size. A large quota improves throughput over multihop routes.

6.4.2   X.25

X.25 is used by DECnet in accordance with the standard procedures already described in the previous chapter. DECnet X.25 implementations are a restricted set of the full specification.

6.4.3   Ethernet/LAT

Ethernets are a main method of interconnecting DECnet nodes. Ethernet parameters are only of secondary importance in determining performance over a route across a WAN, so are not discussed. DEC adds two bytes to the Ethernet header which has to be taken into account in deciding the MTU.

LAT is not a part of DECnet IV in the sense that it does not carry any higher layer routing information, but this is the most appropriate part of the book in which to describe it. Most LAN protocols are extremely inefficient when used with asynchronous data from dumb terminals due to high overheads, but LAT (local area transport) was designed to overcome these deficiencies. LAT allows terminal servers to create multi-user packets containing 60–70 characters with a frequency based on a circuit timer instead of the single character packets characteristic of other protocols. This gives vastly improved performance when bridged across a relatively low-speed WAN link to a remote node. On a 10 Mbps Ethernet with terminal connections at a typical 19.2 kbps, the main delay experienced by a user comes from the circuit timer which determines the interval during which input characters are aggregated. The default is 80 ms, while the character access delay is 0.5 ms and the Ethernet transit delay for a 70 byte packet also adds less than 1 ms. A large circuit timer reduces the processor and network loads, and the default is roughly the largest value that permits an acceptable response time for global echo. The perceived response time for the terminal user is significantly reduced by performing local echo in the terminal driver where possible.

LAT flow control

LAT flow control consists of two parts: XON/XOFF or RTS/CTS at the user terminal and slot flow control. A LAT slot is a block of up to 255 message characters, and a node must possess a credit before it can send a slot, where a credit represents availability of a free buffer at the destination. The destination flow controls the sender by returning credits as appropriate.

LAT service advertisements and group codes

LAT nodes send periodic service multicast advertisements to announce their availability. On large networks this is a problem both for traffic levels and the lack of sufficient memory in terminal servers to handle large numbers of services. These problems can be controlled using LAT's 256 group codes in combination with group code filters on bridges. This restricts multicasts for particular services to the appropriate partition of the network and should be used to minimize traffic over slow WAN bridges.

LAT WAN issues

When LAT is bridged over a WAN the issue of response time becomes extremely critical if global echo is used. A single WAN hop at 56 or 64 kbps adds about 10 ms to the transit time or 20 to the roundtrip, so it it may be desirable to reduce the circuit timer by a corresponding amount to compensate. This will increase both network and processor load. In some cases the WAN link may be congested which will be exacerbated by the increased load caused by reducing the timer. Apart from increasing the WAN capacity, the only other widely available remedy is to use LAT compression on the bridges; this increases bridge processing time by a few milliseconds, but can reduce the required bandwidth by a factor of two.

LAT also uses a retry timer and counter, with the value of the former important for successful WAN operation. The retry timer is started each time that a frame is sent from the host and stopped on receipt of an acknowledgement. If the retry interval is exceeded then the remote device will receive multiple copies of a frame, possibly causing sequence errors. The default retry timer for most systems is one second, which greatly exceeds the 100 ms recommended echoplex roundtrip time, so user irritation will normally give plenty of advance warning of the possible occurrence of these timeouts.

Where a single terminal server has multiple sessions over the same WAN bridge to different hosts, there is liable to be excess echoplex delay whenever the basic frame transmission time across the bridge exceeds the circuit timer value, as frames will then have to queue for the bridge. Typically this happens for speeds below about 64 kbps. If multiple terminal servers are present, then the bridge speed needs to be increased roughly pro rata to prevent excess delay.

Other traffic over the bridge can be disastrous for LAT, as queuing a LAT frame behind a 1500 byte Ethernet IP frame would introduce a wait of 190 ms on top of the normal delay, guaranteeing user dissatisfaction. Bridges need a speed of about 512 kbps before LAT can be mixed tolerably well with file transfer traffic.

Running LAT over multiple WAN hops is very undesirable unless the links approach megabit capacity, so where file transfers take place through LAT, a node needs about three credits initially in order to pipeline data across a single WAN link. The maximum slot size of 255 bytes ensures that few retransmissions will be needed on all but the worst analog links.

6.4.4   Network service protocol (NSP)

NSP is the transport layer for DNA IV. It covers two types of channel: Normal for ordinary data, and Other-data channel for expedited data. There are also two types of flow control with selection at session establishment: these are On/Off Only and Segment with On/Off.

On/Off Only

In this the destination transport layer tells the source when to stop and start sending data.

Segment with On/Off

This provides better throughput since there is a windowing mechanism. In addition to On/Off the destination sends the source a request count which indicates the number of segments that it can accept. There is also another request count to flow-control the Other-data channel.

A retransmission timer is maintained in each case, with unacknowledged data getting retransmitted on expiry.

6.5   TCP/IP

TCP/IP is a major part of the protocol stack of the worldwide Internet with its two million hosts. This section considers the networking aspects of TCP/IP and UDP, while leaving the routing algorithms, such as RIP, to the next chapter.

This protocol stack is not as complete as the later OSI model, and essentially consists of only networking transport and application layers, as shown in Figure 6.4.

The stack can be split into connectionless and connection-oriented parts, with TCP (transmission control protocol) being responsible for the connection-oriented features. In considering the performance-related features, the simpler UDP (unacknowledged datagram protocol) is considered first. This is very simple, and contains no error recovery features, so is only suited to either very reliable media or to applications where a significant proportion of errors do not matter. The advantage is that the packet overhead is small due to the lack of control information, while the

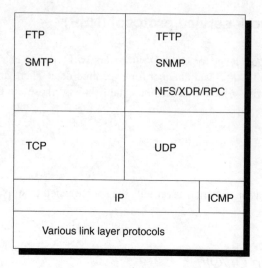

Figure 6.4   IP protocol stack.

absence of error checking allows maximal throughput. The structure of a UDP datagram is shown in Figure 6.5.

The main applications that run on top of UDP are TFTP (trivial file transfer protocol), SNMP and Sun's NFS (network file service). While there is no end–end flow control, link level flow control can be provided by the use of an underlying level 2 that provides this feature, for example HDLC LLC2 for source route bridging (SRB) on Token Rings. A major performance issue that arises with NFS is the use of a fixed NFS intrinsic retransmission timeout of 700 ms. This makes it essential to calculate in advance what the network response time will be on a FIFO basis for the size of datagram to be used. NFS tends to use blocks of 8192 bytes for workstations (but PCs are often 512 or 1024 bytes), so if throughput is less than about 90 kbps a timeout is inevitable. The way to avoid this where low-speed WAN interconnection occurs is either to reduce the size of the UDP datagram or increase the timeout. Reducing the datagram size means that the full block size of 8192 bytes does not have to be fully received at each network node before onwards transmission occurs, but merely the first datagram fragment of the block. On multihop routes this makes a big difference to the time taken for the first response to arrive back at the transmitter, hence preventing a timeout on the FIFO basis (see analogous case in Figure 6.12).

Field	Size (bytes)
Source port	2
Destination port	2
Length	2
Checksum	2
Data	1–1500

Figure 6.5   UDP fields.

6.5.1   IP

IP (Internet protocol) also uses datagrams but, while connectionless itself, it can and is normally associated with the transport layer protocol TCP. The structure of an IP datagram is shown in Figure 6.6.

The total header size is 20 bytes ex options, rising to a possible maximum of 60 if bulky options, such as strict source routing, are used. Most IP networks avoid source routing, but if it is used the extra header overhead is a significant source of delay if small packets are in use.

There are only two fields that have any relevance to network performance optimization. The first of these is the Type of Service (TOS) field, which can be used to select a network route by a path appropriate to the TOS. The TOS field is a single byte whose bit subfields are listed in Table 6.4.

Field	Size (bytes)
Version/Header length	1
Type of service	1
Total length	2
Data unit identifier	2
Flags/Fragment offset	2
Time to live	1
Protocol	1
Header checksum	2
Source address	4
Destination address	4
Options/Padding	Variable
Data	=MTU

Figure 6.6   IP datagram fields.

Table 6.4   IP type of service.

Bits	Field	Values
0–2	Precedence	0=Normal, 7=Top
3	Delay	0=Normal, 1=Low
4	Throughput	0=Normal, 1=High
5	Reliability	0=Normal, 1=High
6–7	Reserved	

The delay, throughput and reliability bits can be used to select a route which meets these requirements, while the precedence field allows a finer degree of prioritization than is possible with the more usual discrimination by well-known port number. The port number allows giving interactive traffic, such as Telnet, precedence over file transfers, such as FTP, but does not distinguish between users. The TOS precedence field could be used to distinguish between different users of Telnet, for example, if they needed different priorities. In practice, the TOS field is rarely implemented in routing for IP version 4, but seems likely to become mandatory with version 6. Many private networks are insufficiently complex to make much use of the feature.

The other feature is the Time to Live field. This specifies the maximum hop-count for a datagram before it is automatically purged from the network. This function is necessary because of the possibility of routing loops resulting from slow convergence of routing tables after a change in topology. The usual default is 16, corresponding to the maximum route length for RIP routing. Changing this to a smaller value corresponding to the maximum actual path length will prevent any misaddressed packets from circulating for an unduly long period, but is only a minor influence on the network. An additional protocol, Internet control message protocol (ICMP), can be used with IP to provide network flow control. The relevant ICMP message for this is the quench. On receipt of a quench, the transmitter reduces its receiver window by a factor of two, down to one eighth of the original value, for each quench recieved. Unlike the TCP flow control (see below) ICMP messages can be sent by any IP nodes that are congested. In practice, this is found to be too drastic a reduction, as there is a delay before any quenches can be received and acted on, so it is rarely implemented.

The main performance factor that can be set on IP networks is the IP frame size. This is set as the message transfer unit (MTU) size in the LAN driver interface. Routers, but not bridges, can fragment packets, so if any translation bridging from Token Ring to Ethernet is involved, then the MTU set for the Token Ring should not exceed the maximum Ethernet MTU of 1492, else the bridges will drop frames. When working with PCs, the MTU is usually set to 576 to allow for TCP/IP and session level headers on top of the typical PC disk block size of 512 bytes. For operations in a WAN environment this is the best value to use. The reason for this is that at each node a block must usually (but not in the case of frame relay) be fully received before it can be onwards transmitted, so that in a multihop slow network, it is quicker if the message is fragmented into relatively small packets despite the extra protocol overhead. In the extreme case of analog WAN links with very high error rates, 576 will be too much, leading to numerous retransmissions. As 576 is often the minimum MTU supported and as overheads would become very high for smaller values, encapsulation in X.25 for multiple hops or PPP (see section 6.5.2) for single hops should be used with an HDLC frame size of 128 bytes. In this case the X.25 forwarder of the router should send a sequence of X.25 packets for each MTU with the M-bit set in all but the last, and the TCP/IP header only in the first for that MTU. The advertised MTU remains at 576 and HDLC handles the retransmissions on a link basis leaving TCP with virtually no error recovery to do, so allowing UDP to be used instead. This avoids the huge overhead associated with a 40 byte TCP/IP header in each fragment.

For high-speed WAN links over optical fibre circuits, however, fragmentation would itself become the major source of delay as it imposes a heavy load on the router or nodes performing it and the subsequent reassembly.

6.5.2 SLIP and PPP

When IP is used for asynchronous or dial-up links, some additional features have to be provided. The serial line interface protocol (SLIP) was originally provided to allow for this. Its main disadvantage was the complete lack of any error recovery mechanism, so that it was reasonable for locally attached asynchronous devices, but not always satisfactory for remote dial up. SLIP flow control is provided by the classical XON/XOFF method. The overhead in SLIP is only a flag at the end of each IP packet, so throughput is good apart from error effects. The absence of error recovery makes SLIP unsuitable for use with applications that use UDP instead of TCP, notably NFS. The maximum packet size for SLIP is 1006 bytes.

The preferred protocol for remote dial up, whether synchronous or asynchronous, is now PPP (point-to-point protocol) which has been standardized both for IP and for various other LAN protocols for which asynchronous serial line access might be desirable. PPP is based on HDLC and entails significant overheads, as shown by the frame structure below.

Field	Flag	Address	Control	Protocol	Data	FCS	Flag
size (byte)	1	1	1	2	Variable	2 or 4	1

Except for very short packets there is no significant difference in performance between SLIP and PPP. The data field of PPP is configurable up to the MTU size for the medium. The optimum size is determined by the bit error rate criteria considered earlier in this book, and is likely to be of the order of 128 to 256 bytes on analog links using modems without forward error correction, but 512–1024 bytes on digital links or on analog links with forward error correction, so 576 would be the normal MTU to use.

When used on asynchronous links, PPP uses exclusively 8 bit characters with one start plus one stop bit in frames otherwise similar to those for synchronous links.

There are three phases to a PPP session; establishment, authentication and network layer protocol. Establishment uses a link control protocol comprising configuration, termination and maintenance packet exchange sequences. Of these, the maintenance echo request is the most significant for PPP performance with configurable intervals between transmissions across the link and with configurable maximum number of requests unacknowledged by echo reply before the link is taken down. Typical intervals are in the range 1 to 100 seconds (usually about 10) with about three unacknowledged.

An important advantage of PPP over SLIP is the ability to avoid routing loops by negotiation of a 'magic number' enabling a device to recognize any looping call.

Another important maintenance factor is link quality monitoring and reporting; this entails sending LQR packets containing counts of incoming and outgoing packets successfully received across the link at a configurable interval, of the order of a few seconds. A rolling average of percentage of packets successfully received is calculated every five reporting periods and compared with a configurable threshold; if substandard, the link is taken down. On error-prone links, the percentage of packets successfully received will increase if the packet size is reduced, so the link can be re-established but using a smaller maximum size specified in the new configuration request.

Both SLIP and PPP support header compression. The compressed version of SLIP is called CSLIP, and typically reduces 40 bytes of TCP/IP headers to 3–5 bytes. The same mechanism, defined in RFC1144, is applicable to PPP. Its main application is to short interactive packets, for example from Telnet, on low bandwidth links.

PPP has also been extended to support payload compression, with the choice of algorithm used being negotiated in an additional header field, thereby allowing higher throughput between devices from potentially different vendors.

When PPP is used with compression over an error-prone analog link it is beneficial to use the 'reliable' (number–mode) version defined in RFC1663, which differs by the additional use of a LAPB error recovery mechanism (as in X.25). This is because many compression algorithms become very inefficient if any packets are dropped (see section 7.5.1).

PPP multilink protocol (MP)

MP is defined in RFC1717 and enables packets to be sent over multiple parallel links with load sharing on a per packet basis and sequencing issues handled by the protocol. Again it has a 'reliable' option. Compression can be used both on a line group basis or separately on the individual links. A design issue for low-end devices is to provide sufficient buffer space in the end-point devices to guarantee detection of any data loss. This is determined from the slippage rates between different channels and the quantity of data that can be queued on each. Slippage is the product of the transmission rate and the transit delay differences between channels. Using an MTU of 576 and a pair of links, one at 64 kbps and one at 128 kbps, the transit delay difference will be of the order of 40 ms and the slippage of the order of 600 bytes. Typically two MTUs could be queued up, so about 1800 bytes is the absolute minimum needed, with twice that value being recommended. In the unlikely case of one link being via satellite and the other a terrestrial link, then about 10 kbytes would be the minimum. For a 19.2 kbps link and one at 64 kbps (both terrestrial) the slippage goes up to about 1600 bytes, so about 8 kbytes of buffer are needed. If more than two links are used, then additional buffering is needed for each link.

6.5.3 TCP

The main factors associated with network performance for TCP/IP come from the TCP component. TCP datagrams are identified in IP by the value 6 in IP's protocol field. TCP also has a normal 20 byte header whose structure is shown in Figure 6.7.

Optional fields

Optional fields were originally defined in RFC793, then extended in RFC1323. The original set only included one of any performance significance, namely the maximum segment size. This is defined in the initial connection request (that is, SYN); for WANs the default of 536 bytes is normally used, but this field enables other values to be specified, typically 1024 which is better for LANs or single-hop high-quality WAN links.

The normal maximum window size is limited by the 16 bit field to 65 535 bytes, but for very high speed links or satellite transmissions this may be inadequate (see Chapter 12), so another option was added in RFC1323. This is the window scaling field. This is a one-byte field preceded in the SYN by similar sized kind-of-option and option-length fields. It takes values in the range 0 to 14, indicating the power of two by which the specified receive window is to be multiplied. Values in the two directions need not be equal. This permits a receive window of up to one billion bytes.

Field	Size (bits)
Source port	16
Destination port	16
Sequence number	32
ACK number	32
Data offset	4
Reserved	6
URG flag	1
ACK flag	1
PSH flag	1
RST flag	1
SYN flag	1
FIN flag	1
Window	16
Checksum	16
Urgent pointer	16
Options	24
Padding	8
Data	Variable

Figure 6.7 TCP fields.

RFC 1323 also includes a TCP timestamp field that can be included in all segments. It enables the TCP sender to set a timestamp on transmission that it can use to calculate the roundtrip time more accurately than would otherwise be possible. The returned ACKs contain the most recent value of the timestamp received. It is important for high-speed networks with large window sizes and potentially variable delays.

This timestamp is also very important for avoiding sequence number problems if packets arrive out of sequence while using a large window scale. As TCP sequence numbers refer to individual bytes it is possible for the sequence number to wrap around under these circumstances, but combining this with the timestamp eliminates ambiguity. This is sometimes called PAWS (Protection Against Wrapped Sequence numbers).

General performance factors

The performance factors are associated with the sequence and acknowledgement numbers, flags and window. The purpose of the flow control associated with these is to prevent a DTE from becoming overloaded, for example rather than network flow control a PC receiving a file transfer may not be able to write to disk nearly as fast as a server can read data to it. In cases where the underlying network and data layers do not provide much flow control, such as frame relay, then TCP may also act to handle network congestion. During the session each DTE indicates how much data it is able to accept by means of the window field which indicates the amount of buffer space allocated to the connection. This is measured in bytes rather than the frames of OSI protocols, and is adjusted throughout the session according to DTE congestion criteria.

Acknowledgements are sent via the ACK sequence number field in normal TCP segments, and indicates the next byte sequence number expected. If an erroneous segment is received, then the ACK merely repeats the sequence number based on the last correct block received, thereby implying that retransmission is required. This error correction aspect is not fully specified and performance problems can result from different TCP implementations reacting differently to each other (see below).

There is not always a segment to return, so TCP also implements a delayed ACK to handle this. It is returned if an ACK is required and no data is due to be sent by the time an internal clock has passed its timeout position. This interval is unrelated to the data flow and has a fixed value for the implementation that must be not more than 500 ms; usually it is 200 ms. This can cause reduction in throughput for unidirectional transactions, such as file transfers.

The MSS and maximum receive window size determine what effect this delay will have. The window size for unrestricted data flow is based on the roundtrip time multiplied by lowest line speed, and must include the average ACK delay, typically 100 ms. The MSS must be small enough to allow a regular flow of segments, and is also related to the maximum IP datagram size by:

$MTU = MSS +$ IP header size + TCP header size

TCP supports an upper layer protocol (ULP) timer, whereby the timer is started when a datagram is transmitted, and retransmission occurs if receipt is not acknowledged within the timeout period.

There are two different strategies for this retransmission; either resend all unacknowledged segments, or only resend the first such segment. Where the two ends of the TCP session use incompatible choices the performance may be very poor.

Unlike most other protocols, the retransmission timer is constantly recalculated on the basis of the observed acknowledgement delay and a standard formula. TCP/IP has undergone several versions, and the timer formula has evolved. Prior to 1989 the formula used was:

$$RTT = A * RTT(\text{old}) + (1 - A) * RT(\text{sample})$$
$$T/O = B * RTT$$

where B was given the fixed value of 2.

This was found to give too rapid a timer back-off and also caused trouble if any retransmissions took place. This led to Karn's algorithm, whereby the timer is not updated for retransmissions and also takes account of the variance of the transmission time. The main version now used is given by the MIL model below.

$$SRTT = A * SRTT(\text{old}) + (1 - A) * RT(\text{Sample})$$
$$T/O = \text{MIN}(UBOUND, \text{MAX}(LBOUND, B * SRTT))$$

This differs from the earlier version by using a smoothed roundtrip time SRTT that avoids over-reaction to sudden changes by the use of bounded values. *LBOUND* is a preset lower bound to the round trip time to use in the calculations, and *UBOUND* a corresponding upper bound. The parameter B is an updated delay variance parameter, usually in the range 1.3 to 2, rather than the previous fixed value of 2. The retransmission timer in the two opposite directions will normally be unequal due to differing average segment sizes and congestion levels, so having different algorithms at the two ends is not a problem.

There are also a few old versions of TCP that do not include any such automatic procedure; in that case a value should be configured that is several times the maximum roundtrip time expected. Loss of a packet usually means congestion, so retransmission must be slow enough to reduce the problem, not exacerbate it.

The other area of importance for performance is the use of the TCP flags. Of the six, four are only used in relation to session set up, but two, PSH and URG are relevant. The PSH flag is important for throughput where the message sizes are smaller than the DTE buffers. By setting PSH, the transmitter forces the receiver to transfer the received data up to the application without waiting for either buffer full or a timeout. This needs to be set for character based applications. URG is used for urgent data that needs to be processed ahead of other data; typically this is associated with session flow control, such as break or interrupt from the terminal.

Port numbers can be used in prioritization (see Chapter 7), and are indicative of a service from a server, but allocated ephemerally on a client.

Silly window syndrome

A problem that can cause inefficiency with TCP is the 'silly window syndrome', where the destination returns a small window size as the buffer space is progressively used up, leading to a succession of small packets, perhaps as little as 10 bytes, being sent by the source. This is cured by measures defined in RFC1122, whereby the destination should quote a window of zero until it is able to offer at least half its normal maximum. Thus a few large packets are sent with low overhead instead of incurring high overheads with lots of small packets. One slight exception to this is in the cases of either very low-quality analog links or multihop routes with links of similar speeds. In each of these cases a smaller fraction of the maximum receive window should be advertised to obtain better throughput despite slightly higher overheads.

Nagle algorithm

Another method of reducing the waste of bandwidth due to small segments is Nagle's algorithm contained in RFC896. This states that a TCP connection can have only one outstanding small segment that has not been acknowledged. Small is relative to the segment size, as in the silly window case.

The main purpose of this algorithm is to prevent the gross inefficiency that occurs on heavily congested networks when several segments timeout and have to be retransmitted before even the first of them has been acknowledged. The Nagle algorithm means that not more than one should have to be retransmitted, and makes a positive contribution to congestion reduction by aggregating multiple small segments, especially when header compression is not used. In general this will cause a reduction in response time on heavily congested networks.

The effect of this on lightly loaded networks is to delay data transmission slightly as well as aggregating transmissions. There are some instances where this increased delay is unacceptable, in which case the algorithm can be disabled on a per connection basis.

6.5.4 UDP (unacknowledged datagram protocol)

UDP is indicated by the value 17 in IP's protocol field. It is much simpler than TCP, with an 8 byte header as shown in Figure 6.8.

Field	Size (bytes)
Source port number	2
Destination port number	2
UDP length	2
UDP checksum	2

Figure 6.8 UDP header.

Port numbers are essentially the same as those used with TCP. The length is that of the UDP header and data combined. The checksum also covers both header and data. It is optional, causing the datagram to be silently discarded by the receiver if there is an error. The lack of acknowledgements means that it is up to the application to request any retransmission.

UDP is more sensitive to server congestion than TCP and packet loss is quite common under these conditions.

6.5.5 IPv6/IP ng (IP next generation)

Currently a new version of IP, version 6, is being standardized and is commonly referred to as IP ng, where ng denotes next generation. The main reason for this is the exhaustion of official Class A and B Internet addresses, coupled with the administrative benefits of a more hierarchical addressing structure.

The main change to the header is an enlargement of the source and destination address fields from 4 to 16 bytes each. Some of the other IP header fields have been made simpler or optional so that the average v6 header is only twice the v4 size despite the quadrupling of the address field. One of the fields that has been dropped is the IP header checksum, so processing by routers will be significantly speeded up. For small packets, such as those often generated by terminal servers, this remains a serious increase in overhead that will reduce performance quite noticeably on slow WANs. If strict source routing were also used, entailing inclusion of the addresses of all intermediate nodes, the effect of this on response time would be little short of catastrophic for interactive traffic. The solution to this will be to avoid source routing and to use header compression on WAN links.

A positive performance benefit of IP ng is that use of a QOS field is likely to become mandatory, so that much finer prioritization discrimination will be possible than is currently usual. This is likely to be based on a 28 bit field (the flow label) in the IP header, and is primarily intended to make it easier to send voice and video traffic over IP networks at acceptable quality. Large IP packets will still make jitter much worse than on an ATM network. Use of QOS for routing requires multiple routing tables, either with RIP or OSPF (see Chapter 7), and hence more memory on routers.

Another performance feature, the maximum datagram size, seems certain to be unchanged at 64K. This is a limiting factor on very high speed networks with large propagation delays and between superservers that can handle bursts greater than 64 kbytes in length unless TCP window scale is used. The WAN aspects of this limit are discussed further in Chapter 12 on ATM, to which the high speeds and propagation delays are particularly relevant.

For large IP networks a major change is the increase in maximum hop count from 15 to 255. For most networks it will be advisable for the network administrator to configure a much smaller value, say twice the maximum hop count expected, in order to prevent misaddressed packets from using up significant network resources before being dropped.

IP ng does not involve any change to TCP.

The benefits of IPv6 will be most apparent on large networks with complex addressing and security requirements but, for small private WANs with slow links, v4 is likely to offer better performance for interactive traffic. For file transfers over high-speed links, the faster router processing in v6 may well offset the delay due to the increased header size.

Further information on IPv6, particularly optional fields relating to security, can be found in RFC 1752 and any later related RFCs.

There are a very large number of books on TCP/IP that can be consulted for further information on IP. For performance issues one of the best is Stevens (1993).

6.5.6 Internet stream protocol (ST2+)

IP Version 5 is reserved for the Internet stream protocol, defined in RFC1190 (ST2) and modified in RFC1819 (ST2+). This protocol relies on resource reservation to stream traffic across a network with provision of end–end response time and jitter guarantees, thus it should be suitable for packetized voice and video. Only the first four bits of the data packet header, the IP version type, are consistent with IP; the rest of the header has an ST version number (3 for ST2+), D-bit, packet drop priority field, total length, header checksum, unique ID and the originating 32 bit IP address. The D-bit (totally different to X.25) distinguishes between data packets (D=1) and control packets (D=0). The priority ranges from 0 to 7, with the lowest priorities being the first to be dropped in the event of congestion. The unique ID and IP address together define a unique stream identifier (SID) that is assigned by the originator at set up.

The protocol is connection-oriented with resource reservation performed via a CONNECT, one of many streams control message protocol (SCMP) elements. From a performance point of view, the key field in the CONNECT is the flow control specification. There are seven possible distinct variants of specification, notably Null (type 0), as ST2 (type 3), as RFC1363 (type 6) and ST2+ (type 7), of which the first and last are mandatory. The ST2+ specification consists of the fields listed in Table 6.5.

Desired and Limit values are set by the source, while other figures are inserted and updated by successive agents on the path. If an actual value is worse than the limit value, then the call is rejected with a REFUSE.

The protocol is intended to provide better service for voice and video across the Internet than the MBONE which uses IP. In practice, agents are usually routers and links are liable to carry other protocols also. In order to achieve acceptable limit values for voice and video, links are likely to need to be at least of E1/T1 capacity, while the routers need to reserve both processor availability and bandwidth to ensure that each data unit is not held up for more than a few milliseconds before onwards transmission (see Chapter 4 for some discussion of packetized voice requirements). As a data unit is liable to have to wait for an MTU in course of transmission to

Table 6.5 ST2 + flow control fields.

Field	Size (bits)	Significance
QoS Class	8	Predictive (=1), Guaranteed QoS (=2)
Precedence	8	Precedence of stream (0 = lowest)
Unused	16	Unused in ST2+, value 0
DesRate	24	Desired transmission rate in messages/s
LimitRate	24	Minimum acceptable rate in messages/s
ActRate	24	Actual rate. Downgraded from DesRate by successive agents
DesMaxSize	16	Desired maximum message data unit size in bytes
LimitMaxSize	16	Minimum message data unit size acceptable to source
ActMaxSize	16	DesMaxSize downgraded by successive agents
DesMaxDelay	16	Desired maximum delay in ms
LimitMaxDelay	16	Longest maximum delay acceptable to source
ActMaxDelay	16	Sum of MaxDelays set by successive agents for each hop
DesMaxDelayRange	16	Desired maximum delay range in ms set by source
ActMinDelay	16	Sum of minimum possible delays set by agents for each hop

complete before being forwarded, the MTUs for any other services may need to be reduced. For example, a 1500 byte MTU would take about 8 ms to transmit at 1.544 Mbps, and a tendency for this to happen on several hops could lead to too much jitter (delay range) for voice, but reduction of MTU to 576 would probably be acceptable in this scenario. Several separate streams sharing the same link exacerbate this problem. A different solution is to use build-out delay to reduce jitter (as in ITU-T G.764 – see Chapter 4).

Internet Streams requires special voice and video applications on top of it. These are NVP and PVP; for definitions see Cohen (1981) and Cole (1981). Some loss of data units is acceptable for voice and video, so ST2+ does not provide resilience, nor is TCP used normally.

6.6   OSI CLNP (ISO 8473)

The open systems connectionless protocol stack was heavily influenced by TCP/IP and is implemented in DECnet Phase V. The stack consists of the connectionless ISO 8473 networking protocol with the OSI transport class 4 frequently used where a connection is required. The structure of the connectionless datagram is shown in Figure 6.9.

Field	Size
Protocol identifier	1
Header length	1
Version/Protocol extension	1
Lifetime	1
S,M,E,T bits	1
Segment length	2
Header checksum	2
Destination address length	1
Destination address	Variable
Source address length	1
Source address	Variable
Data unit identifier	2
Segmentation offset	2
Total pdu length	2
Options	Variable
Data	Variable

Figure 6.9   OSI CLNP fields.

This structure is very similar to IP, with the main difference lying in the variable length addresses supported. The total header size is thus variable, but usually a few bytes more than IP version 4, but less than IP ng. The lifetime field serves a similar function to that in IP, but is formatted in terms of 500 ms units. The transmitting station initializes this field to the maximum acceptable lifetime, then each node decrements the field by one (or more if the perceived link delay is greater than 500 ms) until either the PDU is delivered or the count reaches zero when the PDU is dropped. PDUs are also dropped if the checksum is found to be incorrect. The only congestion control feature in ISO8473 is an optional bit in the options field. Any node that experiences network congestion can set this bit, but the standard does not specify what action the rest of the network should take, although some implementations such as DECnet V do. Some routers implement this congestion feature by setting the congestion bit when the buffer queue in the router exceeds a configurable threshold; it is then up to the ES device to throttle back.

6.6.1   OSI TP4

OSI offers a choice of five transport classes, from 0 to 4, of which TP4 is the most powerful and intended for use with unreliable network services. TP4 establishes a virtual connection between the end stations in a similar way to TCP, but with significant differences. The normal form of header structure for a TP4 TPDU is shown in Figure 6.10.

Field	Size (bytes)
Header length (LI)	1
Fixed part	6
Variable part	0 – 247
Data	0 – (TPDU-LI)

Figure 6.10   TP4 fixed header.

The fixed part contains the type code for the TPDU (for example, connection request or data transport), the initial credit window, destination reference field, source reference field, transport class and options, while the variable part consists of optional less-common parameter codes and their lengths. These extra parameter codes, such as maximum TPDU size, acknowledgement time, residual error rate and so on, are mainly used in the CR and CC (connection confirm), with a typical class 4 CR shown in Figure 6.11.

A data TPDU for TP4 does not carry the source reference, but has an end of TPDU sequence and sequence number field instead. The only variable component is usually the actual checksum (16 bit ones complement), while the remainder is data up to the negotiated TPDU size.

Field	Size (bits)
Header length (LI)	8
Type of TPDU & CDT	8
DST-reference	16
Calling TSAP	
Identifier	16
TPDU size	8
Security	Variable
Checksum	1
Other options (each)	1
Alternative protocol	
class	Variable
Acknowledge time	2
Throughput	12 or 24
Residual error rate	3
Priority	2
Transit delay	8
Reassignment time	2
Data	Variable

Figure 6.11   TP4 variable header.

The TPDU size is a multiple of 128 bytes in the range 128 to 8192. Like TCP, TP4 uses a sliding window credit flow control scheme intended primarily for end-device congestion control rather than network congestion. The value entered in the credit field is the number of TPDUs of the specified size that can be accepted rather than the number of bytes. An initial value for the credit is contained in the CR TPDUs. This window size can be up to 32 767 in principle, making this one of the best protocols to use on high-speed or satellite links where a high throughput is to be obtained from a single connection (see Chapters 9 and 10 for more details).

TP4 also uses a retransmission timer, but unlike TCP or DECnet's NSP, this timer has to be estimated in advance, then set up in the call request as a fixed parameter for the session. The timer, called T1, is defined in terms of the network and processing delays for a data TPDU by:

$$T1 => X + E_{LR} + A_R + E_{RL}$$

where:

X is the local processing time for the TPDU,

E_{LR} and E_{RL} are the maximum expected TPDU transit delays from local to/from remote device, and

A_R is the remote acknowledgement delay.

As TPDUs are of a negotiated fixed size in file transfers apart from fragments, there is less need to revise this timer than in the TCP or DECnet IV cases. In DECnet V, which uses TP4, this timer is automatically adjusted in the light of experienced delays.

TP4 also maintains a reference timer, usually denoted by L, that prevents the reuse of a reference number. L measures the maximum time that a TPDU can possibly remain legitimately unacknowledged in the system. There is also a separate retransmission timer, W, that determines the time that a device will wait before retransmitting an AK TPDU (which is normally shorter than a data TPDU). The AK TPDU is also used to adjust the credit field. As the network is assumed to be unreliable, it is expected that AK TPDUs can arrive in the wrong order and so incorrectly adjust the credit; to counter this each AK carries a subsequence number that is increased for every credit reduction, and only reset to 0 when further DT TPDUs are received. AK TPDUs are only accepted on one of the three following conditions:

(1) It acknowledges DT TPDUs with higher sequence numbers than before.

(2) It acknowledges the same TPDU as before, but with a higher subsequence number.

(3) The same DT TPDU and subsequence number as before, but with increased credit.

This system enables TP4 to resequence out-of-order TPDUs within the same window, before passing them up to the session layer.

An important adjunct of TP4's ability to resequence TPDUs is support for multiple network connections under a single transport connection. This allows multiple links to be used, so that if one is lost there is a reduction in throughput, but no loss of transport connection or higher session. Multiplexing of multiple links or virtual connections also allows higher throughput to be obtained. This is particularly relevant to countries in which there are no fractional T1/E1 services, but a bandwidth of more than 56/64 kbps is needed. Multiple virtual circuits are applicable to any networks in which network flow control restricts the throughput of a single VC to much less than the available bandwidth.

6.6.2   DECnet Phase V implementation of OSI

DNA V does not support all the options of OSI CLNP, but makes some significant improvements also. The major omissions are the options for priorities, security and source routing. ISO 8473 does not actually specify an algorithm for source routing, hence there is no standard method; DNA fills this gap by using the link state routing of DECnet Phase V instead (see Chapter 7).

Congestion control is improved by setting the CLNP congestion bit whenever the buffer queue in a router exceeds a configurable threshold, then using DNA's version of TP4 to reduce the level 4 window size if the number of packets showing congestion exceeds another threshold. Furthermore, if a message is lost, then the window is automatically cut to one.

Other improvements to TP4 in DNA V are the automatic calculation of updated retransmission timers, making TP4 responsive to variable delays, and the use of the extended flow control sequence and credit fields.

For further information on DECnet and OSI see Martin and Leben (1992).

6.6.3   OSI CONS

There are also connection-oriented networks services in OSI that can use transport classes 0,1, 2 and 3 of ITU-T X.224. In these cases error correction and sequencing is provided by the underlying connection-oriented service, that is, X.25 or ISO LLC2, so that the transport layer does not have to provide any flow control. Its only performance parameter is the optional segmentation of higher-level data units. This is determined by the packet/frame size and window arguments already discussed in Chapter 5.

6.6.4   OSI session layer

The influence of the OSI session layer on performance is minimal, but still of some relevance. The session protocol includes minor and major synchronization points, of which the latter requires a wait for an acknowledgement. The maximum size of a session data unit is 65 535 bytes, and in an OSI environment will limit the maximum size of a burst of data sent by a file server. Acknowledgements are optional for minor synchronization points, but if used may reduce throughput.

The situation in which this becomes important is in high-speed links over long distances, where the propagation delay is comparable to the transmission time. Even then, the transport layer will usually be a more severe limit.

6.7   Frame relay

Frame relay can be regarded as a cutdown derivative of X.25 that takes account of the high quality of digital lines and the intelligence of new user devices to eliminate much of the error and flow control that used to be necessary within the network. Where the old conditions of dumb terminals and error-prone analog lines still exist, X.25 will remain preferable.

Frame relay has several performance advantages over X.25. The first of these is that level 3 protocol has been eliminated and level 2 streamlined, with the result that a typical frame relay node can support about five times as high a frame through-put as could X.25 with the same processor. This benefits the user financially through a lower cost per switched frame and operationally through a reduced response time. The biggest performance improvement resulting from frame relay is in multihop networks where the fact that frame relay standards permit a node to commence for-warding a frame before it has been completely received cuts out a lot of the line transmission delay. This is particularly important for upper-layer protocols that lack a windowing mechanism, such as NetWare without burst mode or TFTP. Figures 6.12 and 6.13 illustrate the reduction in response time that results from this feature.

Figure 6.12 shows the benefits to response time on networks with more than three hops of segmenting packets within the network; this is done automatically by

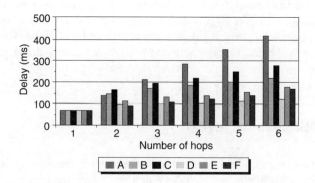

Figure 6.12 Segmentation and transit time.

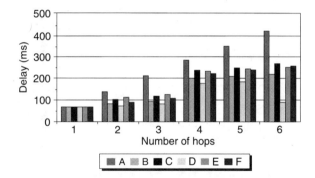

Figure 6.13   Cut-through and transit time.

some public X.25 networks. Response time A (on FILO basis) is that for a 512 byte packet plus overheads being transmitted unsegmented across a multihop network at light loading (no queuing) with 64 kbps links and 1 ms processing time at each switch/router. B shows the effect of segmenting into 128 byte packets at the end of the 64K hop into the network, while C shows the same thing, but with a longer packet processing time of 10 ms. D and E are analogous to B and C, but with 256 K links for all but the first hop, while F shows the 512 byte packet in this scenario, again with 1 ms packet processing time. In general, fragmentation is beneficial for routes of three or more hops provided that the packet processing time is less than the link transit time. If the packet were fragmented before entry into the WAN, then these benefits would apply after two hops instead of three.

Figure 6.13 shows how the response time comes down if frame relay starts to forward the 128 byte fragments as soon as it has received the first 128 bytes, instead of waiting for the full frame (and its CRC check) as X.25 would have to do. FILO response times A to F are otherwise analogous to those in the previous graph. This provides significant improvement over the X.25-style fragmentation above, and would show a slight improvement over fragmentation before entry to the WAN due to a lower frame processing time.

6.7.1   Frame relay congestion control

The structure of frame relay frames is based on the ISDN LAPD standards and defined in ITU Q.922 and ANSI T1.606. This structure is shown in Figure 6.14.

Individual logical circuits are identified by the data link channel identifier (DLCI) field that normally has 10 bits, but which can be extended by either one or two bytes. Most implementations use the basic 10 bit field, so giving up to 1024 DLCIs, of which 992 are available for user circuits. The size of a frame is from 5 to 8189 bytes of data.

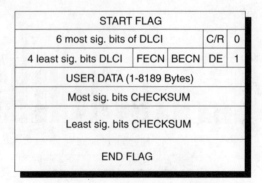

Figure 6.14   Frame relay fields.

Congestion is controlled through the use of the FECN (forward explicit congestion notification), BECN (backward) and DE (discard eligibility) bits in conjunction with a committed information rate (CIR). The FECN bit is set in a data frame by the network to notify the user that congestion avoidance procedures should be initiated for traffic in the direction of the received frame. Similarly, the BECN bit is set to indicate that flow control is needed for traffic in the opposite direction to the received frame. The big problem for frame relay networks is that the FR end-user is often a router that is unable to flow control its own end-point devices and can only do very limited flow control itself. This router flow control depends on a configurable threshold for the number of BECNs received within an interval for a DLCI, after which the router reduces or cuts off the supply of further data to that DLCI until another configurable threshold for the number of frames without a BECN has been reached. The rate at which flow is resumed is normally less than that at which it was reduced; this is in order to prevent recreating the problem.

Where data transits more than one frame relay network there is another useful congestion indicator, the A-bit. Some networks set this to indicate to the originating network that the destination network is congested, thereby preventing the congestion feeding back.

The way in which the FR network does its own flow control is simply to drop frames when it is congested. Ideally this is done by dropping the minimum number of frames that have the DE bit set, while continuing to deliver all others. The DE bit is set by the FR end-device for relatively low priority traffic, and may also be set by the network for user traffic in excess of an agreed CIR. Dropping of a frame will normally trigger a retransmission, but the delay before this happens may be sufficient to bring the transmission rate back within the CIR and possibly eliminate congestion. In the case of OSI TP4 the value of the retransmission timer T1 can be set to be such that if each TPDU has to be retransmitted, then the maximum throughput is within the CIR. For public networks the CIR is part of a contractual agreement between the user and network service provider, while for private networks it is set by the network manager on the basis of expected traffic levels. Frequently the CIR is not defined directly as a bit rate, but rather through three other parameters as follows; the port speed, a committed burst size, B_c, and a critical burst duration, T_c. These are related by:

$CIR = B_c/T_c$, subject to CIR < port speed.

Some networks also add an excess burst size as a safety factor, but its main role is in tariffing. In that case, traffic between the committed and excess burst levels within the critical time has the DE bit set, but is usually carried, whereas anything in excess of the excess size is automatically dropped. The charge for excess data is often less because of the uncertainty. ITU recommendation I.370 proposes that these parameters should be related as shown in Table 6.6 where ACR is the access rate of the line.

If the structure of the applications on each port is well understood, then the burst sizes can be reliably estimated, but in general a few simple guidelines are all that are available. The burst size must be greater than not only the largest frame expected, but also the complete transport level window, as there is no way of controlling the flow at the higher level until the window is exhausted. An upper bound to the burst size is given by circumstances that will automatically give rise to congestion. The typical case of this is where the burst is so large that it occupies the entire route across the network, that is, it is of a size comparable to the product of the port bandwidth and the network transit time, and there are other virtual circuits on that port. Similarly, if the burst occupies the route for more than the retransmission time for other traffic, then that traffic will get retransmitted leading to the possibility of avalanche decay of the network performance. TCP will automatically extend its timer under these circumstances, but that for TP4 is fixed. This must also be taken into account when deciding the retransmission timer for TP4; if N file-servers share a frame relay port, then there is a significant chance of a burst from one being queued behind the remaining $N - 1$. This also tends to require high port speeds for file-servers with 64 kbyte bursts, since the retransmission timers have to be unreasonably large otherwise. Another factor is the buffer space available in the frame relay node, as bursts converging from several trunk directions onto an access line will have to be buffered, and any frames that have to be dropped due to lack of memory will be retransmitted.

Another approach to setting CIRs is to consider the access port speed multiplied by the peak achievable loading (often about 70%) and divide this between the number of virtual circuits defined on the access link, then provide trunk capacity to match. If this rate is less than the CIR deduced from the transport window size and the network response time, then performance may be unsatisfactory. Another such check is provided by dividing this CIR by the burst size for each application, translating this into bursts per minute, and seeing whether this is likely to meet user requirements.

Table 6.6   CIR relationships.

CIR	B_c	B_e	T_c
>0	>0	>0	$T_c = B_c/CIR$
>0	>0	=0	$T_c = B_c/CIR$
=0	=0	>0	$T_c = B_e/ACR$

Congestion bits obviously have to be set before retransmissions or frame dropping start to take place. Where there is a frame relay DTE (as opposed to a DCE like a router), then it should reduce its data flow in accordance with the following algorithm:

> On receipt of consecutive frames with the BECN bit set, the DTE should according to ANSI reduce its transmission rate to the next lower step rate below the current rate; these rates are 0.675, 0.5 and 0.25 of the current rate. The rate can then be increased by 0.125 of the new rate on receipt of two consecutive frames without the BECN bit set. If frames are small compared to the burst or transport window sizes, then this mechanism will lead to a rapid drop to the base level followed by a slow rise after the end of the burst. Response to FECNs is less critical, and it is recommended that if the number of frames with FECNs set exceeds that with FECN clear in a configurable interval, then throughput should be reduced to 7/8th of its current value, increasing by 1/16th after a period with more FECN clear than set.

Routers only have a limited ability to reduce or suspend data flow before their own buffers become full leading to frame drop, so they have to rely on the upper levels. Where they are about to run out of buffers due to frame relay congestion, they should set the FECN/BECN bits as appropriate when a threshold is passed that gives some leeway for corrective action before the need to drop frames arises. In some instances they may also elevate congestion bits to higher-level protocols that support congestion bits, such as OSI CLNP. Frame relay access devices (FRADs), often derived from X.25 PADs, tend to have better flow control and traffic prioritization than routers.

A cruder alternative recommendation for devices that do not implement FECN/BECN flow control is to reduce throughput by a quarter if a frame is lost, increasing again after a period with no losses. Devices with a higher-level protocol window should decrease the window size towards a minimum of one until a number of frames have been returned without FECN/BECN set.

Another factor that limits the usability of FECN and BECN is the need for the data flow to carry the bits. A file transfer will not always have this feature, so ANSI introduced the idea of consolidated link level management (CLLM) to overcome this. In CLLM, DLCI 1023 is used to send regular messages across the network that contain one-byte congestion codes to which standard responses are expected. Most manufacturers do not support CLLM, and use the earlier proprietary local management interface (LMI) instead. The LMI also used DLCI 1023 originally, so is incompatible with CLLM, but should now use DLCI 0. It features regular keep-alive messages that can carry the BECNs, but unlike CLLM is only suitable for PVCs not SVCs. It allows for polling of PVC status, which is returned in a PVC status byte. Bit 1 of this is the R-bit which is used to to indicate that a configurable buffer threshold has been exceeded, thereby giving advance warning of congestion. Bit 2 is the A-bit that shows whether a PVC is active or not.

A further improvement to frame relay management is the Frame Relay Forum's Customer Network Management (CNM) agreement, whereby the user is able to monitor variables relevant to traffic flow on a PVC and to add further PVCs or change the CIR on demand. Another useful feature is the use of A-bit notification to show the failure of a remote link, thereby enabling rapid rerouting, for example by dial up.

Frame relay is not recommended where the bit error rate is more than about 10^{-7} owing to the retransmission overhead on an end–end basis. This limits the window size, so satellite links are limited to fairly low speeds and analog links should be avoided unless good forward error-correcting modems are used.

When frame relay is used over good quality lines with cut-through switching in the backbone, then large frames (several thousand bytes) will give optimum performance for file transfers as on LANs.

When used for LAN interconnection the allocation of PVCs is a significant design issue. If each router requires a PVC over the WAN to each other LAN default router, then the 992 unreserved DLCI limit is exceeded at about 45 sites, so either extended addressing or other techniques are needed. Each DLCI is likely to need the order of 1–10 kbytes of memory so extended addressing capability is limited by router memory. In a client–server environment only e-mail normally supports anybody–anybody communication, so by using a version of mail based on hierarchical post boxes, the number of PVCs needed can be restricted to those needed to enable access to servers and central mail servers instead of all LANs.

Frame relay gives poor quality if used for voice owing to jitter. Best results require voice prioritization, small frames for all traffic and G.764 style build-out delay. For further information on frame relay see Black (1993) and Smith (1993).

6.8 XNS

Xerox Network Systems (XNS) was one of the earliest LAN protocol stacks to be developed.

RIP is the routing information protocol, IDP is the Internet datagram protocol, SPP is the sequenced packet exchange protocol and PEX is the packet exchange protocol. The structures of these are given below.

6.8.1 IDP

IDP is the network level component of XNS, and has a 30 byte header with up to 546 bytes of data. The structure is almost identical to that of the much more widespread IPX (see section 6.9), so is not described here.

6.8.2 SPP

SPP is the transport level component of XNS that is responsible for end-station flow control; its structure is given in Figure 6.15.

Field	Length (bytes)
Conn.control/data type	2
Source connection i.d.	2
Destination conn. id	2
Sequence number	2
Acknowledgement number	2
Allocation number	2
Data	

Figure 6.15 SPP fields.

The sequence and acknowledgement numbers provide for end–end data integrity, while the allocation number is used for flow control in a similar way to the credits of LAT or the later OSI TP4. Acknowledgements can be requested or sent at any time using the send-bit piggybacked onto a data packet or via a separate probe. There is no automatic calculation of a retransmission timer; instead it is recommended to use a small multiple of the roundtrip time.

6.8.3 PEX

PEX is the connectionless transport level protocol in XNS; its structure is shown in Figure 6.16.

The identification number enables responses to be matched to requests, while the client type identifies the type of upper-level service.

This will retransmit packets based on single packet sequences only, hence giving low throughput like TFTP in IP, and does not do any error checking.

XNS is rarely used now, but forms the logical basis for IPX, one of the most common protocols, and also of some parts of Banyan VINES.

For more information on XNS see Naugle (1994).

Field	Length (bytes)
Identification	4
Client type	2
Data	0–546

Figure 6.16 PEX fields.

6.9   Novell IPX/SPX

Novell's IPX (Internet Packet Exchange) and SPX (Sequenced Packet Exchange) are closely modelled on XNS with similar sized headers, but with slightly different field meanings. The IPX header structure is shown in Figure 6.19.

Workstations obtain their network and node numbers from the nearest server, while the socket number identifies the process or application. In IPX there is a difference in the control and type fields as compared to the similar XNS IDP, while the checksum is not used in IPX and is always set to FFFF. The IPX transport control field keeps a count of nodes transited; if it reaches 15 then the packet is discarded to prevent routing loops from getting out of hand. The packet type is used to indicate the higher-level protocol to which the packet belongs, for example 17 for NetWare control protocol (NCP) or 5 for SPX. Normal data field lengths are up to 546 bytes, but with a large packet option, LIPX, in recent versions of NetWare. LIPX is beneficial for LANs, but counterproductive for multihop WANs or single analog WAN links.

In Novell's use of IPX there is no transport level protocol on top of the IPX network layer; instead the session/application levels of NCP, NetBIOS or less frequently RPC (remote procedure call) or LU6.2 talk to IPX. Some third party products use a transport level protocol SPX that is equivalent to SPP in XNS.

There is no equivalent of PEX, and NCP is responsible for most of the performance issues associated with IPX; this is described in detail in section 8.3 in relation to NCP. The data field within an IPX packet is not pure user data as it contains the higher-level NCP header. This header normally consists of 6 bytes including the connection and sequence numbers of the packets plus the type, but rises to 36 bytes for burst mode which is the only form of NCP that uses a window. SPX is not often used because of the numerous broadcasts within NetWare which would require a separate SPX connection for each address, leading to excessive overhead; instead, the acknowledgement requirements within NCP are used to give reliability.

Field	Size (bytes)
Checksum	2
Packet length	2
Transport control	1
Packet type	1
Destination network	4
Destination node	6
Destination socket	2
Source network	4
Source node	6
Source socket	2

Figure 6.17   IPX header.

A major feature of IPX that requires optimization wherever low-speed WAN links are involved is the service advertisement protocol (SAP). SAP updates are normally issued every 60 seconds (as well as triggered updates), with 64 bytes per SAP device, up to 7 SAPs in a packet with 32 byte header. A typical 'server' contains a print server, file server and NetWare server, each of which is a separate SAP device. A single 'server' thus generates 224 bytes per minute of self-advertisements. On large networks with hundreds of servers, this constitutes a major overhead on low-speed WAN links, which can cause congestion. SAPs are propagated between networks by routers broadcasting their SAP tables which contain entries for each active service. These are issued as a sequence of packets; typically at a rate of 20 to 50 per second until the full table has been sent. This causes a period of congestion of a few seconds on 56/64 kbps WAN links that can be very detrimental to users.

There are three ways of reducing this when it becomes a problem: using a long non-standard timer (if permitted by the router software) for regular updates across all links (for example, 10 minutes), the transmission of triggered updates only across slow X.25 or asynchronous links, and the use of SAP filters. Reducing the frequency of updates does not eliminate the congestion but reduces the frequency of its occurrence pro rata. On extremely large networks with several thousand servers this problem extends right up to T1/E1 speeds, so some routers have an option to segment the blocks of SAPs to let other traffic through rather than have users experience timeouts.

SAPs can be filtered outbound on a variety of criteria, such as type and address, dependent on the router's IPX implementation. Some routers also allow a maximum number of hops to be set for each service type or server name. Filters are awkward to maintain from an administrative point of view. The main recognized SAP types are listed in Table 6.7.

The majority of recognized SAPs on most networks belong to types 4 and 7, but they are often heavily outnumbered by special services with type values of several hundred. In many networks the full range needs to be transmitted within a local area, but very few need be sent across the WAN; print services in particular can often be cut by filtering outbound onto the WAN. Type 4 file servers may need to be accessed from a much wider region.

Comprehensive tables of all SAP types can be obtained by searching on Novell's World Wide Web site.

Replacement of RIP for IPX by NLSP (NetWare link state protocol) is the major future way to cut SAPs on the WAN (see Chapter 7).

6.9.1 IPXWAN

This is a standard defined in RFC1634 (amending earlier RFCs) for encapsulating IPX in other protocols for transport across a WAN. Establishment of a network connection contains a timer request that is used to fix the link delay advertised in IPX RIP packets for the duration of the session. This is done using a 576 byte request and

Table 6.7 Common SAP types.

SAP type	Significance
0	Unknown
1	User
2	User group
3	Print queue
4	File server
5	Job server
6	Gateway
7	Print server
8	Archive queue
9	Archive server
A	Job queue
B	Administration
21	SNA gateway
24	Remote bridge server
26	Router server
47	Advertising printer
4B	Btrieve VAP v.5
50	Btrieve VAP v.4.11
9E	Portable NetWare server
107	Remote console
133	Netware naming service
304	SAA gateway
39B	Lotus Notes

response, with the eventual delay and timeout set to a multiple of the roundtrip time that depends on the nature of the connection. This is frequently six times the measured delay, but a fixed value of 55 units of 1/18 seconds (that is, one second) may be used for multiple workstation sessions to prevent timeouts. This system gives an automatic adaptation to initial network conditions, but is not as flexible as PPP's echo requests which can be used to tune a session periodically to adapt to changing conditions.

6.9.2 IPX header compression (CIPX)

Many NetWare sessions use a high proportion of small packets, making header compression important on low bandwidth links. The standard for this is CIPX, defined in RFC1553. The normal IPX header has 30 bytes, which is compressed to between 1 and 8 bytes, with 2 the norm using the main tele-bit option. There is also another option due to Shiva which additionally compresses the 6 byte NCP header (but not a 36 byte burst mode header).

When NCP is used without burst mode, the average packet fill is often only about 26 bytes in interactive applications, so the compression ratio of CIPX is about 2:1 making it very useful on low-bandwidth links. For file transfers with 546 bytes of data, the ratio drops to only 1.04:1, which is not worthwhile.

IPXWAN supports both of these compression modes, using a field in the header to say what, if anything, is being used.

6.10   AppleTalk

AppleTalk uses a relatively complex protocol stack, fairly close to the OSI model, whose components are shown in Figure 6.18.

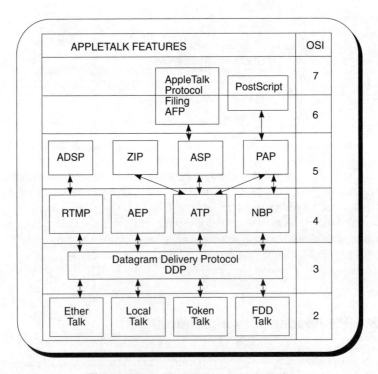

Figure 6.18   AppleTalk protocol stack.

For normal file transfers, the relevant components are Apple filing protocol (AFP), AppleTalk session protocol (ASP), AppleTalk transport protocol (ATP), DDP and the appropriate data link protocol. Printing makes use of PostScript, printer access protocol (PAP), ATP and the same lower layers. ADSP (AppleTalk datastream protocol) is another reliable transport alternative to ATP, but used for datastreams instead of request/response styles of transaction. Datastreams are not normally used in Apple Macintosh applications, and ADSP's main role is in emulations of other systems and in gateways. The remaining components ZIP (zone information protocol), RTMP (routing table maintenance protocol) and AEP (AppleTalk echo protocol) are concerned with location of devices and the routing algorithms which are discussed in Chapter 7.

At the network level, the datagram delivery protocol (DDP) uses 13 byte headers and 0 to 586 bytes of data for all types of traffic. The header structure is shown in Figure 6.19.

Unlike IP or IPX, there is no standard way of compressing this header for sessions using small packets.

Routers do not always support fragmentation of IP datagrams (for example, from Mac IP) so there is a risk of packet loss for systems with large MTUs.

The DDP limit of 586 bytes carries over into EtherTalk and TokenTalk frames, so that the maximum information field in them is only 599 bytes plus 4 bytes of AppleTalk link layer header. On a LAN, AppleTalk is thus less efficient than most other protocols, but the DDP packet size is quite effective on WAN links.

6.10.1   ATP

Of the four level 4 functions, it is ATP that performs the transport class functions for normal data traffic. The 8 byte header structure for ATP is shown in Figure 6.20.

Field	Size (bytes)
Hop count	1
Datagram length	1
DDP checksum	2
Dest. network #	2
Source network #	2
Dest. node	ID 1
Source node ID	1
Dest. socket #	1
Source socket #	1
DDP type	1
Data	0–586

Figure 6.19   DDP fields.

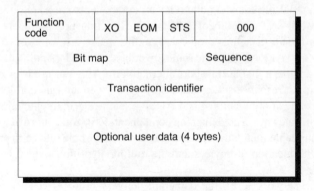

Figure 6.20   ATP header.

There are three possible function codes: transaction request, transaction response and transaction release. The flags XO, EOM and STS denote Transmit Once Only, End of Message, and Status Request, respectively. The request indicates the number of buffers to send by means of the sequence number/bit map field. The responder uses this to put received packets in sequence and request retransmission of any missing packets via a selective reject mechanism.

XO is used for calls which if repeated would lead to a different result; for example, it would transmit a different block of a file to the original.

ATP uses two timers, one for individual packets and the other for transaction release; in the case of XO (only), the 3 zero bits are replaced by binary values indicating from 30 seconds to 8 minutes (although AppleTalk I only uses 30 seconds). The more important parameter for throughput is the packet retransmission timer. This is passed to ATP by its client application, such as ASP or PAP, rather than being part of ATP itself. PAP uses a fixed value of 15 seconds, which is realistic for printers, but potentially too long for other applications making use of PAP across a frame relay network liable to drop frames. ASP does not have a fixed timer, but again relies on its clients to specify a value. For bespoke applications, one option is to send an AppleTalk echo of typical packet size, measure the roundtrip time and then use a small multiple for the timeout. The number of retransmissions can be specified to ATP, and is nominally infinite for ASP, but limited by the fact that ASP uses a tickle timer and packet to check both session ends are alive, which drops a session after two minutes if one end is dead.

6.10.2   ASP

ASP uses eight functions, notably open/close session, tickle and write. The ASP function code goes into the first of the ATP user bytes, while the session ID goes in the second and sequence number into the last two, where applicable. Thus the only overheads associated with ATP are the extra protocol packets. Tickles are sent every

30 seconds when no data is flowing and consist of 21 bytes, so do not impose a significant network load.

6.10.3   ADSP

ADSP requires the opening and closing of its own connection, and like ASP checks its two ends when no data is flowing by a probe every 30 seconds, with the connection being taken down if there is no reply after two minutes. ADSP uses a 13 byte header that contains the fields shown in Figure 6.21.

ADSP packets contain up to 572 bytes of data with bytes being identified by sequence numbers via the byte sequence number field. Flow control is performed by the responder setting the receive window according to buffer capacity plus the setting of an ACK bit in the descriptor field. Packet next receive sequence number specifies the actual bytes acknowledged as the next expected. Frequency of acknowledgements is implementation dependent, but a request will always be made when the sender finds its window exhausted. The maximum window size is limited by the field size to 64 kbytes.

6.10.4   AppleTalk via IP

AppleTalk is sometimes carried in IP using Mac IP which gives some reduction in routing traffic, but has the problem that some implementations do not support fragmentation. As this may be necessary for acceptable performance over a WAN the details of the implementation need to be considered.

6.10.5   AppleTalk via frame relay

AppleTalk is more sensitive to timing problems than most other protocols, and when carried by frame relay where frames are liable to be dropped, usually needs to be given a high priority to minimize this.

For further information on AppleTalk see Sidhu *et al.* (1990) and Steenstrup (1995).

Field	Size (bytes)
Connection ID	2
Packet 1st byte sequence number	4
Packet next receive sequence	4
Packet receive window	2
ADSP descriptor	1

Figure 6.21   ADSP header.

6.11   VINES

VINES offers several alternative protocol stacks, with IP the most important network-level component. Banyan VINES IP supports frame sizes up to 1500 bytes with 18 byte headers and has a fragmentation protocol to handle larger MTUs instead of dropping them. This header only consists of two bytes that contain a sequence number and position flags, so constitutes a negligible bandwidth overhead. Fragmentation does, however, put a considerable extra processing load on a router, typically by a factor of two to three as compared to a normal packet.

VINES has three possible transport modes in addition to TCP and IDP giving different levels of reliability. The most basic is unreliable IPC (interprocess communication) which sends single unacknowledged datagrams of up to 1450 user data bytes. The next is reliable IPC which sends up to four such datagrams in sequence and requiring acknowlegement. Where a long stream of reliable data needs to be sent, SPP is used in combination with reliable IPC. In this a window field indicates the highest sequence number that SPP is prepared to accept at any stage.

At the network level the main VINES protocol is VINES internetwork protocol (VIP); the header structure for this is shown in Figure 6.22.

Servers have a network number plus their host number, which acts as the subnet number for clients. On start up, clients broadcast for servers and adopt the host number assigned by the first to respond as their subnet number as well as taking its network number. The transport field in the header varies according to whether the packet is a broadcast or directed. For broadcasts it indicates the type of nodes that should respond and provides a hop count of nodes traversed to date. Otherwise the node type subfield is replaced by error, metric and redirect bits relating to ICP requirements for routing. The protocol type indicates the transport level protocol to which exception messages for these three conditions are destined.

Multi-interface servers act as routers and help to contain broadcasts by not forwarding them at all if received on a non-optimal path, and otherwise omitting the received path from further flooding.

Field	Size (bytes)
Checksum	2
Packet length of entire VIP packet	2
Transport control	1
Protocol type	1
Destination network number	4
Destination subnetwork number	2
Source network number	4
Source subnetwork number	2

Figure 6.22   VINES IP header.

7

LAN/WAN Interworking

7.1   General considerations

LANs are connected to or across WANs by means of bridges, routers and gateways. In the case of bridges, a pair of remote bridges are required instead of the single local bridge used to connect a pair of LANs directly; likewise routers are used in pairs, but gateways are single entities. This chapter is mainly concerned with the performance aspects of configuring bridges and routers, the main issues being bandwidth, minimization of interrupts on servers and bridge processing power. Before covering these topics a brief summary of LAN performance characteristics is given.

7.2   LAN performance

LAN performance depends on the type of LAN and its bandwidth. The main types of LAN are 10/100 Mbps Ethernet, 4/16 Mbps Token Ring, 100 Mbps FDDI and 100 Mbps 100 Base VG ANYLAN. The main performance limiting factors on a LAN are associated with the workstations and servers rather than the network, hence large message transfer units (MTUs) are used whenever possible to reduce the load on them. These lead to large frame sizes which are likely to give poor response times over the WAN. This is much more of a problem for bridges as they do not fragment frames, whereas routers can normally be configured to split packets into smaller units.

7.2.1   Ethernet

Ethernet performance is usually given in terms of formulae deduced originally by Lam for random communication.

Throughput = $S/(2*A + (1+A)*S)$

where S is $1/e$ (e being the exponential), and

A = Carrier sense time/Average message transmit time

This model is a bit pessimistic for under about 100 stations on an Ethernet, Figure 7.1 shows the variation of throughput with A.

Normally A is in the region 0.01 to 0.3 (see Figure 7.2), but were the speed to be increased to 100 Mbps, the A values rise owing to the reduction in frame transmission time, so that the size of the Ethernet has to be reduced for efficient performance of the standard CSMA/CD algorithm at this speed. This is one of the factors motivating the alternative 100 Base VG standard discussed later. A is also sensitive to distance, and with a maximal 2 km Ethernet backbone efficiency is very low, making FDDI preferable in this role.

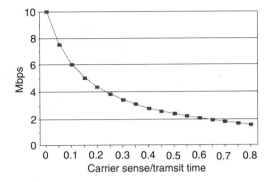

Figure 7.1   Ethernet throughput and A.

For a normal 10 Base T network based on a single hub, about 8 Mbps throughput should always be achievable, but for large 10 Base 5 networks with small frames and many stations, collision back-off causes a big degradation as shown by Figure 7.1. For WANs, the significance of these figures is in assessing what filtering load has to be catered for, and in deciding whether to segment the Ethernet and insert a short WAN bridge.

Most modern Ethernets support client–server communication rather than the random type, so collisions are mainly between servers. This enables much higher LAN loadings to be obtained, with the main design issue being segregation and location of servers.

7.2.2   Fast Ethernet (IEEE 802.3u)

There are two versions of 100 Mbps Ethernet within the IEEE 802.3u specification, 100 Base TX and 100 Base T4. The 802.3u differs primarily from normal Ethernet

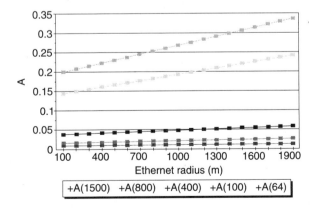

Figure 7.2   Effect of frame and network sizes on A.

by the 100 Mbps speed and the inclusion of a media independent interface (MII) layer between the MAC and physical levels to allow operation over different types of medium, notably category 3, 4 or 5 UTP and fibre. 100 Base TX uses two pairs of category 5 UTP with the proven FDDI PMD coding scheme, so is not suitable for buildings with old voice grade cabling; for these, 100 Base T4 is needed, but with the caveat that four pairs of UTP are required instead of two. The 802.3u standard also includes an autopulse feature that enables the type of Ethernet to be ascertained dynamically.

Permitted frame sizes and workstation to hub distances are the same as for normal 10 Mbps Ethernet, but inter-repeater distances are reduced to only 10 metres over twisted pair, making the maximum station–station distance only 220 metres. This means that either fibre connections or brouters have to be introduced when upgrading some large 10 Mbps Ethernets.

7.2.3 Ethernet switching

Ethernet switching is a proprietary technique for the dynamic switching of stations onto individual LAN segments according to destination address which is implemented in a variety of ways, depending on vendor. The main choice is between cut-through switching, where the frame is forwarded as soon as the header has been read, or full frame forwarding as in bridges. The former gives better response times, but will forward invalid frames such as runts and giants. Switching provides a cost-effective alternative to brouters in a local environment, but is not applicable to the wide area. WAN connections still require brouters, and stations are switched to the segments that support these devices as required, with no significant performance differences from a normal Ethernet scenario. This is also true of Token Ring switching.

7.2.4 Token Ring

Token Ring performance can be written in a similar way according to the formula

$$\text{Throughput} = 1/(1+A)$$

where:

$$A = (P + ((N+24)/V))/(NT * Tm)$$

where:

P is the propagation delay round the ring,

N is the number of stations on the ring,

24 represents the bit latency of the monitor,

V is the speed, that is, 4 or 16 Mbps,

NT is the average number of stations waiting to transmit (depends on traffic load),

Tm is the average message transmission time.

Throughput estimated this way rarely drops below 0.8. The exception is MAN-sized fibre-optic rings with small packets and no early token release, where the large propagation delays cause inefficiency.

As A is heavily influenced by distance this shows that Token Ring is much less sensitive than Ethernet to distance, particularly when IBM's early token release scheme is followed.

7.2.5   FDDI

FDDI's performance is very similar to that for Token Ring above, but with a 100 Mbps speed and early token release. It is possible to use almost the full bandwidth of FDDI. Where the ring uses single-mode optical fibre to achieve its maximum circumference of about 250 km, then throughput for a single session becomes limited by the propagation delay due to the finite velocity of light unless all window sizes are very large. This effect is discussed in detail in Chapter 9 for ATM WANs where it is a key issue.

WAN brouters should be given top priority to minimize congestion.

7.2.6   IEEE 802.12 (100 VG ANYLAN)/demand priority

This is the 100 Mbps upgrade for both 10 Mbps Ethernet and 4/16 Mbps Token ring over UTP and STP. Unlike Fast Ethernet, it is not restricted to the reduced distances of the high-speed CSMA/CD systems on twisted pair. It is also able to perform over bundles of voice grade cabling, for example 25 pair category 3 UTP, although the avoidance of crosstalk on multicasts has some slight adverse affects in this case. Four pairs of twisted pair are required instead of the two of 10 Base T Ethernet.

The main characteristic of IEEE 802.12 is its demand priority system. This makes it practical to run motion video over an 802.12 LAN unlike 100 Base T or 100 Base T4 Fast Ethernet. The principle of demand priority is that a hub maintains a pointer for each of two priority levels with access from attached stations on a round-robin basis. High priority requests take precedence over low priority requests, but do not pre-empt low priority packet transmissions that have already commenced. Hubs can be cascaded, in which case the round-robin priority scheme is extended to cover all members of such a group of hubs in a single table. The top priority traffic has a guaranteed worst case wait before transmission of $N-1$ times the transmission time of a maximum length packet, where N is the number of stations in a non-cascaded hub. Where hubs are cascaded, N is the total number of stations, and in addition there are liable to be small training delays when new hubs come on line.

Bridges provide an alternative to cascading of hubs, but provision has to be made for rigorous maintenance of priority on these (or routers also).

Where 802.12 LANs are connected over the wide area, it is desirable to have separate connections or at least bandwidth reservation to ensure that tolerable response times are available for the low priority service. Using a single connection without bandwidth reservation would lead to the total lock-out of low priority traffic at busy times owing to the arrival of further high priority frames over the 100 Mbps LAN before the completion of transmission of the last high priority frame over the slow WAN, even if there had been time to receive about 50 low priority frames on the LAN.

7.3   Bridges and their performance

Bridges are usually used for interconnection of small numbers of LANs, but routers for large numbers. A bridge operates at level 2, and connects similar LAN types only, with the exception of the special class of translation bridges, pioneered by the IBM 8209. The bridge does not look at any level 3 networking protocol headers, so the processing load for a bridge is usually less than that for a router, leading to a higher throughput for a given processor type than a router, but for WAN communications this difference is unimportant when compared with the slow transmission of the serial WAN link.

Bridges perform two roles, filtering and forwarding. In the case of Ethernets, addresses have to be learned and any address that is unrecognized is forwarded on all bridge ports unless filtered, whereas IBM Token Rings use source route bridging in which the path is explicitly set up by the source station, leading to different performance criteria. The differing LAN types are thus considered separately.

7.3.1   Transparent bridging

Transparent bridging is the technique used on Ethernets and some non-IBM Token Rings. An IEEE 802.3 Ethernet frame consists of a preamble, header, data and trailer as shown in Figure 7.3.

Field	Length (bytes)
Preamble	7
Start frame delimiter	1
Destination address	6
Source address	6
Length	2
Data and LLC control	N (Variable 1–1500)
Padding	N–44 or 0 for N>44
Frame check sequence	4

Figure 7.3   Ethernet frame.

In the case of Ethernet I, the length field is replaced by a type field that identifies the type of traffic, such as LAT. This structure is quite efficient if large quantities of data are available to fill a 1500 byte maximal frame, but extremely inefficient if devices such as terminal servers are inserting single user characters into individual frames. This inefficiency is exacerbated if the frame has to cross a WAN bridge; in the worst case of single character frames, the throughput of a 64 kbps link is only about 110 user characters per second, which is far worse than old technologies such as echoplex or X.25. The remedies available to rectify this are either to change to a more efficient protocol that avoids single character packets or to use compression/truncation techniques to eliminate unnecessary overheads. For terminal server traffic, the main protocol actions are to avoid TCP/IP which tends to generate such packets and to use LAT instead, where multi-user data packets of 60–70 user characters tend to be created, thereby increasing the useful load of the bridge by a factor of about 60. Outside of the DEC–UNIX environment LAT is not available, so truncation and compression need to be used.

Truncation is entirely proprietary and usually consists of removing the Ethernet PAD characters from short packets and possibly compressing the address fields. In the extreme example quoted, this increases the throughput by a factor of about 10 on low-speed WAN links. As the speed of the link is increased, this improvement drops off because of the processing overhead and delay occasioned on the bridge, so that above 256 to 512 kbps it may not be worthwhile.

Compression is applicable to the case of longer data packets where there is little or no padding to strip out. The algorithms are again proprietary, so compression bridges from different vendors cannot interwork. Compression consists mainly of the use of similar methods to those for modems, such as v42bis or Lemple-Ziv, and achieves similar results, that is, compression by factors of up to about 4, but more usually 2–2.5 for text and only 1.5 for binary code such as Windows applications. Again, there is a significant processing overhead on the bridge that reduces filtering/forwarding capability and adds to delay. As a result, compression is not recommended above about 64–256 kbps depending on the processing rate of the bridge unless hardware compression is used.

Filtering

Filtering is used to prevent unnecessary traffic from clogging up low bandwidth bridges and remote Ethernets. Occasionally this is now performed by means of filtering cards on an Ethernet hub, or by means of Ethernet switching, but usually it has to be performed by the bridge. Most bridges are able to filter Ethernet frames at the maximum possible frame rate of the (10 Mbps) LAN, that is, 14 881 frames per second, although as shown in the previous section, the maximum load on an Ethernet is usually only 30–80% of the available bandwidth. Filtering is based on the address fields only for 802.3, but in the case of Ethernet with type fields instead of the length, this field can also be used to select specific protocols. This can also be done where SNAP headers or IEEE 802.2 headers are used. DEC LAT, with Ethernet type field 6004, needs to be prioritized if it is required or filtered out if not. LAT also needs to have its service adverts controlled by filtering on group number.

Most filtering is based on the bridge learning where the MAC addresses are in relation to its ports. Associated with this is an ageing timer, whereby any addresses that have not been used for more than the timeout are automatically forgotten. This enables users to move their stations from one LAN to another without having to wait for a long period before recommencing work from the new location. The normal default is five minutes, but for WAN bridges a longer interval should be configured as users are unlikely to move quickly from one geographic site to another. Even the most mobile such users, peripatetics with notebook PCs, are unlikely to want to login at a new site for at least half an hour, so the ageing timeout should be increased to at least this in order to prevent flooding slow links with traffic for forgotten addresses that are still located on the base LAN. In the absence of peripatetic users a value of greater than one day is desirable to avoid storms at the start of the day. Configuring permanent addresses for servers helps to solve this problem where a short timer needs to be retained.

Filtering imposes a significant load on the bridge, and the maximum filtering rates can normally only be obtained when the bridge is using a single simple filtering criterion, such as one range of addresses. Where a complex criterion, such as several disjoint address ranges, is used the filtering rate drops because several independent tests have to be performed. For this reason it is sometimes desirable to use soft Ethernet addresses instead of the intrinsic MAC addresses if filtering performance is likely to be an issue.

Forwarding rates are rarely critical for WAN bridges as the bandwidth constrains the number of frames that can be forwarded, and tends only to be important for multiport bridges with several T1 or E1 interfaces, but the filtering rate needs to be up to the maximum LAN throughput.

7.3.2 Spanning tree

Ethernet bridges route data transparently and this can lead to broadcast and unrecognized addresses circulating endlessly if there are any loops in the network. This means that where multiple routes connect LANs together in a mesh, some means of eliminating closed routing loops is required; this is done by the spanning tree. The spanning tree algorithm is defined in IEEE 802.1D (but with various incompatible revision levels), which gives rules for the bridges to configure themselves into a tree configuration without any physical loops. When bridges start up, they go into a blocking state in which they do not forward any data, but do send bridge configuration protocol data units (BPDUs) which are used to determine a root bridge and root ports. The root bridge is the bridge whose identifier in the BPDU has the lowest value, while another bridge receiving BPDUs with lower identifier than its own designates the port receiving the lowest value BPDU as its root port, and stops sending BPDUs. This leads to the rapid identification of the root bridge. All other bridges then forward the configuration BPDUs generated by the root with an updated path cost field, while BPDUs from bridges further from the root are forwarded with the

Table 7.1 Transparent bridge timers.

Timer	Default (seconds)	Range
Hello	2	1–10
Listen	2*Hello	
Learn	15	4–30
Forward	15	4–30

path cost replaced by that of the forwarding bridge. The bridges with the lowest path costs go into the forwarding state, while the others go into the blocking state; thus for any Ethernet with multiple bridges, only the one with the lowest path cost to the route will be used. Where two or more bridges have equal path costs, then a priority based on MAC address or bridge identity is used to select one in preference to the others. IEEE 802.1D stipulates that path costs should be in the range 1– 65 535, and gives a suggested formula for relating these to the speed of LAN segments, but many bridges allow network operators to configure their own values in preference. The IEEE formula gives a path cost per segment of 1000/speed (Mbps).

Before a bridge can start forwarding data frames it must go from the blocking state into the listening state in which it waits for any further root path costs, then after expiry of a timer it goes to the learning state in which it updates its filtering database. On expiry of another timer it starts to forward data. The root bridge continues to send BPDUs at a Hello frequency, so that if bridges do not hear from the root within a period, they assume a failure has occurred, and start to reconfigure again automatically. IEEE suggests defaults for these timers (Table 7.1).

Unfortunately there have been a lot of variations on the spanning tree standard, so it is not guaranteed that bridges from different vendors will interwork satisfactorily. Some check on this is provided by the inclusion of a version number in the configuration BPDU format shown in Figure 7.4, but it does not give the full revision.

Field	Length (bytes)
Protocol ID	2
Protocol version	1
BPDU type	1
Flags	1
Root identifier	6
Root path cost	4
Bridge identifier	6
Port identifier	2
Message age	2
Maximum age	2
Hello time	2
Forward delay	2

Figure 7.4 Configuration BPDU.

Flags cover topology change and topology change acknowledgement. Root and bridge IDs are MAC addresses. The message age is usually a hop count from the root, and any BPDUs exceeding the maximum age are dropped.

Spanning tree works well with local bridges, but when remote bridges across a WAN are involved they can be very wasteful in terms of bandwidth and cost. If resilience dictates the existence of two or more parallel bridges or a mesh of triangular configurations, then spanning tree will disable many of them. It is also essential to use a path cost algorithm (such as that above based on segment speed) that ensures that the fastest of the available links is used in preference to low-speed alternatives. The waste of expensive resources can be minimized by using ISDN backup to provide resilience in preference to leased lines and meshing, or to use proprietary load sharing systems.

For wide area spanning trees it is necessary to ensure that both the root bridge and designated bridges for each LAN are suitable to make best use of the WAN links available, that is, block low-speed links in preference to high-speed alternatives. This often means configuring both the overall bridge priority for each bridge (where bridge configuration permits this) and the individual port priorities on multiport bridges. Where these features are available, it is always the lowest priority object which is selected, while the higher ones go into the blocking state.

Traffic in a spanning tree flows towards the root, so the bridges must be configured so that the choice of root matches the required real traffic flow. Usually this means that the root needs to be a large central site bridge. Conversely it is essential to ensure that the root is not at a small dual-homed branch connected over low-speed WAN links. Any assigned bridge priorities must also ensure that in most failure situations, any new root will also meet these criteria.

Many bridges are able to circumvent some of the inefficiencies of spanning tree, by configuring multiple parallel paths between two bridges as a single circuit group for the purposes of spanning tree. Some proprietary algorithm is then used to decide which of the possible paths a given frame should go down. Typically this is based on a specific combination of source and destination addresses, so that a looping frame will automatically be sent to the same circuit group member, where it will be recognized and discarded.

The other issue that the network manager must consider is the downtime resulting from bridge reconfigurations as a result of failures. Based on the IEEE defaults, reconfiguration time is about 30 seconds, while the minimum is about 15 seconds and the maximum around 100. In general the reconfiguration time should be made as short as possible, but the spanning tree parameters configured must take account of the speed of the links, size of the network and the effects of Hellos from the root having to queue behind frames of user data traffic. Reducing the bridge forward delay increases the amount of broadcast traffic on the network, but if there are only a few destinations this will not be a problem. On networks that only handle LAT, there are few hosts and the queuing delays will be small since typical LAT frames are only about 70 bytes long; as the minimum acceptable bridge speed for LAT itself is 56–64 kbps, the minimum values can usually be configured for such networks. If however, there are a lot of file transfers with 1500 byte frames, then allowance for queuing behind several of these over low-speed hops means increasing the timers to several seconds for Hellos. The maximum delays are applicable to networks with 50–100 bridges, file transfers and a significant number of links of 64 kbps or less. The Hello timer needs to be increased for satellite networks also due to the propagation delay.

In order to allow rapid reconfiguration of WAN spanning trees after failure, it is advisable to exclude from the spanning tree all remote bridges with only a single WAN link (sometimes called leaf entries), as they do not contribute to closed routing loops, but do slow down convergence. The typical network scenario is one in which a large number of isolated branches are singly homed (possibly with dial backup) onto a small number of central sites. Exclusion of the branch bridges greatly reduces the number of bridges contending to be the root as well as cutting out the delays associated with slow serial links, thereby enabling shorter timers to be used also. The net effect can be a reduction in convergence time by a factor of up to 10.

If the OSI transport class TP4 is running on top of a spanning tree network, then timers may need to allow for the reconfiguration time if sessions are not to be lost in the event of a bridge failure. Values needed for this purpose are much larger than those for normal data transmission, so a decision has to be made on whether it is more important to maintain sessions or to achieve the maximum flow under normal conditions.

Spanning tree is not very suitable for carrying X.25 traffic as a local link that is up may lead to a remote bridge in a blocking state that is invisible to X.25.

Another problem with spanning tree occurs when bridges connect Ethernet segments that have internal repeater links. In this case, if a repeater is switched off, then switched back on while the bridges are in the forwarding state, a closed loop will be formed leading to storms. This is only likely to happen during maintenance, and could be solved by using a bridge in place of the repeater.

7.4   Source route bridging (SRB)

Source Routing is the normal technique used in IBM Token Ring environments. Instead of the bridges having to learn the device locations as in transparent bridging, in SRB the end-stations send out broadcasts to discover the best route to their intended destination, then put the route to be followed into the Token Ring frame. This avoids most of the loop problems of ST, and enables resilient networks to be constructed in which all bridges can be used simultaneously, which is particualry important where WAN links occur. The main problem with SRB is the broadcast storms that are associated with the route discovery process.

7.4.1   Route discovery

There are two basic modes of route discovery, All routes broadcast and single route broadcast. In each case a station initially assumes that its intended destination is on the same LAN, but when the frame returns unread, it goes into the discovery process. In the All Routes Broadcast (ARB) case, the transmitting station sends out a Link Protocol Data Unit (LPDU) which is then forwarded on every port from each bridge on the ring. Each bridge includes its identity in the frame before forwarding, and will drop any frame that includes its identity already. The destination thus receives as many copies of the original LPDU as there are non-looping routes to it. It then returns one copy of the LPDU on each of these routes to the source, with each LPDU retracing its original path. the source then selects the route that gives the least delay, and enters this into each subsequent frame that it sends to that destination. In the case of single route discovery (which uses spanning tree explorers), the number of frames is halved by sending out the frame by one specific route, then receiving it back by all possibilities as above. In order to do this the source route bridges have to be configured into a spanning tree for the discovery process; this may be done manually or automatically according to the bridge functionality. The decision as to whether to use ARBs or STEs is taken by the end-station rather than the bridge. Manual spanning trees are inadvisable owing to loss of service in the event of a root failure.

The structure of the Token Ring frame is shown below, with the Routing Information Field (RIF) being the part that is set up in this way.

SD	AC	FC	DA	SA	RIF	DATA	FCS	ED	FS

where:

SD is the start delimiter,

AC is the access control,

FC is frame control,

DA and SA are destination/source address,

FCS is the frame check sequence,

ED is the end delimiter,

FS is the frame status,

RIF and Data jointly constitute the Token Ring information field.

The structure of the RIF is shown below.

ROUTE CONTROL	ROUTE DESIGNATOR 1	ROUTE DESIGNATOR 2	——————	ROUTE DESIGNATOR 8

Each Route Designator consists of a 4 bit bridge ID and a 12 bit Ring ID. The route control field consists of 2 bytes that identify the type of LPDU, for example ARB or specifically routed.

This technique clearly means that there can be a maximum of only seven hops on a path, a fact that can cause problems on large networks. This limit is more restrictive than it first appears, as the limitations of the standard Token Ring interface assume that a bridge has only two ports, so if multiport bridges are used, then they must be given an internal virtual ring ID. Most vendors of such products have proprietary schemes that get around this doubling of the hop count in many situations where only their bridges are used. A second obvious limitation is that the 4 bit bridge ID only permits 16 values, whereas a network may have many more bridges. This is not in fact a problem as it is only necessary to distinguish between different bridges when they are connected to the same Token Rings, or in some of the proprietary schemes to distinguish bridges from different vendors. The new draft IEEE 802.5p standard extends the RIF to allow up to 14 hops, but old Token Ring interface chips do not support this. IP encapsulation over a router network is the main way to overcome the limit where it is a problem.

The performance problems that occur with SRB are congestion of slow WAN links by broadcast storms, and the effects that the latter have on low-powered servers.

The techniques for overcoming these problems vary slightly according to the bridge functionality. Most bridges are capable of filtering on the address fields and the route control field. Another technique on some bridges is to configure a maximum hop count on each port, so that the RIF is effectively limited to a much smaller value than seven. This obviously only works if all source stations are situated relatively close to their main destinations. Typically LANs are structured into work groups fulfilling this criterion, but with a need to contact a few remote hosts also, in which case the network topology must be designed to do this by low hop routes. Use of STEs instead of ARBs is another option, while the use of filters specific to a protocol is also important. NetBIOS is the most important such protocol, with name caching and name filters as key elements. These features are decribed more fully under NetBIOS in Chapter 8.

Optimum response time over a multihop WAN bridge requires a reduction in frame size from the LAN norms. The lowest frame size recognized by most bridges is 516 bytes, and this should be used.

7.4.2   SDLC/LLC2 Token Ring interworking

Interworking of IBM SNA over a mixture of Token Rings and serial SDLC links poses specific problems that are often handled by bridges. The obvious problem is simply the different protocols. The simplest way to carry SDLC at the same time as Token Ring traffic is by means of some form of encapsulation, but another that is more effective is SDLC/LLC2 conversion. If a remote host needs to communicate over the WAN by means of SDLC to a workstation on a Token Ring, then there is an issue of timeouts. Both SDLC and SDLC use a retransmission timer T1, but the values for Token Rings are much shorter than for SDLC on account of the difference in line speed. By using SDLC/LLC2 conversion, many of the timeout problems can be eliminated. Effectively the LLC2 session is terminated at the bridge, leaving the bridge to respond to the Token Ring on one side and to SDLC on the other, so that both end-devices can use their normal timeout values without the risk of session loss.

SNA over LLC2 also uses broadcast techniques similar to those for NetBIOS in principle. In this case the relevant frame is an XID with the broadcast bit set to indicate an ARB.

7.4.3   Data link switching (DLSw)

DLSw is the recommended technique by which SNA and NetBIOS traffic is carried over a TCP/IP network. The direct technique of simply encapsulating all LLC2 or SDLC frames in IP is rather unsatisfactory because low-speed WAN links add greatly to the network response time as compared to a LAN, so that retransmission timers have to be increased to prevent retries and session loss. Variable congestion levels mean that these fixed timers have to be set to the maximum applicable values leading to poor performance when bit errors necessitate retransmissions. Router manufacturers have tended to provide SDLC/LLC priority or bandwidth reservation to minimize this problem when such traffic has to contend with other IP traffic, but the result is usually a drop in throughput of at least 10% compared to a dedicated link. A worse problem than this is that when a delayed packet is retransmitted it can cause sequence errors in LLC2 leading to the link and session being taken down.

DLSw overcomes the main problems of IP encapsulation by the use of switch–switch protocol (SSP) between TCP/IP nodes together with local termination of LLC sessions at these points, so that timers do not have to be changed, nor are polls transmitted across the WAN.

A single TCP session is established in each direction between the DLS switches. SNA sessions are established over this via an SDLC TEST or XID triggering a CANUREACH/ICANREACH exchange, while NetBIOS sessions are started by NetBIOS Name_Queries triggering SSP NetBIOS_NQ/NR exchanges. The NetBIOS exchanges are more specific than the All Routes Broadcast of the bridged environment, as once a DLSw switch has learned which other switches are able to reach a name, it only sends the NQs to those switches. Control messages have 72 byte headers, while I-frames have 16 byte headers. The main components of the 16 byte header are the message length and a circuit identifier (remote TCP port) unique to a DLSw switch consisting of 8 bytes defined by a 4 byte DLC port ID and 4 byte data link correlator. This header is smaller than the typical 20 byte IP header of IP encapsulation. Up to four levels of priority are supported via a circuit priority byte at offset 22 of CANUREACH, ICANREACH or REACH_ACK frames. It is up to the originating session to set this at set-up time; typically this would be used to give SNA precedence over NetBIOS, in particular 3270 traffic with small RUs.

A pair of DLSw router ports are connected across the WAN by two TCP sessions, one for receive and the other for transmit. This carries the risk of a single congested LLC2 session restricting the flow of data for other sessions. This problem is partly overcome by the use of very large windows for the TCP sessions combined with separate frame buffers for each SDLC or LLC2 session.

Flow control is provided for each virtual circuit through the use of a flow control byte located at offset 15 in each information frame and most control frames. The structure of this byte is shown below:

Bit	7	6	5	4	3	2	1	0
Field	FCI	FCA	Res	Res	Res	FCO	FCO	FCO

where:

FCI is flow control indicator,
FCA is flow control acknowledgement,
FCO is flow control operator bits,
Res denotes reserved.

The values for FCO and their meanings are:

000 – Repeat window operator
001 – Increment window operator
010 – Decrement window operator
011 – Reset window operator
100 – Halve window operator
101, 110 and 111 – reserved.

A frame with the FCI bit set is called a flow control indicator (FCIND) and controls the data flow in the opposite direction to the frame, while a frame with FCA set is a flow control acknowledgement (FCACK) and controls the flow in the same direction as the frame itself. A single frame can be both an FCIND and an FCACK and is usually piggybacked onto data. The receiver grants permission to send data units by means of FCINDs which the sender must acknowledge via FCACKs. The sender then maintains a count of frames granted (by FCINDs) and the initial and current window size, while the receiver maintains counts of the current window size (in frames) and the number of FCACKs owed by the sender.

This technique minimizes the need to send RNRs across the network and protects other sessions, but imposes a very high memory requirement on the router. SDLC buffers are typically likely to have to allow for seven frames of 265 or 521 bytes, represented here by grants of two or three windows of typical size 2, so support for several hundred such sessions would need about one megabyte to be configured.

Many SNA/SDLC frames are quite small, especially for 3270 traffic, so on heavily utilized links it is beneficial to use packet aggregation. This cuts overheads by combining several small SNA packets into a single TCP packet, and is supported on many routers using proprietary algorithms. Queuing theory indicates that the average number of packets waiting for transmission reaches one once the line utilization gets up to about 50%, so above this level aggregation need cause little extra delay, while reducing response time at near saturation levels over a single link. Packet aggregation is more effective for making efficient use of low bandwidth than in reducing latency, so is more beneficial to file transfers than to interactive traffic.

Details of DLSw can be found in RFC1795, which replaces the earlier RFC1434.

7.4.4   Translation bridging

Another set of issues arises when a network contains several distinct types of LAN, such as Token Ring and Ethernet. Normal MAC level bridges are only able to link LANs of the same type, so translation bridges, commencing with IBM's 8209, have been developed that work at the logical link level by looking at the standard IEEE format frame addresses and converting the frames from one format to the other at either side of a link. In the case of the IBM 8209, this is only done for local bridges, but other vendors have extended it to remote bridges across the WAN. Translation bridging is much more processor intensive than normal bridging, so throughputs tend to be lower and there are also buffering issues due to connecting LANs at different speeds. Ethernet–Token Ring translation entails insertion/deletion of the Token Ring SNAP header that contains the RIF and source/destination service access points, while the bit orders of the source and destination addresses both have to be reversed.

7.5   Compression on bridges

It is advisable to distinguish between two driving forces for compression, financial cost and performance, as there is often a trade-off between the two. Reduction of bandwidth as a result of compression will save on line costs if it allows a lower bandwidth circuit to be used, for example 56/64 kbps instead of 112/128 kbps, but is liable to increase bridge costs through the need for more memory and processing power, while performance should always improve up to a limiting speed. Cost factors on public networks also entail distinguishing between compression methods that reduce the number of characters only, and those that also reduce the number of frames or packets (more especially for router networks).

For interactive traffic where response time is the main issue, the criterion for compression to be useful is that the reduction in frame transmission time due to compression outweighs the increased latency due to the compression process. Compression latency is independent of line speed, so as the line speed increases a point is inevitably reached at which compression becomes counter-productive to response time. For file transfers subject to a good windowing mechanism, the breakeven line speed is much higher than for interactive, since the increased latency acts mainly as a constant retardation that does not reduce throughput. With software compression the aggregate link speed that can be supported is usally much less than that for uncompressed traffic. Compression in hardware is much faster than in software and makes the technique effective at much higher speeds, for example T1/E1.

There are three main types of compression to consider: header compression alone, payload compression and link compression.

7.5.1   Header compression

This is applicable mainly to small frames associated with interactive and terminal server traffic, such as LAT, Telnet, Rlogin and X-Term. Terminal server traffic often leads to single user characters encapsulated in a 40 byte TCP/IP header, padded out to a 64 byte Ethernet frame plus Ethernet header. Without any form of compression, the throughput of a 19.2 kbps WAN link is only about 35 user characters per second, equivalent to the output of about 6 skilled typists. Removal of Ethernet padding and compression of the TCP/IP header can increase this to about 100 characters per second. Where packets contain more than about 64 bytes of user data, the increased processing time for header compression tends to offset the advantage of header reduction. TCP header compression is covered by an RFC for encapsulation in HDLC over serial links, so interoperability applies as part of PPP.

7.5.2   Payload compression

For file transfers the important type of compression to use is payload compression. In principle this can be done by rapid static runtime Hoffman compression or by the slower and more efficient dynamic dictionary-based systems, such as the Lempel-Ziv algorithm in V.42 bis. Many WAN bridges offer proprietary algorithms of the second category, as this gives roughly twice as much compression as the former. Its disadvantages are the longer processing time and the need for greater memory to hold the dynamic dictionary. The degree of compression obtainable depends significantly on both the data type and the implementation.

The most compressible data types are text, while the least compressible are binary applications. Typical compression rates for text are about 3:1, but some bridges are able to achieve about 7:1. As the line speed increases, the benefits of data compression start to become progressively offset by the processing overhead involved (see Figure 7.5). Maximum line speeds supported currently are mostly in the range 64 to 2048 kbps, but should rise as more powerful processors become available in the bridges.

Payload compression can also be performed externally, either in the original data application or by a separate compression box. If compression is performed by the application, for example PKZIP for PC text-files, then additional compression by the bridge is likely to be counter-productive.

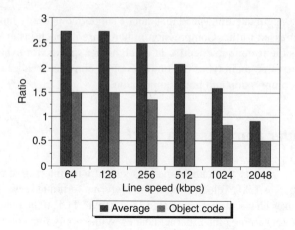

Figure 7.5 Compressed vv uncompressed throughput.

7.5.3 Link compression

In this type, both the header and the payload are compressed as a whole and then encapsulated in another link protocol with small headers, usually PPP. The original protocol headers are just treated as ordinary data in this case, so the frame has to be reconstructed by the remote bridge before it can be forwarded any further, hence the technique is limited to a single WAN hop (or at least performed on a hop-by-hop basis). This is potentially the most powerful of the three approaches, particularly for medium-sized frames.

WAN bridges are often used in preference to routers on low-speed connections where efficient use of bandwidth is critical; thus many bridges support compression. Techniques are normally proprietary, frequently based on the Lemple–Ziv dictionary algorithms as they require little processing power. There are a lot of such algorithms derived from two fundamental types, LZ77 and LZ78, so different implementations do not normally interwork. LZ77 keep track of the last N bytes seen, and the compressor outputs a pair comprising the previous position of a similar phrase in the buffer together with its length, with the inverse lookup for decompression. This allows the dictionary to update itself as the data changes throughout a transmission. LZ78 starts with a 4K buffer of substrings and gradually builds up a larger fixed dictionary of phrases as new combinations occur up to the maximum size permitted. Hybrid techniques also exist.

7.5.4 Compression mode

There are two main modes of operation associated with the Lempel–Ziv algorithms, continuous mode and packet mode, with different performance characteristics. In continuous mode the dictionary is progressively built up during the whole course of a transmission, whereas in packet mode, the dictionary is reset for every packet. The former is potentially much more efficient, particularly if data is sent in short packets. Its disadvantage is that the dictionaries at the two ends of the circuit must be kept strictly in synchronization, else large quantities of data will be corrupted, leading to a requirement both for data retransmission and dictionary reinitialization with serious resultant performance degradation. To avoid this problem, continuous mode needs to be run over a reliable data link protocol, such as X.25 LAPB, LLC2, 'reliable PPP' (see RFC1663) or SDLC, so that errored or lost packets are corrected before passing up to the decompression dictionary where they would cause the major errors. In the case of packet mode, the errors are confined to a single packet, so the consequences are strictly limited, thereby making the method suitable for unreliable data link levels such as LLC1, PPP and frame relay. As a result of these differences, packet mode gives a fairly constant degree of compression throughout a transmission, whereas the degree of compression steadily increases up to a maximum based on the permitted dictionary size in LZ78, but may drop thereafter if the nature of the data changes. Continuous mode LZ77 also improves up to an optimum when the dictionary is first filled, but remains constant thereafter even if the nature of the data changes.

Some bridges and routers also have proprietary modifications to the underlying protocol to enable the high degree of compression of the continuous mode to be used with the unreliable protocols such as PPP and frame relay in particular; this modification is some form of retransmission and will not interoperate with other vendors' equipment.

Compression is memory intensive if a separate dictionary is used for each virtual circuit. Points to check on any bridge or router are the aggregate compressed throughput achievable, any extra memory needed for its use, protocol restrictions and the type of compression used. Manufacturers' figures based on very large continuous mode dictionaries are unlikely to be achieved for short messages and may degrade for long ones unless an LZ77 style windowing mechanism is used.

For more information on compression see Hal[92] and the Frequently Asked Questions (FAQ) of the Compression Newsgroup on the Internet.

7.6   Routers and routing protocols

7.6.1   Bridges v. routers

In large networks bridges run into problems with broadcast storms, while over WANs they are wasteful of expensive bandwidth, so routers are perferable under such circumstances. Routers operate at level 3 of the OSI stack, so are media independent but protocol dependent. As a result they are used when it is necessary to connect different media types, apart from those IBM environments where the 8209 local translation bridge is used. In the previous section on bridges it was pointed out that bridges were only really suited to network topologies with a natural structure resembling a spanning tree; by contrast routers are much better suited to complex meshed topologies. Another reason for using routers in preference to bridges is their ability to control broadcast storms more effectively. The maximum size of a bridged network depends on the ability to avoid both congestion of low-speed links by storms and the number of interrupts hitting low-powered servers. A 286 PC may only be able to process 10 interrupts per second without crashing, so bridges have to be configured to prevent this or correspondingly higher limits for more powerful servers. The rough numerical limit tends to be in the range of 30 to 200 bridges, before routers are essential. There is also a maximum diameter for bridged Ethernet networks of seven hops, but it is usually better to use routers before this limit is reached.

A few protocols, such as LAT and NetBIOS, have no level 3 control, so cannot be routed. For this reason most routers also contain bridging software (both ST and SRB) so that they can support both these and any protocols for which they do not have the appropriate forwarding software. The individual network and transport level aspects of these protocols have already been described in the previous chapter, but in addition each is associated with its own characteristic routing algorithms, and it is these that are discussed here. The issues that relate to the algorithms are their efficiency in finding the best possible route, their ability to load share or not, the network overhead of routing protocol updates, the memory and processor load on the routers and the time taken to reroute in the event of network failure.

7.6.2 Routing principles

Routing protocols are classified in ISO Technical Report TR9575 as belonging to one of five categories as follows.

Static

In this case routing tables are preconfigured by a central management station and have to be recalculated in the event of a failure. This is not satisfactory and not used by major protocols.

Quasi-static

Again routing tables are precalculated by a central management station, but routes include alternatives to be taken in the event of failures. This is used by many packet switch and routing multiplexer networks. The advantage is that rerouting is very quick in the event of failure, but the tables have to be recalculated when new nodes are added.

Centralized

In this case routers or switches pass information to a centralized system that calculates the best current routes and passes this back to the nodes. This is used by a few packet switch networks, but suffers from a single point of failure and from difficulties in reaching the central system in some failures.

Distributed adaptive

This is the category used by modern router networks. Nodes exchange information about their environments and each node periodically recalculates its routes. There are two types of such algorithm, distance-vector and link state. Early algorithms tend to belong to the former, such as DECnet IV and RIP, while most newer ones are link state. In distance-vector algorithms, nodes try to form a comprehensive picture of the network and pass this on to their neighbours as complete routing tables, while in link state they broadcast information about their own neighbourhood states to all routers. Link state is much better for large networks.

For very large networks both of these techniques become very unwieldy, and gateway routing protocols have been developed to handle routing between largely independent sections of the network.

Some distance-vector protocols are based on a Bellman–Ford algorithm that only allows one route at any one time for a source–destination pair. If this route fails, then there is a delay of several router update periods for a new set of tables to converge; during this period there is no service to replace the failed link.

7.6.3   RIP

The routing information protocol (RIP) for IP is both the best known and one of the worst of the routing protocols. It has two main disadvantages from a performance point of view, first that it does not necessarily select the fastest route and second that it is slow to converge. A lesser disadvantage is that it does not support load sharing; each end-station sets up a source route field in the network packets, which is used throughout a session. RIP was initially developed for XNS by Xerox, but was also adopted for TCP/IP which is its main use. The algorithm is based on a simple hop count; the route selected is that with the least number of hops, with a maximum count of 15 and the value 16 used to denote unreachable. Stations are divided into active types (the routers) which broadcast routing information every 30 seconds (configurable to other values on some routers) and passive stations which listen to the broadcasts only. Each router maintains a vector table pointing to the component networks with distance given by the hop count and direction via other routers. A simple example of this is shown in Table 7.2.

The destination is a network rather than an end-station, metric is a hop-count, the next hop is the next IP interface accessed in order to reach the destination,

Table 7.2 Routing table entries.

Destination	Metric	Next hop	Type	Protocol	Age
197.22.1.0	1	197.22.1.45	Direct	Local	
197.22.2.0	1	97.22.2.30	Direct	Local	
129.2.4.0	2	197.22.1.70	Indirect	RIP	
144.45.12.0	3	197.22.1.70	Indirect	RIP	

protocol is local for an interface on the initial router, else RIP, Age is the age of the routing information, and index a typical proprietary identification of the router card-slot and port used.

A RIP message has a 4 byte header followed by up to 25 network/distance entries of 20 bytes each for a maximum 512 byte packet; larger tables require multiple packets to be sent.

Convergence is slow because it is essential not to flood the network with routing protocol packets at the expense of user traffic. Convergence may not happen at all due to ping-pong updates in which a router receives old information just after a failure, then passes this false information around the network, so that the failure is spuriously cancelled, then reinstated, and so on. This and other convergence problems have led to modifications to RIP to reduce their scope. The main features are split horizon, poison reverse, triggered updates and hold-down.

Split horizon

This reduces the ping-pong problem by the router recording the interface over which it has received information about a particular route, then not forwarding its updated information about that route over the same interface. In networks without alternative paths this solves the ping-pong problem, but where loops exist the problem remains.

A second benefit of split horizon is that it reduces the overall routing traffic load.

Hold-down

Hold-down attempts to solve the residual loop problem in large networks by preventing the arrival of delayed routing information from creating routing loops. It does this by ignoring routing information for a set hold-down period following receipt of information that a network is unreachable; in this way it ensures that all routers receive the bad news.

Triggered updates

Triggered updates are arguably the best of these modifications, and entail a router immediately sending out the bad news of a network failure rather than waiting for the periodic update. This greatly reduces the chance of news of a failure from being cancelled out by delayed good news. It also helps to speed up replacement of defective routes when dial backup is being used.

Poison reverse

In this technique a router continues to propagate bad news about an unreachable network for several update periods, even if it receives good information during that period.

On many routers the choice of technique is configurable, and the ones to select depends on the protocol being routed and on the speed of the link. Triggered updates are universally beneficial, but split horizon and poison reverse are mutually exclusive. Poison reverse is usually the default on routers as it gives a faster convergence time than split horizon. The main occasion for use of split horizon is with WAN links at speeds up to about 64 kbps, where it is essential to minimize routing update traffic. It is also preferable for frame relay and SMDS. Hold-down is used in conjunction with split horizon on large unstable networks with slow links, where both congestion and out-of-date information are problems. It has the disadvantage of causing slow convergence.

7.6.4 Static routes

Another way of reducing the routing update traffic and improving the convergence time is the use of static routes. These are manually configured into tables where no alternate route exists. This enables singly connected branch routers to be excluded from the update process. In many networks these are a large majority of the total population, so the effect is quite significant. They are also used for dial-up connections. Default routes also help to reduce table size and are important in dial-up.

Autonomous systems

The number of routes to specify within an IP network is roughly proportional to the square of the number of nodes; hence as the network increases in size the routing tables and traffic volumes start to become unmanageable causing convergence to become unacceptably slow. If the total network can be split into autonomous systems (AS) that converge separately, then this problem is alleviated. This requires the autonomous systems to be connected by special router protocols, of which the main examples are EGP and BGP.

EGP (exterior gateway protocol)

The first such type of interconnection was EGP and is typically used where several AS are attached to a large core backbone. Routers are divided into interior and exterior (to the AS) types, with only the exterior routers exchanging tables with the backbone. Exterior routers advertise their knowledge of the routes within their AS to manually configured lists of neighbours. EGP has its own configurable Hello timer with normal default value of 60 seconds.

EGP exchanges complete routing tables, so is still bandwidth intensive in large networks. It is also liable to require acknowledgements, resequencing and retransmissions.

Limitations of EGP are that it only indicates reachability rather than hop-count and that it does not support mesh networking between autonomous areas and is unable to prevent routing loops.

BGP (border gateway protocol)

The newer BGP provides a more efficient way of performing related functions. BGP has undergone several revisions, with versions 3 and 4 being the main ones at present. After an initial exchange of complete routing information at start up, BGP-3 routers only exchange routing table changes, so are much more efficient than EGP when low-speed WAN links connect the border routers. BGP-3 also carries a list of the AS passed through, so enabling the border routers to eliminate loops. Another advantage over EGP is the use of TCP instead of UDP, so cutting the retransmission and resequencing problems. BGP does not send any routes by default; instead the operator must explicitly configure which updates to accept and which to propagate. Where the links between AS are of low bandwidth this should be used to eliminate information that is not required about remote networks.

The later BGP-4 supports classless interdomain routing (also known as IP supernetting), in which several consecutive IP network numbers can be given a single route where appropriate, instead of having to be reported separately. Again this helps to cut WAN traffic in complex networks provided that the individual networks have been suitably numbered. Primarily this applies to the situation on the Internet where organizations have been assigned contiguous blocks of class C network numbers with only one or two connections to the Internet; giving individual network routing information would clearly be very inefficient in such a case.

7.6.5 Addressing issues

IP addresses are currently (IP version 4) each 4 bytes long and based on the use of four classes, A,B,C and D, for three sizes of network and multicast, respectively. These are illustrated in Table 7.3, where sizes are in bits and the prefix indicates the characteristic first few bits.

Table 7.3 IP address classes.

Class	Prefix	Net ID size	Host ID size
A	0	7	24
B	1	14	16
C	1.1.0	21	8
D	1.1.1.0	Multicast	Address

This scheme has several disadvantages. The first is that there are not enough network identities of classes A and B to satisfy demand; the second is that the structure is not well suited to hierarchical addressing and routing, while the division into network and host parts does not allow enough networks. The simplest modification is that of subnetting, where a bit mask is used to split the host field into a continuation of the network ID and a smaller host field. Subnets are then defined so that each router interface corresponds to a distinct subnet. As a result of points one and two, the whole structure will be replaced by a hierarchical scheme in Version 6 that uses 16 byte addresses akin to those of OSI CLNP. Another problem is that there is no way of including the MAC address. This leads to the requirement for the address resolution protocol (ARP) whereby a station has to send out a broadcast packet (ARP) to find the MAC address of an IP address to which it wishes to send information, unless the router already has this in its tables. This technique adds to session establishment time and can cause congestion on slow WAN links. Some end-stations may be unable to support the subnet mask and so be unable to ARP correctly; in such cases the router can perform a proxy ARP, by replying to the workstations ARP with its own MAC address, then finding the real one, but this is very bad for router performance.

Each WAN IP link has to be given its own IP network number. Many router implementations will provide load sharing over separate WAN links that share the same network number.

Addressing schemes also influence the size of routing tables, convergence speed and router memory requirements. The basic requirement is to ensure that subnets are grouped together geographically so that they can be summarized via their parent network instead of needing to be specified individually in RIP tables.

RIP-2 and CIDR

This principle is carried one stage further with classless interdomain routing (CIDR) and blocks of class C addresses on the Internet, or in other large IP networks. By grouping class C networks (supernetting) together geographically so that they are accessed via a single Internet service provider in the Internet case or via a single area generally, a whole group of networks can be summarized in a single route entry. This is facilitated by RIP-2 which includes a subnet mask in the RIP packets, thereby allowing variable masks in a RIP network.

7.6.6 RIP for IPX

RIP is also used by IPX, but with slight modifications. The hop-count in the routing table is replaced by a tick count, which takes some account of the link speed. The second difference is that split horizon is used, but not poison reverse.

A particular problem that occurs with IPX is that when Novell routers are interoperating with bridges, they do not see the latter, so the tick count in the RIP tables does not get incremented for crossing a bridge. In the WAN context this can lead to exceptionally bad choice of route, potentially allowing a slow bridged WAN multihop route to be used in preference to a single LAN Novell router hop.

A major issue with IPX networks is the existence of large numbers of service advertisement packets (SAPs) and also of NetBIOS storms when NetBIOS emulation is used by NetWare. These storms can be controlled by use of a static, manually created table that enables the router to convert the broadcasts into directed addresses. Routers broadcast their SAP tables every 60 seconds (configurable in some proprietary versions) and these contain entries for each known service, leading to bursts of packets that may cause periodic congestion. Where timer configuration is an option, it is usually best to reduce the frequency of updates on low-speed WAN links to once every five minutes or less to reduce the number of interruptions to normal data traffic. Some routers are able to segment the SAP table broadcasts instead of sending them as a solid block; this is useful if otherwise there would be an interruption to normal data of a second or so.

SAP filters are another key element in controlling the overheads.

Broadcasts of RIP tables are much less of a problem than the SAPs, but can cause congestion on slow WAN links for a second or two on large networks. About 50 IPX RIP routes can be put in a single packet. One factor that can lead to unnecessarily large RIP tables is the use of several of the four possible IPX Ethernet encapsulation modes at the same time on the same segment, as most routers require a separate IPX network number for each encapsulation type.

7.6.7 RIP for XNS

This was the first type of RIP to be developed. The normal frequency for XNS RIP updates is every 30 seconds. Routes are marked invalid if no updates are received for three intervals and removed from the routing table after six.

XNS is liable to have a high number of broadcasts since this technique is used by end-nodes for service discovery. Both the broadcast and the replies can impose a heavy load on slow WAN links, so reduction techniques are advisable.

Broadcasts are of three types as follows:

- local, for nodes on one network only (usually one LAN, that of the originator),
- all-nets, everywhere recognizable by network address FFFFFFFF,
- directed, to one network other than that of the originator.

Some implementations reduce broadcasts through the use of helpering and flooding as appropriate. Helpering is used mainly for service discovery, and amounts to the router blocking the broadcast but redirecting a packet to a specified server which can process and reply to the packet. XNS uses several sub-protocols, so for each helper a protocol list is also configured on the router. In some cases a server might be anywhere in the total network, nor is there any helper; in that case flooding has to be carried out. This should be minimized by only allowing flooding forwards from the port on which a broadcast was received, and blocking it on all paths able to lead back to the originator.

7.6.8 IGRP

The best of the distance-vector routing protocols is Cisco's proprietary IGRP. This uses a far more sophisticated metric than RIP, with the result that it gives much better routing in complex networks. The metric is a 32 bit number that depends on the permissible MTU, the segment delays and the lowest bandwidth of any segment on a potential route. In the special case of a network all of whose links have the same bandwidth and nature, this reduces to the usual RIP hop count.

IGRP routers broadcast updates every 90 seconds, and a route is marked as down if no update is received from the first router for 270 seconds; if no update is received for 630 seconds, then the route is deleted from the table. Network load due to IGRP is less than for RIP due to the reduced update frequency, but higher than for link state methods.

IGRP uses triggered updates, hold-down, split horizons and poison reverse to speed up convergence and cut loops, much as in RIP.

Load sharing is possible based on the IGRP metric, and can be performed unequally between participating links in proportion to their capacity, unlike OSPF (see below).

Enhanced IGRP (EIGRP)

EIGRP uses the same distance vector technology as IGRP, but with improved convergence time and efficiency. Convergence is based on the distributed update algorithm (DUAL) which allows all routers involved in a topology change to synchronize at the same time, while unaffected routers do not have to do any recomputation of routes. It uses five packet types; Hello/acks, updates, queries, replies and requests, and a topology table containing destinations advertised by neighbouring routers. Routes have two states, active and passive. Passive is when the route is stable, and active when it is undergoing recomputation. Routing is based on feasible successors that are neighbours downstream to the destination with respect to the router. Recomputations have to be carried out after a change when query/replies show a lack of feasible successors.

7.6.9   OSPF (open shortest path first)

This is a link state interior gateway routing protocol for IP that is rapidly replacing RIP. Its main advantages are the ability to select a path based on the speeds of the links as well as the hop count, and faster convergence. It also supports separate costs and routing tables for the different IP type-of-service classes and avoids the 15 hop limit of RIP, thereby allowing much greater flexibility in very large networks. A further advantage over RIP is the ability to support multiple subnet masks; this is achieved by broadcasting the mask with the destination, and allows more freedom in subdividing a network. Load sharing is automatically provided over equal cost paths between the same sites, but not for differing costs.

OSPF divides a network domain up into areas within which routing information is distributed between routers. Each area runs its own copy of the OSPF algorithm and each has its own copy of the topological database. Topology of an area is invisible to the exterior while routers internal to an area are ignorant of the external world. Routing updates are immediately flooded within an area on all interfaces except that on which they are received, so permitting much faster response to failures than with RIP, with a low periodic backgound rate for resilience. Each OSPF domain must contain a backbone to link its areas, while routers are grouped into four overlapping categories listed below.

Internal router

This category only interfaces to a single area, including the interior of the backbone.

Area border router

These attach to more than one area and run a separate copy of the algorithm for each area. They distribute their tables to the backbone.

Backbone router

This category consists of the area border routers and any interior routers belonging to the backbone.

AS boundary router (ASBR)

These are any routers that exchange information with any other domains.

There is an analogous subdivision of routing modes as follows.

Intra-area routing

This covers routing between sources and destinations within a single area. Adjacencies are defined between neighbouring routers within the area. Hellos and routing protocol packets are only distributed between adjacent routers. LANs with multiple routers attached elect a single designated router and designated backup router for this purpose.

Inter-area routing

This applies to sources and destinations in different areas. In this case area border routers exchange a subset of their areas topologies.

External routing

Where a router has an external connection it can flood its domain with the external routing information, apart from preconfigured stub areas for which this is barred.

OSPF parameters

This section contains a subset of parameters that are the most likley to be modified in tuning the network.

Link cost

A link cost must be specified for each interface and also for each class of service if OSPF type-of-service is supported. Typical defaults are costs inversely proportional to bandwidth.

Hello interval

The interval between sending regular Hellos should be the same for all routers. The default is 10 seconds for broadcast networks, but for X.25, frame relay and SMDS is 30 seconds. For small networks with high-speed links, a smaller value should be used to give a faster response to changes in topology, but for large slow networks a larger value might be needed to cut congestion.

Link state retransmission interval

This is the time in seconds between transmitting link state advertisements between adjacent routers. This is constant across the network and must be greater than the greatest roundtrip time between adjacencies. In order to prevent futile retransmissions, the value should be several times this minimum. Typical values to use are 5 seconds for LANs and about 15 for WANs.

Transmit delay

Link state advertisements have their age updated each time they are forwarded to take account of the likely propagation and transmission delay. The default is usually one second, and the values are used to timeout old information. For slow WAN links with queuing effects, a value several times higher may be needed. For dial-up links, such as ISDN, there is an OSPF demand extension that has a Do_not_age option for advertisements to prevent updates from keeping the link up.

Router dead interval

This is the time in seconds for non-receipt of a router's Hellos after which its neighbours declare it down. This needs to be at least twice the Hello interval, and the usual default is four Hellos.

OSPF performance

The quantity of routing traffic generated by OSPF also varies enormously according to the architecture of the network. As with RIP it is best to subdivide the network into autonomous systems interconnected by border routers running BGP. The maximum number of routers that can be in a single area is usually limited to about 200 to 300 on performance grounds.

One of the main limiting factors is available memory in the router for the link state database. Typical entries take about 64 bytes per external link state advertisement (see below for types and outline structure) and around 200 bytes for router links, with most entries usally being the former kind. On this basis 0.5 Mbytes of available memory would support 7–8000 entries. With low-speed links a lower limit on external LSAs is imposed by the need not to use up too much bandwidth, for example for a 5% link utilization the limit is about 6000 entries for a 28.8 kbps line and 13 000 for 64 kbps.

Many large wide area router networks consist of a large number of small branch routers feeding by single links into a backbone network. This gives rise to a classical hub–spoke design in which there is a single backbone area and numerous stub areas consisting of branches that feed into a regional border router on the backbone. Only the border routers need full knowledge of the complete network; within the stubs only internal links plus an external default route summary are advertised. This type of design saves router memory (important if memory-hungry features like compression are also running), minimizes waste of bandwidth on unnecessary routing information, and is highly desirable where high line costs restrict the provision of WAN capacity. Stub areas also allow faster operation of the Djykstra route calculating algorithm (see Chapter 14). On some routers only a small number of stub routes can be configured; in such cases RIP-2 external routes provide an alternative with similar benefits.

OSPF reacts to changes much faster than RIP, and on small to medium-sized networks will usually reroute around a single failure in a couple of seconds, while adjacencies over T1/E1 links take the same order of time to establish.

In many medium-sized corporate networks the WAN is the backbone, large offices are areas and small offices stubs.

If link resilience is required it is best provided through direct backup (such as by ISDN) of the single links. Dual-homing of branches to provide resilience leads to a great increase in routing traffic due to the multiple parallel paths generated. This both wastes bandwidth on the WAN and greatly increases memory requirements on the routers, with the consequent risk of data packet dropping due to buffer shortage. Another resilience issue arises in the backbone. Route summarization increases efficiency markedly, but if a backbone area router fails, then there is a chance that some routes previously summarized together will now be accessible via distinct backbone routers. This problem can largely be overcome by only using fully fault-tolerant routers in the backbone.

All OSPF messages have a 24 byte header as shown in Figure 7.6.

OSPF converges faster than distance-vector protocols in general, but recalculation of the shortest path tree can be a serious load on some routers. As a result the frequency of running the OSPF algorithm is configurable on some routers to ensure that they can handle their data traffic. This slows down convergence, so making rerouting slow, and applies particularly to router architectures in which one CPU has to do all the critical processing.

OSPF messages should be assigned top priority on the router interfaces; OSPF is IP type 89. The five OSPF packet types are shown in Table 7.4.

Hellos are sent on all interfaces, and carry the Hello interval, network mask, dead interval, designated router and backup plus active neighbours, leading to at least 24 bytes in addition to the header.

Database descriptions are potentially very voluminous; they contain 8 bytes of further header material plus some or all of the link state advertisements (see below) held, but are only exchanged when establishing adjacencies.

Field	Size (bytes)
Version	1
Type	1
Message size	2
Gateway IP addr	4
Area ID	4
CHECKSUM	2
Authentication type	2
Authentication	8

Figure 7.6   OSPF header.

Table 7.4 OSPF packet types.

Type	Description
1	Hello
2	Database description
3	Link state request
4	Link state update
5	Link state acknowledgement

Link state requests ask for specific parts of a database, with 12 bytes used to specify each part.

Link state updates carry a collection of link state advertisements one hop further than their origin. Each of these adverts has a 20 byte header plus link data.

Link state acknowledgements contain the 20 byte headers of each update that is being acknowledged. Several updates can be acknowledged in one packet, thereby reducing overheads slightly. This bundling is controlled by the acknowledgement timer.

Link state advertisements

There are five types of advert as shown in Table 7.5.

The common 20 byte header identifies the link, the advertising router and update sequence number as well as giving the total length and a checksum.

Router link adverts are generated by each router in an area and describe the state, type and cost of each of its interfaces. If IP type-of-service (TOS) is supported, then there is an entry for each TOS, but many networks only support default type 0. This default case leads to 12 bytes per interface. OSPF currently supports the eight possible combinations of the delay (D), throughput (T) and reliability (R) flags, leading to up to 96 bytes extra per interface. OSPF routing messages themselves belong to TOS 0.

Network link adverts are originated for each transit network in an area, and has 8 bytes for each of the attached routers in the multi-access network.

Table 7.5 OSPF advert types.

Type	Description
1	Router links
2	Network links
3	Summary link (IP)
4	Summary link (ASBR)
5	AS external link

Summary links are generated by area border routers, and are of type 3 if the destination is an IP network, but type 4 for an AS boundary router (ASBR) destination. There are 8 bytes giving the network mask, TOS and metric. Maximum use of summaries minimizes the bandwidth required.

AS external link adverts are generated by AS boundary routers with one advert per known external destination. The advert contains 12 bytes for the mask, forwarding address and an external route tag, plus 4 bytes per TOS.

Most of these adverts are very short to ensure rapid propagation, but some of these packets (database descriptions, link state requests, link state updates and link state acks) can be quite large. In principle, sizes up to the maximum IP datagram size of 65 536 bytes could be sent, relying on IP fragmentation to reduce them as required, but it is more efficient to limit individual packets to the guaranteed minimum MTU of 576 bytes from the outset for operation over WANs. Response times for interactive traffic are also less badly affected if the router is able to intersperse the OSPF protocol traffic with user traffic instead of sending contiguous blocks.

Selection of TOS routes

Where TOS is used, it is desirable to split interactive (D) and high throughput (T) traffic on paths with less than about 256 kbps of bandwidth. The D routes should attempt to give FILO delays of less than 250 ms in general, and less than 100 ms for character mode Telnet. As these packets are small, low bandwidth circuits, for example 56/64 kbps, can be used provided that the TOS routing prevents queuing behind long file transfer packets and bursts. T traffic should accordingly be kept off these routes and put on high bandwidth circuits only. R traffic should be kept off analog links, but be directed towards SDH/SONET circuits and routers with common logic redundancy. In all cases these objectives are achieved by configuring high TOS costs for unsuitable interfaces and low for suitable.

Boundary routers supporting TOS require high processing power and extensive memory since they have to calculate and hold routing tables for each TOS class and each of their areas.

More detailed information on OSPF performance is given in RFC1245 and 1246, while details of the protocol are in RFCs 1583 and 1793.

MOSPF (multicast OSPF)

The rise in videoconferencing and distributed computing make the ability to perform multicast routing efficiently an essential network requirement; in OSPF this is achieved by its MOSPF extension.

The basic performance requirement is to ensure that the network is not flooded with multicast traffic, especially in the case of voluminous video traffic. MOSPF works on the basis of calculating shortest path trees for each combination of a source address and a multicast group address. Unlike a unicast address each multicast router calculates the route relative to the source node rather than itself, so that all produce the same tree, and route duplication is avoided. Unlike OSPF there is also a tie-breaker algorithm to ensure that traffic goes by a unique route where equal multicast paths exist.

MOSPF routers use the IGMP protocol to monitor multicast group membership, and distribute information on the related addresses through a special link state advertisement.

MOSPF updates are sent using an additional type 6 link state advertisement.

The biggest performance issue associated with MOSPF is the effort required to calculate the routing trees in a large network. A sizing argument is given in Internet RFC 1245 where it is estimated that a shortest path calculation for a 200 router network takes about 15 ms on a 10 Mip processor. If a multicast router had to calculate a large number of trees simultaneously this could potentially disrupt its normal forwarding activities when heavily loaded. MOSPF minimizes this risk by only calculating the multicast tree when it is first required, or if the topology subsequently changes. The effect of the calculation on the forwarding activities depend on the router software/hardware structure and the prioritization of tasks. In a multiprocessor router, most forwarding tasks will be unaffected, but in a single CPU system the disruptive potential is greater, and it is probably best to give forwarding a higher priority than multicast tree calculation to prevent packet dropping. In a videoconference call, a multicast tree will be required for each participant to multicast to the others, so a worst case will be simultaneous calculation of about six such trees. In the case of a 200 node OSPF area where each nodal site participates in a videoconference to three local neighbours, the total number of trees to be calculated is 200, equivalent to 3 seconds' worth of processing at the estimated rate.

Another application in which MOSPF has proved useful is in tunnelling of source route bridge traffic through IP networks. Use of MOSPF means that UDP encapsulation can be used without running into packet duplication and sequence error problems.

7.6.10   DECnet Phase IV

DECnet Phase IV is an adaptive routing algorithm that is more efficient than RIP, but which has very high network overheads. The data path through the network is selected on a least cost basis from individual circuit costs which can be set by the network manager. The individual circuit costs are normally proportional to the reciprocal bandwidth. This algorithm would select a two-hop route via T1/E1 circuits in preference to a single 56/64 kbps route, unlike RIP.

Large networks are divided into areas with up to 1023 nodes per area and up to 63 areas per network. There is a corresponding division of routers into level 1 routers that perform routing within an area, and level 2 routers that perform routing between areas. Most, but not all, commercial routers are able to perform both levels within the same unit. Nodes have an ID given by Area #.Node #. The address size is 16 bits, leading to the overall node limit of 64K, and is too restrictive for some networks so that it has been increased in Phase V.

A level 1 router tells each of its end-nodes the nearest level 2 router. Each PC or other end-node on the network advertises itself every hello time (normally 15 seconds). This information is used by the level 1 router to build a level 1 routing table containing the station ID and a hop count. If the router fails to receive an advert within three hello intervals, it sets the hop count to 63 to indicate unavailability. It also sends a triggered update that contains the entire level 1 routing table. This information is sent as a start node number, number of nodes, hop count, hop number and cost. As the node number is not included a full range of unobtainable entries has to be included for non-existent nodes. For a maximal 1023 node area this would amount to about 2 kbytes, and this is sent to two addresses, the normal plus DEC Pathwork's last, for 15 seconds. This overhead is excessive if sent over low-speed lines, particularly if X.25, so it is normal to configure much smaller areas whenever possible. This depends on the DEC node IDs which must be made compatible with the reduced area size; node numbers N.1 and N.1022 would require a full 1023-size area even if there were no other nodes. Minimizing the area sizes is also important on some routers with limited memory because of the consequent reduction in table storage requirements.

Routers normally send their routing tables every 180 seconds, but for stable networks containing slow links, some vendors allow their routers to be configured with longer time intervals to cut congestion.

DECnet is able to avoid the ARPs of RIP by means of its addressing scheme. When a station boots up, it modifies its MAC address to include the 6 bit area number and 10 bit node number, which are modified and appended as two hex digits on to the end of the DEC MACaddress. Another benefit of DECnet over RIP is the ability to perform load sharing over equal cost paths. This works well for VAX nodes which can resequence packets when necessary, but for PCs is risky, since they can often only reorder a maximum of two out-of-sequence packets. Uncorrected sequence errors lead to retransmission with its consequent delays, reduction in throughput and increased network load.

7.6.11 OSI/DECnet Phase V

OSI defines two routing standards that are used in DECnet V: end system to intermediate system (ES–IS) and intermediate system to intermediate system (IS–IS) in ISO 9542 and ISO 10589 respectively. An ES is any node that does not participate in routing, while an IS is any that does.

DECnet V also uses the OSI CLNP (ISO 8473) network level protocol, but with source routing replaced by the two standards above. An important OSI option that is supported is congestion control. DECnet Phase V also uses OSI transport class 4, although DECnet's NSP can still be used instead.

Networks and routers are subdivided into areas and levels as in Phase IV, but with different protocols as above plus an extended addressing structure. Network service access point (NSAP) addresses are used for both routers and end nodes. The NSAPs are at least 10 and not more than 20 bytes long, with the last 9 bytes conforming to the OSI IS–IS requirements

Field	Initial NSAP	LOC-AREA	ID	SEL
Length (bytes)	1–11	2	6	1

where:

Initial NSAP identifies the network and should follow the principles of ISO 8348 Amendment 2,

LOC-AREA defines an area within the network,

ID is a 6 byte node identifier that is usually the DECnet identifier assigned during manufacture to the node in accordance with the IEEE LAN addressing scheme, and

SEL is a selector that identifies the type of transport level protocol associated with the node; 32 indicates DECnet V's OSI TP4, while 33 indicates the old DECnet NSP.

Inclusion of the ID field in the network address avoids the need for ARPs that occurs in other protocols such as RIP and AppleTalk. This avoids storms associated with unrecognized names. DECnet V also supports a distributed naming service that enables users to insert friendly names instead of addresses; the address requests are directed to the nearest name server only, so do not cause much traffic.

Ten categories of routing control packets are used for IS–IS and three for ES–IS.

ES–IS

End-system hellos (ESH) are generated by end-nodes to tell all routers on the data link of the node's existence. Typical hello time is 15 seconds.

Intermediate system hellos (ISH) are generated by the routers to tell the end-nodes of their existence.

A specific feature of ES–IS is a redirect packet, whereby a router tells an end-node of a better route by which it could have sent a packet; this is done by sending the subnetwork address to use in future for the destination.

IS–IS

There are three types of hello: levels 1 and 2 plus point-to-point. The former two are broadcast to obtain the addresses of routers of that level, while the last is sent on a point–point link on receipt of a hello to determine whether the sender is level 1 or 2.

The topological information is sent in link state packets (LSP) for levels 1 and 2. Level 1 LSPs are sent to all routers in an area while level 2 is sent only to level 2 routers.

An important feature of IS–IS is the sending by routers of sequence number packets for levels 1 and 2 to ensure that information is reliable and up to date. Partial sequence number packets (PSNP) are sent to acknowledge receipt of LSPs, while the designated router periodically (usually every 10 seconds) multicasts the sequence numbers of the LSPs in its database by means of a complete sequence number packet (CSNP). An IS whose sequence numbers are out-of-date requests retransmission of the missing material.

The remaining type is an XID for DDCMP links only.

Unlike OSPF, the LSP adverts tend to be very large as all information is sent together, so take longer to propagate and cause more interruption to any interactive traffic. Use of small MTUs permits an LSP to bé broken into up to 255 fragments if necessary.

IS–IS metric

There is a single default metric with a maximum path value of 1024. Each link can have a value of up to 64 that is assigned by the network administrator, the value for a path then being the sum of its link values.

In addition to the default there are three optional metrics based on delay costs, expense costs (that is, tariffs) and error costs that can be related to the quality-of-service field in the CLNP packets to be routed. Delay cost routing is the best for interactive traffic. Expense cost routing enables organizations to make maximum use of their own private lines rather than route via costly public networks, while error cost routing is appropriate for upper-layer protocols lacking resilience.

Congestion control

DECnet V uses the congestion flag in OSI CLNP datagrams to inform OSI TP4 or DECnet NSP as appropriate of the existence of congestion. Either of these transport protocols then responds by reducing the transport level credit window size. DECnet uses the 31 bit sequence number/16 bit credit field option in TP4 in order to be able to handle very high speed networks. The congestion flag is set whenever the buffer queue length exceeds an operator configurable threshold.

If this procedure does not manage to avoid congestion, then the credit is cut to 1 until recovery takes place.

Inter-domain routing protocol (IDRP)

IDRP is the OSI's form of gateway/border routing, and is arguably better than both EGP and BGP-4 and is intended to operate efficiently in networks with billions of nodes. IDRP is based on several additional concepts as follows:

- A border intermediate system (BIS) is any IS that participates in inter-domain routing.
- A routing domain (RD) is a group of ES and IS under the same administration, in particular having a common routing plan.

- Each RD has a unique identifier, the RDI.

- A routing information base (RIB) is the routing database, that is, set of routes, used by a particular BIS based on information from its own RD plus other BIS.

- A confederation (RDC) is a group of RDs whose topology is not visible to RDs outside it. They can be used to reduce routing traffic and to provide security.

IDRP is able to exchange either updates only or full RIBs. Although updates are usually more efficient, in extremely unstable networks, full tables may generate less traffic than individual updates. As with BGP, reliability of update transfer is needed and is supplied through the use of sequence numbers in IDRP packets rather than by a transport level protocol. Like BGP it suppresses loops.

Details of IDRP are given in RFCs 1477, 1478 and 1479.

7.6.12   Netware link services protocol (NLSP)

This is Novell's link state protocol for its routers (that is, servers with routing ability) and should replace RIP for IPX. NLSP is similar in nature to OSI IS-IS. It cuts out the RIP broadcasts associated with RIP for IPX, but not the SAPs. NLSP is not used universally within an IPX network; instead the network is partitioned into regions that use NLSP and regions with RIP with NLSP enabled on appropriate ports of routers that straddle the two types of region. Workstations still use RIP and SAPs to communicate with routers, but backbone and WAN areas use NLSP. SAPs can be filtered to remain confined to their own areas. NLSP has a much lower routing traffic overhead than RIP, as it relies on triggered updates supplemented by routing tables every two hours in the absence of any updates. Another advantage for very large networks is an increase in the maximum number of hops from 15 to 127.

NLSP aims to divide routing into three levels:

- level 1 routing within a single area,
- level 2 routing between areas combined into routing domains,
- level 3 routing between domains of a global IPX internetwork.

Of these, version 1.0 of NLSP only supports level 1. Partitioning into separate areas is recommended if the number of network numbers exceeds about 400. With version 1.0, the associated level 2 routing can be handled by RIP pending this functionality in NLSP. When this is done it is important to avoid having two areas split in the middle of a WAN link as this will lead to a large number of RIP and SAP updates being sent across this connection, potentially leading to periods of congestion. The ideal way of handling the WAN in version 1.0 is to make the entire WAN a single NLSP backbone area with their own routers, while the locally connected NetWare LANs are each made into separate NLSP areas. RIP has to run on the inter-area links, so the distinction should be made that the WAN interface to a LAN is part of the backbone with RIP on a LAN interface.

A further advantage of NLSP for performance optimization is that in the few instances where a network interface on a heavily loaded LAN is the major bottleneck, it supports multiple interface cards on one LAN and performs load balancing between them without the need for any additional NLMs. This balancing is performed by selecting the NIC with the lowest load at the time the initial 'Get Nearest Server' request is received.

Up-to-date information on NLSP can usually be found on Novell's web sites.

7.6.13   AppleTalk

AppleTalk Phase I only covered systems of up to 254 stations and was extended to Phase II which is described here. The protocol stack is fairly complex as is illustrated on Page 114.

Of the four datalink protocols the original LocalTalk is very slow as it only runs at 230 kbps, so the others should be used in preference if performance is poor in a pure LAN environment.

AppleTalk generates more routing overheads than most protocols and is also more time sensitive, so that it often has to be given a higher priority when used in conjunction with others.

AppleTalk networks are conceptually split into zones by the network manager on a basis that logically need have no relation to geography, but should have for optimization of WAN traffic. They are usually related to workgroups and sized to make it practical to scroll through a list of names to find the resource to use. Each router interface must be associated with at least one zone. Zone information protocol (ZIP) is used to record which names are where.

NBP

Name binding protocol (NBP) maps names of services to AppleTalk addresses and is broadcast within local networks; it uses ZIP to find which networks belong to any zone. There are four name binding services: registration, deletion, look-up and confirmation. Any service can register its name by using a registration call to the node's NBP process, but this requires a look-up call to ensure the name is unique. As with NetBIOS name queries, this look-up is usually repeated several times. In a WAN, look-up is sent in the form of directed broadcasts using DDP datagrams. This is carried out by sending a broadcast request to each network within the name's own zone; this then triggers a broadcast or ZIP multicast within each of these networks. The DDP datagram is of DDP type 2 that contains a 4 bit NBP function code, 4 bit tuple count, 1 byte NBP ID and a set of NBP tuples. A look-up only contains one tuple, but each of these contains a 4 byte network address, 1 byte enumerator plus a service name consisting of three strings, each up to 32 bytes long. A look-up and confirm are also used at the start of each session, so potential traffic levels from this source are high.

ZIP

Each AppleTalk network has a zone list of up to 255 from which a node can choose to belong on start up or transfer to. Each router maintains a complete network to zone-name mapping, the zone information table (ZIT). ZIT information is accumulated by ZIP queries and replies after start up, but thereafter no additional traffic is generated except for changes.

AARP

AppleTalk ARP requests are used to find hardware addresses and ARP probes to obtain router addresses. A burst of explorer packets is generated in this way whenever an AppleTalk user clicks on a device under chooser.

Routing is performed by RTMP. Nodes are identified by a 16 bit network number plus an 8 bit node number. RTMP tables are held by each router and contain entries of the form below, with minimum distance vector routing subject to a maximum hop count of 15.

Network	Distance	Port	Next router

Timers

AppleTalk timers are not always configurable. The default for exchange of routing updates is 10 seconds. Routes are normally considered valid for up to two routing update intervals, thus giving a 20 second default. Routes are deleted after three such intervals without update, that is, 60 seconds. These frequencies are about nine times those of IGRP, hence the protocol overhead on the network is much higher.

The retransmission time for an AppleTalk ARP request for a hardware address is freely configurable with one second as the default. This time needs to take account of the slow response times of some devices, and is often increased for printers and for slow WAN links. The AARP probe for a router address has a shorter default, and is not normally changed because of its role in dynamic node assignment.

AURP (AppleTalk update routing protocol)

On many networks AppleTalk coexists with IP and this gives the possibility of some overhead reduction through the use of AURP. This is an encapsulation protocol defined in RFC 1504 for carrying AppleTalk across an IP network with AppleTalk spoofing on either side of the IP cloud. It supports static routes and dynamic via OSPF. Hop-count reduction is also possible, so that AppleTalk's 15 hop limit can be bypassed through AURP.

AURP runs over UDP which is unreliable, so its own header uses sequence numbers and acknowledgements with a window size of one. It uses separate send and receive connections between the exterior routers. Full routing tables are exchanged at start-up, thereafter only updates and the AppleTalk DDP traffic. It is memory intensive on the exterior routers. The window size of one does not apply to the DDP.

AURP uses two timers; a last-heard-from timer that is reset every time any form of data is received, and a tickle timer. The former is configurable with default 90 seconds, and if it expires a tickle is sent, to which a tickle ACK is expected before the tickle timer expires. The connection is taken down after no reply to three tickles. AppleTalk cannot normally be used cost-effectively over ISDN because of RTMP updates every 10 seconds, but by using AURP with the tickle timer set to a long interval, such as one hour, this can be done.

Traffic reduction

On large networks with slow WAN links it may be necessary to minimize the protocol overheads associated with AppleTalk routing. The first principle involved in this is to make the network hierarchical with zones based on workgroups. These zones should be confined where possible to a single network so that name binding protocol broadcasts can be minimized. This minimization uses zone filters to prevent the broadcasts from going to zones in which they are not relevant.

Some implementations of AppleTalk routing allow a cost factor to be configured to each router port which is then added to the hop count used in calculating the minimum distance routes. These cost factors can be used to keep traffic off low-speed WAN links to avoid congestion. Such cost factors need to be kept as small as possible to avoid routes exceeding the maximum hop (+cost) limit of fifteen and so becoming unreachable.

7.6.14   VINES

VINES routing is closely related to RIP for IP, but with specific routing table protocol updates. RTP goes in a normal VINES IP packet that has an additional 4 byte header at the start of the routing data field that describes the nature of the packet, the node type, LAN interface card and processor. Client nodes send out routing update packets every 90 seconds in version 4 (30 in the older v3), and are removed from tables if not heard from for 6 minutes. Routers send out full routing tables on start up, but only triggered updates thereafter, so VINES routing overheads are lower than for many other protocols.

Another benefit of VINES over RIP is the use of delay metrics by VINES servers to calculate timeouts. These numbers can be configured on the router interfaces, with some characteristic Banyan recommendations shown in Table 7.6.

Table 7.6   VINES RIP delay defaults.

Interface	Delay value
9.6 kbps WAN	90
56 kbps WAN	45
4 mbps Token Ring	4
10 mbps Ethernet	2
16 mbps Token Ring	2

7.6.15   APPN and HPR

APPN (advanced peer to peer networking) is IBM's distributed routing protocol; HPR (high performance routing) is an enhanced version of APPN.

APPN

In APPN nodes are divided into end-nodes (EN) and network nodes (NN), with a temporary category of low end node (LEN) for devices which do not support LU6.2. Routing is performed by the NNs, and at any one time an EN is serviced by one NN. The style of routing differs from most of the other protocols above through being intended primarily for connection-oriented network services instead of connection-less. This leads to different addressing capabilities. APPN can maintain dynamic tables of addresses when ENs are moved, whereas protocols like RIP have to have their end-stations addresses modified under such circumstances, although MOSPF keeps this fairly simple.

Nodes communicate at session establishment by means of XID3 variable length information exchanges followed by SNA BIND procedures. When an EN tries to communicate with a destination unknown to its local NN, the NN has to send out a broadcast to try to locate it.

APPN's routing method is called intermediate session routing (ISR) with a routing algorithm of the link state variety, and the shortest path found by means of Djykstra's algorithm. The cost functions are based on throughput and a resistance factor that takes account of congestion levels at call establishment. ISR assigns a label, the FQPCID, at the start of a session to identify the session traffic; a different FQPCID is used for each hop across the network. Each NN creates a session connector to correlate the two FQPCIDs.

Each NN carries out extensive SNA layer 3 and 4 functions relating to error correction and segmentation, so that a heavy processing load results. APPN does not support SNA transmission groups or dynamic rerouting without HPR.

HPR

The capabilities added to APPN by HPR are higher performance, a new end–end flow control and automatic reconnect in the event of failure.

HPR replaces the connection-oriented ISR of APPN by the connectionless automatic network routing (ANR) protocol which is analogous to the techniques of source route bridging. The heavy processing load at intermediate nodes in APPN is drastically reduced by cutting out error checking as well as putting the route to follow in the packet header. The route is indicated by a sequence of labels of 1–8 bytes length each that define the port to be taken for the outbound route from each NN; labels are progressively deleted as the packet is forwarded. Error checking is still an essential requirement and is supplied in HPR by the use of rapid transport protocol (RTP) on top of ANR. RTP provides an end–end full-duplex connection with packet resequencing and the option for error correction. RTP also contains a sophisticated flow control mechanism that predicts when congestion is likely to occur and tries to pre-empt it. Prediction is based on comparison between the rates at which the network is sending data to the receiver node and that at which the receiver is sending it on to the end-node. If the network deduces that the end-node is falling behind, then it will tell the sender to slow down before actual congestion results. This is claimed to allow higher data link utilizations than for other protocols such as TCP/IP.

Another important feature of RTP is dynamic rerouting in the event of failure. Lack of this capability is a major weakness in APPN as compared to most other routing protocols.

7.7   Router performance problems

The main performance problems that occur with router networks are slow network response and throughput for transactions and shortage of memory or buffers on the router; CPU overload only occurs rarely, usually for very short packets. Some router implementations of X.25 are very inefficient, and it is usually much better for response time to use frame relay or IP encapsulation instead.

The principles for network response time and throughput are similar to those already described in previous chapters. Optimum WAN performance often entails reducing the size of packet or MTU from that used in a pure LAN environment to take account of the higher bit error rate and probability of multiple hops over slow links.

Memory and buffer shortages of routers are characteristic of such networks and are most common where the router is required to support several different routing protocols simultaneously. Overall memory shortage results mainly from excessively large routing tables and packet sizes, while protocol-specific buffer shortage results also from an unsuitable distribution of memory between tasks. OSPF and DECnet

IV/V have particularly memory intensive routing tables. Segmentation of a network into smaller routing areas and avoidance of configuring unnecessary interfaces and protocols are the simplest ways of reducing this, along with limiting numbers of virtual circuits of connection-oriented protocols terminating on the routers.

Latency depends on both the router's processing power and its architecture, with single processor models using DMA tending to have the shortest latency, typically equal to roughly the reciprocal of the packet processing rate. Multiple processor models have longer delays in relation to the overall rate since packets usually go through at least two processors as well as some internal queues.

In calculating the effective throughput of the network, the important performance parameter to use is the zero packet loss figure rather than the maximum obtainable. The reason for this is that if a packet is dropped, then either data is lost or a retransmission has to take place depending on the transport layer, and as the proportion of packets dropped can be high this effect is very significant. The main cure is to provide more memory with increased latency, but not enough for the buffer holding time to exceed protocol timeouts.

Congestion control is sometimes achieved by configuring a maximum latency on the router after which any unprocessed packet is dropped. Such values are likely to be of the order of a hundred milliseconds, as compared to the order of one for the actual processing, and allow buffering for a number of packets that is equal to the latency times the interface speed divided by the packet size, subject to sufficient memory being available. Increasing this parameter may improve throughput due to the reduction in the proportion of packets dropped. The same effect can be achieved on other routers by increasing the buffer space per interface directly, but again with implicit increase in maximum latency.

7.7.1   Broadcast/multicast issues

One of the biggest potential performance problems on large router networks is the occurrence of broadcast storms, although these are much less of a problem than with bridged networks. These arise in principle from a router forwarding a broadcast on each of its ports for every copy that it has received from the original source, so that on highly connected networks very rapid frame multiplication takes place. This was a particularly notable problem with early versions of RIP, but has been reduced by better definition of broadcast addresses, the use of multicast and by further techniques to eliminate duplication. Certain types of application, such as rapid distribution of financial information to dealers, also have a major need for broadcast or multicast.

Early RIP simply used all ones in the IP address to define a broadcast, but later versions use a mask that enables the broadcast to be unicast until it reaches a specific network at which it explodes into a local broadcast to all subnets of the network. As the broadcast then goes out on all relevant ports, multiple copies of packets are probable. If the subnets are all locally connected LANs this is not a problem, but if connected by slow WAN links this may cause congestion. Multicasts to group addresses also cause significant congestion, so a number of techniques are used to reduce or eliminate duplication. One of the most widespread of these is to use a spanning tree for the multicast address, so that each copy is received by a single pathway. An example of this is Cisco's UDP flooding. Two slightly better ways are by means of distance vector multicast routing protocol (DVMRP) and multicast OSPF (MOSPF).

DVMRP

DVMRP was invented for the multicast backbone (MBONE) of the Internet and defined in RFC1075. It achieves its reduction in traffic by means of route pruning back from the destination when multiple copies are received.

Hosts belonging to a particular multicast group have to register by sending out IGMP messages, then DVMRP routers build internal tables for all possible sources that specify which multicast groups need to be forwarded on which interface. When multicast traffic is received by the router, it is forwarded on the reverse path from that in the forwarding table (reverse path flooding). If a router receives multicast traffic for which it has no registered downstream users, then it sends a 'prune' message back to the sender, so that multicast traffic gets terminated on that path, thus providing some traffic reduction.

Networks on the Internet that wish to participate in the MBONE dedicate specific hosts to this role; these hosts then register by IGMP messages and use DVMRP tunnels between themselves on the Internet. This technique still leads to a considerable degree of packet duplication.

DVMRP depends on RIP unicast features and is considered to scale badly. Maximum message size is 512 bytes.

Routing loops are a greater risk with DVMRP than with RIP itself, but one way of reducing this risk on small networks is by changing the default unreachable hop-count from 16 down to a smaller value. Increase as far as 255 is also permitted.

Other parameters that affect performance are the update rates and group membership timeouts and query rates. The values to use depend on the stability of the system and the degree of need to respond rapidly or not to changes. The default interval for full updates is normally 60 seconds, but this might be reduced if the multicasts are business critical, for example distribution of stockmarket prices, or increased on low bandwidth networks with non-critical applications. Group membership is normally queried every 120 seconds, but this period could be increased if changes are rare.

Multicasts via MOSPF

MOSPF was discussed in some detail earlier in this chapter and is much more efficient than DVMRP as each MOSPF router calculates a shortest path tree for each source–multicast destination pair. This tree is calculated the first time that such a multicast datagram is received, then cached to cut processing load for subsequent occasions. At present this is the best way of handling multicast traffic. Its main disadvantage is the high processing load on the router. This is minimized by caching of multicast routes, but these still have to be purged and recalculated if the network changes due to failure or additions.

Protocol independent multicast (PIM)

PIM is a technique that is under study by the IETF for multicasting using traffic reduction by pruning that improves on DVMRP. Unlike DVMRP it can work with protocols other than RIP, such as OSPF, IS-IS and IGRP, so avoiding the limitations of the former. It has both 'Dense and Sparse Modes'. The Dense mode is very similar to DVMRP, but the sparse mode, for situations in which the proportion of networks receiving multicast traffic is a small fraction of the total, is much more efficient. In sparse mode rendezvous points are defined for each multicast group. New sources or destinations for the group send joins to these points. Initially traffic flows via the paths defined by these joins, but is then optimized by the destination sending a new join by the most direct route to the particular source and pruning the original, leading to a distribution tree without duplication. This looks as if it should achieve similar final traffic to MOSPF, but without the heavy CPU load potentially associated with MOSPF.

7.7.2 Multiple protocols

Even in the case of single protocols there is normally quite a large variance in throughput according to which is being routed, and where multiple protocols are present these effects are greatly increased. Throughput for an individual protocol depends on the number of fields in the header that have to be processed, the complexity of these operations and the efficiency with which they are handled. Handling efficiency can vary enormously in some router architectures where there is a distinction between fast path processing and slow path, usually involving some form of co-processor. The distinction between processing rates is therefore very dependent on the specific router model, but with a tendency towards the ordering quoted below.

The most basic effect of supporting multiple protocols is simply an increase in the total memory requirements, due to additional code, additional buffering and additional routing tables. When the memory available for buffering becomes marginal, packets are liable to be dropped leading to retransmissions and reduced throughputs, but when adequate there should be little effect on performance. Curing this problem is a combination of checking memory allocations to ensure that none is being reserved for functions that do not need it, and memory upgrades where that is insufficient. DECNET and OSPF are particularly hungry for routing table memory, while anything that terminates TCP sessions at the routers, such as DLSw, requires exceptionally large amounts of buffering.

The next effect is contention for processing power. Some reduction in throughput will always occur when a single processor is handling more than one protocol, due to the need to save and restore resources between using different packet handling modules. Efficiency is therefore greatest when the protocols are separated as much as possible. The major tuning factor in this regard is the setting of protocol priorities.

Most routers are able to assign individual protocols to one of about 5 to 10 priority levels which are then queued separately. Packets are then taken from these queues at relative rates determined by their priorities. The protocols that have to be given the highest priorities are those that are most sensitive to timeouts and rapid acknowledgement requirements; typical such examples are SNA and AppleTalk. More generally it is necessary to be able to distinguish between interactive and file transfer traffic within a single protocol, and to give the interactive traffic a higher priority; for example, within TCP/IP higher priority needs to be given to Telnet and Rlogin than to FTP.

In the mathematical appendix to this book, examples are given that show that prioritization gives great benefits to small amounts of traffic using short packets, but that prioritization of traffic that uses large packets provides a much smaller benefit. This is completely consistent with giving interactive traffic a higher priority than file transfers, as the latter usually have much larger packets and potential throughputs. Another feature that emerges both mathematically and empirically is the tendency of the higher priority traffic to adversely affect, or even lock out, lower priorities. This problem occurs when there is a large volume of high priority traffic, which can easily happen transiently when a high priority file transfer starts up, even though the average load for that protocol is small.

There are two basic solutions to the lock-out problem; the first is to use a bandwidth reservation scheme in addition to the prioritization, so that each protocol can be guaranteed a certain minimum bandwidth in congested conditions, while the second is to distinguish between different transaction types within a single protocol. The latter requires the router to be able to read the characteristic socket number, or equivalent, in each packet.

Where different protocols use packets with widely differing average packet sizes, the ability to guarantee configurable bandwidths to each varies with the type of implementation. Some algorithms are predominantly based on frames sent, while others take more account of the number of bytes. In the unequal length scenario it is the latter type that are more successful in ensuring the right ratios under congested conditions.

Another problem with prioritization is that when self-tuning protocols are given a low priority they are liable to respond by slowing down even further under congested conditions, so that it is not possible to guarantee them a fair share of bandwidth. TCP/IP is particularly susceptible to this.

In addition to protocol prioritization it is worth using address-based priorities to give precedence to WAN traffic on heavily loaded routers with multiple LAN interfaces. Retransmission of WAN data over a slow serial link is more serious than across a LAN, and this reduces the chances of packets of WAN traffic being dropped due to lack of buffer memory.

7.7.3   Load sharing

Both throughput and network utilization can be improved for some protocols by sharing the traffic between parallel paths between the source and destination networks. Some routing protocols, such as RIP, do not support this while sequence errors may make the method ineffective for some packet protocols. In addition to routing protocols, such as OSPF, that do support this, there are also proprietary features on some routers that enable them to load share even in cases where the routing protocol does not. The proprietary approaches usually entail the router having several paths collected into a circuit/transmission group, with the router putting packets onto them in either a round-robin fashion, or according to which has the shortest transmission queue. In general, if there are N parallel paths of similar speeds instead of one, the throughput will be N times as high provided that there is no resequencing work to be done.

There will normally be some such resequencing, as differing congestion levels will occasionally lead to packets arriving out of order, so that either the router or the end-device will have to resequence them. In some cases, notably IBM's LLC2, a sequence error will lead to session loss, so in these it is essential for the router to be able to guarantee resequencing. In some others there is a variable capacity for the end-device to do this depending on its power; for example, many PCs can only resequence two frames, whereas an AS/400 can resequence many.

DECnet phase IV between VAXs, for all but the earliest software releases, allows resequencing of packets and hence use of multiple equal cost paths.

7.7.4   Compression on routers

Compression criteria for routing are very similar to those for bridging, with the benefits being confined to relatively slow links. Router networks are normally larger and more complex than bridged systems, so that multihop issues are potentially more important, although the main use of compression is on single hops from remote branches to central sites. As routers can recognize different protocols and session identifiers, efficient compression by using separate dictionaries for each is more practical, but at the expense of more memory. Compression techniques consist of standardized header compression for various protocols, for example van Jacobsen TCP/IP header compression, plus non-standard data compression as in the case of bridges. TCP/ IP header compression is most useful in the cases of short packets, such as terminal server traffic, where the proportion of overhead is high, but of little value for file transfers, where the processing time overhead may exceed the transmission gain even on 56/64 kbps link.

Compression in software is very processor intensive and can lead to a general reduction in router performance for all tasks supported by the processor. As a result it is better to perform compression in hardware, either in the router itself or an external device that is compatible with the protocols. Compression in hardware is useful at significantly higher speeds than for software, typically up to about 1 Mbps. Special compression techniques for video and image, such as MPEG and JPEG, are performed in external devices for much faster lines. Attempts at further compression in the router are likely to be counter-productive.

The main category of compression used by routers is payload compression.

Link compression is unsuited to router networks, except for single hop or dial-up applications, due to the need to go through the decompression/recompression cycle at each intermediate router. In the case of public cell/frame/packet switch networks it cannot be used, since the public network will not normally have the (proprietary) intelligence needed to carry out these cycles, which are needed to perform the routing at all.

Lempel-Ziv style compression on routers normally uses a separate dictionary for each virtual circuit, leading to high memory requirements. A typical dictionary size is in the range 16 to 64 kbytes, and inadequate memory leads to poor performance or restriction of the number of VCs.

7.7.5   Dial-up links and SVCs

Router protocols pose problems whenever they are used over any form of temporary link. Such links are physical dial-up, such as PSTN, ISDN or inter-PABX channels, or logical switched virtual circuits as in X.25, frame relay or ATM. The issue which arises in each case is the need to prevent the routing protocol from keeping the circuit up with update traffic after the actual data message is completed. In those ISDN networks that allow users to transmit data through the D-channel it may be possible to avoid this problem by passing all the protocol overhead messages through this channel rather than the B-channel.

In the case of RIP, the main technique is the use of static routes for temporary links, so that no update traffic is sent. Many routers support the use of ISDN both for backup and for bandwidth on demand. Backup can either be a parallel link between the same two routers, or else third-party backup to an alternative router, thereby allowing for both link and single router failure; typically of the central router in a local star configuration of sites. Whereas the simple link failure is quickly detected by both ends if intelligent link-testing protocols, such as PPP and frame relay (with A-bit notification), the third-party mode is much slower as it has to rely on the primary route disappearing from tables to initiate backup. There is then a further delay until the new routing tables converge before any traffic can be sent. This normally requires timers and retry cycles to be extended for user sessions to be maintained. In this regard it is similar to the intelligent routing multiplexers and spanning tree bridges. Another issue is the manner in which these routes are held in tables. Third-party routes are normally predefined, but should only be used in the event of either a failure or of excess traffic on the primary path. The third-party routes are usually defined as either static routes (one per remote subnet) or default routes (one in total to another default router), but this raises the question of precedence in IP routing method. IP routers have tables of precedence that determine which of a range of potential routing paths should be used: static IP routes, default IP routes, BGP routes, EGP, RIP, OSPF inter/intra area, OSPF external, RIP or directly connected networks. In addition they also have a weight parameter to select between routes of equal precedence. The problem here is that static routes and default routes are normally of highest precedence (equal to direct connections and OSPF inter/intra area), so would be used in preference to a typical RIP primary unless these precedence tables are reconfigured. The required action is to put the ISDN static and default route precedences at the lowest level instead.

With RIP for IPX a further problem is what to do with the SAP broadcasts. A partial solution is provided by the use of static SAPs, whereby the router sends out adverts locally on the (possibly false) assumption that the server is present, but does not transmit them across the temporary circuit. Associated with this is the ability to receive SAPs at the normal frequency, but to transmit them at a low frequency appropriate to the outgoing interface. Potentially the greatest problem occurs with AppleTalk and its frequent updates, but this can be controlled using IP encapsulation via AURP.

Dial-up ISDN bridges have the same requirements as routers for spoofing the application protocol keep-alive and advertisement features, for example server SAPs for IPX, but not the routing protocol hellos. The issue of avoiding closed routing loops with dial-up bridges is different to the leased line case. Dial-up calls are often short, for instance just a few seconds over ISDN for messages of a few tens of kilo-bytes, compared to the configuration time of the spanning tree algorithm, so it is not practical to use the algorithm. The preferred alternative is for proprietary dial-up bridging software to include the transmission of loop detection frames at the start of a call to a new ISDN number and periodically thereafter, so that the link is taken down again if the loop detector comes back within a configurable timeout period of about one to two seconds. If the loop detection frame is received, then data can be transmitted via some round-about route without the need for a new link.

7.7.6   Buffer memory

An important factor in optimizing router network performance is the amount of memory configured for each interface. The key criteria are to ensure that the router has enough memory to prevent the dropping of deliverable packets, but not so much that it delivers packets which have been held for so long that they have timed-out before delivery. The way in which memory is allocated in the router is proprietary, but the overall principle is that the buffer space per port should be slightly less than the product of the port speed and the timeout. For example, a 64 kbps port subject to a one second protocol timeout would need about 8 kbytes, while a 2 Mbps port sub-ject to a 0.5 second timeout would need 1 MB. To prevent congesting the network with timed-out packets, it is also possible on some routers to configure a maximum holding time after which any undelivered packet is discarded. In this case the buffer size needed is the port speed times the holding time.

For protocols with self-tuning timers and for some connection-oriented sessions terminating at the router itself, such as TCP/IP sessions for DLS, the memory is estimated by a different technique. In this case it is the number of sessions to be supported times the window size in bytes. For example, 100 TCP/IP sessions with 4K window would need 400 kbytes of memory.

Early routers often had insufficient memory to meet these criteria, leading to packet loss and data retransmission degrading network performance. Top-end routers may now have up to 32 Mbytes of memory on a single card, of which only 4–8 is needed for code, leaving the remainder for buffers and large routing tables.

OSPF tends to use more memory than RIP, but by using RIP on external areas this requirement can be reduced somewhat. Use of level 2 frame switching instead of routing on the LANs produces a larger reduction by cutting the number of networks.

On IPX networks SAP tables are liable to use a lot of memory, but this can be reduced by use of SAP filters.

Minimizing the number of routing tables by restricting the number of protocols to one and avoiding class-of-service routing gives a very big reduction where applicable.

7.7.7   Router configuration

The performance of most routers can be optimized by relating the traffic flow over their interfaces to the processing architecture. Many routers give best performance when traffic enters and leaves by the same interface card, as this minimizes bus and inter-CPU traffic. Extensive logging of diagnostic information will degrade the performance of any CPU that is involved in the process. These problems are more criticial for heavy LAN–LAN connections than for low-speed WAN links, so CPUs that are primarily concerned with WAN traffic are the best candidates to do the logging work where a choice is applicable.

7.7.8   Further reading

A good general reference on routing algorithms is Steenstrup (1995), while basic principles are covered in Schwartz (1987). DECnet routing is covered in Martin and Leben (1992) and APPN in Nilausen (1994).

8

Networked Applications

8.1   Introduction

This chapter looks at the networking consequences of using various possible application architectures and structures. Historically WANs were largely used for data entry to remote hosts using protocols that imposed minimal overheads on the network in order to save costly bandwidth. Recently many other applications have evolved in the LAN arena that take advantage of the low bandwidth costs of local cabling and the lower processing costs associated with PCs instead of mainframes. Gradually these LAN techniques are being extended across enterprise networks despite not being designed for this role; this imposes a requirement to minimize their network load wherever possible.

8.2   Client–server architecture

The most important alternative to the old mainframe communications is client–server computing. This is not a precisely defined concept, but usually refers to cooperative processing of networked workstations, typically for a departmental workgroup, in which a graphical user interface is provided by the client while the processing is carried out in the server. Common server processes are file management, printing, database maintenance, mail handling and some remote communications.

Within this umbrella definition, about four levels of client–server variations can be picked out:

(1) A GUI in the PC and all other processing in the server;

(2) Cooperative processing in which applications are split between the client and the server;

(3) Simple client–server processes in which the data is split and calls are only made across the network when data is required;

(4) Data distributed across the network between clients and server.

Of these, (1) and (3) are the most widespread, with (1) being characteristic of many PC remote access packages, where it avoids the need to send large quantities of mouse and cursor information to the server. Adminstrative control issues are providing pressure to produce applications in category (2) in which the proportion handled by the server, and thus easily controlled, is increased.

8.2.1   RPC (remote procedure call)

One of the main elements of the client–server architecture is the RPC. There are three basic types of RPC as follows:

- asynchronous RPC without reply,
- asynchronous RPC with reply,
- synchronous RPC with reply.

Asynchronous RPCs allow the client to continue operations without having to wait for a reply, while in the synchronous case the client has to wait for a reply. In a local environment the difference may not be very great, but for operation over a WAN the additional latency makes the asynchronous RPCs much preferable whenever possible.

An additional degree of optimization is possible for the asynchronous RPCs by batching together any that occur within a very small interval, such as 0.1 seconds, into a single message to the server. As many RPCs are very small, around 50 bytes, this leads to a big reduction in bandwidth; for example, four such separate RPCs in TCP/IP amount to 360 bytes, whereas when batched this drops to 240.

An important special case of client–server architecture is the use of DDE (direct data exchange) or OLE (object linking and embedding). In this the user's application acts as the client and when updating embedded information from another application forms a link to that application as server, possibly to another host over the WAN.

There are two performance aspects to consider; one is the optimization of the client–server process itself, and the other is the impact of the application on other WAN traffic. Performance optimization depends on identifying the bottlenecks, then optimizing bottleneck throughput. Where LANs are linked across a WAN with T1/E1 links or slower, the WAN is almost always the bottleneck. The most important single factor is to use applications that minimize the transfer of data across the network, and to avoid transferring OLE files, whereby a small data file could drag across several bulky applications. From a networking point of view the older DDE link is more efficient than OLE, because the application remains on the server, but from a user's point of view the need to have both source and client applications open at the same time is a major disadvantage that led to the change. Other factors that are important in the LAN environment are the server CPU performance, buffer size, available memory and communications controller throughput. These topics are outside of the scope of this book, which concentrates instead on the WAN bottleneck. Many of the performance optimization aspects have already been covered in earlier chapters, but there are specific features associated with the architecture and with individual network operating systems.

Traffic loadings are almost entirely dominated by the number of servers and not the number of clients, since at any one time each server network adaptor is supporting one client only. On Ethernets where collisions may be a problem, optimization often amounts to segmenting the network so that there is only one server on a segment. This may require a superserver to handle all the traffic.

Some of the other important issues are summarized below.

8.2.2   Application structure

Applications for distributed processing differ from old mainframe programs in that they event driven by user actions instead of requesting the user to enter data. The structure of the application requires a greater degree of function modularity, since the location of functions should be locatable anywhere in the network according to efficiency criteria that may vary. Data entry, request entry and ouput display will almost always be on the client, and most of the file I/O and computation in the server, but some aspects of these could be in either location according to circumstances. When operating on a LAN data can easily be accessed by redirection to another server, but over a WAN this is liable to be impractical, so the application must be able to cater for differences in virtual file structure.

8.2.3 Data location and replication

One of the key decisions in a cost-effective network with adequate performance is on the siting of data and the degree of replication. The factors that determine this are:

- update frequency,
- degree of sharing,
- available bandwidth, response time and cost,
- security,
- business structure.

Information that is not updated very often, such as pricing files, can be downloaded periodically to many locations and accessed as locally as possible from a replica database. Conversely, information that quickly gets out of date, such as stock or credit, has to be located centrally as frequent downloads of the up-to-date file are impractical; instead either the relevant records only are downloaded when needed or, better, the update information/request is transmitted to the centre and the result returned. Where synchronous RPCs are used it is best to have local replica databases from a performance point of view but for some applications, such as credit checks, this is impractical. This example leads to delays at supermarket checkouts, and requires the use of network performance optimization to compensate.

Resilience may require that there be at least two databases that are kept in synchronization by the application. More widely distributed synchronized databases are not recommended as they are difficult to maintain and generate high levels of traffic throughout the network due to synchronization. Where multiple replicas are synchronised, there are two main approaches:

- a hierarchical approach with multicasts to a few central masters, thence a second multicast to the peripheral replicas,
- non-hierarchical multicast to neighbours who propagate the updates to adjacent replicas.

Of these, the former is easier to control and has a lower maximum update delay.

Sharing of data between applications means that its location must be made practical for all users; usually implying a tendency towards centralization.

The main problem is the trade-off between bandwidth costs and the required response time. Usually there are clearcut requirements on response time plus budgetary constraints, so the aim is to minimize data flow across the WAN to give the best result. Many 'network aware' applications have been written for LANs, where only record locking is required, and fail to meet this criterion. A lesser issue in this category is storage capacity which may limit the data locations.

Security requires that confidential information only be held on systems that have adequate precautions, for example RACF on IBM mainframes. This tends to lead to centralization, so is minimized by not imposing unnecessary restrictions. If security is defined on a data field basis, then a greater degree of delocalization may be possible, by imposing a simple block on access to sensitive fields for the versions held on unsophisticated machines.

Divisions within a company are likely to affect the choice in ways that may not be compatible with network efficiency.

Further extensive information is provided in Cou[94].

8.2.4   Data transaction processing monitors (DTP)

The two-tier client–server architecture is often extended to three by the use of DTP monitors where it is necessary to update data in two or more unrelated databases. Typically, the transaction can only be completed if both databases are able to perform the required updates (two-phase commit), and it is the DTP monitor which controls the process. These monitors have some impact on performance, both through additional load balancing capabilities and through their own communication techniques.

Dynamic load balancing is provided on some monitors, by which they check the utilization of all servers executing an application and send requests to the least loaded, thereby minimizing server delays.

Communication between server and monitor inevitably adds some network delay, and this is compounded if the DTPs rely entirely on remote procedure calls (RPC) for this. The problem of RPCs is that they are synchronous in the sense that the relevant programs must be running simultaneously in both machines, and the requesting RPC is held up until it receives its response, leading to server delays. Some DTP monitors add asynchronous messaging functions to get around this issue.

8.2.5   Client caching

A useful technique for minimizing network traffic is caching by the client. This requires the client to have sufficient memory to hold data or code that is not currently required in order to avoid calls across the network for such items that have previously been obtained. It is best for read-only items, such as price-lists and application code.

The downside to caching is that for information that gets updated by multiple users, the cached version quickly becomes out of date.

8.2.6 Server optimization

This is a major topic in its own right that is outside the scope of this book. The slowest operations are often disk I/Os, so these are the most important to optimize. Ideally there should be a separate disk controller for each disk, while using a faster drive obviously helps at extra expense. Use of relatively large block sizes, combined with avoidance of fragmentation also cuts the number of I/Os. Other elementary techniques likely to be beneficial are eliminating unnecessary macros and daemons, as well as minimizing paging. Detailed description of UNIX server optimization is covered in Lou[92].

8.3 Network operating systems

A network operating system is the extension of the client workstation's operating system to the LAN, such that remote files and processes appear to the client user as if they were resident on the client. The most ubiquitous of these is Novell's NetWare which effectively extends a PC's DOS operating system to the LAN; other examples are LAN Manager, LAN Server and so on. Associated with these are the NetBIOS and NetBEUI protocol stacks.

8.3.1 NetBIOS

NetBIOS is an IBM program for peer–peer networking of PCs that is also emulated by other vendors' products, such as NetWare. NetBIOS provides an API for session, transport and network layers, but does not contain any routing information. It also has a set of network services that are defined in the IBM PC LAN support program. It is intended for peer–peer networking and contains no concept of hierarchical addressing. As a result, broadcasts have to go everywhere, unlike RIP's ARPs which stop at the default router. When a connection is to be made, the PC has to send a broadcast (ARB) containing the NetBIOS name of the intended destination (see section 7.4) to which the latter responds, while bridges insert their identities in the RIF field. This procedure causes heavy network loads and frequently suffers from NetBIOS timeouts over a WAN. There are 22 different NetBIOS commands, of which Add Name Query, Add Group Name Query, Name Query and Name Recognized are the most significant protocol overhead.

The Add Name Query at the start of NetBIOS sessions is to check the uniqueness of the workstation's name; as it treats no answer as meaning unique, it is repeated up to ten times at 0.5 second intervals, with the typical defaults equal to three or six to allow for packet loss. The same is true of Add Group Name. Once uniqueness has been established the station sends a Name Query to locate the destination (usually a server). This responds with a Name Recognized frame as an SRB that contains the quickest path RIF. Each of these NetBIOS frames has a size of 44 bytes, giving a minimum of 65 bytes when level 2 headers are included. Other similar, but less common broadcast frames are Group Name Query and Status Query. Once the name has been recognized, a session is established; thereafter frames with session numbers instead of names in the header are used, leading to a drop in header size from 44 to 14 bytes.

The most drastic effects are on low-speed bridges and on low-powered servers in the network. The servers are potentially the greatest problem as a 286 PC with unintelligent interface card may only be able to handle about 10 interrupts per second without crashing, while this level of traffic would only amount to about 5000 bits per second. The use of filtering, spanning tree and hop-count limits on bridges were described in Chapter 7 as means of controlling the level of broadcast traffic. Another technique is the use of NetBIOS name and RIF caching on the bridges. In this a bridge learns both the name and location of a NetBIOS station, and responds to the ARB itself by setting up the known best route within the BPDU as well as dropping all but the first name request. In the typical situation where most communication is destined for a small number of servers, this can reduce the level of broadcast traffic very significantly. The age limit for the name cache need not be more than five seconds to eliminate the multiple name queries. If the number of name queries sent is configured to be only one, then name caching has little advantage, but changing the configurations on all workstations is tedious and difficult if remote sites are involved.

NetBIOS supports the use of LLC2 link level over the Token Ring as well as IBM PC baseband and broadband networks, with the exception of the queries which use unacknowledged LLC1 instead. Interface parameters are set in the Token Ring or Ethernet driver as appropriate. Key parameters in throughput optimization for old versions are the transmit buffer size, retransmission timer and window sizes; parameters are set in the device driver. Buffer size is set by the DHB (data hold buffer) size. The size of datagram transmitted is then usually equal to DHB minus 86 bytes of buffer header information, subject to a maximum value of 512 bytes. The transmit window size is given by DLC MAXOUT with default 2, and the maximum that can be received without acknowledgement has to be less than this, that is, one normally. Larger values are not normally applicable as the NetBIOS command set only allows one buffer to be sent by the SEND command and two by CHAIN SEND. As a result, throughput for file transfers will be poor on low-speed WAN connections.

NetBIOS in TCP/IP

RFCs 1001 and 1002 define the encapsulation of NetBIOS in TCP/IP and UDP. The basic features remain the same, but there are NetBIOS name and datagram distribution servers that may be used to cut broadcast traffic. This leads to three types of associated nodes:

- P nodes that use directed datagrams under TCP,
- B nodes that use broadcasts for discovery and advertisement, but only in a restricted broadcast area,
- M nodes which use a mixture of the two techniques, starting with broadcasts and sending directed enquiries to servers if no reply. B and M nodes must not be mixed else name conflicts may arise.

Traffic optimization requires as high a proportion of P nodes as possible, particularly in the WAN. P and M nodes require the presence of NetBIOS name servers and NetBIOS datagram distributors. Names are registered with the name server instead of a station having to broadcast a name query, while any NetBIOS broadcasts are sent as IP broadcasts by the datagram distributor.

A large network uses NetBIOS scopes based on the Internet domain concept to define the areas for which sets of names are applicable and to which broadcasts should be confined. This leads to a name based on a combination of the basic name and the appended scope identifier subject to detailed modifications defined in RFC1002, such that the full Internet name may be up to 255 characters long. The broadcast traffic is encapsulated in UDP with very high overheads consisting of at least 20 bytes IP header, 14 bytes NetBIOS header, 8 bytes of UDP header and up to 255 bytes each for full Internet source and destination names. Individual scopes should be confined to LAN regions to prevent these bulky broadcasts from going onto the WAN; furthermore most NetBIOS implementations are able to use pure NetBIOS in such scopes.

Unfortunately these standards are rather complex for end-stations, so are rarely implemented. This leaves a situation where broadcasts are encapsulated in UDP/IP and sent across the WAN to obtain IP addresses as well as the pure NetBIOS activities. This can be minimized by the use of NetBIOS name caching within IP by routers with this functionality as well as by use of PC LAN Support's remote name directory facility, whereby an end-station can save up to 255 names.

Broadcast reduction is more easily accomplished where NetBIOS is encapsulated in IPX (as with NetWare) than in IP. In this case a router can be configured to convert an encapsulated NetBIOS broadcast into a directed datagram.

Windows NT uses the B Node version of NetBIOS in TCP/IP, but overcomes WAN broadcast issues by allowing remote names and IP addresses to be set in the LMHOSTS file.

8.3.2   NetBEUI (NetBIOS extended user interface)

NetBEUI is an enhancement to NetBIOS developed by Microsoft for the OS/2 operating system. Its big advantage over a WAN is a sliding window with values up to 18 possible, and self-tuning, leading to much better performance. Even so, it is not intended for WAN use due to its broadcasts and lack of hierarchical addressing, and systems like LAN Manager default to TCP/IP in preference to NetBEUI for such routes.

In the case of Windows NT NetBEUI is completely distinct from NetBIOS.

8.3.3   NetWare

NetWare improves on IBM's basic input/output system by communicating with the PC's hardware directly, with the result that it gives better performance on the LAN. About 70% of the DOS market uses NetWare, making it of paramount importance. Unfortunately, prior to releases 3.12 and 4, NetWare was not written to take account of well-known WAN optimization techniques, so performance problems are frequently encountered when its traffic has to cross a WAN. Flow is controlled by the NetWare control program and prior to the development of Novell's burst mode in 3.12 and 4 it had no windowing mechanism, and hence required an individual acknowledgement for each packet sent. As shown in earlier chapters this has a horrendous effect on throughput over multihop WAN routes. Optimum performance in the pure LAN environment usually means using as large a packet size as possible, for example with LIPX preventing the old segmentation into 512 bytes, but on a WAN this will be subject to long forwarding delay and the possibility of retransmission due to errors. The best performance will result when the packet size for the LAN transmission is reduced, either by fragmentation by a router or gateway (bridges will not support this) or in the network interface card of the device.

Where burst mode is available, the optimization problem changes to configuring this feature. Burst sizes of from 2 to 10 are available on the server for reads of up to 64 kbytes using 512 byte packets and optimization can increase throughput by about 300% as compared to the old window size 1 scenario. This is still not quite as good as a sliding window, as an acknowledgement has to be received for each burst, leading to a pause after the last packet of the burst has been transmitted. There is also an option to set an interval between individual packets of a burst; this is mainly for end-stations with limited buffering. As with WAN protocols the window must not be made so large that a large number of retransmissions occur due to bit errors; thus the optimum burst window is smaller for analog dial-up applications than for connections across digital links. With NetWare 3.12 and NetWare 4.0 or later this optimization is made automatic with inclusion of several desirable features. Firstly, the window size is reduced to one in heavy congestion, thereby greatly reducing the chances of avalanche decay due to large window retransmissions, and secondly, selective reject is used at the shell's transport level for errored data.

Burst mode is not operative for messages of less than 4K, so there is a range of message sizes below this where response time remains poor due to individual acknowledgements. Where only a single slow WAN hop occurs, performance will be improved by the use of LIPX provided that the link quality is good enough not to cause retransmissions. On a very good link, a single packet for the entire message would give the best result in this case.

The main parameters that can be configured are the maximum packet size limit in SHELL.CFG or NET.CFG and the PBurst buffer window, if applicable. The range of packet sizes is from 576 to 6500 bytes, with typical default 4160. Over any analog WAN links or multiple low-speed digital links, 576 is likely to be the optimum packet size for the workstation, with 1024 for single digital WAN hops. The packet size is negotiated with the file server during batch initiation (see below). Where burst mode is available (that is, versions 3.12, 4.x or later and BNETX in the workstation and PBURST.NLM in the file server for version 3.11, standard on 4) the configured window size determines the initial behaviour of the transmission, so is critical for short file transfers, but becomes optimized during longer transactions. A value of zero disables burst mode, so setting the window equal to one permanently. Optimum values are likely to be in the range from 2 to 4, depending on the need to keep the window open, but to minimize retransmissions over error-prone WAN links. The latter constrains the total segment size (that is, buffer window times the packet size) not to be more than about 10% of the average number of bytes per bit error (typically this gives about 2000 bytes for analog WANs and 10–20 000 for digital). The maximum burst size is 64 kbytes, with particular applicability to satellite links and long-distance ATM links.

Where burst mode is not available, some windowing is available on WANs that provide packet fragmentation and protocols with a windowing mechanism, for example X.25 and IP tunnelling. This is beneficial on multihop WAN routes, but ineffective for single hops. NetWare IP is available as an alternative to IPX from version 4.1 onwards, but this is only recommended for UNIX environments where IP is the only protocol used on the WAN. The problem with NetWare IP is that it simply encapsulates IPX packets within IP, thereby adding overhead, while retaining the underlying NCP flow control. This typically causes a 10–15% hit on response time.

NetWare/IP does however provide some tuning parameters accessible on the server from the UNICON utility for UNIX systems. The main parameters are the number of ticks (units of 1/18th second) between nodes on (a) the same IP subnet, (b) the same IP network, (c) between IP networks, with respective defaults one, two and three ticks. Actual delays can be found by pinging nodes in each of the three categories and allowing for any difference in size between the ping echo packet and the user packets. Some increase in default is likely to be desirable if more than one hop is traversed at 64 kbps or less. Adjusting these parameters should largely eliminate any timeouts on file transfers. In this slow WAN link scenario any servers acting as IP/IPX gateways are also liable to require their tick values to be modified via the slow link customization menu.

The initiation of NetWare batch file transfers also requires optimization on low-speed WANs. This process starts with a broadcast SAP (socket 452h) looking for the workstation IPX driver, followed by a RIP broadcast (453h) from the workstation to determine the nearest file server. This is followed by unicast packet size negotiation, route description and time of day update. The part that requires optimization is the broadcast section, as these messages are often far more extensive than needed, and waste bandwidth. In the previous chapter, the use of IPX filters on routers was described as one way of improving this situation, but another alternative is to define filters in the file server. In either the SAFILTER.NLM of NetWare 386 multiprotocol router enhancements, or SERVMAN.NLM of NetWare 4, it is possible to restrict SAPs to specific networks. SERVMAN also provides access to similar network statistics to MONITOR.

NetWare print files sometimes consist of exceptionally small packets because the byte-by-byte transmission mode of a parallel printer port is retained when sending data to a network interface card. This can be overcome by using the block mode feature of the NetWare API instead of byte mode.

Another area of NetWare performance that is amenable to tuning is the frequency of updates between primary servers and any secondaries. The default query interval between servers is five minutes, but if these updates take place over congested WAN links, it is worth reducing the frequency to conserve bandwidth, or in the case of dial-up links to prevent unnecessary reactivation of the link.

8.3.4   LAN Manager

A major difference with LAN Manager is that it supports NetBEUI on a LAN and TCP/IP over a WAN. Use of TCP/IP means that a windowing mechanism is automatically available with a self-tuning retransmission timer. LAN Manager supports a maximum packet size of 2000 bytes, which while restrictive on a LAN is still larger than the optimum over a WAN. The NetBEUI driver supports large window sizes with six the default, so avoiding interruptions to data flow across the WAN due to acknowledgements. Over most WANs, a value of at least four is needed to avoid interruptions.

The LAN Manager operating system is also self-tuning for optimum performance.

A specific problem that occurs with NetBIOS over IP from LAN Manager is the subject of broadcasts. Although there are two RFCs (see section 8.3.1), to deal with this topic they are both too complex for most end-stations and as a result special features are needed in the router. The main element of broadcast reduction is the use of a special UDP port number to support NetBIOS over IP. Broadcasts are then enabled for that port number, but not for any others.

8.3.5   DEC Pathworks

This is essentially similar to LAN Manager, but used for PCs in a DEC environment. Versions exist for different environments including DECnet.

8.3.6   LAN Server

LAN Server is intended for operation on LANs, usually with the server and workstations on the same segment, so when used over a WAN the defaults often have to be changed. LAN Server performance over a WAN is highly dependent on version. Version 2 uses NetBIOS on top of LLC in such a way that there are two sets of acknowledgements, one at the NetBIOS layer and the other at LLC level. Combined with the maximum normal NetBIOS window size of two this leads to interruptions in transmissions over a WAN as well as the overhead of a large number of small acknowledgement packets. Later versions of LAN Server that use NetBEUI instead of NetBIOS have much better WAN performance on account of the NetBEUI sliding window, so any of the early version should be upgraded. Packet size is normally restricted in early versions to 512 bytes, and this is quite adequate for WANs. Early versions of LAN Server are not self-tuning.

LAN Server 4 also supports NetBIOS over TCP/IP in line with the procedures of RFCs 1001/2 as well as native TCP/IP and TCPBEUI. These are stated to be up to 200% more efficient than earlier versions of these for OS/2. It behaves as if 9 bytes of IP routing had been added to each NetBIOS packet.

Version 4.0 has a feature called Tuning Assistant where entry of the configuration leads to appropriate parameters being set, but for earlier versions changes must be done manually. The main parameters liable to need changing are the maximum data frame size (MAXDATARCV), link level response timer T1 and NetBIOS TimeOut. MAXDATARCV should be reduced from the default of 4168 to a lesser value such as 512 or 1024 bytes for analog links or multihop routes. T1 and the NetBIOS TimeOut need to be increased. PiggyBacks and SideBanding should be enabled to cut delays waiting for acknowledgement and reduce the protocol overheads. Network statistics are obtainable via use of the Net Statistics command on the workstation and from SPM/2 on OS/2 workstations. OS/2 Warp Server uses Tuning Assistant and the same file and print services as LAN Server 4.

For tuning the servers and further details see Chambers *et al.* (1995).

8.3.7 Banyan VINES

VINES offers a choice of WAN protocol comprising any of NetBIOS, TCP/IP, X25 or VINES ICP. The API allows the programmer to buffer up to 5800 bytes at a time, allowing the equivalent of ten 512 byte blocks of data plus header. VINES has a maximum IP packet size of 1500 bytes, which is perfectly adequate for WAN operations, with reduction to 576 giving better performance for multihop WAN routes. Its maximum datagram size is 1450 bytes. The VINES network management system option is useful in deciding how to tune the operating system.

8.4   LU6.2 and CPIC

IBM's approach to distributed processing is based on the use of type 2.1 nodes and LU type 6.2, with the programmer's interface either directly through LU6.2 verbs, or indirectly via the standard CPIC interface. This section does not give a comprehensive description of these, but selects out those verbs which are primarily associated with throughput considerations. LU6.2 covers levels 4,5 and 6 of the SNA protocol stack, with most of these effects taking place at level 5. Most end–end flow control is covered by the normal pacing considerations, but this may be influenced by the way in which verbs are used.

LU6.2/CPIC lie beneath the transaction services layer of SAA and many programs will make use of DDM and DRDA. One major effect that they have on network load is that they are record-oriented, so the data volume transmitted across the network will be much higher than for some UNIX programs that are able to pick out individual fields, but much less than simple-minded LAN applications that pull a whole file across.

The initial session establishment uses the Allocate verbs and is of little relevance to performance optimization.

The area that affect performance are instructions which enforce a wait for some form of acknowledgement and those that force data transmission earlier than would normaly occur under buffer flow control.

SEND_DATA only sends data down to the buffer, and does not transmit it across the network, hence a file transfer coded in terms of this verb will exhibit normal data flow control. If the FLUSH command is used, then data will be transmitted immediately even though the buffers may not be full; sequences of FLUSHs would tend to produce a higher proportion of small packets and increased network overhead, but better response time. Applications running over analog WAN links need to use a buffer size or FLUSH frequency that keeps packet size down to around 500 bytes to avoid a high rate of retransmission due to error. Buffered data is automatically sent by DEALLOCATE and CONFIRM also.

Any pauses while waiting for special acknowledgements over and above pacing considerations will reduce throughput. The main verb in this category is CONFIRM.

Programs will also run faster if there is a minimum number of direction changes unless the newer full duplex options are used. This option was introduced in CPI; version 2.0 enables both simultaneous send–receive and the use of expedited data to bypass flow control for urgent data; use of these features is important to high performance servers.

8.4.1   APPC/PC

One of the most important LU6.2 applications to optimize is APPC/PC as this is often run over relatively slow WAN links. The general principles are essentially those described earlier under SNA tuning, but the key features in this case are the particular aspects of PACING that are applicable in this case. The general description in Chapter 6 gave hints on fixed pacing window sizes, but many APPC/PC implementations on modern equipment are also able to use dynamic pacing, whereby the window size is varied according to instantaneous memory availablity. Dynamic pacing defaults back to fixed if the other computer is unable to support the newer technique. The fixed pacing window needs to increase with the number of hops, with a tendency towards allowing one frame to be present at each intervening line or network processor if each component has comparable latency. Where response time is dominated by one slow link, this size drops to the order of the response time divided by the latency of the slowest component. Use of dynamic pacing allows this to be reduced automatically when memory shortages occur.

8.5   Types of application

This section considers the networking consequences of certain common types of application.

8.5.1   General interactive applications

One of the most essential requirements on a network is to achieve acceptable response times for interactive applications. The extreme cases of echoplex and LAT have already been discussed in earlier chapters, but in the modern world of LAN interconnection, a similar, but less spectacular situation exists in relation to Telnet and other interactive applications.

It is usually quite easy to provide acceptable response times, typically under 250 ms, for short messages on their own, but the problems arise when they compete for bandwidth with file transfers or multimedia. The reason for the problem is that optimum throughput for the file transfers entails the use of large packet sizes, typically at least 576 bytes for all LAN protocols and up to 9188 for SMDS. Even in a prioritized system an interactive packet will have to wait for completion of

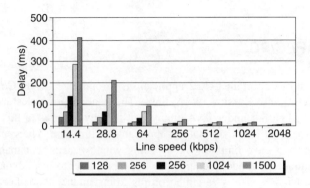

Figure 8.1   Packet delays.

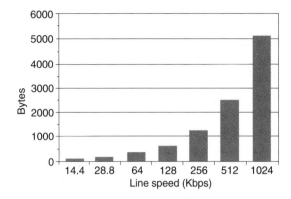

Figure 8.2   Safe packet size.

transmission of a large file packet, so if a heavy load exists it will be delayed for up to the transmission time of such a packet on each link. The delays for various common packet sizes for file transfers are displayed graphically in Figure 8.1 for a variety of WAN link speeds.

It is immediately apparent that the size of packet that can be used for file transfers without degrading prioritized interactive traffic too much increases with line speed. In a worst-case scenario of an analog bridge at 14.4 kbps, a complete Ethernet frame has a transmission time of over 0.8 seconds, so interactive applications will be totally unsatisfactory even with prioritization. To mix the traffic types at this speed a router must be used that can fragment the Ethernet frames into packets of about 128 bytes, intersperse them with interactive packets, then reassemble them at the far side of the network. In this way the queuing delay for the interactive packets can be kept down to about 75 ms. A very crude rule of thumb for the maximum file transfer packet size compatible with acceptable response times for prioritized interactive traffic is that the size in bytes should not exceed one hundredth of the bit rate of the line. This is illustrated graphically in Figure 8.2.

This shows that the normal packet sizes for TCP/IP, AppleTalk, Banyan VINES and NetWare of 536–586 bytes become roughly compatible with interactive applications at about 56 kbps and above, while Ethernet bridging needs over 128 kbps and SRB more than 192 kbps with defaults of about 2000 bytes.

These figures still require all interactive traffic to be able to pre-empt any queued file transfers, and many priority mechanisms do not do this. A minimum requirement is that the priority queue for interactive traffic must be processed at least as fast as the transmission time of the file transfer packet; again not all schemes do this. Obviously very light file transfer traffic does not matter much as the chance of an interactive packet getting stuck is small. The point at which it becomes irritating to users is when about one in 20 interactive messages gets held up; this will occur when the load due to file transfers reaches about 10% of line capacity.

In order to use routers to support interactive traffic over the same links as file transfers at speeds below about 256 kbps, the router must be able to do the following:

(1) recognize interactive traffic types within a protocol, for example distinguish Telnet from FTP in IP;

(2) examine the interactive queues at least once every 50 ms;

(3) provide pre-emptive priority for these queues;

(4) for operation below 56 kbps, they must also fragment large packets.

RLogin

RLogin was formalized in RFC1282 and enables a user to log in to one local UNIX host, then from there perform a remote login to any other such host. Recently it has also been extended to some non-UNIX hosts. It is characterized by the exchange of numerous small packets, so is susceptible to queuing delays caused by large packets from other applications; this means that its well-known port number of 513 should be prioritized.

Characters entered locally by the client are echoed globally by the host, leading to very high bandwidth overheads due to the headers. This is minimized by enabling the Nagle algorithm, whereby multiple characters are blocked together and sent as a single segment, and this should be used on low-speed networks. Header compression techniques, such as the use of CSLIP on dial-up links, are also helpful at low speeds.

Telnet

Telnet is much more general than RLogin, as it applies to virtually any operating system, but has rather similar characteristics and needs.

Telnet has IP port number 23, which should also be given precedence over others such as 20 for FTP data, 25 for SMTP, 69 for TFTP, 80 for HTTP, 103/104 for X.400 mail and 138 for NetBIOS data. Where the IP type-of-service field is supported, Telnet should set it to indicate low delay.

Telnet itself can be optimized by selecting the best mode of operation of the network virtual terminal protocol that is associated with it. Most terminal servers come up in character mode, whereby individual characters are inserted in TCP/IP headers, and this should be changed to line mode for most applications so that groups of characters terminated by a carriage return or timeout go into the packet instead. This can easily reduce associated WAN traffic by a factor of 10. Echoing in this mode is performed locally once the initial password has taken place, so network response time is much less critical than for character mode.

Some applications, notably those associated with full screen editing, can only operate in character mode with global echo. In this case the response time for an echo must be less than about 160 milliseconds to avoid irritating the user and causing typographic errors.

Telnet also has two other modes, half-duplex and kludge mode. The latter is a vaguley defined precursor to Linemode, with similar characteristics, while half-duplex is rarely used now. It uses local echo, but waits for a GO-AHEAD command from the host before sending a line of data. As most terminals are now full-duplex, it has been effectively replaced by Linemode.

8.5.2   X-windows

The X-windows protocol is used by clients to send requests to the server to manipulate windows, generate text or graphics, and to communicate with other clients as well as receive responses from the server. It differs from many client–server applications through the keyboard, mouse and window being controlled from the server. In order to operate easily over networks, the protocol is asynchronous in the sense that the applications can carry on while waiting for a response. X-windows requires to be carried in a networking protocol that provides guaranteed reliability and sequencing. Usually this is TCP/IP, and less often DECnet. It requires very short response times, particularly for mouse movements.

Requests are relatively short with a 4 byte header that includes a 16 bit length field expressed in units of 4 bytes, so the maximum length is 1020 bytes, with many requests much shorter. Replies have a 32 bit length field, so can be up to several hundred kilobytes long in principle. There are also 32 byte event messages and error reports.

One important X-windows application is the terminal emulation program X-term, which has very high overheads. It involves global echo like character-mode Telnet, but in addition to the TCP/IP headers, each keystroke is converted into a 32 byte X-message, thereby creating a total overhead of 71 bytes per stroke. Header compression is obviously vital for this, but is not fully available until release 6 with its Low Bandwidth X.

X-windows is an exception to the general rule that the Nagle algorithm (see Chapter 6) should be used with TCP/IP; here it must be disabled, else the possible delay of 100 to 200 ms in updating mouse movements would be unacceptable.

In practice, X-windows usually generates heavy traffic with a high proportion of short messages, so for best performance it should be given a high priority to minimize queuing behind long packets belonging to file transfer applications, although the asynchronous operation means this is not critical. Where the messages are predominantly short, TCP/IP header compression, for example by CSLIP or PPP, will provide a worthwhile reduction in bandwidth. In general, operation over line speeds of less than 56–64 kbps are likely to be unsatisfactory.

Some performance improvement is obtained by using Low Bandwidth X introduced in Release 6 of X-windows. It is derived from the proprietary XRemote. In addition to header compression this offers caching and the sending of only differences from previous packets. It also features X-payload compression using the Lempel-Ziv methods, and is better in this regard than a modem or router, as performing compression at the application level eliminates the buffering delays associated with external equipment. These delays are not very important for file transfers, but in the case of the short packets, characteristic of X, are of major importance.

8.5.3   File transfers

The next biggest area in which optimization is called for is in file transfers; unfortunately this may clash with optimization for interactive traffic. The basic network level features have already been described in earlier chapters; the aspect discussed here is the tuning of parameters set within the application.

The most important factor outside of network flow control is the requirement for block acknowledgements. If the block acknowledgements are more frequent than the various level 2, 3 or 4 window sizes, then a reduction of throughput will occur. A hypothetical example of this would be a disk block read of 512 bytes requiring an individual acknowledgement while the network use a TPDU of 512 with window 2, accompanied by packet size 256 and window 4. The effective window size would only be half of that configured for the network in this case.

At the opposite extreme, some protocols such as NFS try to send large quantities of data in too short a time for a WAN, leading to retransmission timeouts. Features of some of the main protocols are listed below.

NFS

NFS runs over UDP as a default, so all acknowledgements and retransmissions are its responsibility rather than the network. Normally NFS uses blocks of 8192 bytes and expects to receive an acknowledgement within 700 ms. Excluding network overheads this amounts to a throughput of over 93 kbps, so any WAN link of less than about 128 kbps will inevitably cause timeouts, while many higher speed links will do so due to other traffic and possible multihops. The solution to this is either to reduce the UDP datagram size or to increase the timeout (where possible), of which the former is better because of the probability of bit errors in the WAN and the reduction in throughput on multihop paths due to the need to receive fully a datagram before forwarding onto the next link. Reduction of the packet size usually has to be done by setting a 1024 byte block size for read/writes in the initial NFS Mount sequence. The precise options of this command vary with implementation, but for System V the read and write sizes Rsize/Wsize can be set to any sub-multiple of 8192 that is divisible by 1024, while the timeout, Timeo, is configurable in tenths of a second, with 7 as the normal default. The effectiveness of any choice of these parameters can be checked by looking at the NFS statistics field 'nfsstat': if there are a large number of retransmissions or timeouts, then Timeo needs to be increased. Although NFS is often a lot faster than NetWare on a LAN, having to cut the block size in this way puts it on very much of a par with the 512 byte packets of NetWare.

Most recent implementations of NFS allow TCP to be used instead of UDP, in which case it can be changed to this in the Mount command. This will give better flow control than the basic UDP version.

The influence of server load on the performance can be checked from 'nfsstats', which provides comprehensive information on buffer and CPU loads. Similarly most UNIX hosts contain network statistics in 'netstat'.

NFS also provides for interactive networked applications based on remote procedure calls (RPC). In these only a minimum of information is passed from the client to the server; typically a call for an application to be used plus pointers to the data to process. RPCs are the best basis for client–server processing across a WAN because of the low data flow, and are much more network-efficient than OLE.

Version 3 of NFS allows block sizes of up to 65 536 bytes instead of 8192. This will give better performance for file transfers over satellite or high-speed links.

TFTP and BOOTP

TFTP also runs over UDP, but does not have the awkward defaults, nor does it have any error checking. TFTP uses a datagram size of 512 bytes with an acknowledgement for each being required before the next can be sent. This makes throughput low, particularly on multiple hop paths, just as with early NetWare.

TFTP is used by BOOTP, so the latter inherits the low throughput. BOOTP is based on the use of broadcasts, so it is important to tune the network by setting the paths over which BOOTP can run to those on which it is needed. Most routers will automatically block the all-ones broadcasts, so this is a question of specifically enabling interfaces for BOOTP.

Another performance disadvantage of TFTP is that it contains no sync-pointing, so if a failure occurs in the middle of a file transfer, the whole process has to recommence from scratch.

FTP

FTP runs over TCP/IP so error checking and flow control is performed by the network with the retransmission timeout automatically updated in accordance with the observed transit delay. The only tuning lies in the IP MTU; normally this is set at 576 bytes to take account of a 512 byte disk block plus protocol overheads. Where more than one WAN hop below about 200 kbps occurs a smaller packet size will improve throughput due to the need to receive fully before transmission, unless a large segment window is specified. Alternatively frame relay could be used across the WAN in which case this would not apply and the normal size would be preferable.

One common problem with FTP over WANs is that when a new session is started to a remote destination, TCP usually sets the retransmission timer to the value of its other sessions, which are often on a LAN and hence quite short. The result of this is that the initial window times-out and gets retransmitted, possibly several times, until the timer eventually tunes itself to the WAN conditions of the session. The simplest way round this problem is to configure the initial value of the timer for a session to be sensible for WAN operations, but many implementations of TCP lack this feature.

The same type of problem also occurs if TCP has been used for Telnet sessions across the WAN using small buffers; if a UNIX host then advertises a 4K buffer, then the same timeout will be used as for the Telnet sessions, leading to timeout and retransmission; again the initial timer should ideally be changed.

FTAM

This is the OSI file transfer program which is intended to run over the OSI protocol stack, notably the TP4 transport layer and CLNP network level. Arguments for its optimization are essentially the same as those for FTP above. FTAM is slower than FTP because it has higher protocol overheads in the upper layers.

Where FTAM is much better than FTP is in its flexibility; in particular, it allows individual records to be requested and transferred instead of the complete file, thus potentially offering much more efficient use of the WAN for database updates.

Apple filing protocol (AFP)

AFP and the printer access protocol (PAP) are called up transparently by the user through AppleShare device selection. This does not offer the user any configuration options. AFP and PAP both use the Apple transaction protocol (ATP) to transmit data reliably. The data packet size is 586 bytes, including AppleTalk upper-layer headers, with a window size of up to eight. A large file transfer takes place as a set of consecutive transactions initiated by a transaction request, TReq, which includes a mask specifying up to eight packets and a transaction ID. This is followed by a transaction response for each packet specified, and acknowledged via a transaction release. Selective reject of missing or illegal packets is requested through the bit mask. This is followed by the next TReq/TResp/Trel sequence until transmission is complete. A common window size is four, making the sequence very similar to Vines apart from a smaller packet size. Over sequences of WAN links the packet size is quite adequate, although inefficient in a pure LAN environment.

The total volume of data transmitted in a file transfer is much greater than that of the file for small file transfers. This is because AFP has about 60 possible calls which may be used in setting up the transfer, so that the first few ATP transactions will be for volume headers, directory structures and parameter exchange rather than actual data.

PC comms packages

This category includes many applications based on protocols such as XMODEM, YMODEM, ZMODEM, KERMIT and various more proprietary protocols used by more modern packages, such as PC Anywhere and Carbon Copy. XMODEM was the earliest widespread PC file transfer program and requires a block acknowledgement for each 128 byte block, with a fixed retransmission timer of 10 seconds; this gives very low throughput by modern standards.

YMODEM is an improved version of XMODEM that includes a CRC checksum and allows use of 1024 byte blocks also.

ZMODEM is a further improvement that gives high performance due to automatic adjustment of block size in relation to the error rate experienced.

KERMIT is very similar in operation to XMODEM and gives low throughput, but with a Super Kermit improved version also.

A major factor to consider when using file transfer or remote control software is the option of data compression by the application. In Chapter 2 of this book the question of data compression by the modem was discussed, and it was pointed out that sometimes the additional propagation delay caused by the extra processing offsets the gains. In such cases it may be better to use the PC to do the compression instead where this option is included in the comms package. The most common package for this is PKZIP at the transmitter and PKUNZIP at the receiver. This will also be the case where the PC has a powerful processor, but only a 38.4 kbps serial port so that it is unable to take advantage of modem data compression with V.32 bis or V.34 which entail 57.6 or 115.2 kbps ports for maximum advantage. Even at these port speeds some compression capability is lost, as a typical file will contain a few tracts that permit more than the 3:1 (equal to 4:1 when start–stop bits are included) overall degree of compression. In such cases the port will be unable to send information to the modem as fast as it can transmit it. If data compression is done in the PC, then the port speed should match the line speed, with 28.8 kbps the maximum for these modem standards. PKZIP gives a factor of 2 to 3 compression for most files, but up to 10 for some database applications. Decompression is much faster than compression.

Attempting to compress the data twice, once in the PC and again in the modem, is counter-productive. It does not increase the degree of compression achieved, but reduces throughput by introducing extra processing delays in the modems. The V.42bis algorithm is able to detect some forms of compression, such as ZIP files, and turn itself off, so avoiding the counter-productivity. ZIP compression tends to give a faster file transfer than V.42bis in the modem as well as being more suitable for use with ISDN TAs.

Print files

A special case of file transfer is remote printing. The particular issue that arises is the question of hard or soft fonts. Many print applications, such as Postscript, send soft font information to the printer in addition to the actual text to be printed. This leads to a print file often being twice the volume of the original text, and up to 10 times as much in some cases. In order to cut unnecessary WAN traffic, hard fonts stored on the printer should be used if there is network congestion.

8.5.4 E-mail

This ubiquitous application is extremely variable because users are free to send anything they like, unless prevented by network management controls. Usage often starts at very low levels with users sending short messages, but then builds up as users start to send diagrams, spreadsheets, applications and videoclips across to each other.

The main issues are the location of mail servers and controls to ensure that the more bulky transfers are carried out off-peak (or even banned) where bandwidth is limited. If videoclips are allowed to be attached in e-mail, then ATM is likely to be required, but elementary text usage is undemanding.

E-mail packages can in principle be either centrally located, distributed peer to peer or hybrids. The earliest systems were all central, but most modern systems are hybrids in the sense of having multiple strategically sited servers that interact on a peer–peer basis. Usually the files are held on a server, and a pointer passed to a user's mailbox. Many applications, such as Windows, do not support direct receipt of unsolicited files and must execute a fetch instead.

Traffic to and from a server may be very high, so this traffic should be concentrated into the server via a LAN with multiple WAN ports to other servers rather than concentrated via WAN links. Mail servers tend to be very expensive, so the main design factor is the trade-off between high server costs for a large number of regional centres on one hand, and high WAN line costs on the other when use of a small number leads to local traffic going via a remote server. For best performance the WAN should only be used for server-to-server traffic.

When deciding the bandwidth required for e-mail it is important to note that the header overheads for short messages are extremely high. The most extreme case is probably X.400 e-mail, where a message of 100 or 200 data bytes leads to the transmission of 10 times as much due to the headers.

8.5.5 Electronic software distribution

This is a special case of file transfer in which the application handling the file transfer is also able to recognize its target environment and selectively update files there. Typical applications in this category are NetView Distribution Manager and HERMES.

This type of application is characterized by long periods of inactivity, with occasional bursts of very heavy traffic when a new software application gets distributed. Bandwidth on demand via dial-up circuits, such as ISDN, or SMDS are the main WAN requirement. Capacity has to be such that the software gets distributed to all relevant stations and checked within a period of a few days for new applications, or hours for retail pricing change files.

The most efficient style of downloading is by means of a cascaded process. Normally a host will have only a limited number of ISDN ports available, so that a purely central process will require many remote sites to be downloaded sequentially from a single port. If the application supports a cascade from an intermediate set of sites, then the process will be much faster. For example, if a bank downloads a new 100 Mbyte version of branch application code to each of 900 branches from a single host with 30 64K ISDN ports, allowing for retransmissions this will take about 7 days to complete; however, if cascaded via 30 regional branches, each with 30 ISDN ports, the time drops to half a day, which is much more practical from a business point of view. The alternative to this is usually to distribute disks or CDs by mechanical post, leading to at least a week's delay to allow for errors.

A lot of early PC ESD packages do not support cascaded operation, hence are not suitable for large networks; one such package that does is Navigator.

8.5.6   Diskless PC operation

Security and cost considerations have led many organizations to use diskless PCs in their networks. In a pure LAN environment this is usually very satisfactory, but can cause major problems over a WAN. The main problem is in loading up the software, particularly if Windows is used. Several megabytes of information may have to be downloaded to the PC. If this had to traverse a 64 kbps WAN link, then at the maximum achievable useful throughput of around 50 kbps this would take about five minutes, while if around 50 such stations were contending for the bandwidth at the start of the day, it would be several hours before all were loaded up. Even with the smaller DOS file volumes, it would still take about half an hour in the latter case. For this approach to be at all practical the WAN links would require to be of T1/E1 type or better.

One of the main forms of optimization in this case is to ensure that the PC has a large amount of RAM which can be used to cache application code for DLLs. In the case of a single user over a 64 kbps link, there will be a loading time of the order of one minute for a single application, followed by several glitches of 5–10 seconds while DLLs are loaded for some previously unutilized operation. These glitches are not repeated if the DLL is then held in cache memory unless it gets overwritten. In the case of a shared link, the associated reduction in network traffic may be vital in providing an adequate quality of service.

8.5.7 Remote LAN access

This is liable to encompass any of the preceding applications, but has special features of its own. Often traffic is too intermittent to justify a permanent leased line, so the issue is how to make the most efficient use of dial-up access or of a public network. Dial-up can be based on either modems, ISDN or switched 56. There is little to choose between the latter two on throughput, but modems are more limited. The short call set-up time of ISDN means that sessions can be spoofed into staying up permanently although the link is only brought up when there is actual data to transmit. These spoofing requirements are listed in Table 8.1 for some of the major protocols. Spoofing the responses to keep-alives locally also leads to higher throughput than transmitting them end–end.

These techniques reduce line costs and potentially the central equipment costs, the latter through the reduction in the number of access ports required where multiple sessions can share ISDN channels in line with Erlang quality-of-service criteria (see Chapter 4). The grade of service for this must be much higher than for traditional voice traffic, as each session is equivalent to a large number (hundreds) of separate ISDN calls for sub-messages with the session failing if any one of these is blocked. Economies are only possible with very large central sites and rather inactive applications.

In the case of NetWare 4.0 and 4.1, there are liable to be additional non-information frames over and above those listed; to prevent them from keeping an ISDN link up, patches, Timesync, Pingfet and DSFILTER from Novell needs to be installed on the stations.

If routing is used on these ISDN networks, it is also advisable to have any routing updates sent across the network on the back of data transfers to prevent bringing the link up unnecessarily; this functionality is included in OSPF demand circuits.

Compression is advantageous for file transfers, but for short interactive transactions can lead to an increase in response time, especially for primary rate ISDN as some brouters are insufficiently powerful to support all the B-channels with compression.

Table 8.1 Protocol spoofing.

Protocol	Features to spoof
X.25	X.25 level 2, with level 3 call request sent when data to send
IPX, SPX	SAPs, RIP, NetWare serialization, IPX/SPX watchdogs
NetBIOS	Session keep-alives, adverts
TCP/IP	RIP, Optional keep-alives where used
DECnet	Service adverts, keep-alives
LAT	Service adverts, keep-alives
AppleTalk	RTMP and tickles through use of AURP and IP

8.5.8   Document image processing (DIP)

DIP is another application that puts heavy pressure on a network. Many institutions find it desirable to store letters and third-party documents in electronic form to allow rapid retrieval should the need ever arise, but these items are very voluminous. The answer is to make as much use of compression at the application level as possible, so that documents are both stored and transmitted in compressed form and only expanded by the reading/printing application. There are two main sets of standards for image compression, the fax standards and the JPEG standard.

Fax compression

The fax standards are Group 3, Group 3bis and Group 4. They are intended for black and white text and give poor graphical representation. For PCs Group 3 is usually performed by a fax modem at either end of an analog link, while Group 3bis and Group 4 are mainly implemented by the appropriate type of fax machine. Group 4 compression is also an option at the application level in some commercial DIP packages. In general these standards can give compression by a factor of 20–30.

The main modem types to use for this are V.17 at 14.4 kbps or V.34.

When fax is sent across a voice/data network through a PABX whose channels are subsequently compressed by a multiplexer, throughput is likely to drop by a factor of about two due to incompatibilities between the compression algorithms for voice and fax. Ideally the fax traffic should be sent by a fixed subset of PABX ports, so that the PABX can set a class of service field in the initial service request (with DPNSS signalling) packet to enable intelligent multiplexers to recognize the fax traffic and avoid trying to compress it.

JPEG (Joint Photographic Experts Group)

The JPEG standard is more comprehensive than the fax methods, and much better for documents that contain diagrams and photographs. Several options are available for configuring JPEG. The maximum degree of compression is destructive, in the sense that when the image is expanded some detail will have been lost. For most purposes, such as letters and documents in general, this will not matter, but for engineering diagrams the detail is vital, so non-destructive options exist also.

Using the current version of JPEG with maximum compression an A4 typescript takes about 45 kbytes, while a similar document with some greyscale images occupies about 60 kbytes; similarly the image of two sides of a cheque takes about 12 kbytes. Colour images require more space due to the extra pixel information, typically about 200 kbytes for an A4 colour page and 60 kbytes for two sides of a cheque.

JPEG is an option in most commercial DIP applications.

The original JPEG algorithms are based on a technique called discrete cosine transform (DCT). This is based on comparison of adjacent pixels, and becomes very grainy at high degrees of compression. An enhanced version of JPEG with higher degrees of compression is likely before long, probably based on the newer fractal transform technology (FTT – see section called Proprietary standards below). FTT can give two to three times the degree of compression of DCT and has a more pleasing appearance as it does not appear grainy at high resolution.

Although JPEG is primarily intended for still images, it is also sometimes used with video to give higher quality images than with MPEG (see below), but using higher bandwidth. Non-destructive compression can be configured to give a reduction by about 4:1 to 15:1, as compared to about 30:1 for the document image applications. This 'motion JPEG' is used in quite a lot of video-conferencing applications.

In video applications with motion JPEG, the ratio of the largest JPEG frame to the smallest is about 3:1, so if carried on an isochronous channel, the bandwidth needs to be about 50% higher than the average throughput to allow frames to be presented at a uniform rate.

JBIG (Joint Bilevel Image Group)

This is another set of image compression standards based on DCT. This standard covers bilevel images plus some colour and grey scale. Its best level of compression is on grey scale images, where its factor of 30 gives superior results to fax.

Even when compression is used, DIP is still much more bandwidth hungry than ASCII text files, since an A4 page of text only requires about 3 kbytes. Printer text files using soft fonts, such as PostScript, increase this to at least 6 kbytes. Allowing for network overheads a 64 kbps WAN link can only support a throughput of about 6 JPEG black and white pages per minute. The response time at this speed for an office worker faced with a customer would be about the worst that might be acceptable.

Proprietary standards

The use of advances in the mathematical theory of fractals for compression runs ahead of most standards bodies, so greater degrees of compression can be obtained by the latest non-standard FTT techniques. The extreme case is the (destructive) compression of an A4 page of black and white text to only 2–3 kbytes, as for native ASCII text, with special image-enhancing software to improve the transmitted image.

Fractals provide a more natural look than JPEG for still images, but despite this are probably less accurate than JPEG for degrees of compression below 30–40:1. Thus they are better for things like advertising copy that need to look nice, but worse for engineering drawings. A disadvantage of fractals is that early algorithms are very processor intensive.

Wavelets are another emerging non-standard technique offering high compression.

8.5.9   Graphics imaging

The image quality required for some applications such as medical X-rays and CAD/CAM coloured diagrams has a much greater bandwidth requirement than the DIP systems above. Before compression, the volume of a single full image is in the range 1–10 Mbytes, with non-destructive compression reducing this by a factor of about 10. Acceptable WAN performance for transfer of such images will need at least T1/E1 bandwidth, and considerably more if heavy use by multiple users is anticipated.

8.5.10   Video-conferencing

Video-conferencing is a special case of multimedia that allows a much greater degree of compression than would be possible in general. This results from the relatively static nature of the proceedings, whereby it is only necessary to transmit the part of the information that has changed from one frame to the next. This will be facial and body movements, but not the large volume of background information. Special standards apply, of which the most important is ITU-T H.261/320. H.261 supports two scanning modes, CIF (common intermediate format) with 288 lines of 320 pixels per line, and QCIF (quarter CIF) with 144 lines of 176 pixels per line. CIF requires at least 128 kbps, preferably 384 kbps, while QCIF, which is used for small-screen video-telephony, rather than multipoint video-conferencing, can run tolerably well over 64 kbps, with 128 kbps preferable. Some proprietary standards incorporate the latest technology advances and offer better quality, but H.261 is probably more efficient than motion JPEG.

H.320 can also be used at the top end of its bandwidth range for video, although for rapid motion it is not as good as MPEG (see below). H.262 is closely aligned with MPEG-2 for higher resolution.

There is also an emerging H.263 standard for QCIF video-conferencing over V.34 modems. This uses about 6.5 kbps for voice and 20 kbps for video, with some pre-standard versions already available.

ATM switches for multpoint video-conferencing need to be able to support cell replication multicasting as well as AAL1 constant bit-rate operation; many early implementations do not do so (see Chapter 9 for features of ATM and its performance).

8.5.11   Multimedia

Multimedia, particularly full motion video, imposes the greatest strain on the network, but compression is again of vital importance. There are several standards, listed below.

MPEG 1 (Moving Pictures Expert Group)

This standard, based on DCT, allows full video to be transmitted at about 1.5 Mbps to correspond to the normal data rate of a CD-ROM drive, giving quality comparable to VHS home video recordings. This transmits one full frame (image-frame) every 12 frames, and fills in with two types of highly compressed frame (P-frames and B-frames). The overall compression rate is about 20:1, with a maximum of about 200:1. Cuts and sudden movements both cause a temporary degradation of picture quality with this as with any video compression technique. The standard resolution is suitable for quarter screen images, and when used for full screen images these are created by interpolation between the quarter screen bit values, so the extra information is not carried across the network.

There are three possible levels of compression for the audio component, with important differences between them (Table 8.2). Only the first is suitable for interactive use due to problems of lip synchronization with the higher delays of the others.

Almost all MPEG-1 implementations are of a restricted subset, the constrained parameter bit rate (CPB) for 352×240 pixels at 30 frames/s, rather than the maximum $4095 \times 4095 \times 60$. This is for conformance with the CCIR-601 digital TV standard.

The bit rate of MPEG transmissions is variable, with maximum to minimum frame size ratio of about 6:1, and to ensure quality of reception in isochronous systems the maximum bandwidth must be allocated at all times, that is, 1.5 Mbps. This applies to protocols such as IEEE 802.9 (see Chapter 10), ATM AAL1 (see Chapter 9) and circuit switch connections, whereas anisochronous variable bit rate systems, such as ATM AAL2 (if it is eventually implemented), may only average about 1.2 Mbps depending on material.

MPEG-1 is usually regarded as slightly better than ITU-T H.261, particularly if there is a lot of motion, and motion JPEG. Motion JPEG is occcasionally marketed as 'MPEG', but is actually quite different and incompatible.

MPEG 2

This newer standard is intended to provide broadcast quality video over the network. The basic principles of the standard are similar to MPEG 1, but incorporate both empirical improvements to the algorithms and numerous extensions, although MPEG 2 decoders remain backwards compatible with MPEG 1 encoders.

Table 8.2   MPEG audio compression.

Type	Target bit rate	Compression	Min. Delay	Likely delay	Application
Layer 1	192 kbps	4:1	19 ms	50 ms	Digital compact cassette
Layer 2	128 kbps	6–8:1	35 ms	100 ms	DSS satellite broadcast
Layer 3	64 kbps	10–12:1	59 ms	150 ms	ISDN, satellites

MPEG 2 distinguishes between program and transport streams, with the former carrying information about the channels and viewing rights, and the latter carrying the video images. It is thus suitable for much more complex applications than MPEG 1. It will support chrominance formats 4:2:0 and 4:2:2. The normal WAN transport method is again via TDMs or ATM, with inefficient bandwidth utilization due to the variable bit rate.

The transport stream uses 188 byte packets that can be mapped into blocks of four ATM cells in ATM AAL1 or a pair of packets into eight cells with AAL5 (see Chapter 9 for ATM). The ability to use AAL5 is the result of the transport packets containing timing information in three fields, namely the program reference clock (PCR), decoding timestamp (DTS) and presentation timestamp (PTS). This timing information is much more comprehensive than that present in ATM's AAL1 cells, so AAL5 is slightly preferable to AAL1 on account of its ability to support variable bit rates and the 32 bit CRC field which provides some error correction. The disadvantage of AAL5 is that, in most implementations, it is given a lower priority than CBR and hence a greater probability of cell loss; in addition its headers are too simple to allow description of all MPEG 2 functions. Some ATM switches however have the option of treating AAL5 VBR services on the same priority as CBR or to use proprietary VBR modifications to AAL1, so the best transmission technique to use is dependent on proprietary switch features at present.

PCR allows accurate matching of transmit and receive clocks, while the timestamps allow some correction for variable ATM cell delay plus the ability to support programming features such as slow motion and pause.

Video quality is related to the compression options used, influencing the bandwidth needed and degree of buffering in the decoder. High degrees of compression require more buffering in the decoder and also entail longer delays. This is particularly associated with the B-frames in MPEG. For interactive real-time displays these delays of 50–150 ms are a major problem, but not an issue for replay of recorded material.

MPEG 2 also has the ability to support data partitioning so that different aspects of the data can be sent across different paths between transmitter and receiver, or with different priority levels over the same path according to importance. This feature could be used to ensure that the vital I-frames had precedence in the event of network congestion, thereby making the best use of bandwidth.

MPEG 3

This standard intended for HDTV has been dropped in favour of MPEG 2.

MPEG 4

This is a projected low bit rate standard, intended to enable some form of motion video to be carried across dial-up or mobile communications links with about 4.8 up to 64 kbps of bandwidth. The target quality of MPEG 4 is 10 frames per second of resolution 176 × 144 pixels.

Indeo III

This is Intel's standard for full motion video on PCs. The bandwidth required is again around 1.5 Mbps to conform with CD-drives.

Proprietary standards

The reading rate of CD-drives for PCs is rapidly increasing, with speeds up to about 6 Mbps fairly common. Where such devices are networked there will be a corresponding WAN bandwidth requirement if the superior quality is to be maintained across the network.

Granny phones

Very poor quality moving images can be sent over analog links with modems, the traditional application being to enable grannies to see their descendants who live a long way off. The main criterion is to choose the best modem possible for the job; this is normally V.34. MPEG 4 over basic-rate ISDN should be slightly better than this.

Interactive video games

The minimum human visually detectable interval is about 35 ms, so for optimum performance of arcade-style games over a network it is desirable that the roundtrip delay should not exceed this. As most such games are played from home this is difficult to achieve. High-speed modems can be counterproductive due to their high latencies, where the filter delays alone exceed this. As the bursts of data representing joystick movements are very small it is best to use a lower-speed standard with small filter delays, such as V.29 or V.32 at 9600 bps, on a modern multistandard V.34 modem rather than V.34 itself. Error correction and data compression should be switched off for minimum latency. A much better solution is to use ISDN, as the latencies of an ISDN card or terminal adaptor for a single 64 kbps B-channel is only a few milliseconds.

8.5.12   Security issues

Where security is important additional delays will be incurred. The first of these occurs at log-on. The sequence for this is liable to involve exchange of encryption keys plus the issue of a privilege access certificate (PAC). The PAC enables unitary login, whereby the user can log on to any other host directly by hot-keying and sending the PAC to the new host without having to repeat the security exchanges individually. The typical size of a PAC is in the region of 1000 bytes, so it is a significant source of session establishment delay on slow WAN links. Negotiation and PAC distribution is liable to take one or two seconds.

Use of datacryptors also adds significantly to transmission delays, usually by a few milliseconds. Another performance factor associated with datacryptors is the effect of encryption key changes. This usually causes a loss of service for 0.5 to 2 seconds so, to prevent loss of sessions, the transport protocol parameters need to be set to allow for this.

9

Cell Relay Networks

9.1 Introduction

With all of the network technologies discussed so far in this book, the WAN has been the main bottleneck, but with cell relay this may no longer be the case. Cell relay is designed to take advantage of the high bandwidths potentially available from optical fibre. A typical bandwidth of an individual fibre is 25 GHz, while the financial cost is largely that of the installation of the fibre. This raises the possibility with cost-based tariffs of very much lower charges per unit bandwidth than has hitherto been available over the WAN.

The principles of cell relay are very similar to those of frame relay, but with short fixed length cells. The reason for this structure is to keep queuing delays short and hence eliminate jitter on multimedia services. A second important advantage is that it makes it much easier for the routing of cells to be implemented in hardware, thereby allowing operations at higher speed than would be possible for something done by software.

There are three main cell relay technologies, IEEE802.6 MAN (metropolitan area network), SMDS (switched multi-megabit data services) and ATM (asynchronous transfer mode). This chapter examines the overheads and performance issues associated with each. What is common to all three is the use of 48 byte cells with 5 bytes of additional header, however there is also control information within the cells that depends on the protocol.

9.2 IEEE 802.6 MAN

The MAN is based on the dual queue dual bus architecture in which there are two independent queues, one onto each bus. The technique is normally provided as a public network service with range up to 250 km and speeds initially from 34 Mbps access up to 155 Mbps, with 622 Mbps later. Two types of service are provided, pre-arbitrated (PA) and queued arbitrated (QA). Of these the former uses reserved bandwidth for constant bit rate services like voice and video, while the queued service is used by variable bit rate activities, such as LAN interconnect. MANs are normally configured as looped bus topologies (see Figure 9.1) in which single faults are isolated.

In Figure 9.1 the heads of buses A and B are both at Node 0, with the dotted line at that node indicating a logical break. When a failure causes a physical break, then the logical break is sealed and the two heads move to either side of the break. Nodes are attached to both buses and attempt to put traffic onto both as indicated by arrows.

Data is input to the MAN in the form of normal level 2 MAC frames, usually referred to as service data units (SDU), which can contain from 1 up to 9188 bytes. The MAN protocol stack adds large initial MAC protocol data unit headers and trailers to form the IMPDU, which is then segmented into 48 byte cells. The

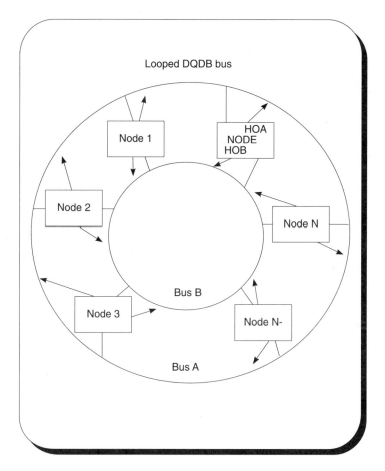

Figure 9.1   Looped DQDB BUS.

IMPDU header is from 24 to 26 bytes long with its structure as shown below, while the trailer has a further 4 bytes.

Field	RES	BEtag	BAsize	DA	SA	PI	QOS	BDG	HDRex
Size	1	1	2	8	8	1	1	2	0–2

Of these fields, the first three form the common PDU header, while the remainder constitute the MAC convergence protocol (MCP) header which depends on the MAC level protocol. The RES field is reserved, BEtag is a beginning/end tag used in reassembling cells into IMPDUs, BAsize is a buffer allocation size for the original data unit, DA and SA are destination and source addresses, but with undefined format, PI is a protocol identifier for the upper layers, QOS is an undefined quality of service field to which the header extension length is appended, BDG identifies the bridging protocol used between LANs and HDRex is an optional header extension. The trailer has a reserved one-byte field, a matching BEtag and a length field for the MCP header plus data.

Each level 3 IMPDU is then segmented into individual 48 byte cells, consisting of up to 44 bytes of the IMPDU plus level 2 header and trailer data as shown below:

Field	ST	MID	IMPDU data	PL	CRC
Size (bits)	2	14	352	6	10

where ST denotes the type of segment, that is, beginning, continuation or end of message, MID is a message identifier, PL is the length of the payload field and CRC is the cell checksum. Each cell then acquires a 4 byte cell header consisting of a network-wide virtual channel identifier, payload type, priority and their own checksum. A one-byte access control is then prepended for MAN slot control.

The large volume of header information means that performance can be wasteful of bandwidth with some traffic types. The extreme case is TCP/IP terminal server traffic with one user byte per Ethernet frame. In addition to the 64 byte Ethernet frame there now has to be added 24 bytes of IMPDU header and 4 bytes of trailer, giving a total of 92 bytes before segmentation into cells. Each cell contains 44 bytes of payload, so three cells are required, entailing a further 27 bytes of header, so each user character ends up with 118 bytes of overhead. Because of the high speed of the MAN, performance will still be perfectly acceptable at up to 40 000 user characters per second on a 34 Mbps MAN, but the costs may not be. Delay sensitive interactive QA traffic can be given priority over QA file transfers by means of the priority field.

For file transfers with large frame sizes and video traffic the overhead is proportionately reasonably small, being about 2% for the IMPDU headers and 20% for the cells, and these are the types of traffic for which the MAN is really intended. Jitter is eliminated for the video traffic by the use of the pre-arbitrated slots, whereby traffic is sent at regular intervals rather than with variable delay. Even the QA slots would give acceptable jitter at all but very heavy loads, because of the short cells and high bandwidth as the maximum acceptable value of 20 ms corresponds to about 1600 cells at 34 Mbps, or 6400 at 155 Mbps. Using MPEG compressed video a MAN could support about 10 video channels (plus some QA data) at 34 Mbps and 40 at 155 Mbps.

PA slots for isochronous traffic are not sent at a completely uniform rate, but rather at a guaranteed average rate that depends on the head of the bus. This guaranteed rate for isochronous traffic is based on using 'M slots every N frames', where the minimum set of such rates that the DQDB head of bus must support is shown in Table 9.1.

The minimal rate is thus suitable for an uncompressed digital voice channels, while the higher rates are those typical of video-conferencing, compressed video and PABX backplanes. Some implementations provide additional rates, such as 32 kbps for ADPCM. Apart from these basic rates, compound rates of the form 'M1 slots every N1 frames plus M2 slots every N2 frames...' can be created to give more flexible definition of isochronous channels. The basic frames have a 125 microsecond duration as in digital voice.

Table 9.1   DQDB slot frequencies.

Data rate (kbps)	M	N
64	1	48
192	1	16
384	1	8
768	1	4
1536	1	2
2048	2	3
6144	2	1
9216	3	1

The original DQDB protocol and an upgrade, usually referred to as new DQDB, both show a bias towards the stations near the head of the bus as regards throughput and access delay at very high loads, so IEEE 802.6 uses a further modification to minimize this. The extra feature is the bandwidth balancing module (BWB), with which is associated another counter, the bandwidth balancing counter, and a bandwidth balancing modulus parameter. The value of this parameter controls efficacy of the BWB; zero deactivates it and higher values increase the effect, while 8 is the recommended value. This value is the same for both buses and all nodes. A transmitting node increments the bandwidth balancing counter each time that it captures a free slot until the count reaches 7; the node must then skip a free slot on its next turn to transmit, whereupon the counter is reset. This mechanism leads to equal throughputs and access delays provided that there is only one priority level. DQDB supports three levels of priority in principle, but bias reappears in the lower priorities if they are implemented. In the QA prioritization suggested above, this will mean that file transfer throughputs are dependent on station position on the bus when the MAN approaches saturation, but at light loads there should not be a problem. The stations near the head ends are the beneficiaries, and those in the middle the losers.

9.3   SMDS/CBDS

SMDS (switched multimegabit data services) and its European equivalent, CBDS (connectionless broadband data service), use the same dual queue dual bus technology as the MAN initially, but without pre-arbitrated slots and other minor differences, and support data only. As such, SMDS/CBDS is strictly a set of service definitions rather than an independent technology, and can run over ATM in future. CBDS encompasses a wider range of potential services than SMDS, but coincides apart from terminology for the LAN interconnect service defined by SMDS. It is

Table 9.2   Standard SIRs.

Class	SIR (Mbps)
1	4
2	10
3	16
4	25
5	34*

intended to run at lower speeds than a MAN initially, typically from 2 Mbps up to 45 Mbps, with easier implementation. The physical medium used consists of mainly T3 (45 Mbps) circuits in the USA and E3 (34 Mbps) in Europe. The user subscribes to any one of several subscriber interface rates (SIR) as shown in Table 9.2 that correspond to common LAN speeds.

Of these classes, the last is not available in Europe owing to the lower speed of an E3 circuit. Some European services offer an E1 interface with SIR of 1.47 Mbps also; the reason for this being less than 2 Mbps is the need to allow for the high overheads of SMDS. In addition to these main classes, a lot of carriers have also introduced lower rates, such as 0.5 Mbps.

SMDS uses a subscriber interface protocol (SIP) that is very similar to that for a MAN, but with different interpretations of some of the IMPDU header fields. Unlike a MAN, the format of the address fields is specified for SMDS, with each address split into a 4 bit type field and a 60 bit address conforming to a 10 digit address. The main differences are that the header extension field is used and contains the SMDS version number and carrier selection information.

The cell structure comprises standard 53 byte ATM cells (see Section 9.4) consisting of 5 bytes header and a nominal 48 bytes of payload, which has to contain another 4 bytes of control information; this is the cause of the SIRs being a lot less than the theoretical circuit bandwidth. The level 2 headers for these cells are also slightly different to those for 802.6 and are shown below.

Field	AC	NC	ST	SN	MID	DATA	PL	CRC
Size	8	32	2	4	10	to 352	6	10

AC, ST, MID, PL and CRC are as in a MAN, but the remainder differ. The NCI field (network control information) is not actually used, SN is a sequence number.

Performance considerations are fairly similar to a MAN for data, but SMDS does not have the notion of PA slots and is not intended to carry constant bit rate traffic such as voice and video, although the European CBDS definition does allow for this.

The IEEE 802.1D standard for spanning tree is being extended to cater for MAN bridges. Interconnection via routers is possible using high-speed interfaces, such as HSSI at 52 Mbps.

A fundamental difference between SMDS and ATM is that the former is connectionless, thereby making the support for traditional LAN protocols easier, but

Table 9.3   SMDS error guarantees.

Fault	Max ratio allowed
Containing error	5 in 10^{13}
Misdelivered	5 in 10^8
Not delivered	1 in 10^4
Duplicate	5 in 10^8

leading to heavier loads on the WAN. The main function of SMDS services is to provide LAN interconnect at higher speeds than frame relay can provide. The normal LAN interface is via a DSU and a router that supports DXI on high speed, such as HSSI, interfaces. The DXI interface only requires the router to support variable length frames with a specific HDLC header for SMDS along with some extra network management features; all the cell segmentation and reassembly is performed by the DSU.

A significant drawback of SMDS is the lack of any congestion control, with adherence of users to agreed SIRs the only limiting factor. As a result, networks supporting SMDS need to be designed to operate at lighter loads than would be the case for more controlled protocols, while users need to have end protocols that support their own flow control, such as TCP/IP but not UDP.

9.3.1   Performance guarantees

The SMDS specification guarantees several quality-of-service parameters. The FILO transit time of SMDS for DS3 access/egress (that is, T3 in USA and E3 in Europe) is 95% within 20 ms for a maximum 9188 data byte L3 IMPDU. Some networks also quote figures for slower speed access, such as 140 ms for T1 access/egress and 80 ms for T1 at one end and T3 at the other. The other guarantees are for the proportion of PDUs that are unsatisfactory, as shown in Table 9.3.

9.4   ATM

Asynchronous transfer mode is the basis for broadband ISDN and has also been developed for high-speed LANs. Unlike MANs the hardware architecture does not have a shared bus; instead cells are switched by the hardware on the basis of their header information. Cells are divided into isochronous and anisochronous. The former are provided at constant intervals to carry the constant bit rate traffic, while the latter are used for the variable bit rate traffic. ATM is entirely connection oriented, with users identified by virtual channel information in the cell headers. There is no error correction, so this must be provided by the upper layers of the user protocol. Cells that display a CRC error are merely dropped.

ATM cells have 48 bytes with a 5 byte header, so that level 2 overheads are always at least 12%, which is higher than old packet protocols. Some proprietary implementations of ATM only use the 48 byte cells at the network periphery, and have larger cells on internal trunks to increase efficiency for data-only services. The structure of the header varies according to whether the cell is at the user network interface (UNI) or an internal network-node interface. These two header types are shown below.

Field	GFC	VPI	VCI	PT	R	C	HEC	DATA
Size (bits)	4	8	16	2	1	1	8	to 352

GFC is a generic flow control field for helping to control access to the network. In the ATM Forum's UNI version 3.0 the GFC is set to zero. VPI identifies the virtual path, which is a bundle of virtual circuits that have the same network end-points. The virtual channel identifier is a unidirectional link identifier of a virtual circuit that is set up at the time that a VC is switched. The set of all VCIs for a given call across the network is the virtual channel connection (VCC). VPI and VCI are specific to individual links, and change across the network, so do not constitute an addressing limitation. PT is the payload type, where 00 stands for user traffic. R is reserved and C is the cell loss priority bit (CLP) which controls load shedding in a similar manner to frame relay's DE bit. HEC is an error check field for the header (only).

Within the network the GFC field is dropped and the VPI field extended to 24 bits.

The payload type is important to the limited congestion control available in early versions of ATM. The individual bit patterns and their interpretation is shown in Table 9.4.

In this table, type 1 cells are the last for the higher-level packet to which they belong, while the remainder, including the first, are type 0 continuation cells. The end ATM device passes all accumulated cells up to its segmentation and reassembly (SAR) layer on receipt of a type 1 cell. ATM switches set the second bit to one for these cells if they experience congestion, but do not reset them if already set. This means that the receiver obtains an indication that congestion exists within the ATM network; it is then up to the receiver to pass this back to the sender in order to reduce the traffic. In early implementations this information is usually ignored.

Table 9.4   ATM payload types.

Value	Interpretation
'000	User data cell type 0, no congestion
'001	User data cell type 1, no congestion
'010	User data cell type 0, congestion experienced
'011	User data cell type 1, congestion experienced
'100	Management cell for segment
'101	Management cell for end–end flow
'110	Explicit forward congestion indicator (EFCI)
'111	Reserved for future use

The explicit forward congestion indicator (EFCI) is analogous to the FECN in frame relay, and is the most basic of several mechanisms for congestion control within the ATM network used with the ATM Forum's UNI version 4. It requires that the end-station cut back transmission in a series of steps until the EFCI is reset for a significant number of cells.

Routing is performed at the VC level, with incoming VCIs on one link switched by hardware to VCIs on outgoing links. Two different VCs that belong to different VPs at a particular node are allowed to have equal VCIs there. Best switch performance occurs if as much as possible of the routing is done by means of the VPIs without having to go down to the individual VCIs, however switch processing time is negligible compared to propagation delay.

The most complex part of ATM is the ATM adaption layer (AAL) at the periphery of the network where external traffic is formatted for the ATM network, with many issues still surrounding the conversion of connectionless LAN traffic to the connection-oriented form for ATM. Typical problems are the need for cell replication where multicast or broadcast connectionless traffic occurs, with greatest efficiency occurring where as much as possible of this functionality is spoofed using address caching facilities at the periphery.

One of the biggest factors affecting performance is the question of dropping cells. Normally a higher-level, typically transport layer, data unit will contain many cells and, if any one of the cells is dropped, then the entire data unit will be retransmitted, possibly causing the congestion to become much worse. For this reason it is important that as much congestion control as possible should occur at the edge of the ATM network, so that whole data units are dropped at the periphery instead of isolated cells in the middle. Sensitivity to dropping cells varies according to the type of traffic. The ITU-T standards define four classes of traffic, A to D, with differing performance criteria as listed in Tables 9.5 and 9.6, to which the ATM Forum added class X with class Y appearing for available bit rate service.

Table 9.5   ATM traffic classes.

Class	Features
A	Constant bit rate, connection-oriented e.g high resolution video
B	Variable bit rate, connection-oriented, timing coordination e.g interactive compressed video
C	Variable bit rate, connection-oriented, no timing coordination e.g X.25, TCP, frame relay
D	Variable bit rate, connectionless, no timing coordination e.g LAN traffic without transport layer
X	Undeclared bit rate, no timing coordination, low priority

Table 9.6   Principal ATM performance parameters.

Call parameter	Connection parameter	A	B	C/D
Throughput	Peak rate	X	X	X
	Sustainable cell rate	–	X	X
	Committed burst size	–	–	X
	Minimum burst size	–	–	X
Delay	Mean transit delay	–	–	X
	Maximum transit delay	X	X	–
Accuracy	Rate of cell loss	X	X	X
	Bit error rate	X	X	–

Cell loss is much less critical for classes A/B than for C/D since the human senses readily gloss over small quantities of missing information, whereas computerized data transactions have to be accurate in most cases, particularly Class C. As a result, classes A/B should have a higher cell loss priority than C/D, although their timing requirements are much stricter.

The AAL provides five formats, AAL1– AAL5 for these four classes of traffic, plus another called AAL0 for future applications that interface directly to an ATM API. AAL1 and AAL2 are for A and B respectively, but AAL5 is a low overhead alternative to AAL3/4 for classes C/D. These formats for the 48 byte data part of an ATM cell are shown in Table 9.7.

In this table, SEQ. PROT denotes a protection field for the Sequence number that is checked at each ATM node, the Length field refers to the length of data in the payload field, while for AAL4 the full header should be concatenated to become equivalent to the message identifier (MID) of MANs and SMDS. Using AAL4 for general connectionless LAN traffic would be very inefficient on account of the large header within the 48 byte cell, so AAL5 has been developed for those protocols that do not need the sequencing and checking procedures and to allow payload alignment with computer word boundaries; most current protocols that have a connection-oriented layer are likely to use it. The CRC error checks in types AAL2-4 are able to correct single bit errors.

Table 9.7   ATM adapation layer types.

AAL1	SEQ. #	SEQ. PROT	–	Payload	–	–
Length	4 bits	4	0	47 bytes	0	0
AAL2	SEQ. #	Not defined	–	Payload	Length	CRC
	4	4	0	45 bytes	6	10
AAL3	SEQ.TYPE	SEQ. #	Reserved	Payload	Length	CRC
	2	4	10	44 bytes	6	10
AAL4	SEQ.TYPE	SEQ. #	Part of MID	Payload	Length	CRC
	2	4	10	44 bytes	6	10
AAL5	–	–	–	Payload	–	–
	0	0	0	48 bytes	0	0

Such cells are corrected before being passed up to a higher layer in the ATM switch, while cells with multiple errors are dropped. In AAL5 the last of the cells defining a single data unit contains padding and a 32 bit CRC check for the whole unit.

These standard formats were still under study at the time of writing, with the expectation of further changes. In particular, AAL2 does not appear to be very useful and may be dropped altogether, while AAL3 is likely to be merged with AAL4, with AAL5 used as the main format for CONS data services.

For early data applications, UBR class X traffic using AAL5 is the norm. The cell loss priority is always set to one for UBR traffic, so these cells are the first to be dropped if congestion occurs.

AAI for voice is inefficient and costly as it uses nailed up bandwidth, especially with PVCs, like an old fashioned TDM. For T3 and above it is scarcely necessary to use CBR, and proprietary VBR for voice with extra priority and timing is much more cost-effective. The emerging AAL6 for low bit rate voice will be better.

9.4.1   Physical medium

ATM was originally designed to carry broadband ISDN over SDH/SONET networks, but the greater drive for high-speed LAN interconnection has led to other media also being used. These include the T3/E3 circuits of the older PDH system, local fibre with 4B/5B or 8B/10B encoding, STP with 8B/10B , UTP level 5 over SONET STS-3c and posibly UTP level 3 over SONET STS-1. Each of these standards has its own framing structure.

Several of these coding schemes are associated with specific ways of implementing local ATM. The lowest speed seriously proposed for this environment is 25.6 Mbps by IBM, and is now accepted by the ATM Forum. This uses the same 32 MHz transceivers and UTP/STP wiring as for 16 Mbps Token Ring, but with 4B/5B instead of Manchester encoding. The 32 MHz frequency should be free from emission problems. The relatively low speed should be suitable for workstation clients, but not for multimedia servers nor for many isochronous services.

The lowest LATM speed proposed by the ATM Forum was originally 51.8 Mbps, over category 5 UTP or STP type 1, but the lower speed of 25.6 Mbps (not a submultiple of 51.8) was subsequently adopted also. This is intended for multimedia workstations, with servers using 155.3 Mbps.

ATM cells over SDH/SONET were originally expected to be identified by means of a pointer in the SDH path overhead, but this idea has been dropped in favour of a method of hunting for the header error check (HEC) of the cell and relying on the standard length to confirm this, by locating subsequent HECs in the expected positions. Timing issues regarding maintenance of the transmitter clock require that the cell payload be scrambled when using SDH/SONET; this increases the processor load significantly unless performed in hardware.

Scramblers themselves can go wrong if the cell being transmitted contains the polynomial scrambler itself. An alternative approach to timing is the use of block coded transmissions. This is the principle that is used in ATM over fibre or STP. Cells are delineated in these systems by means of control codes that do not correspond to any possible user data.

Each of these encoding techniques entails a significant overhead. In the case of SDH/SONET STS-3c, a 2430 byte frame contains 9 rows, each of which has 10 bytes of overhead and 260 of payload, so that only 149.7 Mbps of the 155.5 Mbps bandwidth is available for the 53 byte cells. Similarly, for ATM over DS-3 circuits, each 53 byte cell also has a 4 byte DS-3 header, so that out of the total 44.7 Mbps, the part available for the user cells is about 41.5 Mbps.

9.4.2   Call set up

This is one of the areas in which a great deal of standardization remained to be agreed at the time of writing. Early implementations employ PVCs only, with the intention to support SVCs through a development of ITU-T's Q.931 signalling scheme for ISDN. The ITU-T protocol is called Q.2931 (formerly Q.93B), and will support multiple types of network address, but probably not multicast. The latter is vital for traditional LAN traffic, so will be supported in an alternative standard from the ATM Forum. In the case of PVCs multicast is supported by replicating cells onto different VPI/VCI at each switch in a preconfigured manner analogous to that for frame relay.

Congestion control was also still under definition at the time of writing; in particular the contents and usage of the GFC field in the ATM header were undefined. In the absence of standards various proprietary schemes are being used. One of the most logical is to use management traffic to signal back congestion levels in the network whenever a threshold is exceeded that is liable to cause cell loss. The peripheral nodes then drop complete incoming frames for AAL3–5 on a priority/route basis to ensure that loss of a single cell does not entail retransmission of the entire frame across the congested area; furthermore they should ideally recognize that a cell has been dropped when that happens and stop further transmission of cells belonging to the same frame, that is, until after the next type 1 cell. If this is not done, then in the worst case of a 9188 byte IMPDU loss of one 48 byte cell would entail retransmission of amost 200 times as much, thereby making congestion worse. This multiplier effect means that random dropping of cells is far more serious in ATM than the widespread dropping of frames by bridges and routers in response to congestion. Some pioneering networks just duck the issue by designing the network for low traffic levels throughout, so that there is little possibility of congestion occurring, but it is difficult for carriers to provide competitive tariffs on a long-term basis this way.

Cell loss is much less reliable for congestion control than dropping frames in frame relay, and whatever proprietary scheme is used it has to be able to at least concentrate on dropping cells for specific VCIs rather than at random, even if it cannot select cells belonging to specific frames.

The main form of congestion control proposed is to monitor the rate of data access in relation to an agreed sustainable cell rate, and to tag any cells in excess of this rate. If congestion occurs, these cells should be dropped in preference to untagged cells. This mechanism does tend to tag all the cells in a frame, so long as the time intervals used in checking the traffic rate are long compared to the transmission time of a frame. This does not prevent retransmission of affected frames, but does achieve the concentration effect, provided that the core ATM network has been designed to carry all the full subscribed rates simultaneously.

Version 3.0 of the ATM Forum's user network interface specification defines the quality-of-service parameters:

- Sustainable cell rate (SCR) is the upper limit for transmission of ATM cells. It should be used by the network to allocate sufficient resources.

- Peak cell rate (PCR) is the maximum manageable rate of cell transmission.

- Minimum cell rate (MCR) is a minimum cell rate specified by the user and relevant to ABR.

- Cell transfer delay (CTD) is the maximum permissible cell transfer delay specified on a FILO basis.

- Cell delay variation (CDV) sets a limit to the jitter for various classes of traffic.

- Cell loss ratio (CLR) is the percentage of cells lost in the network due to errors or congestion.

- Burst tolerance (BT) is the maximum burst size that can be sent at the peak rate.

- Maximum burst size (MBS) is the maximum number of back-to-back cells that can be sent at the peak rate.

BT and MBS are related via the formula:

$$BT = (MBS - 1) * (1/SCR - 1/PCR)$$

Associated with these parameters are a number of procedures for congestion control, notably the following:

- Connection admission control (CAC) which checks to see if sufficient resources are available before setting up an SVC.

- Usage parameter control (UPC), whereby connections are monitored to stay within the specified quality-of-service parameters negotiated, for example PCR and MBS.

- Traffic shaping, whereby buffering at the edge of the network is used to bring excess traffic within the specified parameters.

Some early implementations also use other monitoring functions. For example, AT&T's Reliaburst mechanism. In this the access and egress ports are both monitored on a millisecond basis, with information from the latter as to capacity in relation to CIRs being passed back to the former. This indication of spare bandwidth is then used to decide how much of any excess over their CIRs the users can transmit into the network. The disadvantage of this is that it uses a significant amount of bandwidth itself.

9.4.3 ABR (available bit rate) flow control

Flow control becomes both more important and harder for those services that set up SVCs to use available bandwidth rather than PVCs as traffic is much less predictable. Without good congestion control there would be a very serious risk of avalanche decay resulting from dropping of a few cells leading to massive retransmissions of frames.

In order to achieve this there is an initial cell rate (ICR) to ensure that an especially low start-up rate is used and additional resource management (RM) cells within the network to control changes of rate. These are sent at regular intervals by the source, and contain fields such as a congestion indicator (CI), no increase allowed (NI), explicit rate limit (ER), current cell rate (CCR) and the MCR. If backwards CI and NI are both zero, then a source can increase its traffic in steps based on an agreed additive increase rate (AIR). If the destination sees the EFCI bit set in ordinary cells or CI in RM cells, then it should set CI in return RM cells to tell the source to slow down. ATM network switches set the EFCI, CI and NI fields in the light of the current situation. They can also trigger a faster response to congestion by reducing the explicit rate field, particularly by generating backwards RM cells containing the reduction.

This mechanism works on a per VC basis and gives much finer control than is possible with EFCI alone.

Full details of this scheme and its efficacy were not available at the time of writing of this book.

9.4.4 Support for other services

Unlike IEEE 802.6 and SMDS, ATM is suitable for the transport of other services. The use of AAL3/4 cells to carry 802.6 and SMDS cells has already been mentioned. In addition, there is an emerging standard, ITU-T I.555, for the transport of frame relay traffic over ATM. This adds ATM headers to those already present for frame relay so for a given speed is less efficient than pure frame relay. The reason for using it is that ATM services run at much higher speeds than frame relay, so response time will be reduced by going over a high-speed ATM backbone. As both frame relay and ATM are connection oriented, no special problems arise from this. Frame relay makes use of AAL5 cells, so the extra overhead is about 11%.

This is not the case for LAN emulation, where Ethernet or Token Ring is being transported. The simplest effect is the addition of a LAN emulation cell identifier to each frame. This identifier consists of two bytes for Ethernet, but four for Token Ring, while FDDI is not supported in the first version.

Frame relay over ATM

Frame relay is transported over ATM using AAL5 via an ATM DXI interface to a T1/E1 DSU, with the flags and CRC of the frames dropped before segmentation. There are two multiplexing options that can be used, (a) one frame relay DLCI to one ATM VPI/VCI, and (b) many DLCIs to one ATM VPI/VCI subject to the DLCIs all having the same destination. The latter is less resource intensive, and cheaper on public networks, but if different quality of service or destination is needed, then the former has to be used.

Frame relay support over ATM uses schemes for mapping the FECN, BECN and DE bits into associated ATM bits, the EFCI and CLP. For the transition from frame relay to ATM, the DE bit is copied to the CLP bit of each of the cells associated with the frame, and similarly for the FECN and EFCI bits. ATM has no analog of the BECN, so this is simulated by setting the EFCI bit in the last cell (that is, Type 1) of a frame going in the opposite direction. For the reverse transition from ATM to frame relay, the CLP bits of all the cells of a frame are OR'd together, so that if any one CLP bit is set, then the frame DE bit is set, and similarly for the EFCI bits and FECN. More details of this can be found in the Frame Relay Forum's document FRF.5.

The above approach is based on the the the use of the ATM DXI interface at the periphery of a high-speed ATM WAN, but there is another standard for low-speed (fractional T1/E1) WAN access to an ATM core; this is FUNI (frame relay user network interface). ATM overheads are too high to be desirable on low-speed access circuits, and segmentation/reassembly is done on the switch using FUNI frames. FUNI frames do not use FECN/BECN and DE bits, but a CN congestion bit analogous to FECN and CLP bit that map directly onto ATM equivalents.

Effect of data protocol windows

Because ATM runs at very high speeds, the effects of propagation delay and end–end windowing flow-control mechanisms are exceptionally drastic on such WANs. The high speed means that for long-distance circuits, the main network source of delay is the propagation delay rather than the data transmission time. In many instances segmentation and reassembly in the ATM adaptor card will also cause a delay of several milliseconds, but switching time in ATM hardware is negligible. The window size required to give uninterrupted throughput is, as usual, given by the bit rate of the circuit times the response time. Figure 9.2 shows the window size required to obtain T1, T3 or OC-3 bandwidth saturation via a single virtual circuit for various lengths ignoring the adaptor delays which make the situation worse.

In the extreme case of a terrestrial international circuit of 10 000 miles length, the window size needed is about 4 megabytes for T3 throughput, far exceeding the maximum for many current protocols. This means that an application such as financial database synchronization between London and Tokyo which might require 100 Mbps throughput could not achieve more than about 300 kbps over a

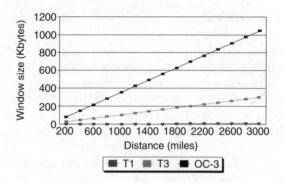

Figure 9.2   Line saturation window size.

single ordinary TCP/IP session, with even lower values for many other protocols as shown later. In the case of TCP, the window size problem is solved by the optional window scale factor; using the maximum permitted window scale factor the peak configurable window size is just over 1000 Mbytes.

The best other protocol with end–end windowing is OSI TP4, using large packets and windows as for satellite links, where a similar phenomenon occurs at much lower speeds (see Chapter 10). With TPDUs of up to 8192 bytes and windows of up to 32 767 such units and corresponding end-station buffering, TP4 can provide the full bandwidth on a single connection. The other rate limiting factor for a single ATM VC is the bit error rate. For a mixture of optical fibre trunks and local UTP wiring, the best error rate obtainable is likely to be about 1 in 10^9, thereby limiting the window size to about 10 Mbytes. To go above this it is probably necessary to use end–end optical fibre.

For more normal links of a few hundred miles or kilometres, many end–end flow control mechanisms still limit the maximum throughput of a single circuit to

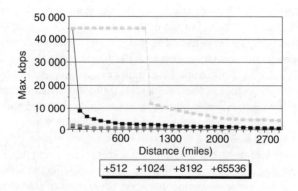

Figure 9.3   WIndow size and ATM throughput.

much less than OC-3 capability, and some examples are shown in Figure 9.3 for various distances. Window size of 512 bytes is characteristic of TFTP and IPX ex burst mode, 8192 bytes for NFS version 2 and 65536 for NFS version 3, IPX burst mode and TCP/IP ex window scale.

In many cases, the buffer capacity of a server limits the effective maximum window to 64 kbytes, so that the data communications protocol does not introduce a limitation not already inherent in the system. For more powerful super-servers this buffer limit is at least a megabyte, so several guidelines have to be observed when running long distances over OC-3 or faster circuits:

- Restrict major synchronization point frequency to less than once per megabyte.
- Either avoid other forms of end–end acknowledgement, or find a protocol stack, such as TP4 or TCP plus window scale, which allows a total window of at least a megabyte.

Protocols like IPX, AppleTalk and VINES require modification to support end–end windows of at least a megabyte if they are to be usable for very high speed file transfers over ATM (or anything else operating at high speeds). The forthcoming IP ng does not do this itself as it is a TCP function and covered by the window scaling option defined in RFC 1323. This is a one byte field used at connection set up to indicate that window sizes returned in TCP segments are to be multiplied by a power of two specified by the value of this field. To allow windows of one megabyte, window scales of at least 4 are needed .

New native ATM AAL0 file transfer applications seem the proper long-term solution to this problem, along with AAL5 for OSI TP4 or TCP/IP with window scaling and timestamp.

Voice and video do not normally have any problems of this nature owing to the lack of any end–end acknowledgements.

LAN bridging over ATM networks

The simplest method of carrying LAN traffic over an ATM WAN is through a transparent pipe as defined in RFC1483. This is currently the best method for most LAN protocols, but for IP there is a more complex standard (see next section).

Each network level PDU has an 8 byte header prepended, consisting of a 3 byte LLC header and 5 byte SNAP header that contains a 3 byte organizationally unique header (OUI) and 2 byte protocol identifier. RFC1483 recommends use of AAL5, so the bandwidth overhead on a 512 byte PDU due to use of ATM is about 1.6% for the LLC/SNAP headers plus 10.4% for the ATM cell header plus a variable figure up to about 10% (only 1.6% for the precise 512 byte case) for padding and CRC check in the final cell of the sequence. Throughput depends on transport level flow control factors for the particular network protocol.

RFC1483 uses PVCs between the LANs, so there is no additional set-up delay at the start of individual calls over the ATM network.

IP over ATM

This is defined in RFC1577 to connect logical IP subnetworks over an ATM LAN. A logical IP subnet (LIS) has a single IP subnet number and unique subnet mask, so is normally confined to a local area. The main performance factors are the time required to carry out an ATM ARPprocess, the header sizes in encapsulation and the windowing aspects already described above. The TCP window size extension defined in RFC1323 is key to high throughput over ATM. An IP client sets up an ATM call to its local logical ATMARP server (normally the local ATM switch) and registers its address by replying to an inverse ATMARP from the server. When the client wishes to send IP traffic to an IP address for which it does not have the ATM address, it sends an ATMARP to the server to obtain this. Where an ATM SVC is set up, the time required for this process is shown by the first ping to the destination, which is much longer than for the subsequent pings after set up.

Attempting to use this technique over a WAN requires either the use of traditional routers to connect the IP subnetworks, or the use of a proposed next hop routing protocol that generalizes the ATMARP concept. Until the latter is available, the use of RFC1483 bridging techniques is likely to give better performance over the WAN than RFC1577.

LAN emulation (LANE)

LANE works at the MAC level to emulate legacy LAN operation and thus provide ATM transport for the whole range of LAN protocols, even where the ATM network extends across a wide area.

The standard defines additional headers for each frame, consisting of two bytes of LECID (LAN emulation client identifier) to identify the sender and a PAD byte also for Token Ring frames. Additional control frames are defined with characteristic LECID of 0xFF00 followed by 14 more bytes of header that identify transaction type, status and server, plus variable control fields. Three types of server are defined: LAN emulation server (LES), LAN emulation configuration server (LECS) and broadcast and unknown server (BUS). In principle all services can be provided by a single processor, but the heavy processing load means that early implementation tend to use separate devices for the functions.

The header overhead is less than for RFC1483 and 1577, but the complex SVC set-up procedure based on the three servers as appropriate means that there can easily be a quarter-second delay to perform this.

The main design issue for ATM LANE is the ability to re-establish virtual circuits quickly after the failure of a major node in order to prevent higher-level sessions from timing out. Increasing the power of the servers and efficiency of the software are the main methods of improving this.

Importance of API

ATM offers multiples classes of service, but for SVCs this is only of value if the application programming interface is able to specify the quality-of-service parameters that it needs. Apart from APIs intended for IBM's APPN, most early APIs do not offer this capability since most routing protocols are unable to use it. One of the first widespread APIs to offer this capability is Winsock-2, so it should be used in preference to earlier interfaces such as the original Winsock. For PVCs the API does not matter, since the requisite type of circuit is set up by the network manager. Other emerging APIs written specifically for ATM, such as that by Fore Systems, also meet this criterion.

9.4.5 Further reading

General principles of ATM performance and digital video can be found Leduc (1994), Partridge (1994) and Onvural (1994). As this is a very rapidly evolving area, up-to-date information can best be obtained from online sources on the Internet, such as the web pages of the ATM Forum and the ITU-T, which are the main standards bodies for ATM.

10

Emerging Technologies

10.1 IVD LANs

10.2 Wireless LANs (CLAN)

10.3 ANSI high performance parallel interface (HIPPI)

10.4 ANSI fibre channel standard (FCS)

10.5 ESCON

10.6 High bit rate digital subscriber line (HDSL)

10.7 Asymmetric digital subscriber line (ADSL)

10.8 Community antenna television (CATV)

10.9 Satellite networks

10.10 SDH/SONET

This chapter is intended to show what sort of performance can be expected from the technologies described rather than give any advice on their optimization. Several of those described are for very short distances only, and being of high performance will not themselves be the bottleneck normally.

10.1 IVD LANs

Integrated voice data (IVD) LANs are intended to provide limited support over local area networks for constant bit rate applications, such as voice and video, without the need for the use of cell relay techniques. The basic principle involved is the use of time division multiplexing techniques to divide the bandwidth into components suitable for normal LAN data traffic and for the constant bit rate types. This work is standardized by IEEE 802.9, but with several variants.

The first of these is 802.9A ISO-Ethernet which is a derivative of Ethernet with modified coding that runs at 20 Mhz instead of 10. Out of 20 Mbps it typically provides 6.3 Mbps of TDM bandwidth for isochronous applications, while leaving the remainder for normal Ethernet data usage. This isochronous channel is equivalent to 96 ISDN B-channels, one D-channel and one M-channel. The TDM bandwidth can be used for a large number of ADPCM voice channels, numerous video-conferencing channels or three to four compressed video channels of approximately domestic VHS quality. The draft standard does not fully address the issues of timing in relation to external WAN communications using the H.221 and H.261 principles, so should normally be confined to a single LAN. Where external WAN access is used it should be based on H.320. The timing issue that has to be addressed to prevent possible data loss, is synchronization to the multiplexer network rather than to individual asynchronous Ethernet frames. Onwards transport across an ATM network is also possible using the AAL1 isochronous adaptation layer.

IEEE 802.9B is a closely related variant that describes access unit to access unit multimedia communication across a single LAN. Again, the initial draft does not address the timing issues for WAN communications.

A draft exists for a comprehensive 802.9 standard that is suitable for WAN communications also.

Some non-standard schemes and servers exist to provide multimedia service over ordinary Token Rings or Ethernets. These are adequate for still CD-ROM images, but for full motion video they only work if there is no significant data traffic present at the same time, and give bad quality if they have to contend with large file transfers; ideally they should be used on a dedicated LAN only. The Ethernet version at best can carry only about half as much video traffic as 802.9A, while the Token systems rely entirely on prioritization.

10.2   Wireless LANs (CLAN)

In some types of business environment, such as retail stores, it is not practical to have a normal structured cabling system and some form of wireless network is desirable. The options available are still being standardized under IEEE802.11, but various proprietary systems are already used. There are three main forms of CLAN:

- spread spectrum
- infrared
- narrowband.

Of these, spread spectrum has the lowest bandwidth, with early implementations offering speeds from 38.4 kbps up to about 6 Mbps. The frequency switching inherent in this approach make it well suited to relatively secure communications requirements.

Infrared has potentially the highest throughput with bandwidths up to 16 Mbps in early implementations, while narrowband runs at 5.7 Mbps in its main early implementation.

The draft standard supports spread spectrum technolgy with speeds of 1 and 2 Mbps. The advantage of a low bandwidth is that more independent CLANs can run within a single building if the frequency available is split between several low-speed systems instead of a single high-speed CLAN, as well as a longer range at low speed. Some modifications to TCP/IP have been proposed to make it more effective for mobile CLAN terminals.

Interaction with the WAN is by bridges or routers with 802.11 interfaces. CLANs have higher error rates than LANs as well as lower speed, so performance optimization is more like that for a pure WAN, with the need to minimize both store and forward delays and retransmissions by use of smaller packets than normal for a LAN.

10.2.1   DECT (Digital European cordless telecommunications)

Another technology that provides for local mobility is the new DECT standard. DECT is predominantly intended for voice, but can also carry data. It uses an OSI style protocol stack with a MAC layer between the physical and data link levels. The structure of a DECT packet consists of a 48 bit header, 16 bit CRC, 320 bits of data and 4 trailing collision detection bits, to which are added 32 bits of MAC header.

DECT uses time division multiplexing and dynamic channel allocation operating at around 1.8 GHz. Ten radio frequency carriers are used, and 10 milliseconds frames are divided into 24 timeslots. Digital telephone connections work at 32 kbps, implemented through 400 microsecond bursts every 10 milliseconds. These

226

10 ms intervals are sufficiently short not to cause noticeable jitter or delay. Link set up only takes about 50 ms, but portable set verification is much slower. Higher bandwidth aggregate links are also possible.

DECT itself is confined to very short ranges, but can interact with the WAN via PABXs.

10.3   ANSI high performance parallel interface (HIPPI)

HIPPI is intended to provide very high speed interconnection of supercomputers over very short distances using a LAN style of structure. Twisted copper pair circuits are used with a maximum segment length of 25 metres. This very short distance limit has led to the evolution of proprietary serial extensions of HIPPI using fibre optic cable, but these are largely replaced by the fibre channel standard (see section 10.4). Speeds range from 800 Mbps using 32 parallel circuits to 1600 Mbps using 64. HIPPI has a level 2 framing protocol, HIPPI-FP, that splits unlimited size packets into 1024 byte bursts consisting of 256 words each of 32 bits (800 Mbps case), with at most one short burst fragment per packet at the beginning or end to allow for arbitrary length packets. The only form of error correction consists of longitudinal and horizontal parity checks.

HIPPI has three alternative higher-level layers for interfacing to other systems. HIPPi-LE provides an interface to IEEE 802.2 logical data link control structures, while HIPPI-FC provides the interface to fibre channel, and HIPPI-IPI gives the interface to intelligent peripherals.

10.4   ANSI fibre channel standard (FCS)

FCS is also intended to provide interconnection between high-speed computers and their peripherals, but with fewer distance restrictions than HIPPI. Fibre-optic cable is used to support serial connections over distances from 2 metres up to 10 kilometres, and speeds from 100 Mbps up to 800 Mbps. The initial implementations support a speed of 266 Mbps, making this a more attractive technology for connecting clusters of computers over these distances than early ATM.

The FCS protocol stack has six levels as shown in Table 10.1.

FC-2 frames have a common structure as shown below.

SOF	Header	Data field	CRC	EOF
4 bytes	24	0–2112	4	4

Table 10.1 FCS protocol stack.

Level	Features
FC-F	Switch functions
FC-4	Channel protocol, peripheral interface
FC-3	Common services, e.g multicast
FC-2	Signalling and frame structure
FC-1	8B/10B transmission coding
FC-0	Signalling/data rates

SOF/EOF are start/end of field indicators while CRC is a cyclic redundancy code. Frames consist of both data frames and control frames, with acknowledgements and responses in the latter category.

Three types of service are supported:

(1) dedicated connections

(2) multiplex connections and

(3) connectionless.

Of these, the dedicated provides guaranteed delivery in the correct sequence, multiplex guarantees delivery but not sequencing, while connectionless guarantees neither.

10.5   ESCON

This is a proprietary IBM standard somewhat analogous to FCS. It supports distances up to 60 km, but at lower speeds than FCS. The current maximum ESCON channel speed is 17 Mbps, while ESCON cluster controllers such as the IBM 3172 and some 3174 only support 1.5 Mbps.

10.6   High bit rate digital subscriber line (HDSL)

HDSL is a technique for using existing copper pair cable to connect user premises to a local exchange. The HDB3 and AMI coding used for PCM systems over copper between exchanges are not suitable for the thinner and more irregular subscriber cable that is also liable to have open taps. Instead it uses two-pair copper cable with

1B1Q coding for full duplex transmission with echo cancellation at T1/E1 speeds over distances up to 3 km without repeaters. Each pair runs at 1040 kbps (E1 case) and data output onto both to produce the 2048 kbps channel. Bit error rates are lower than for modem links over copper circuits, but higher than fibre-optic links.

The main reason for using this service is that it is potentially cheaper than normal T1/E1 services and may be available where they are not. The higher error rate means a slightly lower throughput than T1/E1 using smaller packet and window sizes for the optimum performance.

10.7   Asymmetric digital subscriber line (ADSL)

This is another technique for delivering high-speed services over ordinary copper subscriber link cable but using only one pair, which is currently being standardized by ANSI. In this case the bandwidth is unequal in the two directions; typically about 28 kbps into the exchange and 1.5 Mbps to the subscriber (but potentially up to about 6 Mbps when it can carry MPEG 2). The main use for this service is to provide dial-up video on demand to roughly home-movie VHS standard, interactive video games, Internet access and home shopping. The technique is rather sensitive to impulse noise, so proximity to power cables or lightning strikes may make quality unacceptable.

The maximum range of ADSL is about 3–4 km, so its use is limited to copper pairs between the end user and a reasonably close exchange or else a kerbside junction box. Onwards communication uses the other technologies appropriate to the backbone, such as ATM over optical fibre.

ADSL does not interfere with the normal operation of a telephone conversation over the same wire.

10.8   Community antenna television (CATV)

CATV is a long established broadband technique for distributing TV over cable, but it has a new relevance for data communications as a means of providing relatively high speed data access to the home. A typical system provides 10–27 MHz capacity from a head-end to several hundred cable modems used by the subscribers. This allows the order of 100 kbps capacity to individual subscribers that can be used for the same functions as ADSL, but reducing the number of users sharing the head-end increases the throughput pro rata. Capacity can be either symmetric or asymmetric between input and output.

Some cable modems are able to support 10 Mbps operation over distances up to 300 km, but services based on this were not available at the time of writing.

Early cable modems are entirely proprietary, but a standard may emerge under the IEEE 802.14 aegis.

10.9   Satellite networks

These are already widespread for geostationary orbit satellites (GEOs) and likely to become available through low earth orbit satellites (LEOs). They are especially important in areas of the world that lack a leased line infrastructure. The main characteristic of these networks is the long propagation delay that requires specific optimization techniques. In the case of GEOs the characteristic delay for a single hop to and from a satellite at a height of 22 400 miles is 270 ms, while those for LEOs are much less on account of the lower orbit, but still significant ranging from about 10 ms for the lowest possible height up to 100 ms for the highest postulated orbital height of 8000 miles.

Satellite networks can be either one-way only (for centralized distribution) or two-way interactive. Standard terrestrial components are remote VSATs (very small aperture terminal), centralized hub with 5–10 metre antenna, network control system (NCS) and switch interface to central computers. The main technology used is traditional TDMA, but some voice systems use demand assigned multiple access (DAMA) instead, whereby satellite channels are allocated as required, thus providing greater bandwidth efficiency and lower cost. In the case of TDMA, stations wait for their allocated timeslot, then transmit complete buffers in a single burst using the full bandwidth. In addition, spread spectrum code division multiple access (CDMA) is used for low bit rate transmission to multiple groundstations.

Both star and mesh topologies can be supported, but in the former case anywhere–anywhere communication will always need at least two hops. VSAT availability is usually high, of the order of 99.9%, so that star configurations are quite acceptable on reliability grounds.

A wide range of bandwidths are offered in contemporary GEO services, ranging from 1200 bps to T1/E1 megabit rates, usually with bidirectional traffic capability although this is barred by licensing restrictions in a few places.

Satellite networks can carry any protocols, but polled systems are rather unsatisfactory unless spoofing is used to avoid the 270 ms propagation delay. There is also a small bandwidth overhead due to proprietary satellite addressing protocols on the links.

There are a small number of key principles that must be observed in order to obtain good performance:

- use local poll spoofing for polled protocols,
- large level 2 window size,
- large level 3 window size,

- large level 4 window size,
- large file transfer block size,
- longer than normal timeouts.

The size of window required depends on the bandwidth and frame/packet size used. The basic requirement is to ensure that an acknowledgement is received from the far end before the transmission window has been exhausted, else a gap in transmission will occur until it arrives. In the case of X.25 and SDLC, windows should be modulo 128 rather than modulo 8. Figure 10.1 illustrates this effect subject to BER of 1 in 10^6, demonstrating that at T1/E1 speeds unrealistically large windows would be required to meet the acknowledgement criterion. In many cases the window limit arises from the transport level or the block size.

Case A represents 512 byte IPX traffic for NetWare ex burst mode, B is 512 byte X.25 frames with common maximum window size of 15, and C is 1024 byte IP packets with total segment size 8192 bytes. For example, NFS version 2 has a normal transport window of 8192 bytes, so from Figure 10.1 it can be seen that there is little point in using more than 200 kbps for such file transfers over a GEO link. NFS version 3 allows a window of up to 65 535 bytes, so it can support rates eight times as high as version 2. One protocol stack that can be used to obtain the full bandwidth of a link is OSI with TP4 over the CLNP datagram network service. The maximum window size of 32 767 data units far exceeds anything required on such links, so the limiting factor is the bit error rate. Another unlimited protocol is TCP/IP provided that the window scaling option is used.

TFTP and early NetWare prior to burst mode both require end–end acknowledgements for each 512 byte block. This effectively sets a limit to the satellite bandwidth worth using that depends on the number of simultaneous connections to be supported, with only about 7.4 kbps for a single session.

For a two-hop satellite link to the opposite side of the world these throughputs would be halved.

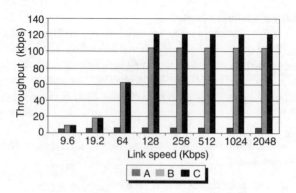

Figure 10.1   Satellite link throughput.

NetWare 4 does not have the full restrictions of the earlier version and can reach about 100 kbps for a single session. Optimum performance requires the maximum burst size of 64 kbytes, possibly with an inter-packet gap if the end-station is unable to handle a burst of this size in one go.

At the high speed/large window end of the spectrum, it is also necessary to take account of the retransmissions resulting from bit errors which limit the quantity of data that it is worth trying to send in a single uninterrupted sequence. This effect was discussed in some detail in Chapter 3. Satellite links suffer considerably from noise to atmospheric and ionospheric effects resulting in high error rates. Unlike terrestrial links these errors tend to occur at random rather than in bursts, so are relatively easy to detect and correct. Most VSAT transmission systems automatically provide forward error correction. As a result, the BER for satellite links is about 1 in 1 000 000 to 10 000 000. This makes the maximum window that can be used without degradation due to retransmissions about 10 000 to 100 000 bytes. Selective Reject is significantly better than Go-Back N on satellite links, as the latter requires retransmission of the complete post-error window. Combining these arguments on acknowledgement delays implies that the maximum bandwidth usable for a single session is in the range 256 kbps to 2.048 mbps, depending on quality, for applications with very large windows, but only about 7 kbps for 512 byte windows. Multiple sessions make better use of bandwidth.

Some satellite service providers can offer special equipment with more complex forward error correction to reduce the bit error rate further.

10.9.1 Memory requirements

One limitation on the number of sessions that an end-device can support is the amount of memory available for buffering. Each session needs buffer space equal to its full window size; for example, 1 MB buffer is needed to support 100 sessions with 10 kB window.

10.9.2 Ku-Band and C-Band

GEO systems can use either of two main frequency bands, C-Band at 4/6 GHz and Ku-Band at 11/14 GHz, where the higher frequency is for the up-link and lower for the down-link. The first networks were based on C-Band, but suffered from problems due to terrestrial interference. These problems can be greatly reduced by the use of spread spectrum technology, but for terminals in crowded areas the more highly directional Ku-Band is preferable. Ku-band is less susceptible to interference, but is prone to drastic loss of quality during heavy rain or thick fog. Many satellites carry transponders for both types of band, so many networks consist of a mixture of VSATs of the two varieties according to location characteristics. Congested areas with heavy rainfall are not well suited to either, but usually have leased line services available as an alternative. If VSAT services are used in such locations, then either C-Band with spread spectrum, or Ku-Band with extra large aperture (for example, 3 metres instead of 0.6–1.8) is required.

Another problem with GEOs is that for a few minutes each day around the equinoxes, the satellite will be in line with the sun, whose strong radiation drowns the satellite transmissions. The system must switch to an alternative satellite on these predictable occasions.

10.9.3   LEOs

LEOs are being developed largely to support terrestrial mobile communication systems, with which they share a number of common features. Apart from the reduction in propagation delay from 270 to tens of milliseconds, the main characteristic of a LEO system is that an individual satellite is not in the field of view of a station for more than a few minutes at a time. As a result there has to be a handover from one satellite to another, analogous to that between base stations for the basic terrestrial systems. The number of satellites in a LEO constellation and the inclination of the satellite orbits to the equator are chosen to ensure that reasonable coverage is provided for all latitudes; typically at least 48 satellites with orbital inclinations of about 50 degrees are proposed. This means that there should always be two or three satellites of the constellation in view (barring obstructions) at any one time, with the ground station selecting whichever gives the best reception at any instant.

Signal losses occur whenever a satellite disappears behind a local obstruction or during handover, so data performance is likely to be poor, with a need for full transport-level recovery and retransmission. The system is mainly intended for voice, for which these problems are less critical and outweighed by the reduction in the propagation delay.

Where data services are offered, they are likely to be of low bandwidth only, typically about 4.8 kbps; again this is only likely to be suited to mobile communications.

The main users are likely to be aircraft, ships and vehicles in sparsely populated areas of the earth where terrestrial cellular services are not practical.

Tuning of data transmissions is comparable to that for mobile terrestrial services. A transport layer is required which can handle interruptions of the order of a second while switching between satellites.

10.10   SDH/SONET

Until the early 1990s the level one portion of digital public networks was based on a plesiochronous digital hierarchy (PDH) with differing standards throughout the world. SDH (synchronous digital hierarchy) and SONET (synchronous optical network) are two compatible standards that overcome many deficiencies in the older PDH networks.

The basic principle of the PDH networks is that they are almost synchronous, but because of the differing bit rates of nominally equivalent pieces of equipment, they have to make bit corrections. This correction occurs when multiplexing together 2 Mbps E1 circuits in Europe or 1.544 Mbps T1 in the USA by the addition of 'justification bits' in each such channel. The consequence of this is that whenever a PTT with very high speed circuits, such as 34 or 140 Mbps in Europe or 45 Mbps in the USA, wishes to provide an E1 or T1 circuit to a customer, the entire high-speed circuit has to be demultiplexed through each of the intervening E or T levels, then remultiplexed back to the original level once the customer's circuit has been dropped and inserted. This scheme is very impractical as it requires a sequence of multiplexers appropriate to the range of levels. In addition to not being able to identify individual E1 or T1 channels, the PDH does not provide any monitoring of error rates; thus a customer may observe high error rates on individual circuits through end-point equipment statistics, but the PTT has no way of checking claims or performing pre-emptive maintenance.

SDH and SONET rectify these deficiencies through the use of a management structure that enables monitoring and identification of individual E1 or T1 channels. They also retain the ability to carry PDH circuits through a packaging structure defined in ITU-T G.709 for SDH and ANSI standards for SONET. SDH defines a series of basic transmission rates called synchronous transfer modules as shown in Table 10.2, along with the corresponding SONET optical carrier rates and synchronous transport signals (STS).

Additional rates, such as OC-9, are defined but seem less likely to be used than those quoted in Table 10.2. The main difference between SDH and SONET is that the lowest level of the latter is one third of that for the former, plus some slight differences in the use of pointers in the data structures and also nomenclature. Lower rate channels, such as 56/64 kbps circuits, are accommodated through the use of virtual tributaries (VT) or containers (VC).

Table 10.2 SDH/SONET rates.

SDH level	OC level	STS level	Rate (Mbps)
–	OC-1	STS-1	51.84
STM-1	OC-3	STS-3	155.52
STM-4	OC-12	STS-12	622.08
STM-8	OC-24	STS-24	1244.16
STM-16	OC-48	STS-48	2488.32
STM-64	OC-192	STS-192	9953.28

10.10.1 STM-1 structure

All plesiochronous channels between 1.544 and 140 Mbps can be accommodated within an STM-1 frame of 270 nine byte lines via the use of containers. Each container carries a plesiochronous channel plus its bit justification, but adds control information, known as the path overhead, as well. It is the path overhead that enables a network operator to identify and monitor the channel and its error rate. The container plus its path overhead together form a virtual container. Figure 10.2 shows the structure of an SDH STM-1 frame; STS-1 in SONET is similar except that it uses 90 lines. Both SDH and SONET transmit at 8000 frames per second.

The section, line and path overheads are related to the operation of the SDH/SONET network components as indicated in Figure 10.3.

The section overhead contains two framing bytes, a frame identifier, a parity bit that describes the status of the previous frame plus several bytes intended to provide voice and data maintenance/administration channels. It controls the section of line between regenerators and eachother or line terminating equipment.

The line overhead is used by the line terminating equipment, such as SDH/SONET multiplexers, and consists of payload pointers, error checks, monitors and diagnostics. The payload pointers allow the user information channels to be placed anywhere in the payload area of the frame, and hence can accommodate the time slippage of plesiochronous systems. The line header also contains its own parity check. Most of the bits are, however, used for the maintenance and monitoring channels.

The path overhead runs from end to end between the initial and final multiplexers. There are four different possible classes of path overhead according to the type of payload. Again there is a parity check and monitoring functions; one byte is used for network provider specific overheads.

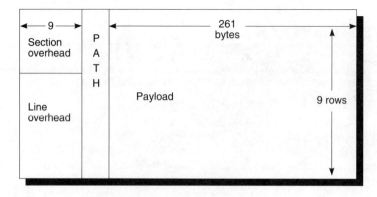

Figure 10.2   SDH/SONET overheads.

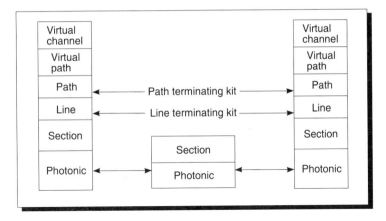

Figure 10.3   SDH/SONET protocol stack.

10.10.2   Performance aspects of SDH/SONET

As far as the user of an SDH/SONET network is concerned, there are two main benefits. The first is that the software-controlled structure of the circuits means that network carriers should be able to provide bandwidth on demand for purposes such as video-conferencing through direct signalling, instead of having to reserve the capacity a considerable time in advance. The second is that the enhanced monitoring capability means that carriers should be able to detect and rectify faults much faster than for PDH networks, leading to reduced downtime. It will also be easier to reach agreement with carriers as to whether contractual quality-of-service agreements have been met, basing much of this on ITU-T recommendations M.2110 and M.2120. The downside of SDH/SONET is that the overheads required to enable this functionality occupy about 4% of the total bandwidth.

11

Network Management and Analysis

11.1   Introduction

Performance optimization depends on knowing what is going on in the network; this is determined by the network management system and by additional monitoring tools. Network management traffic can sometimes impose a significant load on the network by itself, or even be a source of congestion, so this aspect is also considered here.

Performance monitoring has always been a high priority for WANs, but for LANs the relatively high bandwidth has meant that it is only recently that this has become important for them. As a result, LAN performance analysis is much more rudimentary than that for WANs.

Prior to the early 1990s almost all network management consisted of proprietary systems applicable only to one manufacturer's equipment or even just one particular subset of the range. Some of these systems, such as IBM's NetView, are sufficiently important to be considered in this chapter but most of the emphasis is placed on the emerging common standards. There are two main strands of common approaches, SNMP (simple network management protocol) developed in the Internet, and CMIS/CMIP (common management information system/protocol) developed by the International Standards Organization (ISO).

11.2   SNMP

SNMP is a very basic management system that contains only the bare essentials. In its original version it is based on five types of command: GET REQUEST, GET NEXT REQUEST, GET RESPONSE, SET and TRAP. Of these commands, the two types of GET REQUEST enable a manager to see the configuration state of the networking equipment as well as a limited amount of traffic statistics for some types of equipment such as bridges and routers, while SET enables the configuration to be changed. TRAP is used to send alarms whenever certain preset events occur. Standard sets of information to be made available are included in MIB II (Management Information Base II), with additional proprietarily selected information in a MIB extension. Most of the information relevant to performance analysis is in MIB II for bridges and routers. The information that is needed is the numbers of frames of different types (both protocol and function) per port, the number of bytes transmitted and received per port, CPU and memory utilizations of the bridge/router and ideally the peak values over a period of a few minutes. Delay information would be useful also, but is rarely available. The act of obtaining these statistics can impose a heavy load on the network, particularly in the case of large networks. Part of the problem lies in the structure of the command set; to obtain a large block of data, SNMP uses a sequence of GET NEXT commands which leads to a UDP datagram for every variable, with enormous consequent overheads. If the information has to transit a low-speed WAN link in order to reach the network management centre, then it is likely to have an adverse effect on other data traffic. This defect has been rectified in SNMP version 2, along with other features such as security, so making the protocol more suitable for large networks. The change to the GET command is a GET BULK, which enables a single command to be used to get a large block of data, such as the packet statistics by means of a single command. Recently SNMP has also been supplemented by the RMON standard, which provides for the remote monitoring of Ethernets and Token Rings, but not the intervening WAN links.

11.2.1 RMON features

RMON features are divided into nine groups for Ethernet and ten for Token Ring, all of which are optional, so claimed RMON conformance needs to be examined in detail when assessing a product. These groups are as follows: segment statistics, history, host table, host top N, traffic matrix, alarms, filters, packet capture and events. All groups are potentially useful in tuning network performance, with functionality sketched in Table 11.1.

Table 11.1 RMON groups (Ethernet).

Group	Data	Function
Segment stats	Packets/segment: multicast, broadcast collisions, errors, size	Show traffic load and character
History	Segment stats at periodic time	Show trends in traffic
Host table	Stats per node	Traffic distribution
Host top 10	10 nodes with most errors	Pinpoint problems
Traffic matrix	Traffic amount by node pair	Critical routes
Alarms	Thresholds exceeded	Automatic warning of problems
Filters	Templates for defining packets to trace	Support for packet capture function
Packet capture	Trace of packet sequences	Vital function for diagnostics
Events	General event reports	Supplements SMNP polling correlate with diagnostics

Extensive use of the packet trace facility can impose a heavy load on the network, so it needs to be used carefully if the network is congested. More detailed comparable information is also provided by protocol analysers (see later in this chapter). Traffic figures are only available on a node or segment basis, so additional information on per port statistics will often be required. Such extra data can be obtained from the bridge/router statistics.

Simply having RMON agents on the network is not sufficient; what is also required is a user-friendly application to present the information in easily understood format. Basic features needed from this point of view are the ability to translate raw statistics into line loadings and to perform trend analysis. Line loadings need to be further subdivided into contributions from different protocols and different source/ destination pairs, so that the network manager can see who is responsible for peak loads and understand their impact on other users. A particularly important feature is to see how file transfers are affecting interactive traffic, as burst from file servers over low-speed links can have a devastating effect on the latter. The performance analysis application also needs to be customized to handle the additional proprietary information from the bridges and routers.

Where SNMP and RMON commands are used to monitor LANS across a WAN it is vital to use proxy-agents (sometimes also called superagents) to perform the basic tasks, rather than send polls and especially complete RMON files across the WAN. The proxy should then report important changes in status back to the management centre, together with digests of any RMON data requested. A few minutes of a raw packet trace from a LAN is likely to contain many megabytes of data, and if transmitted whole could saturate a slow WAN for several hours.

RMON 2

From the point of view of WAN optimization, a very important extension to RMON is provided by the later RMON 2 standard. Whereas RMON only applies to level 2 of the OSI stack, RMON 2 provides analogous statistical information from level 3 (the network layer) up to the application level. It is therefore capable of giving end–end response time and congestion information, as well as distinguishing between network delays and server delays.

RMON 2 statistics provide a good standard for baselining WAN performance. By keeping a full record of network history a network manager can relate user satisfaction levels to objective data, and distinguish between user complaints arising from real network issues and those that are more the symptoms of some other work grievance.

Monitoring public networks

An important recent addition to SNMP's capabilities is the adoption of a standard MIB, defined by the IETF in RFC1604, for public networks to enable network users to monitor any permanent virtual circuits to which they subscribe, and to obtain extra PVCs or bandwidth on demand. The first technology to take advantage of this is frame relay as customer network management (CNM), but it should become important for other public services offering PVCs with agreed information rates, such as SMDS and ATM.

ICMP

In addition to SNMP, IP networks also have controllability through the use of ICMP (Internet Control Message Protocol). The structure of an ICMP datagram is shown below.

Field	Type	Code	Checksum	Parameters	Data
Length (bytes)	1	1	2	4	Variable

The main types of ICMP message are:

- datagram lifetime exceeded,
- parameter unintelligible,
- destination unreachable,
- source quench flow control,
- echo and reply,
- redirect,
- record route,
- timestamp and reply.

Timestamps potentially give more information than the echo, which may be just that. A packet is stamped on receipt and on transmission, so allowing the end-station processing delay to be determined. It also contains timestamps from intermediate nodes, but as clocks are not accurately synchronized this is of little value, except for measuring the delay across a specific device. It also suffers from a limitation to four hops in each direction because of the permitted field size, as does record route.

11.3   CMIS/CMIP

The CMIS/CMIP acronyms are often loosely used to cover the whole range of OSI network management functions covered by the X.700 series of standards. The part that is most relevant to performance optimization is X.739, the standard for work-load monitoring. These standards are not nearly so widely supported as SNMP because they require very large quantities of memory on each system that actively participates, and are totally unsuited to simple devices such as modems and terminal adaptors and barely applicable even to routers. The protocol itself also carries higher overheads than SNMP because there is a header for each layer of the OSI protocol stack. The trend in industry is to have a proxy agent for CMIS/CMIP support running in the network management system that gets or sets device data in a memory and network efficient manner, but presents a standard OSI interface to the network manager; an example of this is the Network Management Forum's OmniPoint system, where Omnipoint means Open Management Interoperability Point.

11.4   HP Open View

A *de facto* standard largely based on the SNMP and CMIP protocols is Hewlett-Packard's Open View. This enables information from either of the two types of management system to share common high-level applications for data analysis on a single management platform. The raw information has no additions, but the added value of analysis has its costs potentially shared over many users in a way that would not be practical for proprietary systems. In particular, it is likely that performance analysis tools will become available that run under HP Open View.

HP themselves do provide some performance optimization in the special case of systems that support their EASE (embedded advanced sampling environment) algorithms for sampling and analysing network behaviour. The UNIX-based OpenView Traffic Expert analyses the EASE data and recommends current modifications to the network, such as additional capacity or brouters. Similarly, the Openview History Analyser performs trend analysis for general capacity planning.

11.5   NetView

NetView is the generic name for IBM's collection of network management programs. The most important component for the optimization of WANs is NetView Performance Monitor. This provides detailed statistics for utilizations and response times, and is an extremely powerful tool for this function.

11.6   Network performance statistics

This section summarizes the type of information that is likely to be available for different types of network component (Table 11.2).

Table 11.2 Performance statistics.

Device type	Hardware statistics	Line statistics per port
Multiplexer	Bandwidth	Bandwidth per trunk
X.25 switch/pad	Total CPU load, CPU load per protocol, memory use	Level 3 packets TX & RX, level 2 frames TX & RX, bytes TX & RX, errors & retransmissions
Frame relay switch	Total CPU load, CPU load per protocol, memory use	Frames dropped with DE SET, Frames dropped without DE SET, Level 2 frames TX & RX, bytes TX & RX, errors & retransmissions, CIR exceeded
Bridge	CPU load, memory	Frames filtered, Frames TX & RX
Router	CPU load per protocol, Total memory use, Memory per route table	Packets TX & RX per protocol
ATM switch	CPU load, memory	Cells TX & RX, Cells dropped, Payload bytes TX & RX

The level of detail within each category varies significantly according to the individual type of machine. In extreme cases the hardware loads are subdivided into specialized software task contributions to enable the operator to tune the internal scheduling of modules for optimum performance, but the opposite case of only an overall loading is more common.

Some devices have a trace facility which enables a record to be maintained showing what packets/frames were processed on which ports during a short interval. This type of information is very useful when investigating questions of low throughput, as it shows the exact sequence of frames and acknowledgements, albeit at the expense of a significant extra processor load that will cause a slight perturbation from normal operation. In general, this type of information has to be obtained by means of an external protocol analyser or monitor.

For frame relay it is extremely important to know how many frames are dropped and how often the agreed CIR is exceeded. Frame dropping causes retransmissions and delays that may easily be outside the quality-of-service requirements. The cause of frame dropping is likely to be traffic that exceeds the agreed CIR but, while ideally the frames dropped should be those that exceed the CIR or else those with the DE bit set, it is difficult to guarantee that this will always be true.

In the case of ATM switches cell dropping is even more crucial, as dropping a single cell will lead to complete frames being retransmitted.

11.6.1   Determining response time

Another major quality-of-service factor is the network response time. Often it requires a special application, but for LAN interconnection it can often be checked by means of a ping command. This was originally introduced as a simple 16 byte ICMP echo request to test the reachability of a remote IP station, but it has become generalized to provide more information. A number of implementations allow the user to specify a configurable quantity of data from 16 up to perhaps 1024 bytes, while the roundtrip time is also recorded along with the path, sometimes being quoted as average, maximum and minimum. Analysis of this for a range of ping sizes and routes provides much of the information needed to tune performance. Ping is available for other protocols also, such as IPX, AppleTalk, OSI and VINES using the appropriate echo request. APPC also has an analogous APing command.

If a ping is sent to a router, the response time may be significantly longer than the response time for a similar-sized data packet as most routers give replying to pings a very low priority. The extra delay is likely to be of the order of 5 ms, but depends on both router and traffic level.

Use of ICMP timestamp instead of ping allows the elimination of end-station response time; for T1/E1 networks or faster this is an important difference as the main source of delay may be a congested file server.

Some TCP/IP protocol stacks provide a ping function with options to implement ICMP record route and timestamp. Another very useful option is the ability to increase the data field length within the ping. Field sizes such as 512 allow a much better idea of the delays likely to be experienced by file transfers, particularly TFTP which uses this packet size. Use of several ping sizes allows a rough estimate of the queuing delay before transmission; as for isolated pings this is largely determined by the background traffic, whereas the transmission time is proportional to the length of the packet. The router delay is also largely independent of the packet size, and can be estimated by pinging the IP interfaces on either side of the router.

Often the delays that need to be investigated are between sites other than that containing the management centre; to assist with this scenario, some devices support proxy ping. In this, the network operator sends a command to a suitable proxy on a LAN at one end of the troubled path to ping a device at the far end; the proxy then returns the measured delay to the operator. Sun workstations are mostly capable of performing this proxy role. Most UNIX systems also support remote shell or rlogin commands that allow this function subject to permissions.

The most powerful technique on multihop routes is a TCP/IP application called TRACEROUTE. This sends out a series of pings with successively greater time-to-live values in the header, starting at one. The first few cause ICMP 'Destination Unreachable' messages complete with roundtrip response time, until the TTL is large enough to receive an echo back from the destination. Comparison of the roundtrip times for the various nodes gives a good indication of where network bottlenecks are occurring in addition to showing the route taken.

Another useful command in TCP/IP is Spray. This is available mainly on Sun workstations, and allows the operator to measure the response time for a configurable number of packets of specifiable size that are sent as a single burst. This is more useful for tuning file transfers than ping, and is particularly applicable to NFS. Care is however required as some delay between packets usually has to be specified to prevent large quantities of packets from being dropped, even where two Suns are connected back to back. The default command has no inter-packet gap, so will lead to frame dropping even on an unutilized Ethernet. The delay set between packets should also be verified with a sniffer as this interval does not always match that set in the command. The normal file size used is 100 kbytes with a packet size of 86 bytes, but these can be varied, thereby enabling the optimum to be determined. Use of the ICMP option within Spray allows a full two-way data flow. Spray is also a very good way of generating traffic to stress test a system.

It is also useful to have a standard file for network performance checks and maintain baseline records of file transfer times for the main routes across the network, so that advance warning of performance degradation is available before users start to complain.

RMON 2 probes provide a large amount of information about the delays and traffic levels current on the network. Where this information has to be obtained across the WAN these statistics themselves produce a major network load unless T1/E1 lines are available. If there is already thought to be congestion on these links, then the statistics requested should be restricted to the bare essentials.

A few programs also exist to help in tuning, notably Perform 3 for NetWare which automatically varies the buffer size used for a standard transaction and outputs the result as a graph. If Perform 3 is used in conjunction with data compression on the WAN, it should be noted that its packets are much more compressible than average data traffic and may give an over-optimistic impression of the benefits likely from compression, for example 15:1 for Perform 3 but 2:1 for more typical data.

Another program that helps is HP's Netperf, which is applicable to TCP and UDP for BSD UNIX systems, Windows NT (rev 3.5 or later), Fore ATM API and HP HiPPI. This provides throughputs and latencies for bulk file transfers and responds normally to compression. It is available free from HP (at least in late 1995) on the Internet:

http://www.cup.hp.com/netperf/NetperfPage.html

For some BSD UNIX, SunOS, Ultrix and HP-UX systems the program tcpdump enables detailed analysis of TCP/IP traffic.

The other main method of determining response times is by the use of analysis tools as listed in the following sections.

11.7 Network monitoring tools

The most important class of network monitoring tools are simply the device statistics above which are collected and viewed via the network management system, but other functions have to be provided also. The main absentee from Table 11.2 is any information on response time, as this is rarely maintained within the network.

11.7.1 Host tools

In a traditional mainframe environment, packages are available for may hosts that can provide detailed response time and other statistics. For VTAM hosts, such information is provided by NetView Performance Monitor, NetSpy and Netmaster. For each line, PU or LU it is possible to obtain overall traffic statistics, average response time, 95% response time and the numbers of transactions that exceed preset thresholds.

For front-end processors with serial WAN links, the utilization figures from these packages are used for periodic rebalancing of the individual port loads to allow for changes in traffic levels after the initial configuration as well as for trouble-shooting.

VTAM and NCP tuning

ACF/VTAM itself provides useful information for tuning purposes in its tuning statistics. Much of this information is intended for optimizing the host CPU and storage loads rather than explicit network performance, but one statistic is extremely important to end-users of legacy systems; this is NCP Slow Down. This condition results from the front-end running short of buffers on the outbound side, and does not readily clear up. The NCP response to buffer shortage is to slow the rate of polling and to request the host to stop sending data, leading to a very poor response time for users. Simple solutions that are not always applicable are increasing the memory on the front-end and increasing the line speed to reduce the buffer holding time, while the other alternatives involve tuning of the system if this has not already been carried out. Some possible changes may have adverse effects on other parts of the system; for example, reducing the DELAY parameter for data going from NCP into the host will reduce the NCP buffer requirement and hence slowdowns, but will also increase the host processor load by reducing coat-tailing. Slow-downs are also reduced by decreasing the parameter MAXBFRU if this is unnecessarily large. Optimization of this parameter requires knowledge of the the average inbound and outbound message sizes. Where these are roughly equal, the buffer size UNITSZ is set to this size, otherwise to about five times the inbound size if the outbound messages are far longer; NCP then sends MAXBFRU*UNITSZ of data to the host when either it has accumulated or DELAY has expired. Reducing MAXBFRU thus reduces the storage required by NCP. Reducing the VPACING value cuts the amount of data that the host can send to NCP, so reducing NCP storage and slowdowns, but increasing both the overall outbound response time and the host processor load. If host CPU load is not a problem DELAY should be set to zero for optimum performance, while unnecessary NCP slowdowns can be avoided by cutting the configurable free buffer threshold at which it starts to about 6%. A value in the region of 32 for VPACING is likely to optimize file transfers if sufficient buffering is available.

Buffer utilization is optimized on the output side by the analogous parameters BFRS for NCP buffer size and INBFRS. AS NCP buffers are not shared between PIUs, the value of BFRS needs to he set to be an approximate submultiple of MAXDATA, the PIU size. For low-speed WAN applications 84 and 128 are the most suitable, but 240 for modern high-speed systems. Of these 84 is preferred if NCP slowdown is a problem, as it reduces buffer space wasted on short SNA commands and responses. INBFRS is set to match VPACING PIUs.

NCP also contains a set of parameters called T2TIMER with format (T1, T2, W), where T1 is the acknowledgement timeout for traffic on the local LAN, T2 for remote LANs and W is the received acknowledgement count for each link. An ACK is sent when either the appropriate timer expires or the count W is reached. For remote WAN connectivity values of T2 and W in the region of 3 seconds and a count of about 16 are likely to be optimal for file transfers.

This process is simplified for NCP parameters by using NTuneMON and NTuneNCP which are recent IBM packages running with ACF/NCP versions 4 to 7 initially and permitting dynamic changes from version 5 onwards.

Analogous information is available for various other hosts using specific proprietary packages.

In a client–server environment such tools have only recently started to appear in significant numbers. Most packages are for the UNIX market and concentrate more on remote servers than on the clients. This category is expanding rapidly so it is not possible to give a comprehensive survey here. Some of the early packages include online monitors from HP (Perfview), Legent (LanSpy and Paramount Performance Manager), Tivoli (Sentry), IBM (Systems Monitor/6000), DEC (Polycentre), BMC (Patrol) and Compuware (Ecotool). Off-line analysis is provided by Best/1 from BGS and Performance Collection Software from HP.

Novell's NetWare has its own network management system (NMS) as well as specific modules such as Lanalyser and Lantern. These provide detailed traffic analysis on LAN segments as well as statistics on the servers, but are limited on WAN functionality.

11.7.2   Protocol analysers and monitors

A very wide range of stand-alone testers, monitors and analysers exist, with most being specialized for one type of network. For example, line monitors and testers check the quality of lines at the physical level, while protocol analysers are mainly concerned with the data link and network levels of packet switch systems. Within each of these categories there is further specialization, such as OTDRs for optical fibre or ISDN testers for ISDN links.

BERT testers

One of the most fundamental functions required on a network is to check the bit error rate, which is done by a BERT tester. These transmit standard patterns, such as the 511, appropriate to the type of line being tested. Error rates above that expected for the given transmission medium imply defective equipment, undue proximity to a power cable, crosstalk or poor wiring, while knowledge of this error rate allows calculation of the optimal frame and window sizes using the principles described in earlier chapters.

Protocol analysers and sniffers

The main category for network tuning is that of protocol analysers and sniffers. Early systems were entirely proprietary, but the RMON standards (see above) now provide a common information format for this category. In order to find out why a particular application is giving poor response time it is usually necessary to obtain a trace of all the traffic on its route, then consider the types of interaction. For example, a poor Telnet response time might result from the short frames involved getting stuck behind large Token Ring file transfers using the same route across a slow WAN link. In order to know where to locate the analysers in a complex network it is very useful to be able to trace the route taken: for many protocols there are software modules to determine this, such as TRACEROUTE for IP on Sun workstations in particular.

Another essential feature for performance optimization is the ability to trigger on a specific packet or frame, then terminate on the acknowledgement for that frame and record the time elapsed. This is particularly important for protocols like X.25 and frame relay that do not have ping commands.

Most packages include a packet capture facility that allows the information to be analysed in detail offline. The analyser requires to have both a large memory and large hard disk as it is normally placed on a LAN which may easily be carrying 0.5 to 1 Mbyte per second of traffic. Normally all traffic is recorded over a period of a few minutes to ensure examples of the traffic types of concern are recorded. Use of filter options in the display allow the important types to be isolated, and for this it is essential to have a wide range of protocol decodes available with filtering options available for protocol subtypes, such as different IPX SAP types. Once a general understanding of the protocol distribution has been obtained, further packet capture with application of filters allows study of particular features of interest over longer periods of time.

WAN traffic usually has to be isolated on the basis of source-destination addresses. Use of timestamps in the package enables the delays in transactions to be readily observed. Once this has been done it is straightforward to see whether small interactive packets are being held up by large file transfers and so on, or if any application is using an excessive amount of bandwidth. It is helpful to have additional software to translate these WAN traffic traces into line loadings and response times, but this is often not included in the basic package.

Detailed study of the higher protocol layers, for example server message block commands for PCs, is helpful in optimizing file transfers. This shows whether low throughput results from complex data file header read/writes or from pure network causes, and whether print files are carrying a lot of soft-font information that could be eliminated by working only with hard fonts on the printer.

ATM monitors

ATM monitoring is required to ensure that the quality-of-service (QoS) parameters specified by a user's service agreement are met. The usual parameters involved are those that are specified in ITU recommendation I.356. For the ATM layer these are: cell delay, cell delay variation, cell loss ratio, cell misinsertion rate and errored cell ratio. An ATM generator is required that can ideally produce each of the five AAL types of ATM, and as a bare minimum at least VBR and CBR types. In addition to generators sufficient to produce the required load, there must be ATM monitors that can test each of the quoted QoS parameters.

A requirement also exists for testing the layers, such as SDH or SONET, beneath ATM, since they may be the source of any observed cell errors. The technique depends on the level 1 type, but for SDH, the main features to check are frame alignment, bit errors, frame pointers and alarm criteria. New standards for monitoring public circuits are available in ITU-T recommendations in the M.2100 series, particularly for SDH/SONET circuits where they are much more easily checked than for the older PDH.

The most fundamental check to perform is to use the ATM generators to show that the contracted traffic rate can be transmitted across the ATM network without cell loss.

The next feature to check is that this rate can be transmitted at peak times without exceeding the agreed cell delay or agreed jitter, the latter being easily measured via the cell interarrival times.

More detailed aspects of performance are tested through the use of operations and maintenance flows, with F4 for virtual paths and F5 for virtual connections being the most relevant.

Traffic generators

Performance analysis often requires the ability to generate heavy loads, often beyond the capability of an ordinary monitor. The traffic generator modules within PC-based protocol analysers can usually produce a few megabits per second. Often hosts, host emulation pckages and packet switches have to be used for this purpose, either to produce greater loads or to produce specific protocols.

11.8   Performance troubleshooting

This section gives some guidelines for handling common problems.

11.8.1 Slow file transfer

There are three main network reasons for this problem, as well as the possibility of an overloaded server:

- bottlenecks
- retransmissions
- unsuitable parameters.

The first of these is the most important. Use management commands such as traceroute or ping to find the route followed, then check the line speeds and packet switching rates of individual components. Where RIP is used, a common cause is simply that the least hop route uses a low bandwidth route instead of a high bandwidth path with more hops. The maximum possible throughput is equal to the throughput of the worst bottleneck *en route*, but in practice will often be much less. The reason for the further reduction is that the file transfer has to share the bottleneck with other applications. For example, suppose the file transfer has to share a 64 kbps line with other traffic that produces an average loading of 50% on that line, then the bandwidth available to the file transfer with equal priorities will be about 32 kbps. Checking the utilizations of all the slower components should identify the worst bottleneck, and file transfer time ought to be in the region of the file size divided by the adjusted bottleneck throughput. If it is, then the solution is either to introduce data compression or to increase capacity at the main bottleneck, possibly repeating this at progressively lesser bottlenecks.

If throughput is a lot less than predicted by the above bottleneck analysis, then likely causes are packet retransmissions or server congestion. The former will happen if the bit error rate is too high for the packet size used, or if congested switches are dropping packets due to lack of memory or transmission timeouts, or with some cabling faults. Putting a scope on the line will indicate any end–end retransmissions. If they are occurring, then a BERT test will show the error rate, while switch statistics will give transmission errors and possibly memory utilization. High BER may result from cabling faults, but otherwise is difficult to rectify. Shortage of memory can often be handled by a processor upgrade. Server congestion is more likely to arise from LAN traffic than from the WAN, but will affect both.

Low throughput may also occur if the window size is inadequate to allow pipelining of data, so that flow is interrupted by the need to wait for end–end acknowledgements. This is very common on satellite links and to a lesser extent international cable trunks. Use a ping command to find the response time for packets of the size in use, then check the window size against this. The solution is usually to increase the window size, but subject to its not being so large that retransmissions become common. In extreme cases this will require a change of application; for example, NetWare without packet burst mode has a window of 512 bytes and upgrade to 3.12 or 4 is needed to overcome this. For TCP/IP the use of window scaling as per RFC1323 may be the cure, while for NFS upgrade from version 2 to 3 allows window size to go up from 8192 to 65 536.

An alternative is sometimes to segment the packet size where transmission has to go through a multihop network (see the example in Chapter 6) in order to get a faster transit time. Another alternative is to replace end–end acknowledgements by local ones, such as resetting the D-bit in X.25. Retransmissions for a given BER can be reduced by lowering the packet size and by changing to a protocol that provides Selective Reject instead of Go-Back N.

11.8.2   Slow interactive response time

If this is a lot worse than expected from the capacities of the network components *en route*, then the most likely cause is getting held up behind large packets for other applications. Pinging all intermediate nodes in turn will give an indication of where the biggest delays are coming from, and monitoring the traffic in that region should show the cause. Solutions are to prioritize the interactive traffic, reduce the packet size for other applications (possibly detrimental to them) or increase capacity.

Intermittent problems of this nature may be caused by periodic broadcasts on the network, especially IPX SAP broadcasts from a router which often congest low-speed lines for several seconds per broadcast interval. Filtering, prioritization or a change to a less broadcast intensive protocol, such as NLSP in the IPX case, are possible solutions.

11.8.3   Switch overload

Suspected overloads should be visible from processor and memory statistics from the switch or router. In router networks memory shortage is likely to be the main form of overload associated with WAN links, unless the processor is shared with direct inter-LAN links. Memory tuning is very product-specific, but making routing tables more compact and cutting any unnecessarily large port allocations will make better use of what is available. Prioritizing WAN links at the expense of LAN–LAN in the CPU may make WAN performance acceptable while having little effect on the latter in some architectures. CPU overload is more common in X.25 networks, and specialized techniques are quoted in Chapter 5 of this book.

Router throughput is often much less than the advertised datasheet value where multiple protocols or intensive filtering occur. In these cases rationalization or separation of protocols is beneficial, with co-processors sometimes a reasonable cost upgrade solution.

Cabling effects on performance

In a few newly installed networks, unexpectedly low performance may be due to errors in cabling. Poor quality cabling can lead to various forms of noise on the line, accompanied by frame errors leading to retransmissions and the observed low performance. Examples of this are the use of aluminium or the incorrect grade of copper for basic rate ISDN wiring, or of excessive untwisting of UTP cables in high-speed LANs. Where category 5 UTP is installed for a LAN, not more than 13 mm should be stripped back on punchdown blocks, but often this is exceeded. The result is likely to be excessive emissions and crosstalk, with the latter most noticeable with multicast transmissions. Other possible problems are damage to shields on STP cables, excessively sharp bends in cables and excess proximity to power cables. CRC errors are sometimes the early symptom of a network adaptor card that is about to fail, so it may be worth changing this to see if the problem disappears.

11.9 Network modelling and capacity planning

Small networks can be designed on the basis of meeting port count requirements and a few rough calculations, but complex networks require detailed analysis of likely traffic flows and their impact on the networking equipment, for which a modelling package is needed. Comparison of some plausible rough and ready designs for networks with several hundred end-points with results from a modelling package showed a tendency for the rough versions to cost about 10 to 20% more than the optimized designs.

Modelling tools are usually specific to a given type of network, such as circuit switch or X.25 or router, and can be based on either analytic techniques or simulation. For initial network design analytic tools are essential, but once a detailed design has been determined it can be refined by the use of simulation. Simulation can be used to test the detailed behaviour of a small number of possible network configurations, but is impractical for testing large numbers. Topological optimization is usually performed analytically using common heuristic algorithms such as ADD, DROP or 'rolling snowball aggregation'. ADD works by gradually working out from a central node of a star by adding the next most cost-effective link, whereas DROP progressively eliminates the next most cost-ineffective node from a design with nodes at far too many sites. These algorithms only work well where an almost continuous range of equipment sizes is available in the vendors product suite to cover alterations to node size as other sites are added or dropped; this usually means that several models must be considered for each node down to the card level. Snowball algorithms are more decentralized and look for aggregation points for a mesh network. Some additional information on these topics is provided in the mathematical appendix to this book.

In the cases of circuit switch multiplexers and X.25 switches the routing algorithms and device processor operation are proprietary, so detailed modelling often requires a package that takes these features into account. Such packages are sometimes available from some of the larger vendors, but in general less accurate commercial packages have to be used.

Commercial packages have to be made available at a price that the market will bear and running on widely used platforms, particularly PCs; this means that functionality is not as great as is sometimes required. These packages have to make plausible assumptions about the routes followed and the overall processing loads and delays; usually they give quite a good picture of line loadings, but can be in serious error for the device processor loadings which depend heavily on the hardware and software architectures. Best results are obtained when the main performance limiting factors are the transmission lines rather than the networking devices. Users have to rely on the vendors' understanding of their own equipment to get the initial design right in this respect if networking kit is the limiting factor, unless a customized package is available; thereafter the device statistics can be used to check for potential overload situations. Router networks are better in this respect because of the standard routing algorithms used, but again equipment loading requires detailed treatment specific to the individual router architecture. Some of the main current commercial design packages are listed below, but it should be noted that this area is subject to rapid change, so that some models will disappear and others be produced that are not referred to here. Where some feature of a package is criticized here, there is a good chance that an improved version will already be available.

11.9.1   Netsolve from Quintessential

This program running under either Windows or Motif was the major *ab initio* design tool for X.25 and multiplexer networks, giving minimum costs topologies and estimates of throughput and response time. Its main role now appears to be in linecost optimization for which monthly tariff database updates are issued.

11.9.2   Autonet

There is a range of modules under the Autonet banner from Network Design and Analysis, covering US and international tariffs, hierarhical and backbone WAN design as well as performance estimation. The performance module, Performance-3, can use both expected data and real traffic from network analysers to do what-if calculations.

11.9.3   Quartz

This is a package from SIMULOG that enables a user to check the likely performance of X.25 networks analytically with inclusion also of OSI Transport classes 0 or 4. It can be adapted to give similar information for other similarly structured protocols, such as TCP/IP.

11.9.4 NETDA and NETDA/2

These programs are for the design of SNA networks only. NETDA/2 is the PC deriv-ative of the earlier MVS mainframe NETDA program, and runs on OS/2 platforms with 486 or better processors and at least 16 Mbyte RAM. The programs are the most comprehensive widely available tools for such networks allowing the designer to optimize both topology and performance.

Inputs include site locations, traffic and its features, such as priority and security, node types, line types and design constraints. These constraints include the proportion of existing networks that must be used as well as response times and reliability.

Outputs include network topology, loadings, delays, costs, uptime and specialized SNA features such as VTAM and NCP PATH statements. Graphic displays can be obtained if Graphics View/2 is also used.

Intervening networks, such as X.25 or IP, have to be treated as a special type of node in this model, so it is rather limited when used for multiprotocol networks instead of pure SNA.

11.9.5 Other packages

A large number of other models have been produced, particularly in relation to line costing for specific regions of the world. One of the main US items for this is MIND-Pricer (other modules also available) and Autonet, which designs a least-cost network. Within the UK, Cristie's line costing program is one of the most widely used.

BEST from BGS provides an alternative to NETDA for design of SNA networks.

11.9.6 Simulation models

Once the main features of a network have been designed, it can be checked and fine-tuned using a simulation package. Whereas analytic packages only give a steady state picture of a network, simulation provides the ability, at least in principle, to study what happens when a failure occurs and a network reconfigures itself. Unfortunately this requires detailed knowledge of the precise routing, reconfiguration and congestion control algorithms of the equipment being used, so it is rarely available in practice. The main commercial packages at present are CACI's COMNET III, Netmaker XA from Make Systems and BONES from Alta Group. Again, the need for customization arises if the lines are not the limiting factor.

Netmaker from Make Systems

Netmaker XA (and the earlier Netool) is aimed at TDM and router networks, and has plug-in modules for some of the more widespread networking devices in these cat-egories such as IDNX multiplexers and routers from Cisco and Wellfleet. It contains an object-oriented database that supports traffic templates, the loading of logfiles from devices on the actual network and descriptions of equipment characteristics. In addition to simulating a given network, the package will make suggestions for how the design can be improved. What-if calculations are performed on a point and click basis. For networks in the USA, there is also some tariffing information for the major carriers, enabling the network manager to see the financial consequences of design changes as well as the performance. The hardware platform is a Sun Sparcstation 10/40, preferably with about 256 Mbyte RAM.

Router simulation is closely related to specified software releases of the supported devices and the main network protocols, making this arguably the most reliable off-the-shelf package for understanding a router network.

A fairly extensive protocol library is available, but source route bridging is absent on account of routing being determined by end-stations.

COMNET III from CACI

COMNET III is the latest in CACI's range of network simulation packages, replacing COMNET II.5. Versions exist for a wide range of hardware platforms ranging from 16 Mbyte 486 PCs up to Sparc and HP workstations.

COMNET III handles most current technologies including X.25, ISDN, SS7, frame relay, ATM, FDDI, DECnet, SNA, TCP/IP, 802.3/802.5 LANs and satellite networks. The network simulation is set up graphically by pointing and clicking on a variety of types of links and nodes. The model has the option of geographic maps, although many of the backgrounds must be created by the user. Nodes are either application nodes or communications nodes, of which the former accept processing, read/write and transport commands from applications, while the communications nodes perform switching as well as acting as sources and sinks.

Communications nodes are further subdivided into the various networking devices, such as packet switches, multiplexers and routers. Each of these types is given a standard set of the main parameters for its class, which the user can set to those characteristic of any particular vendor's equipment. Idiosyncrasies of a particular vendor's switch architecture is outside the basic model, but an optional extendable code module should enable a very sophisticated user to add such features. This is done by specifying node objects and link objects which inherit the main features of the object-oriented model, but have modifcations and additions to the bandwidth or switching parameters respectively.

Packet switching can be defined on a per port basis, thereby enabling the model to distinguish between the different switching rates displayed by a single device in different contexts, such as an X.25 switching PAD supporting SDLC/QLLC encapsulation, X.25–X.25 switching and X.25–Trunk switching on different ports. Only a single protocol is allowed on any one port, so the user has to work out an average processing rate for a mixture of call set ups and packet switching.

Routing libraries exist for the main routing protocols, RIP, OSPF, IGRP and IS-IS. The basic router object is characterized by port–port switching rates for traffic entering and leaving by the same card, and by a packet size divided by BUS rate for inter-card switching. No distinction is made between different types of traffic on the same port except for allowing different priorities. Multiple parallel routes are catered for in the model, but on the assumption that the end-stations automatically resequence traffic; this is all right for TCP, but wrong for LLC2 end-stations where session loss may occur. Other limitations in the initial version are the simplistic treatment of errors on the line, the lack of modelling of retransmissions due to time-outs at level 4 and the omission of any modules to calculate convergence times for router or bridge reconfiguration. It is, however, very easy to use.

BONES and PLANnet from Alta Group (formerly Comdisco)

Alta supply a sophisticated customizable simulation model, BONES_DESIGNER, and a standard network simulator called PLANnet. Both of these use a block-based graphical user interface. Blocks have a hierarchical structure so that subnetworks can be created at each of the nodal points of the top level. The blocks are constructed out of library blocks that represent the fundamental features of the simulation, notably:

- random number generators
- traffic sources
- queues
- servers
- timers
- memories
- delays
- probes
- data structure accessors and modifiers.

Connections between the blocks are then set up to represent data paths.

The simpler of the two packages is PLANnet which contains modules for Ethernet, 10 Base-T hubs, 4/16 Mbps Token Ring, FDDI, local bridging, multiport routers and point–point WAN links. This will give a general simulation of the effects of connecting LANS over WAN links, but the lack of support for individual WAN protocols means that it is not suitable for performance tuning.

The more sophisticated package, BONES_DESIGNER, is intended for more general-purpose simulations than just networks. For networking applications it contains essentially the same modules as PLANnet, but with additional modules for frame relay and ATM, as well as a specific e-mail model. The most promising of these for WAN optimization is the ATM application; this concentrates on three main performance issues: end–end cell delay, cell loss and cell delay variation. Call set up of virtual circuits is excluded from the simulation, and the GFC header field is not used since standards are not yet defined. Initially the model only deals with AAL 5

Table 11.3   Settable parameters.

LAN	WAN
Token holding time	Network address list
Token R propagation delay	Cost matrix
CSMA/CD propagation delay	Peak bit rate memory
Max. queue size (LAN)	Theory arrival time memory
Packet length	Link propagation delay/unit length
Interarrival mean time	Link length
	Max. number marked cells in queue
	Switch delay/cell
	Network link capacity
	Interworking unit link capacity
	B-NT2 capacity
	Max. ATM queue size

traffic from LAN to LAN via ATM. The main parameters that can be set are shown in Table 11.3.

In this model the B-NT2 is a PABX-like device that concentrates connections, while the interworking unit converts LAN protocols into cells and the ATM switch performs the network switching and routing. In many real situations these functions will be represented by different modules in a single switch.

There is also a specialist satellite network modelling module for BONES, namely SatLab. This is mainly concerned with visibility, channel quality and routing in mobile satellite systems, such as LEOs. The main access methods, TDMA, DAMA and FDMA, can all be modelled.

WorkBench from SES

This simulation model is also provided by ERA Technology in the UK. It is oriented slightly more towards LAN and server issues than the others, and provides a more sophisticated treatment of priorities in FDDI and Token Ring. Customization to individual requirements can be provided.

OPNET from Mil3

This uses an X-based graphical interface and runs on major UNIX platforms. Its WAN protocol suite comprises ATM, TCP/IP and X.25. It differs from some of the other early ATM models in including the effects of segmentation and reassembly (SAR), which imposes a heavy load at the edge of the network. The model is able to import sniffer files. It is expected to be provided with a tariffing module from MIND in the near future.

IBM's Snapshot

This is a sophisticated simulation model of IBM mainframes, servers, databases, networked applications and SNA that runs on IBM mainframes. It is used by IBM to provide consultancy to its customers, but is not currently available as a product.

Modline from SIMULOG

This is a general-purpose tool for modelling and performance analysis of discrete event systems that can be used for data communications. It is an object-oriented derivative of the earlier QNAP2 model that contains four main modules:

- QNET – a graphical construction interface;
- Experimenter – an analytical tool for creating events;
- Analyzer – to analyse results;
- Reporter to produce graphics or textual reports.

Modline is available for Sun, RS/6000, HP 9000/7000 and DEC/Ultrix workstations.
     Data communications objects are not predefined, so must be created by the user.

Optivity Network Designer

This is a module in Bay Networks' Optivity network management package. Although originally developed for LAN applications of Bay Networks (Synoptics) hubs it is applicable to any network devices that support RMON or RMON 2. It uses these statistics for live network traffic to enable the network manager to do what-if calculations for related scenarios, such as increasing types of traffic, changing media speeds or moving devices. Initially it only applied to the LAN, but inclusion of routers has led to an increase in scope.

11.10   Further reading

More information on network management is given in Dah and Sudama (1992). Troubleshooting NetWare is covered in Now (1994) and The (1995), DECnet/OSI in Mar[92] LAN Server in Chambers *et al.* (1995) and general principles of troubleshooting internetworks in Miller (1991). Network modelling is discussed in Har[93], Spo[93].

12

Public Network Issues

12.1   Introduction

Most private networks have a limited requirement to attach to services that are only available on a public network, while individual PC users often only have access to external services via such a network. Some corporations also find it convenient to outsource their networking requirements to a public service to facilitate cost control or adaptability. This chapter describes these factors, but omits any detailed description of either the networks available throughout the world or of their tariffs. The reason for this omission is that these features change so fast that reliable data can only be provided by dedicated publications with monthly updates, rather than by a textbook. Two such publications that are recommended for this purpose are *Tariffica* and *DataPro*.

The first requirements in selecting a public network are obviously to ensure that the network is able to support the required protocols at the right geographical locations; in some cases, particularly with microwave links, this will entail site surveys. The next selection factor considered is usually the tariffs entailed, leaving network performance as the last factor. In some large countries, such as the USA, it is often possible to minimize tariffs by making use of several different carriers instead of a single public network, but this frequently has negative effects on performance. Carriers in the USA are divided into local exchange carriers (LECs), which serve individual LATAs, and inter-exchange carriers (IXCs) which provide inter-LATA communications and intra-LATA calls that cross state boundaries. The main LECs are the seven regional Bell companies, while the three main IXCs are AT&T, MCI and Sprint.

Performance over a public network is governed by the same issues as for private networks, but the scale of the networks and the restricted scope for tuning makes the relative importance of factors differ. Response times on old public networks are often poor owing to the large number of hops to traverse the system as compared to a smaller dedicated private network. Security is often an issue on public networks. The simplest form is to use virtual private networks in which security is provided by means of software functions such as closed user groups and password authentication. Data confidentiality is then provided by means of encryption if required.

The following sections of this chapter consider the performance aspects of public networks according to their type in the same order as the types were considered earlier in this book. Access may either be by means of dial up or by a permanent connection.

12.2   Dial-up issues

12.2.1   PSTN

Compatibility of modems and compression standards are major factors for public dial up. The V series of modems and V.42bis compression are reliable standards that should enable successful interworking, but proprietary standards such as the V.FAST intercepts of V.34 will normally only work to another modem of the same type so will not normally be fully usable in the public arena. In most cases they will fall back to a V series standard recognized by the remote modem, but the added value and cost of V.FAST will be wasted.

In some instances of using a public network to obtain information from a third-party service provider, the latter's charges may be based on the total holding time of a port on the information server. If that is the case, then it is important to use a modem that offers a quick call set up, notably V.34 for which the set-up delay is about five seconds, while avoiding V.32bis in which the set-up time is around 20 seconds. This applies even more to the providers of services with short transaction times, such as credit checks, as the number of host ports that they require will be determined largely by the set-up time. Public networks normally only charge from completion of set up, so that in their case this is not a problem.

12.2.2   ISDN

The best form of dial up from the point of view of set-up time is ISDN as a single B-channel can usually be established nationally within 0.5 to 2 seconds, which is much faster than any modem. International ISDN calls take longer to set up than this, with up to 20 seconds in the worst cases.

ISDN services consist of both basic rate with two B-channels and primary with 30 B-channels; most carriers provide both. Primary rate benefits from economies of scale, and has the property that its B-channels can be independently routed, so many organizations use primary rate ISDN at central sites and basic at remote sites. The only disadavantage of this is that supplementary services for basic rate are not normally available for primary rate, while in the UK there is the additional disadvantage that most primary rate services are based on the proprietary DASS2 standard instead of Q.931.

The supplementary services at basic rate are as follows:

- calling line identification provision and restriction (CLIP and CLIR),
- subaddressing, and
- multiple subscriber number.

Closed user groups should become widely available for primary rate.

A useful option that is becoming widely available is the use of the D-channel to carry low throughput user packet data traffic as well as the Q.931 signalling traffic. Higher volumes of X.25 data are carried over an ISDN network by means of B-channels according to the ITU-T X.31 standard. This allows for both dedicated B-channels across the network and for a packet switching version, with routing within the network. Most carriers offer the former, which is simpler and provides a lower response time, but the switched option is more flexible.

12.2.3   Tariffing

Dial-up tariffs are usually based on the call duration and distance, both often in terms of bands rather than a continuous gradation. Initial connection and rental charges for ISDN are usually higher than for PSTN, but the usage charges are frequently the same, making ISDN better value. In the UK both BT and Mercury tariffs now use a basic call duration of one second. In some European networks the basic unit is of the order of 15–200 seconds depending on distance. Most international ISDN calls use a charge interval of six seconds, but with a high initial charge equivalent to about a minute's duration. Where a long basic unit is used, it is important to take account of this in configuring dial-up applications. A timer should be used so that the call is taken down, if inactive, just before the end of a time unit.

Supplementary services usually have small fixed charges of the order of 5% of the rental cost.

Data compression is a useful technique for minimizing the charges for file transfer across dial-up networks. For highly compressible textfiles this can divide usage costs by up to four, while for binary files the reduction will be much less but still significant.

The crude order of magnitude for ISDN tariffs in the USA is about $50 per month for a single B-channel or $2000 per month for full 23 B+D primary rate ISDN. Where packet-based traffic such as frame relay or X.25 is carried there may also be a usage charge of the order of $0.01 per kilo-segment.

Minimal bandwidth international video-conferencing over ISDN at 112/128 kbps costs in the order of $100–150 for half an hour.

12.3   Cellular networks

Peripatetic network users, such as salesmen and field service engineers, often have a requirement for both voice and data communications while on the move and use this type of network. The types of network available can be divided into analog voice/data, digital voice/data and analog data.

Typical analog voice/data networks are the AMPS services in the USA, TACS in Europe and Australia and NMT in Scandinavia. These offer both voice and data services via a single network access unit with data transmission at speeds up to 2400 or 4800 bps according to network. Use of MNP 10 modems with high maximum speeds may appear to offer the possibility of higher throughputs than these figures, but in practice will drop to these low rates. Network protocols are usually specific to a single network, so that in many areas, especially Europe, a given set of equipment can only be used within the restricted region of its network. This type of network is thus unsuited to those with international mobility requirements. Within the USA a major enhancement of the AMPS networks is the use of US cellular digital packet data (CDPD) which provides more effective data communication by using a wider range of frequencies and by making use of channel hopping. Special modems permit nominal transmission rates of up to 19.2 kbps, while its use of the existing AMPS networks should provide high coverage at relatively low cost.

A greater degree of mobility is possible for the pure data services, with RAM operative in several European countries, Scandinavia and the USA. Data transmission rates are higher than for the mixed voice/data analog networks, with speeds up to 19.2 kbps, so that a user with no voice requirements will normally find these better than basic AMPS, TACS or NMT, but not CDPD which should offer comparable quality at lower cost and higher geographic availability.

International mobility within Europe, Asia and the Middle East is provided by the digital GSM (global services mobiles) networks. These again provide for voice or data from a single network interface, with data transmission speeds up to 9600 bps and data confidentiality provided by a proprietary encryption standard. Subject to acceptability of the tariffs, these should be preferable to the earlier analog networks, with much lower bit error rates. Initial data tariffs have tended to contain a large element proportional to the duration, making the service unattractive for anything other than intensive data transfers.

Within North and South America there is a natural evolution path form the current AMPS services to the US digital communications standard (USDC). Performance of USDC is comparable to GSM, with both voice and data rates of up to 8 kbps and a low error rate.

12.4   Circuit switch public networks and leased lines

Minimum performance standards for such public networks are recommended in X.130 and G.821. In general, performance of such networks is very good except where satellite links are involved, with throughput determined primarily by the speed of the access line and secondarily by retransmissions due to errors. If a third-party service is to be provided over such a network, then it will be useful to know the rerouting time of the network. This information may be used to tune timers and retransmission counts to ensure that service is not interrupted by rerouting if that is fast, or else to take down the connection quickly if slow rerouting is going to lead to the user incurring futile heavy connection charges.

Relatively few such networks exist, as compared to packet switch. Datex covers Scandinavia, while similar networks exist in Germany; connection speeds are mostly low in the range 300 to 9600 bps. German 64 kbps circuit switch connections are being replaced by the ISDN service.

An interesting international circuit switch network is Mercury's Switchband service from the UK to Europe, USA and Hong Kong, as it is the first international variable bandwidth service. The user subscribes to a variable number of lines (minimum charge for 10) over a 2 Mbps connection allowing bandwidths of 64, 128, 256, 384, 512, 768, 1472, 1576 or 1920 kbps according to requirements. Calls are charged according to bandwidth and duration, subject to a minimum charge of about £550 per month in addition to the connection rental. This allows a user to have intermittent use of a variety of bandwidths for different applications at a much lower cost than for dedicated circuits for each.

Circuit speeds in Europe are still mainly based on PDH with rates 64 kbps, 2.048 Mbps (E1), 8.192 Mbps (E2), 34 Mbps (E3) and 140 Mbps, with some carriers, such as BT and Mercury in the UK offering N × 64 Kbps up to 1024 kbps, mainly as private leased lines. SDH circuits from 155 Mbps (STM–1) are just beginning to appear. US circuit speeds are based on 56/64 kbps DS0, fractional T1 from 112/128 kbps up to 1288/1472 kbps, 1.544 Mbps T1 and 45 Mbps T3/DS3; Wiltel and AT&T also provide fractional T3. SONET circuits from 51.8 Mbps upwards are also becoming available. Japan uses 64 kbps, 1.544 and 6.3 Mbps (J2) circuits in the PDH hierarchy. PDH hierarchies throughput the world are not directly compatible, unlike the new SDH/SONET standards.

When international trunk cables are used, large window sizes are necessary because of the propagation delay, although this is not as extreme as for satellite links. An 8000 km intercontinental trunk will have delay of 40–50 ms for this reason.

The main long-distance carriers in the USA are MCI, Sprint and AT&T. Elsewhere national PTTs are the main circuit providers, except for the UK where Mercury, Energis and Sprint provide competition for BT nationally, with additional competition in urban areas from CATV providers such as Colt and US West who own the franchise for that area. CATV services are usually much less expensive where they are available.

12.4.1   Leased line tariffs

In much of the world tariffs are based on distance bands, with a high proportion for the shortest band, but in the USA the IXCs are moving towards fixed rates throughout the country. There is also a tendency towards provision of customers with a single service plan for all of their requirements instead of separate ones for each type of traffic.

In the UK the reduction of incremental tariffs with distance often makes it better to extend a leased line than to aggregate it into a trunk at a concentration point unless utilization is very low or the length less than about 15 kms (for BT). This is illustrated by the sample of BT tariffs for 1995 shown in Table 12.1.

Analog A and Analog B, which stand for Standard Keyline and Keyline3/ network keyline respectively, both have a reduced incremental charge of £12.48 per km above 175 km.

In other countries the distance effect is less marked; for example, Japan's NTT prices lines according to 10–20 km bands with only a gradual reduction with increasing distance.

Table 12.1 Sample BT line tariffs.

Service	Min rent pa (£)	Band (kms)	Add rent (per km)	Band (kms)	Add rent (per km)	Band (kms)	Add rent (per km)
Analog A	346	0–5	100	6–15	75	16–175	13.68
Analog B	540	0–5	140	6–15	94	16–175	13.68
Kilostream 64K	1600	0–15	112	15+	6.75	–	–
Kilostream N 512K	5920	0+	72	–	–	–	–
2M Megastream	5886	0–15	325	16+	160	–	–

12.5 X.25 networks

The biggest advantage of X.25 over circuit switch is its ability to provide any-where–anywhere connectivity via SVCs. Where users do not have sufficient traffic to saturate a dedicated circuit for long periods, X.25 is also likely to be more cost effective than circuit switch. Other types of network that effectively statistically multiplex traffic are also available, and X.25 is the best choice for low throughput traffic that lacks a transport layer to guarantee integrity.

These networks are very widely available, but often give poor performance, although with wide differences in this respect. A typical order of magnitude for the transit delay is 200 ms. This is an area in which detailed questions about performance and tuning options need to be put to the public network provider. Minimum standard for response time and connection availability are specified in X.135 and X.136 as quoted in Tables 12.2 and 12.3.

Table 12.2 Response time recommendations (X.135).

Statistic	National A	National B	Internat A	Internat B
AV.	350 ms	650 ms	215 ms	950 ms
95% response	525 ms	825 ms	215 ms	1200 ms
AV. throughput	3000 bps	2400 bps	2000 bps	1800 bps
95% throughput	2400 bps	2000 bps	1800 bps	1500 bps

Table 12.3 Availability of connection (X.136).

Statistic	National A	National B	International A	International B
Set-up error	10^{-5}	2×10^{-5}	–	2×10^{-5}
Set-up fail	5×10^{-3}	10^{-2}	–	10^{-2}

These figures from X.135 and X.136 are worst-case recommendations for public networks. In practice, most are significantly better than these minima.

- National A denotes terrestrial connections via an access network.
- National B refers to either an access network with one satellite link, or to a terrestrial network comprising an access section and a transit section.
- International A refers to an international network with direct circuit connection (and no virtual circuit, hence no contribution to X.136).
- International B denotes an international connection via two satellite links and one transit section, or by one satellite link and two or more transit sections.

The effect of response time on throughput when using end–end acknowledgement (X.25 D-bit set or occasionally a higher-level mimic) and default packet/window sizes is quite drastic and shows that it can sometimes be quite futile to pay for more than 4800 or 9600 bps access using the defaults. Increasing the window size is possible on most networks, but usually incurs an additional charge. By contrast, if the public network allows local acknowledgement, then fast access can be quite worthwhile even with the default packet and window sizes. Increases of packet and window size improve throughput in the end–end case until retransmissions due to errors intervene (see Chapter 3), but will either not be available or else at an increased tariff. Best throughput/price performance is likely to be from networks that offer local acknowledgements and access speeds of 56/64 kbps. Local acknowledgement does mean that there is an increased risk of loss of data, but it is still very small.

It is also worth asking what the trunk speeds are and what size of packet is used on the trunks, as these have a big influence on the response time for short interactive messages against a backgound of file transfers. Some networks accept packets of up to 4096 bytes from users, but then fragment them into 128 byte packets within the network and reassemble before delivery. This prevents the interactive traffic from experiencing long delays on the trunks while waiting for a complete 4096 byte (worst case) packet to be transmitted across a trunk, which in a 56/64 kbps probable worst case would take about half a second. Fragmentation also improves throughput for file transfers with end–end acknowledgements and small windows, provided that the switch packet processing time remains small compared to the line transmission time. Within the UK, part of AT&T's Istel network provides exceptionally low delays for X.25 interactive traffic over 64 kbps circuits, by virtue of using a proprietary multi-user trunking protocol instead of the more common X.25/X.75 derivatives (in late 1995).

In any event, the user should obtain a service agreement that states what the average and 95% response times should be, together with some method of monitoring it.

VPNs based on X.25 are an option for most service providers. Security is based on X.25 closed user groups (with incoming/outgoing features), while a dedicated management terminal is also a common option. This management terminal normally allows the user a complete view of the VPN, sometimes accompanied by the option to carry out a limited set of configuration changes on the end-points.

Most networks offer a range of access speeds from 4.8 kbps up to 56/64 kbps (occasionally to 256 kbps or even 1920 kbps for the French Transpac network), with PAD options for other traffic types, such as asynchronous, SDLC and BSC. Added value functions, such as e-mail and EDI, are also available in many cases. X.25 and asynchronous dial-in (X.32 and X.28 respectively) is also supported in many cases, as well as the permanent connections. The main performance factors associated with dial-in are the call set-up time of the modem and the bandwidth.

The main X.25 network providers in the USA are Sprint, BT, Advantis/IBM and Compuserve, with Stentor Datapac and Unitel in Canada, while in Europe service is based primarily on national PTTs. Major international networks are also provided by AT&T, GEIS and Infonet. Within the UK, X.25 networks are also provided by Mercury, Racal Network Services and AT&T Istel. Many of these service providers also offer frame relay, but the main such service in the USA is from MCI.

12.5.1   X.25 tariffing

Public X.25 networks normally have a basic connection and annual rental charge for the access circuit based on its capacity, plus additional charges for usage and extra facilities. Dial-in services also have a duration charge.

Usage charges are normally based on the number of data segments sent, where segments are blocks of 64 characters rounded up to the nearest integer in Europe, but kilocharacters in the USA. In some cases there are also duration and minimum charges for switched virtual circuits, but not for PVCs.

The range of extra facilities varies significantly between networks. The most common options are additional logical channels, closed user groups, PVCs and reverse charging, while others include fast select, hunt groups, incoming/outgoing barring, larger packet and window sizes and various PAD types. In some instances, the basic connection charge is for a specified bundle size of logical channels, rather than just one.

The additional costs of these extras tend to be around 10% on average, but PVCs are liable to be 50–500% more expensive as fixed charges since they are free from duration costs.

Use of relatively high speed access circuits, for example 48–64 kbps, is often only worthwhile when at least 10 logical channels are subscribed to, owing to the limited throughput possible if end–end acknowledgements are used. For example, in the UK British Telecom uses end–end integrity, while Racal Network Services provides local acknowledgement, so users of the former could only make use of high access rate by multiple circuits, whereas those of the latter could in principle get up to about 65% usage from a single VC.

Data compression is important for minimizing network usage bills as well as for improving throughput. Ideally the X.25 DTE should compress the data before packetizing it, as in this way it reduces both the number of bytes transmitted and the number of packets, hence it cuts the bill in two ways. Compression after packetization should only be used on networks that do not have any per packet charge.

12.6   LAN interconnect

Many public networks now offer services optimized for LAN interconnect. These services usually assume the existence of a transport layer in the user's equipment and aim to provide a fast, but not reliable delivery mechanism. There are four main types of such service: TCP/IP, frame relay, SMDS and ATM, often used in different parts of the same network.

12.6.1   TCP/IP

This is the protocol used on the ubiquitous Internet, and also offered by some carriers. It has the advantage of being thoroughly understood and widely supported, but as a packet switch protocol does not offer such rapid transmission as the frame/cell relay techniques.

The main TCP/IP public commercial network in the USA is provided by Sprint.

Sweden has a public TCP/IP network, SWIPnet, that also provides commercial interconnection with the Internet.

Many other carriers are also producing IP services, usually with connectivity to the Internet.

12.6.2   Frame relay

Frame relay is an alternative to the traditional circuit switch TDM network. Its main advantage in this regard is its greater cost-effectiveness through the ability to share trunk bandwidth with other users where throughput is well short of the access circuit speed. Response times are slightly greater than for circuit switch networks with comparable access speed, and there is a risk of frames being dropped when congestion occurs. As compared to X.25, frame relay offers higher access speeds and throughput, but lower reliability; early frame relay networks also only provide PVCs between fixed predefined end-points, but anywhere–anywhere SVCs are becoming available. Typical access speeds are 56/64 kbps up to T1/E1 speeds, but with the expectation that T3/E3 will be offered when demand justifies it.

Most such networks offer the user a committed information rate (CIR) per PVC, such that any traffic up to this limit should be delivered, whereas no guarantee is provided if the limit is exceeded. The CIR is related to the size of a burst of traffic (typically from a file server) within a characteristic time (see Chapter 6) and some network tariffing also provides for an excess burst size within the same period above which traffic is liable to be automatically dropped or surcharged if it can be carried. The network user needs to understand the operation of the LAN servers in order to decide what CIR is needed, and Chapter 6 provides some guidance on this.

Frame relay tariffing

Tariffing policies vary widely in relation to CIRs and the attitude to excess traffic. Some networks offer a fixed price per connection, while others charge also on the basis of the CIR and the actual traffic carried. CIRs for individual PVCs tend to be limited to a maximum of about 70% of the access bandwidth.

Many networks oversubscribe circuits so that the sum of the CIRs to be carried over a given circuit exceeds the available bandwidth by a factor of about two to three. The rationale for this is that the CIR needed to avoid dropping traffic in the middle of a burst is usually significantly higher than the average throughput of the PVC, even during the peak hour. Many networks estimate the levels that can be used on the basis of the statistics for frames dropped, and try to ensure that the loadings keep this figure very small.

Some public networks, such as Sprint, offer the option of zero CIR at a relatively low tariff. This service provides no guarantees against dropping frames nor any specific throughput, but is a good option for traffic where these are not likely to be an issue. Quality of service obviously depends on the day-to-day loading of the circuits, but early Sprint users were said to be able to achieve 60–70% of the wire speed most of the time.

Most European PTTs now offer frame relay services, while in the USA the main such networks are MCI, LDD/Wiltel, AT&T and Sprint.

A feature to check is the number of frame relay VCs permitted in the basic and incremental charges for a single network access point. Some routers require multiple VCs per destination in order to give adequate quality of service for different protocols supported on the LAN, and this can have a significant impact on network costs.

12.6.3 SDH/SONET

Since 1994 most major European and US networks have started to introduce fibre-optic network elements based on SDH/SONET in preference to the older PDH. This provides core networks using predominantly STM-1, STM-4 and STM-16 trunks, with bandwidths from 155 to 2488 Mbps. These cores are used mainly as the basis for superior switched voice services and for SMDS and ATM.

In the UK British Telecom is using SDH as the basis for a high resilience 2 Mbps MegaStream service called Genus, which should provide 99.995% availability, coupled to rerouting in under 200 ms in the event of failures. The majority of the new local cable providers in the UK are also offering SDH in their areas, while Energis has based its new national network entirely on SDH.

Early US tariffs for dedicated SONET lines were rather high, an extreme example being about $5 000 000 per annum for a coast-to-coast link at 155 Mbps.

12.6.4 SMDS

SMDS overlaps in access speed with the upper end of frame relay and the lower end of ATM, so that there is a risk of its being squeezed out. Most initial services are in

Table 12.4   SMDS classes.

Access class	Rate (Mbps)
1	2
2	4
3	10
4	16
5	25
6	34

the range T1/E1 to T3/E3, but with a probability of services up to 155 Mbps later. As a connectionless service, SMDS allows flexible high-speed LAN interconnect without the interoperability issues associated with ATM's LAN emulation.

Compared to frame relay its advantage is a higher access speed, but with the disadvantage of higher overheads in the region of 25% instead of less than 5%. Like frame relay it does not guarantee to carry all traffic; instead there is a subscribed information rate (SIR) analogous to the CIR. Tariffs are normally based on this SIR, with additional charges for such features as closed user groups. Most services only offer a small range of SIRs as shown in Table 12.4 that match the speeds of LANs and associated links.

As demand grows, higher-speed access is likely to be added. SMDS only provides a variable bit rate data service, so cannot be used for carrying isochronous traffic with strict jitter and skew requirements. At the highest speeds, that is, T3/E3, queuing delays are sufficiently small for compressed video to be transmitted satisfactorily over SMDS, since the buffering used by the compression algorithms compensates for the small variability in the queuing delays.

Some European carriers may offer the wider CBDS service definition which allows for isochronous services.

A big deterrent to the use of some of the early SMDS services is that some carriers require users to pay for a permanent T1/E1 to T3/E3 access line to the nearest exchange that supports SMDS in addition to the SIR charge, whereas what the user often wants is occasional use of very high bandwidth. As most of the cost of a leased line is incurred over short distances, this makes the service uneconomic for such potential users. In the USA the regional Bell operating companies tend to offer fixed costs per port regardless of actual usage. In the UK BT has introduced an element of usage-based charging for the 16 and 25 Mbps SIRs.

As with X.25 and frame relay, security can be provided by means of VPNs.

SMDS tariffs

The basic component of SMDS charges are:

- registration charge to open account,
- installation/connection charge depending on SIR,

- periodic rental charge depending on SIR and distance,
- usage charge,
- supplementary features such as multi-addressing and CUGs,
- discounts based on time of day, number of connections.

As an example, the initial charges of BT in the UK in 1995 are quoted in Table 12.5.

An ITC is an identified traffic connection between two fixed sites only. Discounts of 5% were available for 5–15 connections, 10% for greater than 15, with 10% for a five-year contract.

Another example is Germany's Datex-M which had SIRs of N × 64 kbps, 2 Mbps and 34 Mbps with standard connection and rental charges for each covering data usage up to 10 Gbytes per month, but with additional charges for each further 10 Gbytes/month.

12.6.5 ATM

ATM networks were originally intended to carry broadband ISDN traffic at speeds of at least 155 Mbps over SDH or SONET optical fibre networks, but the desire to satisfy the LAN interconnect market with a future-proof service has led to its introduction at much lower speeds that compete directly with SMDS. Again cells are liable to be dropped if the access traffic exceeds a subscriber agreement.

The advantage over SMDS is that ATM should provide for both constant bit rate isochronous traffic and variable bit rate data, although the initial networks mainly tend to support the latter. An important feature of ATM is that it can be used as a carrier for both frame relay and SMDS, so that low-speed access traffic can enter by these means, but be converted to appropriate cells for transport across a high-speed backbone.

Most of these initial services use the AAL5 format for data, wherein all cells except the last use the full 48 byte payload for data, while those carriers that support CBR services use AAL1 for this purpose. SMDS can in principle be carried directly over ATM by means of AAL3/4, but initially this type of cell structure is only offered by a few mainly European service providers.

Table 12.5 Sample BT SMDS tariffs.

SIR(Mbps)	Connection (£)	Rent pa (£) up to 25 km	Extra rent per km >25	Fixed ITC rent pa	ITC rent per km
0.5	9 000	8 250	63	–	–
2	9 000	16 000	165	–	–
4	33 000	43 000	2 004	–	–
10	33 000	55 000	2 004	–	–
16	33 000	36 000	2 004	26 400	696
25	33 000	36 000	2 004	39 600	1 080

Widespread use of broadband ISDN services is unlikely before the year 2000, so the short-term advantage of ATM over SMDS is its early capability to carry pure voice without gaps in transmission, plus its guaranteed upgrade path. Cell structure for the LAN interconnect traffic is similar to that for SMDS leading to comparable overheads using AAL3/4, but these drop to about 12% for native CBR cell traffic or AAL5.

ATM networks are starting to become fairly widespread, particularly in North America. By the end of 1995, there were four nationwide ATM networks in the USA, namely AT&T, LDDS Worldcom, MCI and Sprint, while in Canada both Stentor and Unitel offer fairly wide coverage. The US networks all provide CBR and VBR services at 45 or 155 Mbps, and MCI also offer UBR. Within the envelope possible with these line speeds, most carriers offer a wide range of cell rates, varying from about 4 kbps up to the order of 10 Mbps. For long-distance circuits it is usually necessary to have either multiple VCs or else no windowing in order to make use of the highest throughputs (see Chapter 9). Europe is less advanced in this respect, but many PTTs and other carriers have more limited networks, notably Swiss PTT, Deutsche Telecom and Telecom Finland.

Early services are mostly based on use of PVCs, with public SVCs still at a very experimental stage.

ATM tariffs

Most early ATM tariffs were unpublished and varied widely between providers, both as regards tariff structure and overall cost. Thus some early tariffs included examples of about $60 000 per annum for unlimited use of a local 45 Mbps circuit in the USA, while Finland Telecom was offering 155 Mbps at about $40 000 per annum. Instead of a flat rate some carriers offer tariffs based on port speed, access link length and usage, which is better for low utilization VBR services. MCI also offered a relatively low tariff for their UBR service, but the downside of UBR is that all cells are marked as low priority with CLP bit set to one, so that in congested conditions they will be dropped.

SVCs with individual classes of service and usage-based tariffs seemed likely to appear in 1996, particularly for ABR services. RM cells for ABR flow control are normally chargeable as well as the user data.

New companies offering ATM in niche markets have the best opportunity for low tariffs, whereas established carriers have the problem of relating tariffs to those of their other competing services. Rapid evolution of ATM tariffs seems probable with sharp falls where competition becomes intense.

12.7   Satellite services

In many developing countries, and also Eastern Europe, the most effective method of obtaining high bandwidth connectivity to all but a few central locations is the use of VSAT technology. This also applies to connections to these countries from others with a wider range of services.

These services can be either one-way, suitable for centralized information distribution, or interactive also in a high proportion of cases. Bandwidth is much more flexible than terrestrial leased lines, and it is often possible to obtain increased bandwidth at a few days' notice instead of the few weeks or months often needed for the leased lines. The main type of network available at present is that based on GEOs, characterized by its long propagation delay of 270 ms per hop.

The cost of the central hub of a VSAT network (very roughly one million dollars) means that usually of the order of 100 end-stations are needed to make private VSAT networks economic where an alternative exists. Public VPN satellite networks are also an option for smaller networks. Costs are often independent of distance and underlying protocol, and are significantly less than those for dedicated leased lines. Tariffs for point–multipoint one-way distribution are less than those for point–point two-way interactions, and often provide the least expensive solution to centralized distribution requirements.

The main public VSAT networks quote availabilities in the range 99.5% to 99.96%, which is significantly greater than leased line services in most countries. Almost all use forward error correction, without which quality might be unacceptable. The most common data transmission rates are 19.2 kbps, 56/64 and 128 kbps, but other rates as low as 1.2 kbps and as high as 2.048 Mbps can be obtained by selecting the right network. Provision of unequal data rates in the in/out directions is widespread. Satellite transmissions are very easily intercepted, so in cases where data confidentiality is important encryption is essential. Some US services provide DES encryption, but restrictions on overseas sale of DES means that most have proprietary encryption options. Some networks provide security through spread spectrum techniques instead of encryption.

The main applications for which VSAT is ideal are one-way video distribution, especially training material and presentations, and disaster recovery.

Another use of such public networks is to interconnect national sections of an international terrestrial network, as satellite links are often less expensive than terrestrial alternatives of comparable capacity for long-distance intercontinental trunks; within Europe, however, cables are cheaper. Comsat is the main international service with regulated services through Intelsat and Inmarsat.

The main VSAT networks in the USA are AT&T Tridom, GTE Spacenet, Hughes Network Systems and Scientific-Atlanta with a large number of other smaller competitors. European VSAT services were hamstrung for a long time by regulatory issues that prevented national terrestrial services from being bypassed, so are less widely used; PTTs are again the main providers. Some network providers have several distinct VSAT networks, usually for reasons of growth, but offering slightly different services.

LEOs with much lower delays are becoming available, principally to support mobile voice communications.

12.7.1 Satellite tariffing

Satellite links are charged on a basis of their bandwidth, with cost roughly proportional to the bandwidth. Costs for international links are comparable to those for terrestrial links in many cases, but about 10% higher in other short-distance cases, and less for long distances like UK to Japan or Singapore.

12.8   Internet access

The rapid growth of services on the Internet has led a high proportion of public networks to provide gateways to the Internet. Many carriers provide such access from each of their other types of access; thus PSTN, ISDN and frame relay access is widely available, while others such as SMDS and CATV are more localized. Dedicated Internet access providers usually make use of public dial-up access to their own gateways. Cable modems and Novell's NEST powerline technologies offer considerable hope for reasonably cost-effective high bandwidth access from the home.

The main applications are e-mail, which uses little bandwidth, and World Wide Web access, which is extremely intensive.

Almost all Web sites provide users with data in precompressed form, such as ZIP or Stacker files, JPEG still images and MPEG movies, so what the user requires is a corresponding range of PC applications plus web browser and FTP program, rather than data compression software in the networking kit.

The other technique for minimizing costs for the home user is optimization of the receiving window size. This should be at least four times the TCP/IP MTU, that is, typically four times 576 bytes, and preferably about eight times the MTU if the PC (or equivalent) is not being used for much else at the time.

Within urban areas cable modems seem likely to become established as the most cost-effective means of obtaining high bandwidth access to the Internet. Early services seem likely to include symmetric in/out bandwidth of 500 kbps and 4 Mbps, with an asymmetric service based on about 27 Mbps in to the user and 768 kbps out. In the latter case the bandwidth is shared between numerous users so that each is likely to see about 1.5 Mbps in and 60–100 kbps out. Suggested initial tariffing for this service is comparable to that for a single ISDN B-channel, making this far more attractive for users wishing to obtain video services.

12.9   Further reading

The material in this chapter dates especially quickly, so the reader is referred to *Tariffica* and *DataPro* periodicals for more up-to-date information, and to the World Wide Web sites of the public network providers.

13

Conclusions

13.1 General remarks

13.2 Modem issues

13.3 Multiplexers

13.4 Packet switch and router networks

13.5 General principles

13.1   General remarks

This chapter summarizes the overall conclusions reached in earlier chapters. In attempting to optimize performance it is essential to distinguish between what is optimum for a LAN and what is optimum for a WAN, as well as to distinguish between the needs of interactive traffic and of file transfers.

On a LAN the best performance is usually obtained with very large packet sizes, as this optimizes server performance and minimizes protocol overheads, but on a WAN this often breaks down due to transmission errors and store and forward delays on multihop routes. Transmission errors are important on all WAN links other than optical fibre and constitute the size limiting factor on single hop routes. On multiple hop routes, the need to completely receive a packet in a switch or router before commencing onward transmission reduces the optimum size still further, so that on many slow packet switch networks the optimum size is only 128 or 256 bytes. The drawback to this is the increased processing and header overheads associated with small packets, so it is essential to see which is most important out of optimizing response time, bandwidth used or switch processor load. As the WAN is the bottleneck in LAN–WAN communications, it is the one that has to be optimized where a conflict in techniques arises, but subject to distinction between the modes above. Packet fragmentation at the edge of the WAN, for example via X.25 M-bit, allows the retention of optimal large server packets if necessary. Frame relay is an exception to the response time argument provided that the implementation uses cut-through switching instead of store and forward, and it is essential to check this point when purchasing such equipment if response time over multihop routes is important to the business.

When interactive traffic shares low-speed WAN links, at 64 kbps or less, with file transfers, it is also necessary to use small packets plus prioritization otherwise the response time for the former will be severely degraded by the latter.

With ATM these problems cease to apply as ATM is usually run over optical fibres with very low error rates, while the high transmission speeds and small cell sizes mean that interactive and file transfer traffic can easily be mixed.

The general rule of WAN optimization is to look for bottlenecks, solving the worst one before going on to the next.

13.2   Modem issues

In many parts of the world, analog links are still the most readily available means of connection to networks, so despite the superior characteristics of digital transmission, modems remain extremely important. Over the years there have been a succession of modem standards offering progressively higher bit transmission speeds. For file transfers it is almost always the case that the higher the bit rate, the lower will be the transmission time, but for short interactive transactions this is not so true. The problem is that the faster bit rates depend on much more complex processing in the modem which introduces a significant delay on both transmission and reception, thereby offsetting some of the benefit of the higher speed. Modems for the faster line speeds also use more powerful processors for this reason, but more complex line sampling criteria prevent the total elimination of this effect.

For a few applications, such as credit card verification, a low call set-up time may be more important than the actual transmission rate, as it is the main factor determining how long a host port is held open and how long a checkout operator has to wait to complete a customer transaction. Faster modems have tended to have longer set-up times, particularly so with V.32bis, but this problem has been addressed with the later V.34 standard whose typical 5–10 second call set-up time is less than those of the older slower standards. Nevertheless, V.34 is much slower in this regard than ISDN, where national calls usually take less than two seconds to set up.

As V.34 also tolerates higher noise levels than V.32bis as well as operating twice as fast, it promises to be something of a panacea. For asynchronous traffic, V.34 with compression can produce comparable throughput to ISDN from V.110 terminal adaptors (which often lack compression), but much less than the later V.120 terminal adaptors on which compression is commonplace.

13.3 Multiplexers

Multiplexer networks offer very little opportunity or need for tuning, as a circuit switch network has largely fixed delays depending on bandwidth, multiplexer latency and propagation delay. When remote sites are first connected across such a network it may be necessary to increase retry timers to allow for rerouting in the event of failures and, particularly at high bit rates, to increase window size to overcome reductions in throughput due to propagation delay.

Some multiplexers offer considerable line cost savings through the use of such techniques as reading inter-PABX signalling to free up voice channels, packetized voice and frame relay. All of these will give some degradation of performance, but to a calculable degree.

13.4 Packet switch and router networks

Most contemporary data networks belong to this category, which includes such traditional protocols as frame relay, X.25, SNA, TCP/IP and IPX among others. These have a very large scope for tuning, with the main features of packet and window sizes already referred to in the introduction to this chapter.

SNA/SDLC was the earliest of these protocols and arguably offers the best throughput due to its self-adjusting Pacing mechanism, but with poor resilience and rerouting capabilities, and is restricted to IBM environments. Many performance monitoring and tuning tools are also available for this. APPN+ (that is, with HPR) should provide resilient LAN–WAN interworking that retains the high performance of SNA.

X.25 was the most widespread type of network for a long time due to the support of the protocol on almost all vendors' hardware, although this position is now being challenged by TCP/IP. It was designed to meet the requirements of poor quality low-speed analog lines and dumb terminals; as a result it has more error checking and flow control features than are needed for modern workstations communicating over good-quality digital links. Associated with this is a reputation for poor performance that is not entirely deserved, as a modern network can be tuned to provide high throughput over T1/E1 links if powerful switches are used in conjunction with large packet window sizes. The X.25 D-bit is used to provide end–end flow control for individual virtual circuits to dumb equipment, but should not be used for intelligent end-stations with a transport level protocol. When operating over satellite or intercontinental trunk links, the extended window size options should be used. Typically this entails a level 2 window size of 127 and a level 3 window of about 15 to allow decent file transfer performance. The general rule of thumb for estimating the window size needed to give uninterrupted throughput with end–end flow control of any form is

Window size (in packets) $\geqslant$ Line speed $\times$ Response time (FILO basis)/Packet size

The OSI protocol that was designed to replace X.25 by cutting out its unnecessary features is frame relay. This is a level 2 protocol that is intended to give circuit switch type performance for short bursts of traffic while still providing the cost benefits associated with the statistical multiplexing of virtual circuits. This is achieved by means of the committed information rate (CIR) whereby the network guarantees (if correctly designed) to transmit a burst of data up to a specified size across the network in a critical time, the ratio of which is the CIR. Frames exceeding the CIR are liable to be dropped. The burst size depends on the end-station, and is usually up to 64 kbytes with the time parameter dependent on access line speed. A frame relay switch can handle roughly five times as many frames as an X.25 switch with comparable processor, and can also gain considerably in performance on multiple hop routes by the use of cut-through switching (if implemented) whereby a frame is forwarded as soon as the header has been read instead of waiting for the checksum at the end. The reduced error checking capability means that frame relay needs better quality lines than X.25, with a bit error rate (BER) of less than 1 in 10^6 or 10^7 which rules out many analog circuits.

End–end flow control with frame relay is expected to be provided by a transport layer protocol, such as TP4 in the OSI case, or SNA or TCP. This layer will handle retransmission of packets that are dropped due to errors or excess rate. TP4 is largely derived from TCP and is the most comprehensive of five transport classes defined in ITU-T recommendation X.224. It provides a credit window for transport level data units that should be set by the same rule of thumb for uninterrupted flow as for X.25 above.

TCP was designed to provide reliable transport over a resilient but unreliable medium, namely the early Internet with IP as the network level protocol. TCP/IP was widely adopted in the UNIX and Ethernet arenas from which it has expanded to become the *de facto* open standard for LAN interconnection. Its performance characteristics differ considerably from X.25 as the minimum packet size is usually 576 bytes with end–end flow control either determined by TCP's Receive Window segment or absent if UDP is used instead of TCP. 576 bytes is a minimum for efficient operation on a LAN, but too large for poor analog links and for multihop store and forward operation across a WAN. Fragmentation of IP datagrams is inefficient as a means of overcoming this due to the large headers, and cut-through frame relay encapsulation (avoiding the need for fragmentation) is the recommended technique for IP transportation across multihop digital networks, using TCP but not UDP. For single-hop poor-quality analog links encapsulation in PPP is best, while multihop analog routes are likely to be best in X.25 with X.25 packet segmentation. Larger packets, such as 1500 bytes, can easily be used with low-error digital links, provided that the network path does not contain a lot of slow hops.

IPX, prior to NetWare version 4, and AppleTalk, prior to AppleTalk Link State protocol, were designed for operation in a LAN environment and are both inefficient on a WAN. Early NetWare core protocol (NCP) has a fixed window size of one that requires an acknowledgement for each packet; this gives a dreadful response time over slow multihop WAN routes that is sometimes blamed on X.25. In fact X.25 is much more efficient in that environment and the best remedy is to encapsulate in X.25 with packet segmentation and a large X.25 window or to upgrade to a later version of NCP. For message sizes up to about 4000 bytes X.25 may remain the better option, whereas longer messages will be better handled by the packet burst mode features of NetWare 4 or later.

13.4.1   Mixed traffic types

Where networks support mixed traffic types with differing quality-of-service needs, there are conflicts to resolve. With data only networks the main problem is the clash between interactive and file transfer traffic, where congestion due to the latter is liable to cause unacceptable response times for the former. The solutions are either to use quality-of-service based routing and different paths for the two types if available, or more often to use prioritization of the interactive traffic plus a smaller packet size than normal for the file transfers.

When voice is mixed with data, the delay and its variance become even more acute issues. The only satisfactory solutions are separating the two types on the links, as in the traditional TDM approach, or to use ATM, where the small cells, guaranteed bandwidth and high transmission speeds with AAL1 adaption eliminate the problem. Packetized voice/data systems running at T1/E1 speeds are often reasonable at light loads but poor under heavy loads, usually also with an additional problem of clipping.

13.5 General principles

This section summarizes the general principles and rules of thumb that apply to optimization issues.

13.5.1 File transfers

For file transfers the main performance criterion is throughput. For a given network configuration this is maximized by ensuring that there are no delays due to waiting for acknowledgements. This is achieved by setting;

$$\text{Window size} = (\text{Roundtrip time}) \times \text{Bandwidth}$$

where the bandwidth is that of the slowest link.

Data compression improves throughput by a factor between about 1.3 and 15 depending on the nature of the data, with a value of 2 typical.

Increasing the bandwidth available on the slowest link allows throughput to be increased on most networks. Exceptions to this are GEO satellite links and long-distance ATM links where most of the delay is propagation delay due to the finite velocity of light (and hence of data signals); in such cases window size determines the throughput achievable on a single virtual circuit.

Buffer space, protocol capability and retransmissions due to errors limit the window size that can be used; selective reject is better for this than Go-Back N in this regard.

13.5.2 Interactive traffic

For interactive traffic the key factor is response time. This is optimized by minimizing the latencies of individual components, cutting store and forward delays by choice of technology and packet size, and minimizing queuing delays. Use of data compression on modems or routers increases latency by more than it reduces transmission time for very short messages, so is often best switched off for this traffic. Store and forward delays on multihop networks are minimized by use of small packets, provided that switch packet processing time remains smaller than the packet transmission time. Queuing delays are minimized by prioritizing interactive traffic above file transfers and servicing this priority queue at least once every 50 ms.

13.5.3   Session maintenance

Where it is important to keep sessions up, it is often necessary to increase retry intervals and retry counts when operating over the wide area. A small increase may be needed to accommodate the longer response time of a WAN as compared to a LAN, and a much larger increase to allow for some forms of rerouting round a network failure. Network devices that take intelligent collective decisions on how to reroute, as opposed to being table driven, may take several minutes to re-establish connection; the product of retry interval and retry count should thus exceed this time. Examples of where this is necessary are intelligent multiplexers, spanning tree bridges and most routers. Rerouting time is minimized by intelligent logical structuring of the WAN and by choice of protocol, for example OSPF instead of RIP.

13.5.4   Bandwidth utilization

Where bandwidth is the critical factor, overheads should be minimized by avoiding packet segmentation, filtering out unnecessary broadcasts and using data compression.

13.5.5   Router/switch CPU load

If CPU load is the main issue, large packets should be used and additonal processing such as filters, priorities, security checking and network management kept to a minimum.

13.5.6   Router/switch memory

If memory is critical, then window sizes, routing table sizes, numbers of distinct protocols (especially connection-oriented) and compression dictionaries should be minimized. Aids to this process are multiplexing different traffic sources onto single virtual circuit, SAP filters on IPX networks and subdividing networks into independent routing areas.

13.5.7   Quality of service

In order to ensure that diverse quality-of-service criteria can be simultaneously supported on a large network it is necessary to have a wide choice of routes and the ability to select the path on this basis.

13.5.8 Choice of WAN protocol

The main protocols supporting a wide range of quality-of-service criteria are ATM and APPN+ (subject to bandwidth availability). OSPF routing also supports quality of service, but its restriction to IP imposes the limitations of the latter. Developments like ST-2+ and RSVP for the Internet give some hope of supporting constant bit rate services over such networks provided high-speed links are used throughout. TCP/IP itself is a good WAN protocol for data traffic with optional features for high-speed operation and satellite links, as well as being ubiquitous.

Frame relay is ideal for LAN interconnect over good quality lines, but poor for constant bit rate services and a bit clumsy for multicasts.

X.25 is good for low-quality lines, and when run over the fastest links that it can support (256 kbps to 2 Mbps) in conjunction with large windows and M-bit usage also for LAN interconnect. It is unsuitable for constant bit rate services and for multicasts.

Polled protocols like SDLC and BSC are not suited to modern high-speed WANs, and in the SNA environment are best replaced by frame relay or APPN+.

Broadcast-rich protocols designed for easy use on LANs, such as NetBIOS, AppleTalk and to a lesser degree IPX, are poor on WANs, and should only be used when the applications require them.

SMDS service using DQDB or ATM technology is good for LAN interconnect, giving roughly the same functionality as ATM AAL3/4, but with inherent support for multicasts without the complexity of ATM LANE. Its main weaknesses are limited congestion control and geographically restricted availability.

14

Mathematical Appendix

This chapter covers the mathematics which is likely to be of use to network designers and others with a greater need for understanding the principles underlying performance optimization. The two key areas in which more detailed knowledge is worthwhile are routing together with its relation to network design, and queuing theory which is applicable to congestion control.

14.1   Routing theory

The basic principles of routing were outlined in Chapter 7 along with a description of the main router protocols; what this chapter adds are the main mathematical principles. A network designer has to be able to calculate how much traffic there will be at each point of the network in order to produce a viable cost-effective design. In a few cases vendors may provide a network design tool that includes an accurate model of the algorithms used by their kit, but this is rarely the case.

Routing can either be based on virtual circuits or on individual packets. In the former case the route is decided at the time of call set up and followed by all packets until the end of the call or a network failure that leads to rerouting; obviously this is only applicable to connection-oriented protocols. The second technique, which applies both to all connectionless protocols and to some connection-oriented, routes each packet independently. The latter is much more sensitive to short-term fluctuations in traffic levels but can sometimes become unstable, leading to sudden changes in transit time and hence to the possibility of retransmissions. In either case it is necessary to work out the best possible route, and the main computational method of doing this is the use of Djykstra's algorithm. This algorithm is applicable to link state routing protocols in which each node calculates its own shortest paths, and to centralized systems where calculations are done offline for each node.

14.1.1   Djykstra's algorithm

This is one of the quickest ways of finding an optimum route given as the least cost path between source and destination with respect to some cost function. The cost function is characteristic of the networking device and protocol, and does not itself form part of the algorithm. An indication of the nature of some cost functions was given in Chapter 7 for some of the main protocols.

Each node in the network has a list of all others, their interconnections and associated costs which it uses as the basis for its calculation of its own shortest paths. The algorithm starts at the source node, then gradually works out step by step from its nearest neighbours until eventually all remote nodes have been covered. The shortest path is defined to be the least cost route between the two nodes, with distance equal to the sum of the costs of the intervening links.

Let $D(B)$ be the distance from the source node, A, to node B,
let (I,J) be the cost of the link form node I to node J,
let $\{S\}$ be the set of nodes whose routes to A have been determined in the iteration.

The algorithm consists of an initialization step, followed by an interative step as below.

Initialization

Put $\{S\} = A$,
for each node not in $\{S\}$, i.e all others initially, put $D(B) = C\,(A,B)$,

where $C\,(A,B)$ is infinite if B is not directly linked to A, and otherwise equal to the specified cost (e.g reciprocal of link speed).

Iterative step

Find a node, N, that is the closest to the source, not yet included in $\{S\}$, add it to $\{S\}$ and update the distances $D(B)$ of the remaining nodes to allow for the possibility of a short indirect path via N, by putting

$$D(B) = \text{Min}\ [D(B),\ D(N) + C(N,B)]$$

In the event of two nodes, N and M, being equally close, simply select one at random. This step is repeated until all nodes are included in $\{S\}$, with distances $D(B)$ equal to the final values calculated by the iteration and routes via those intervening nodes, N, that enabled the distance function $D(B)$ to be reduced for node B in any iteration. An example of this is shown for five nodes A to E with link costs as indicated in Figure 14.1.

The steps in generating the shortest paths are tabulated as successive rows in Table 14.1.

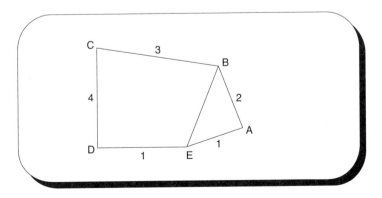

Figure 14.1 Network example.

Table 14.1 Route calculation steps.

Step	Set {S}	D(B)	D(C)	D(D)	D(E)
Initial	A	2	–	–	1
1	A,E	2	–	2	(1)
2	A,E,D	2	6	(2)	1
3	A,E,D,B	(2)	5	2	1
4	A,E,D,B,C	2	(5)	2	1

Other shortest path algorithms also exist, notably Bellman–Ford.

See Steenstrup (1995) for more details on various routing algorithms.

14.2   Backbone network design

Given a routing algorithm and a traffic matrix it is easy to calculate the traffic distribution within the network. In old centralized private computing environments the network usually consisted of a few star configurations centred on mainframe sites, with a minimal number of crosslinks to provide resilence. In such cases little sophistication is needed to work out what extra links have to be added to the basic stars to provide the final design, but for public networks in general or for modern client–server based private networks, the data flows are much more complex and need some additional design principles.

The basic principle used is the maximum flow minimum cut theorem that states that the maximum amount of traffic that can flow between a source and destination is equal to the traffic capacity of the minimum set of nodes and links whose failure would completely cut off the source from the destination. This set of nodes and links is known as a cutset for the source–destination pair. In the case of a source and destination connected directly by a single link, this is obviously just the link, while the capacity is the capacity of the single link, but computer analysis is normally required to determine this in general. In a router network this type of analysis is applied both within the autonomous areas and between them; the areas themselves being determined on the basis that most of their traffic is internal. For a given initial topology this sort of analysis will show that some cutsets are saturated in the sense that they have to carry at least as much traffic as their capacity. The network is then improved by adding one or two links to increase the size of the cutset until the capacity of the cutset matches the peak traffic flow. Similarly, some cutsets may have excessive capacity, in which case some trimming down is performed. The whole process is iterative, and must also take account of the response time requirements.

14.2.1   Provision of resilience

Most networks require an availability that can only be met by providing some form of redundancy. There are two main techniques of providing this: network redundancy and equipment redundancy.

In the case of network redundancy, the switches or brouters have little or no intrinsic redundancy, and resilience is provided through the existence of sufficient spare nodes and trunks to provide alternative routing in the event of node failures. The degree of redundancy required is determined through the above cutset analysis applied to failure situations. Node failures are much more drastic than trunk failures, so tend to be the driving factors in the eventual design. This is the technique most often used in large X.25 networks, particularly complex public networks. A disadvantage of pure network redundancy is that it requires alternative paths from peripheral sites, that may entail drastic changes to the routing, for example dial-out from nominated centres to cover access node failures, which require sophisticated network management.

Equipment redundancy uses nodal switches with no single point of failure, combined with dial backup (typically basic or primary rate ISDN) to cover link failure. This normally entails higher equipment costs than network redundancy, but allows faster recovery from failure and simpler routing. Apart from equipment cost, its major disadvantage is that it does not provide resilience against physical disasters, such as fires, that destroy equipment completely.

14.2.2   Design factors for private networks

A high proportion of private networks have a relatively simple structure due to the nature of the corporation. Retail operations usually have a large number of remote branch sites plus a small number of regional or headquarters sites. In such cases the structure of the network consists of a number of stars centred on the main sites, together with a mesh interconnecting the latter, and relatively complex LANs within these centres.

The WAN design process entails finding the flows within each star, a traffic matrix for the inter-star traffic and selection of entry points to the central LAN complexes.

User data, based on transaction size and frequency, is scaled up to include the various headers and trailers of the communications protocol stack, then additional protocol traffic, such as broadcasts and router updates added in the light of the overall network structure.

Further information on network design is given in Tanenbaum (1988) and Spohn (1993).

14.3　Queuing theory

Network response times at very light loads can easily be calculated by adding up the processing and propagation delays for each component on the shortest path, but as the load increases allowance must be made for congestion. When congestion occurs data is placed in a queue for processing rather than being handled immediately; the response time then consists of the basic processing time plus the additional waiting time. It is rarely cost-effective to operate a network at such a light load that congestion can be ignored, so it is necessary for network designers to be able to estimate in advance what effects it will have in order to provide adequate quality of service. In a few cases the response time estimate will form part of a contractual commitment to users that is subject to penalties for under-performance, so understanding of queuing theory and its limitations is essential.

14.3.1　Classical queuing theory

Classical queuing theory predates electronic computers and consists of closed analytic formulae applicable to simple types of situation that can be evaluated by means of simple arithmetic and tabulated trigonometric functions. Their value to the network designer is that they can be very easily applied and used as a basis for understanding congestion effects, and, when related to the specific flow control features of a given protocol, used to optimize the network performance. Where they break down is in heavy congestion or where the randomness assumptions implicit in them fail to apply, for example traffic generated by a small number of file servers.

There are three main types of classical queue that are of relevance to data-communications: M/M/N, M/D/1 and M/G/1. M denotes Markovian, implying a random process in which events are independent of past history, D denotes deterministic and G general. The first of the three letters refers to the arrival rate characteristics, the second to the processing time, and the third is the number of servers for the queue (such as processors).

M/M/1

The simplest case is M/M/N for a single server, that is, M/M/1. The random data arrival rate is described by a Poisson distribution, wherein the probability $P(K)$ of K data frames arriving within an interval T is given by

$$P(K) = (E(A)*T)^K * \exp(-E(A)*T)/K!$$

where $E(A)$ is the average arrival rate of frames and exp denotes exponential.

The random processing time in M/M/N queues is assumed to be exponentially distributed, so that the probability $P(t)$ of a packet taking a time t to be processed is given by

$$P(t) = \exp(-t/E(S))/E(S)$$

where $E(S)$ is the average service time for a frame.

In datacommunications it is a reasonable model for transmission lines that handle a large mixture of different frame sizes, but errs by allowing for non-existent jumbo packets that exceed the maximum permitted packet size, thereby making it rather pessimistic as to queuing delays.

The average waiting time at utilization U is given by

$$E(W) = U * E(S)/(1-U)$$

Users are more often concerned not so much by the average wait, but what happens in the worst of about 20 cases; in order to estimate this it is necessary to know the variance of the wait and to use this to determine the 95th percentile behaviour. For an exponential distribution, the variance V and average are related by

$$V(S) = E(S)^2$$

from which it can be shown that the variance of waiting time, $V(W)$, is given by

$$V(W) = E(S)^{2} (2 * U - U^{2})/(1 - U)^{2}$$

A further assumption must then be made in order to obtain the 95th percentile wait. The usual assumption is that the waiting times constitute a gamma distribution, in which case the 90th, 95th and 99th percentiles are given by adding the multiples of the variance quoted in the first row of Table 14.2. Sometimes it is assumed that the distribution is normal; for example, this is suggested in recommendation X.135, in which case the multiples are smaller, as quoted in the second row.

The difference in multiple resulting from the choice of probability assumption serves to highlight the sorts of error that are implicit in the use of simple queuing models.

The model M/M/N is widely used in telephony theory, where it is known as the Erlang-C model, to determine the number of operators or lines needed, but its use in datacommunications is largely restricted to X.25 multilink queuing delays, SNA transmission groups or the number of dial-up ports needed. Some people tend to apply it to multiple processor packet switches also, but this is usually invalid because most such devices send a packet to one specific processor depending on the incoming path, rather than to the first free processor.

Table 14.2 Percentile examples.

Type assumed	90th percentile	95th	99th
Gamma	1.3	2	4
Normal	1.27	1.6	3

M/D/1

Packet processors are often modelled by the M/D/1 queue because the processing time is a fixed period determined by the work to be performed on the headers, rather than a variable time depending on the packet size. This model gives an average waiting time that is half that of the M/M/1 for the same average service time, that is,

$$E(W) = U * S/(2 * (1 - U))$$

where the average service time is equal to the fixed value S.

The variance of the waiting time, $V(W)$, is given in this case by

$$V(W) = (S/(1 - U)) + (4 * U - U^2)/12$$

In order to calculate the percentile delays, the same assumptions and multipliers apply as in the case of M/M/1 above. This queuing model is usually overoptimistic about waiting times when applied to data communications. A better but more complex model, lying between these two extremes, is the M/G/1 model.

M/G/1

In this model the frame arrival rate is again assumed to be a Poisson distribution, but the service time is assumed to be determined by a general distribution of times, that on datacommunications lines represent specific categories of frame sizes, such as X.25 levels 2 and 3 RRs plus typical data packet sizes. Similarly for X.25 packet processors, there would be separate times for packet processing and call request/clear processing, possibly with further subdivision according to trunk or access roles. In the case of routers, different service times would be used according to the data packet protocol and for router protocol packets.

The average wait is given by the following formula, often called the Pollaczek–Khinchine formula after its discoverers:

$$E(W) = E(S) * ((1 - U * (V(S)/E(S))2)/^2)/(1 - U)$$

where $V(S)$ is the variance of the service time that is calculated from the relative numbers of frame for each processing time. This result is accurate to about 10–15% when applied to networks up to network load factors around 60%; above this, protocol-specific flow control mechanisms tend to come into play that reduce its applicability.

Queue lengths

Another important factor is the average number of frames queued at any one time. This is the factor that determines the probability of protocol acknowledgements being piggybacked, thereby increasing the efficiency of some protocols. In all queuing models this is related to the average wait by Little's Formula:

$$E(K) = E(W)/E(S)$$

where $E(K)$ is the average number of frames waiting, $E(W)$ the wait and $E(S)$ is the service time. This is also useful in determining how much buffer space is likely to be used at any one time, although the amount configured should allow for full window sizes. If the average queue length is calculated to come out to a larger value than the appropriate window size, then flow control will limit throughput to less than would otherwise be expected, and the window size probably ought to be increased.

14.3.2 Prioritized queues

In many practical situations it is desirable to assign different priorities to diverse processes, and the basic consequences of this can easily be understood with the aid of analytic queuing theory. Queues that are used in datacommunications are normally of the non pre-emptive type in which a low priority process is allowed to complete rather than be interrupted by a higher-level task. Data packets for the high priority are always queued ahead of the lower in the simplest case, which is discussed below.

In the simplest case of an M/G/1 queue with two processes, such as IP and IPX packet processing, with utilizations U_1 and U_2 and average service times $ES1$ and $ES2$, the average waiting time in the absence of priorities is given by the equation above where $E(S)$ is the weighted average service time. In the case of non pre-emptive priority the two waiting times become

$$E(W_1) = E(TR)/(1 - U_1)$$

where $E(TR)$ denotes the average residual processing time of packets of all types in the system remaining before top priority processing of a new packet can start.

$$E(W_2) = E(W_1)/(1 - (U_1 + U_2))$$

More generally, the waiting times in queues with larger numbers of priority classes are related by

$$E(W_n) = E(TR)/((1 - L_n) * (1 - L_{n-1}))$$

where $L_n = Sum(U_k)$ for $k=1$ to n, and n is the priority class immediately below $n-1$.

Figure 14.2 illustrates the effect of prioritizing 50 byte interactive traffic over 1000 byte file transfers on a 64 kbps line, where the interactive utilization is 10% and the file transfers 40%.

It is apparent that the most effective usage is to provide fast, lightly loaded processes with the highest priority, whereas giving a high priority to a slow heavily loaded process would have negligible benefit to it, but a considerable detriment to any fast process. In cases of multiple priorities, those at the bottom can be severely degraded.

Many practical prioritized systems, such as routers, differ considerably from this simple model. In some cases the prioritization is much weaker as the higher

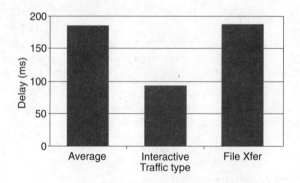

Figure 14.2   Effect of prioritising interactive traffic.

priority queues are not given complete priority but merely checked more frequently, while in others a certain minimum bandwidth may be reserved for each protocol to prevent lockouts.

14.3.3   Sequences of queues

Data communications across a network entails the data passing through a sequence of processors and transmission media, with each of which is associated a queue. The usual assumption that is made in defining the interaction between the queues is that they are statistically independent. This means that the average total waiting time is equal to the sum of the average waiting times for the individual queues. In order to determine the various percentile dealys, such as 95th, the variance of the waiting time has also to be calculated. This entails slightly more detailed assumptions about the statistical processes; usually that they form incomplete gamma distributions. This leads to the variance of the sum of the waiting times, $V(Q1+Q2+...+QN)$, to be related to the individual queue variances by

$$V(Q1 + Q2 + ... + QN) = V(Q1) + V(Q2) + ... + V(QN) + \text{Sum}(\text{Cov}(Qi,Qj))$$

where $\text{Cov}(Qi,Qj) = \text{Corr}(Qi,Qj)V(Qi) * V(Qj)$ is the covariance of queues i and j. If the covariance is zero for two queues, then the 95th percentile of the waiting time for the composite queue is about twice the square root of the sum of the individual variances, whereas if the correlation coefficient is one, then this percentile delay is the sum of the individual percentiles, which is much greater. Where large numbers of links branch out from each switch or router, the covariance of the media transmission queues is close to zero; but for a roundtrip there is likely to be strong correlation between the queue lengths at a switch (especially a single CPU model) on the two halves of the journey.

ITU-T recommendation X.135 Annex C gives some examples of this and their relation to throughput to which the interested reader is referred. Their example quotes the normal distribution, which gives slightly lower delays than the assumption of a gamma distribution, thereby illustrating a degree of arbitrariness and opportunity for specmanship in this parameter.

14.3.4   Limitations of classical queuing theory

The biggest limitation of classical theory is simply the very restricted range of models that permit closed analytic solutions, hence a correspondingly restricted range of real situations that can be described. Most data-communications systems are far more complicated than these simple models; the main differences being:

- many queues in a single packet processor, typically of the order of 100;
- restriction to equilibrium situations only;
- scheduling loops that depend on load levels;
- upper bound to arrival rates due to limited line speeds;
- finite limits to real queue lengths due to buffer limitations and protocol windows;
- non-random arrival rates associated with servers;
- at least three significant protocol levels;
- error correction techniques;
- congestion and flow control mechanisms.

The situations in which the models work well in practice are those in which most of these limitations refer to small side effects, such as a single transmission line with large level 2 window being fed by a powerful packet processor with many lightly loaded inputs. In this case the M/G/1 model is accurate to about 10% for response time. Calculation of throughputs or total transaction times for multipacket processes will also be reasonable if the level 3 window size is large enough not to cause any intersequence delays. Another reliable situation is a packet processor that handles essentially one category of packet, with a uniform amount of work on each packet header, in which case M/D/1 works well until congestion control effects come into play.

Probability distributions, such as the Poisson distribution and exponential distribution, tend to introduce effects of impossible situations that can seriously distort calculated results. The arrival rate is usually modelled in terms of a Poisson distribution and this is illustrated in Figure 14.3 for the probability of the displayed packet arrival rates when the mean is one of the three values 10, 30 or 50 packets per second. If the arrival rates are assumed to refer to 128 byte packets on a 64 kbps line, then the mean rates are quite realistic possibilities, but the Poisson distribution for the 50 packets per second case shows a significant probability of arrival rates above the line capacity of 63 such packets per second.

The exponential distribution for service times for the M/M/1 model is shown for various mean rates for a 64 kbps line in Figure 14.4. In this case the errors are

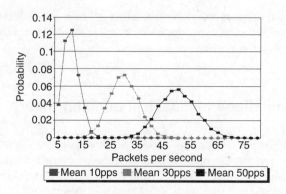

Figure 14.3   Poisson arrival rate.

packet sizes greater than the configured maximum for the line, plus a considerable discrepancy from realistic distributions that take into account protocol acknowledgement frames.

14.4   Simulation models

Electronic computers allow the network analyst to escape from the restriction of queuing theory to the simple closed models described above. A sufficiently powerful computer can simulate the exact operation of any decidable system, either in or out of equilibrium. One of the biggest advantages of simulation is the departure from equilibrium, as the most critical events on networks are often their responses to a failure of a component by rerouting traffic. A typical such situation that is beyond the scope of analytic models is the development of queues and timeouts, while spanning tree bridges recalculate their tables after failure of the root node.

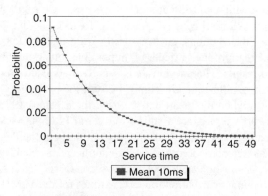

Figure 14.4   Exponential service time.

A full simulation of a network would require the simulator to run software equivalent to the sum of the software modules for all of the nodes it was modelling, as well as having an event-scheduling module to ensure processing in the correct order. Such a system would have to be more powerful than the sum of the network processors to do a computation in real time, so the art of creating a practical simulation model is to include only those aspects of the network that have a significant impact on the performance. This means that level 3 and 4 queues usually have to be monitored relative to their window procedures, but that in a well-tuned system level 2 can be treated as an overhead only as, except for satellite systems, the level 2 default windows are large enough to prevent the system having to wait for level 2 acknowledgements.

Switches and routers have to be modelled in such a way as to take account of their detailed internal architecture unless loading is very low, as their performance limits often arise through the interaction between different internal processes and from the ways in which buffers are utilized. A critical shortage of buffers for one process can severely impact performance even if there is plenty of memory available in total, but allocated for other tasks. Performance also varies drastically if the internal data flow is liable to pass through several processors instead of one. The degree of customization required to take account of differing switch architectures is one of the main difficulties with general purpose communications simulation packages.

Some of the most important network events are associated with the behaviour of the end-point devices, so these also have to be included in many simulations. An example of this is that except with very low bandwidth bridges, the usual performance problem on source route bridge networks is not bridge or transmission line congestion, but the inability of some servers to handle the interrupts associated with a large number of responses to advertisements or NetBIOS broadcasts. It is not practical to treat all the end-stations individually on large networks, so this type of traffic is sometimes treated as an aggregate for workstations on each LAN, with the server destinations being considered either individually or as similar aggregates.

A wide range of books give detailed information on queuing theory and probability, notably Kleinrock (1975; 1976), Schwartz (1987) and Harrison and Patel (1993).

14.5   Error correction

An important consideration in detailed optimization of a network is the effectiveness of different error correction mechanisms, as some algorithms are much more powerful than others, for example OSI CRC checks as compared to TCP/IP. Another factor is the use of forward error correction (FEC) instead of ARQ retransmissions. In responding to a sophisticated invitation to tender for a network, a designer sometimes has to quote likely residual error rates, so some of the main factors are discussed here.

14.5.1 Character mode checks

The most elementary correction method is echoplex, whereby the destination echos back each character received to the sender, who retypes it if it appears incorrect. The error may occur on either the outbound or the return path. Correcting a false error from the return path is harmless, but residual errors arise if an outbound error is corrected by a corresponding error on the return path. Using 7 bit ASCII characters the chances of this happening range from about 5×10^{-7} at BER of 10^{-4} to 5×10^{-11} at BER of 10^{-6} for each character. The chances of this happening to at least one character in a block of 100 is thus 100 times as great.

The next type of test is a parity check using 8 bit characters, with retransmission if an error is detected. This is of comparable sensitivity to echoplex, with false correction on the return path being eliminated, but the possibility of two cancelling bit errors on the outbound path arising instead.

Addition of a longitudinal check eliminates most of the self-cancelling parity errors.

14.5.2 CRC checks

The most widespread form of error checking in current data communications is the use of cyclic redundancy checks. There are several versions of this, notably:

- CRC-12 with polynomial $1 + x + x^2 + x^3 + x^{11} + x^{12}$
- CRC-16 from $1 + x^2 + x^{15} + x^{16}$
- ITU (CCITT) CRC from $1 + x^5 + x^{12} + x^{16}$
- CRC-32

The CRC codes are designed to be efficient at handling the bursts of errors that occur on terrestrial lines due to impulse noise. The size of burst that can be detected is related to the degree of the generator polynomial, so that CRC-12 is able to detect all error bursts of up to 12 bits, most of those of 13 and a significant fraction of those greater length, while for CRC-16 and ITU CRC these limits go up to 16 and 17 for each and extend to 32 and 33 for CRC-32.

The degree 16 CRCs have been extensively studied as to the number and type of residual errors. The overall residual error rates for typical frame sizes and error rates are listed in Table 14.3.

CRC-16 is used by DDCMP in both header and data field checks, whereas ITU CRC is used in most ITU protocols, notably X.25 and frame relay. CRC-32 has been proposed for data checks for blocks of cells conforming to AAL5 in ATM, with the check at the end of a group of cells belonging to the same higher level data packet, as well as for SMDS L3_PDUs. The ATM cells themselves also contain a CRC-8 check, the HEC, but this only applies to the header. Because of the short length of this header the check is not very efficient; it can correct all single bit errors

Table 14.3 Undetected error rates.

Frame size	Bit error rate			
(bytes)	10^{-4}	10^{-5}	10^{-6}	10^{-7}
128	4×10^{-7}	4×10^{-8}	4×10^{-9}	4×10^{-10}
256	6×10^{-7}	6×10^{-8}	6×10^{-9}	6×10^{-10}
512	1×10^{-6}	1×10^{-7}	1×10^{-8}	1×10^{-9}
1024	2×10^{-6}	2×10^{-7}	2×10^{-8}	2×10^{-9}
2048	4×10^{-6}	4×10^{-7}	4×10^{-8}	4×10^{-9}
4096	8×10^{-6}	8×10^{-7}	8×10^{-8}	8×10^{-9}

and detect all 2 bit errors, but there is a 1 in 256 chance that a random sequence of five octets will look like an HEC. This is important because location of a field that looks like an HEC is the means of identifying an ATM cell in a SONET VC4 container. The ambiguity means that a few cells at the start of a message may be dropped until a consistent position for the real HEC is found.

14.5.3   Block interleaving

Where very high BERs are encountered, it is useful to have another way of breaking up long bursts of errors so that a relatively simple error check will suffice. This is the case in mobile data communications where the BER may reach 1 in 50. None of the normal modem error correction techniques are viable under these circumstances owing to the high chance of long bursts of errors, so dedicated cellular modems interleave bits from sequences of codewords of data as well as using forward error correction. This improves data integrity, but at the expense of response time. The extra delay is equal to the transmission time of the reordered sequence plus the interleaving/deinterleaving processing time, and can be as much as 200 ms for a pair of modems.

14.5.4   One's complement

This is a much more basic check that lacks any form of error correction in its normal form. Addition is performed modulo $(2^N - 1)$, where N is the number of bits in the field, to provide a checksum. This is used in IP for the header of a datagram. OSI TP4 optionally uses addition modulo 255 of the octet values and the octet values times their positions to give two checksum components as the number required to be added to give zero modulo 255 in each case. This gives a chance of around 1 in 65 535 of an error being undetected. The advantage is the ease of computation in software as compared to the more sophisticated CRC checks.

14.5.5   Complex error correcting codes

In a few specialized applications, error correction by retransmission is totally impractical, so elaborate forms of forward error correction have to be used that can correct multiple errors. The main example of this is data communications with space probes. A variety of sophisticated codes exist, with common characteristic that a large amount of redundant information has to be added to the underlying data, so that throughput of the real data is greatly reduced.

More information on error correction can be found in Ha[92].

List of Abbreviations

AAL	ATM Adaptation Layer (in ATM q.v.)
AARP	AppleTalk Address Resolution Protocol
ABR	Available Bit Rate (in ATM q.v.)
ACF	Advanced Communications Facility (for IBM systems)
ACF/VTAM	ACF Virtual Telecommunications Access Method (host program)
ACF/NCP	ACF Network Control Program (in front-end processor)
ADP	AppleTalk Datagram Protocol
ADPCM	Adaptive Differential Pulse Code Modulation
ADSL	Asynchronous Digital Subscriber Line
ADSP	AppleTalk Data Stream Protocol
AEP	AppleTalk Echo Protocol
AFP	AppleTalk File Protocol
AMPS	Advanced Mobile Phone System (analog)
API	Applications Programming Interface
APPC	Advanced Program-to-Program Communication
APPN	Advanced Peer-to-Peer Networking
ARP	Address Resolution Protocol
ARQ	Automatic Repeat Request
ASP	AppleTalk Session Protocol
ATM	(1) Asynchronous Transfer Mode
	(2) Automatic Teller Machine
AURP	AppleTalk Update-based Routing Protocol
BCH	Bose, Chandhuri and Hocquenhem
BECN	Backwards Explicit Congestion Notification
BER	Bit Error Rate
BERT	Bit Error Rate Test

BEtag	Beginning/End Tag (field in IEEE 802.6)
BGP	Border Gateway Protocol
BPDU	Bridge Protocol Data Unit
BSC	Binary Synchronous Communications
CAC	Connection Admission Control (ATM)
CATV	Community Antenna Television
CBR	Constant Bit Rate (as applied to ATM)
CCITT	International Telegraph & Telephone Consultative Committee (renamed ITU-TSS q.v.)
CCR	Current Cell Rate (ATM)
CCS	Call Century Seconds (100 seconds of call)
CDLC	Cellular Data Link Control
CDV	Cell Delay Variation (in ATM)
CDPD	Cellular Digital Packet Data (mobile communications standard)
CELP	Code Excited Linear Prediction (voice digitization)
CI	Congestion Indicator (ATM)
CIR	Committed Information Rate (in frame relay)
CLAN	Cableless Local Area Network
CLNP	Connectionless Network Protocol (OSI protocol)
CLNS	Connectionless Network Service
CMIP	Common Management Information Protocol
CMIS	Common Management Information Services
COS	Class of Service
CPI-C	Common Programming Interface for Communications (for IBM)
CPU	Central Processing Unit
CRC	Cyclic Redundancy Check
CTD	Cell Transfer Delay (in ATM)
CTS	Clear To Send (modem signal)
CUG	Closed User Group
DA	Destination Address (field in MAC frame)
DAMA	Demand Assigned Multiple Access (satellite communications)
DCE	Data Circuit Terminating Equipment (part of network)
DDCMP	Digital Data Communications Message Protocol
DDE	Dynamic Data Exchange (a Microsoft PC protocol)
DDP	Datagram Delivery Protocol (in AppleTalk)
DE	Discard Eligibility (in frame relay)
DECT	Digital European Cordless Telecommunications (mobile communications standard)
DES	Data Encryption Standard (uses 64 bit key)
DIP	Document Image Processing
DLCI	Data Level Channel Identifier (in LAPD and frame relay)
DLE	Data Linking and Embedding
DNA	Digital Network Architecture

DQDB	Distributed Queue Dual Bus
DS-0	Digital Signal level 0 (64 kbps in America, Europe)
DS-1	Digital Signal level 1 (1.544 Mbps in America, 2.048 Mbps Europe)
DS-2	Digital Signal level 2 (6.312 Mbps in America, 8.448 Mbps Europe)
DS-3	Digital Signal level 3 (45 Mbps in America, 34 Mbps in Europe)
DSP	(1) Display Systems Protocol
	(2) Digital Signal Processor
DTE	Data Terminal Equipment
DTMF	Dual Tone Multifrequency (analog voice signalling)
DTR	Data Terminal Ready (modem signal)
DVMRP	Distance Vector Multicast Routing Protocol (for IP)
E1	2.048 Mbps plesiochronous circuit in Europe
E2	8.448 Mbps plesiochronous circuit in Europe
E3	34.368 Mbps plesiochronous circuit in Europe
EFCI	Explicit Forward Congestion Indication (in ATM)
ELLC	Enhanced Logical Link Control (in IBM's NPSI X.25)
EGP	Exterior Gateway Protocol
ENQ	Enquiry (typically in BSC q.v)
ER	Explicit Rate (ATM)
ES-IS	End System to Intermediate System (in OSI routing)
ESCON	Enterprise Systems Connection (IBM)
ESD	Electronic Software Distribution
FCA	Flow Control Ack (in DLSw)
FCACK	Flow Control Acknowledgement (DLSw)
FCI	Flow Control Indicator (in DLSw)
FCIND	Flow Control Indication (DLSw)
FCS	(1) Frame Check Sequence
	(2) Fibre Channel Standard
FDDI	Fibre Distributed Data Interface (100 Mbps LAN standard)
FDX	Full Duplex
FEC	Forward Error Correction
FECN	Forwards Explicit Congestion Notification
FEP	Front-End Processor
FIFO	First-In-First-Out (queuing mechanism)
FILO	First-In-Last-Out (queuing mechanism)
FMH	Function Management Header (in SNA)
FRAD	Frame Relay Assembler Disassembler
FTAM	File Transfer Access and Management (OSI standard)
FTP	File Transfer Protocol (in IP)
GEO	Geosynchronous Orbit
GHz	Gigahertz (1 billion cycles/second)
GSM	Global Service Mobile (Digital mobile communications standard)
GUI	Graphical User Interface

HDLC	High-level Data Link Control
HDSL	High Bit Rate Digital Subscriber Line
HDX	Half-Duplex
HPPI	High Performance Parallel Interface (also HIPPI)
HPR	High Performance Routing (in APPN)
HSSI	High Speed Synchronous Interface
ICMP	Internet Control Message Protocol
ICP	Internet Control Protocol (in Banyan VINES)
ICR	Initial Cell Rate (ATM)
IDP	Internet Datagram Protocol (in Banyan VINES)
IEEE	Institute of Electrical and Electronic Engineers
IGRP	Interior Gateway Routing Protocol
IMPDU	Initial MAC Protocol Data Unit (in IEEE 802.6)
IP	Internet Protocol
IPC	InterProcess Communications (Banyan VINES)
IPX	Internet Packet Exchange
IS-IS	Intermediate System to Intermediate System (OSI routing)
ISDN	Integrated Services Digital Network
ISO	International Standards Organisation
ITU-T	International Telecommunications Union – T
IXC	Inter-Exchange Carrier (mainly in USA)
JBIG	Joint Bilevel Image Group
JPEG	Joint Photographic Experts Group
Ku-Band	12–14 GHz frequency band (satellite communications)
L-Band	1 GHz frequency band (satellite communications)
LAPB	Link Access Protocol Balanced (subset of HDLC)
LAPD	Link Access Protocol (subset of HDLC)
LAPM	Link Access Protocol for Modems (subset of HDLC)
LAT	Local Area Transport (DEC proprietary standard)
LATA	Local Access and Transport Area (mainly in USA)
LEC	(1) Local Exchange Carrier (mainly in USA)
	(2) LAN Emulation Client (in ATM q.v.)
LEO	Low Earth Orbit (satellite)
LES	LAN Emulation Server (in ATM q.v.)
LIFO	Last-In-First-Out (queuing mechanism)
LILO	Last-In-Last-Out (queuing mechansim)
LIS	Logical IP Subnetwork
LLC	Logical Link Control (level 2 HDLC protocols)
LRC	Longitudinal Redundancy Check
LU	Logical Unit (in SNA q.v.)

M/D/1	Markov Deterministic queue with one server
M/G/1	Markov General queue with one server
MHz	Megahertz (1 million cycles/second)
M/M/N	Markov Markov queue with N servers
MAN	Metropolitan Area Network
MCR	Minimum Cell Rate (in ATM)
MIB	Management Information Base (mainly in SNMP q.v.)
MID	Message Identifier (field in IEEE 802.6 cell)
MNP	Microcom Networking Protocol (proprietary standards)
MPEG	Motion Pictures Expert Group
MTBF	Mean Time Between Failures
MTBSO	Mean Time Between Service Outages
MTTR	Mean Time To Repair
MTTSR	Mean Time To Service Restoral
MTU	Message Transfer Unit (in IP)
NAK	Negative Acknowledgement
NBP	Name Binding Protocol (in AppleTalk)
NCP	(1) Network Control Program (in DNA and IBM's ACF/NCP) (2) NetWare Core Program
NetBIOS	Network Basic Input/Output System (PC communications standard)
NFS	Network File System (UNIX file transfer program)
NI	No Increase bit (ATM)
NLSP	Netware Link Services Protocol
NPDU	Network Protocol Data Unit
NPSI	Network Packet Serial Interface (IBM X.25 program)
NSAP	Network Services Access Point
NSP	Network Service Protocol (DECnet)
NT	Node Type (in SNA)
OC-n	Optical Carrier level n (in SONET q.v.)
OLE	Object Linking and Embedding (Microsoft linking standard)
OSI	Open Systems Interconnection
OSPF	Open Shortest Path First (routing protocol for IP)
PA	Pre-arbitrated (slot type in IEEE 802.6)
PAD	Packet Assembler Disassembler
PCM	Pulse Code Modulation
PCR	Peak Cell Rate (in ATM)
PDH	Plesiochronous Digital Hierarchy (circuit aggregation principle for TDMs)
PEX	Packet Exchange protocol (in XNS)
PPP	Point-to-Point Protocol (HDLC-style encapsulation for router protocols)

PSTN	Public Switched Telephone Network
PU	Physical Unit (in SNA q.v.)
PVC	Permanent Virtual Circuit
QA	Queue Arbitrated (slot type in IEEE 802.6)
QLLC	Qualified Link Level Control (in IBM's NPSI X.25)
QOS	Quality Of Service
QSIG	A European PABX signalling standard
RELP	Residual Excited Linear Prediction (voice digitization)
RIF	Routing Information Field (in source route bridging)
RIP	Routing Internet Protocol (for IP, IPX, XNS)
RM	Resource Management cell (ATM)
RMON	Remote Monitor (information standard for protocol analysers and monitors)
RPC	Remote Procedure Call
RTMP	Routing Table Maintenance Protocol (in AppleTalk)
RTS	Ready To Send (modem state)
SA	Source Address (in MAC frame)
SAP	Service Advertisement Protocol (NetBIOS and NetWare separately)
SAR	Segmentation and Reassembly (in ATM)
SCR	Sustainable Cell Rate (in ATM)
SDH	Synchronous Digital Hierarchy
SDLC	Synchronous Data Link Control
SDU	Service Data Unit (MAC frame in IEEE 802.6)
SREJ	Selective Reject (retransmission procedure for errors)
SIP	Subscriber Interface Protocol (in SMDS/CBDS)
SIR	Subscribed Information Rate (in SMDS/CBDS)
SLIP	Serial Line Interface Protocol (for IP)
SMDS	Switched Multimegabit Data Service
SMTP	Simple Message Transfer Protocol (mailing application for IP messages)
SNA	Systems Network Architecture (IBM's legacy architecture)
SNAP	Subnetwork Access Protocol
SNMP	Simple Network Management Protocol
SNMP v2	Enhanced version of SNMP
SONET	Synchronized Optical Network
SPDU	Session Protocol Data Unit
SPP	Sequenced Packet Protocol (in XNS and Banyan VINES)
SPX	Sequenced Packet Exchange (in NetWare)
ST	Segment Type (field in IEEE 802.6 cell)
STM-n	Synchronous Transport Module n (in SDH q.v.)
STS	Synchronous Transport Signal (in SDH)
SVC	Switched Virtual Circuit

T1	1.544 Mbps plesiochronous circuit (America)
TACS	Total Access Communications System (mobile analog system)
TCP	Transport Control Program (over IP)
TDR	Time Domain Reflectometry
TDM	Time Division Multiplexer
TFTP	Trivial File Transfer Program (IP application)
TIFF	Tagged Image File Format (image compression)
TPDU	Transport Protocol Data Unit
UBR	Unspecified Bit Rate (in ATM)
UDP	Unacknowledged Datagram Protocol (alternative to TCP over IP)
UPC	Usage Parameter Control (ATM)
USDC	United States Digital Communications (mobile communications standard)
VBR	Variable Bit Rate (in ATM)
VCC	Virtual Channel Container (in ATM)
VCI	Virtual Channel Indicator (in ATM)
VLAN	Virtual Local Area Network
VPI	Virtual Path Indicator (in ATM)
VPN	Virtual Private Network
VSAT	Very Small Aperture Terminal (for satellite link)
VTAM	Virtual Telecommunications Access Method (=ACF/VTAM)
XNS	Xerox Network Service
ZIP	Zone Information Protocol (in AppleTalk)

Glossary of Terms

AC13 Early, but still quite common, automatic two-wire analog voice signalling system.

AC15 Modern standard for inter-PABX analog voice signalling.

Adaptive pulse code modulation (ADPCM) Encoding technique for digitizing analog voice, based on 8 kHz sampling.

Adaptive equalization Modem technique for adapting to changing line conditions.

Adaptive routing Routing algorithms that automatically adjust to network failures and varying traffic loads.

Address resolution protocol An Internet protocol to map Internet addresses to MAC addresses.

American Standard Code for Information Exchange (ASCII) An 8 bit code giving 128 characters covering both data transmission and control.

Analog Transmission technique whereby information is conveyed by modulating either the amplitude or frequency of a wave.

AppleShare Apple software to enable sharing of files in the Macintosh environment.

AppleTalk Seven-layer communications protocol for Macintosh environment.

Application layer   The top layer of the seven-layer OSI protocol model.

Application Programming Interface (API)   Language to define the interface between the operating system and a high-level programming language.

Advanced peer-to-peer networking (APPN)   IBM's first wide area peer-to-peer communications protocol.

Asynchronous   Without regular timing; for example, transmission of characters as they are typed using start/stop bits to delineate the characters.

Asynchronous transfer mode   Cell switching technique using 53 byte cells.

Attenuation   Decrease in signal intensity due to transmission medium, usually expressed in decibels.

Automatic repeat request (ARQ)   Error correction technique based on retransmission of blocks of data shown to be in error by a block check.

B-channel   64 kbps data or voice channel used in ISDN.

Bandwidth   Range of frequencies expressed in hertz that can be used for transmission, alternatively in bits per second for digital signals.

Baud   Unit of signalling speed, indicating the number of analog signal state changes per second.

Binary synchronous communication (BSC/Bisync)   Early IBM character-oriented half-duplex communications protocol.

Bit error rate (BER)   The proportion of transmitted bits of data that are in error.

Bit interleaving   Method of time division multiplexing wherein inputs are sampled so that the sequence and number of bits is maintained.

Block check character (BCC)   A control character appended to a block of data in a character-oriented protocol to allow error detection.

Border gateway protocol   Interdomain routing protocol implemented in TCP/IP networks.

Break   Interruption to transmission.

Bridge   LAN interconnection device operating on the basis of level 2 addresses.

Broadcast Transmission of a message to all the stations on a network segment.

Brouter Loose term for a device that can act as either a bridge or a router.

Byte Small group of data bits that are treated as a single unit; normally 8 bits.

C-band Region of electromagnetic spectrum between 4 and 6 GHz used for satellite communications.

Cableless local area network (CLAN) Local area network based on radio, microwave or infrared transmission instead of cables.

Call century second (CCS) Unit of voice traffic equal to one call for 100 seconds.

Carrier Continuous frequency capable of being modulated.

Carrier sense multiple access LAN access method where stations are able to detect each other's transmissions and wait for inactivity.

Cell relay High performance transmission technique whereby voice and data are sent in short frames called cells, normally containing 48 bytes plus a 5 byte header.

Centrex Telephone service that enables each subscriber to be directly dialled from outside.

Circuit switching Formation of temporary connections of channels between two or more points.

Clear to send (CTS) (aka Ready for sending) Modem signal state indicating that data can be sent. Used with RTS to flow control half-duplex lines (ITU-T V.24 circuit 106).

Client/server model Division of computing application between the user (client) computer and the server source of most of the data or application.

Closed user group (CUG) Restriction of communication to specified groups of users in packet switch networks.

Cluster controller Device that handles the communications for multiple dumb terminals or workstations, notably in SNA.

Coax Coaxial cable based on inner and outer conductors separated by insulation.

Codec Coder/decoder device for conversion of analog music, television or speech to digital form or vice versa.

Common management information protocol (CMIP)   Recommendation for an open standard protocol for network management.

Common management information services (CMIS)   Recommendation for an open standard set of network management services.

Comité Consultatif International de Télèphonie et Télègraphie (CCITT) Advisory committee for international telecommunications standards, renamed the ITU-T in 1993.

Common channel signalling (CCS)   System for signalling in circuit switch networks in which the control information for all channels is passed over a single common channel.

Common channel signalling system 7 (CCSS7)   A specific example of a CCS defined by the ITU-T and widely used between exchanges.

Compression   Reduction in volume of data to be transmitted by the elimination of redundancy.

COMSAT   Communications Satellite Corporation. A private US company established as the exclusive international satellite carrier.

Concentrator   A device that funnels the communications from several lines down a smaller number that is normally one or two.

Conditioning   A procedure for improving the quality of a telephone line to lie within specified limits.

Connection   The establishment of a specific communications path between two devices.

Connection-oriented network service (CONS)   A network service that uses real or virtual network connections.

Connectionless network service (CLNS)   A network service that does not use real or virtual connections.

Contention   Method of line control for multiple devices where each has to request to transmit.

Control character   Character that is inserted into a data stream to signal a control instruction.

Conversation   Term used in IBM's SAA to indicate communication between two logical units.

Cordless telephony   Techniques for telephone connections without physical wiring. CT2 and CT3 are two such standards.

Crosstalk   Unwanted transfer of energy from one circuit to another.

Cyclic redundancy check (CRC)   Error detection technique using a polynomial to generate block check characters incorporated into the end of a frame.

Data carrier detect (aka Received line signal detect)   Modem signal state indicating receipt of incoming signal of adequate quality (ITU-T V.24 circuit 109).

Data circuit terminating equipment (DCE)   Network equipment that terminates a circuit, such as a modem or packet switch.

Data link control   The second layer in the OSI reference model.

Data service unit (DSU)   Access device for transmitting digital data across a private leased line (particularly in the USA).

Data set ready (DSR)   Modem signal state indicating that the modem is fully viable (ITU-T V.24 circuit 107).

Data terminal equipment (DTE)   End-user equipment, such as a workstation, that connects to a DCE to communicate over a network.

Data terminal ready (DTR)   Modem signal state indicating that the data terminal is ready to transmit. (ITU-T V.24 circuit 108.2). Used to make modem or terminal adaptor dial a call.

Decibel (Db)   Unit of signal strength, defined as times the logarithm to the base 10 of the ratio of the power to a reference level.

DECnet   Digital Equipment Corporation's family of peer-to-peer communications protocols.

Demand assigned multiple access (DAMA)   Technique for allocating satellite time to earth stations as the need arises.

Demodulation   Process of retrieving information from a modulated carrier wave.

Dial tone   Signal sent to an operator to indicate that a switch is ready to receive dial pulses.

Digital data communications message protocol (DDCMP)   A character-oriented synchronous protocol developed by DEC.

Digital European cordless telecommunications (DECT)   A European standard for digital mobile communications in the 1880–1900 MHz frequency range.

Disk operating system (DOS)   An operating system that resides in memory or on disk.

Diskless workstation   Workstation lacking either hard or floppy disks that resides on a LAN and obtains all its software from a server.

Distortion   Unwanted change in the shape of a waveform.

Distributed queue dual bus (DQDB)   Medium access control technique used in IEEE 802.6.

DNA   DEC's multi-platform digital network architecture.

Document image processing (DIP)   System for scanning, digitizing and storing images of documents without having to recognize individual characters.

Downtime   The time that a system is out of service due to failure or maintenance.

DPNSS   Digital private network signalling system widely used between PABXs in Europe.

Dual tone multifrequency signalling (DTMF)   Signalling system for push-button telephones that uses two sets of frequencies to transmit numerical addresses.

Duplex transmission   Two-way simultaneous transmission, also called full-duplex.

Dynamic data exchange (DDE)   A communications link between applications that allows information changed in the originating file to be also changed in the receiving file.

Dynamic routing   Routing technique that selects the most appropriate path at the time instead of a fixed route.

E&M   'Ear & Mouth' analog voice signalling technique, often with signalling system DC5.

Echo cancellation   Technique used by some modems that removes the unwanted signal energy due to echoes from the transmitted signal.

Echo request   Control data packet used with many data communications protocols requesting that the packet be returned to allow measurement of delay and route; often called 'ping'.

Echo suppression   A mechanism used for suppression of interference on long-distance voice circuits, but incompatible with most data transmissions.

Echoplex   Simple error-correcting protocol for terminals based on returning each character received and retyping if in error.

EIA interface   Interface with signal characteristics conforming to a standard from the Electronics Industries Association; for example EIA232, EIA530. Formerly referred to as Recommended Standards, for example RS232.

Electronic mail (e-mail)   Electronic transmission of messages between computers.

Encryption   Process of encoding data so that an unauthorized party cannot interpret it.

End system to intermediate system (ES-IS)   Network layer OSI routing protocol between an end device and a routing node.

Enquiry (ENQ)   A request for a response from another terminal in character-oriented protocols.

End of message (EOM)   End of message indicator in character-oriented protocols.

End of transmission (EOT)   End of transmission indicator in character-oriented protocols.

Equalization   Compensation for variations with frequency of attenuation or delay of a signal.

Erlang   Unit of traffic intensity corresponding to continuous occupation of one channel, equivalent to 36 call century seconds.

Erlang-B   A traffic engineering formula for random traffic with blocking instead of queuing of calls when busy.

Erlang-C   A traffic engineering formula for random traffic with queuing instead of blocking when busy.

Exterior gateway protocol (EGP)   Internet protocol used by routers linking autonomous areas, largely superseded by BGP.

Fast packet switching   A generic term for a range of packet switch technologies with low functionality for improved performance, including frame relay and cell relay.

Fibre distributed data interface (FDDI)   A token-based LAN standard operating at 100 Mbps over predominantly fibre-optic media.

File transfer access and management (FTAM)   The OSI protocol for file transfer.

File transfer protocol (FTP)   A file transfer service running over TCP/IP.

Forward error congestion notification (FECN)   A bit used in frame relay to indicate congestion in the forwards direction.

Forward error correction (FEC)   A technique based on appending extra data bits to provide error correction without retransmission, used particularly with modems and satellite links.

Frame   (1) A sequence of bits bounded by beginning and end flags defining a level 2 data unit; (2) a set of consecutive digital time slots identifiable by reference to a framing signal.

Frame relay   A level 2 transmission protocol with minimal error checking.

Frequency modulation   A way of making a carrier wave transport information by varying the frequency.

Front end processor (FEP)   Dedicated communications system that handles the communications requirements of a host computer.

Full-duplex (FDX)   Two-way simultaneous communications, sometimes also called duplex.

Gateway   A network station that enables communication between two otherwise incompatible network systems.

Geostationary satellite (GEO)   A satellite in an orbit about 35 800 kilometres above the equator which appears stationary relative to a point on the earth's surface.

Gigahertz (GHz)   One billion (10^9) cycles per second.

Global system for mobile communications (GSM)   A European standard for digital mobile communications.

Grade of service   Quality of telephone service defined as the probability of a call encountering a busy condition.

Half-duplex (HDX) A circuit for alternate transmission in one of two directions at a time only.

Handoff Transfer of duplex signalling as a mobile terminal moves from one cell to another in a cellular network.

Harmonic distortion Presence of harmonic frequencies in a signal due to non-linear characteristics of a transmission line.

Header The initial part of a data unit that contains control information.

Hertz (Hz) Unit of frequency equal to one cycle per second.

High level data link control (HDLC) Bit-oriented level 2 protocol developed by ISO, subsets of which form the bases for many other protocols.

Hunt group A set of ports that can be accessed in turn using a common address.

IEEE Institute of Electrical and Electronic Engineers.

IEEE 802.1 IEEE control standard.

IEEE 802.2 IEEE level 2 standard for logical link control.

IEEE 802.3 IEEE CSMA/CD standard protocol, of which Ethernet is one trademark version.

IEEE 802.4 IEEE standard for broadband bus and broadband token bus.

IEEE 802.5 IEEE standard for Token Ring network operating at 4 or 16 Mbps.

IEEE 802.6 IEEE standard for metropolitan area network based on DQDB technology.

IEEE 802.9 IEEE standard for 96 isochronous 64 kbps integrated voice/data channels over 802.3 LAN.

IEEE 802.10 IEEE standard for security on LANs that is also used as the basis for some LAN switching techniques.

Integrated services digital network (ISDN) Digital network carrying voice and data in integrated fashion. There are two main variants: Basic rate with two 64 kbps B-channels and a 16 kbps D-channel, and Primary with 30 B-channels and a 64 kbps D-channel.

Interior gateway protocol (IGP)   Protocol used by interior routers within the Internet to move traffic within a single area.

Interior gateway routing protocol (IGRP)   A routing protocol defined by CISCO.

Intermediate system to intermediate system (IS-IS)   An OSI link-state routing protocol between routers that makes end-stations responsible for error correction.

Internet control message protocol (ICMP)   Part of the Internet protocol suite that covers control functions.

Internet packet exchange (IPX)   A widely used data network protocol from Novell, derived from Xerox's XNS and running under NetWare.

Internet protocol (IP)   The network-level datagram protocol in the Internet protocol suite.

International Standards Organisation (ISO)   An agency of the United Nations responsible for open standards including the OSI reference model.

International Telecommunications Union-T (ITU-T)   Formerly the CCITT; an advisory group within the ITU responsible for data communications standards recommendations.

Inter sequence delay (ISD)   A gap in data transmission due to the need to wait for an acknowledgement from the destination.

Isochronous transmission   Transmission where the signal recurs at regular intervals. Used for traffic where variable delay is unacceptable.

Jitter   Time or phase movement of signal that is liable to lead to loss of synchronization.

Joint Bilevel Image Group (JBIG)   A joint ISO/ITU-T standard for image storage, display and transmission of fax.

Joint Photographic Experts Group (JPEG)   A joint ISO/ITU-T standard for compression of still images.

Kilobit per second (kbps)   A thousand bits per second transmission rate.

Kermit   A file transfer protocol developed by Columbia University.

Ku-Band   Section of the electromagnetic spectrum between 12 and 14 GHz used for satellite communications.

LAT   Local area transport protocol developed by DEC.

LATA   Local access and transport area. A geographic area within the USA within which Bell operating companies can offer exchange facilities.

Leased line   A dedicated circuit between two points rented from a carrier.

Lempel–Ziv   Compression algorithms named after their inventors; developed by British Telecom to form the basis of ITU-T V.42bis.

Logical link control (LLC)   A protocol developed by IEEE 802 for data link control for all its local network standards. It includes LLC Type 1 for unacknowledged connectionless traffic, LLC Type 2 for connection-oriented and Type 3 for acknowledged connectionless traffic.

Logical unit (LU)   IBM SNA term for the user interface.

Longitudinal redundancy check (LRC)   An error check character at the end of a block of data based on the bit values for each position within a character.

Media access control (MAC)   Bottom part of OSI layer 2 controlling access of a station to a LAN.

Management information base (MIB)   Collection of information about all managed objects in a system, notably for SNMP.

Mean time between failures (MTBF)   The average length of time that a system works without a fault.

Mean time between service outages (MTBSO)   The average time that a system works without loss of service to a specified pair of users.

Mean time to repair (MTTR)   The average time to repair a fault, normally including the time taken by service personnel to reach the system as well as the actual repair time (ATTR).

Megabyte   Approximately one million bytes (1 048 576).

Megahertz (MHz)   One million cycles per second.

Metropolitan area network (MAN)   High-speed network within city or metropolitan area up to 50 km in diameter, often used for IEEE 802.6 standard.

Microsecond   One millionth of a second.

Millisecond   One thousandth of a second.

Modem   Modulator/demodulator used to send digital signals across analog lines.

Motion Picture Experts Group (MPEG)   Defining body for a group of video compression standards labelled MPEG x.

Multidrop   A communications arrangement where multiple devices share a line though only one can transmit at a time.

Multimode fibre   Fibre optic cable that carries multiple frequencies.

Multiplexer   A device that splits bandwidth between multiple circuits so that all can transmit simultaneously.

Negative acknowledgement (NAK)   A return message that indicates that an earlier outgoing message had an error condition.

NetWare   A network operating system devised by Novell for LANs and subsequently extended for WANs also.

Netware core protocol (NCP)   The part of NetWare responsible for end–end flow control and routing.

NetBIOS   Network basic input/output system. An interface and peer–peer operating system devised by Microsoft and IBM for LANs.

Network file system (NFS)   A machine independent protocol devised by Sun for remote access to shared file systems, widely supported by UNIX workstations.

Network layer   The third layer in the OSI protocol stack.

Network operating system (NOS)   Software that controls the sharing of resources and files across a network.

Network terminating unit (NTU)   The part of the network equipment that connects directly to the data terminal equipment, particularly with reference to European digital leased lines.

Object linking and embedding (OLE)   Set of procedures for linking applications with differing formats devised by Microsoft for personal computers.

Open shortest path first (OSPF)   A link state routing protocol used with TCP/IP.

Packet assembler/disassembler (PAD) A device that provides access to a packet switch network by means of protocol conversion and packetizing/depacketizing.

Packet switch A network device that routes data on the basis of header information within individual packets.

Parity bit A check bit that is added to an array of binary bits to make the sum of all bits, including the parity bit itself, either always even (even parity) or always odd (odd parity).

Permanent virtual circuit (PVC) A virtual connection between two stations that is established permanently.

Phase jitter Random variations in the phase of a signal.

Physical layer The bottom layer of the OSI protocol stack dealing with media issues.

Physical unit (PU) Set of processes in an IBM SNA device for network access.

Ping General term used for sending an echo request across a network.

PKZIP A proprietary file compression protocol used with PCs.

Plesiochronous Almost synchronous, having more than one clock source.

Plesiochronous digital hierarchy (PDH) The range of line speeds supported on plesiochronous circuit switch networks.

Point-to-point protocol (PPP) An encapsulation method for carrying various data protocols across a WAN.

Primary rate Term used in ISDN for multiple B-channels with signalling in a 64 kbps D-channel.

Prioritization Procedure for giving some specified traffic types precedence in a queued system.

Private automatic branch exchange (PABX) Telephone switch providing connections within an organization.

Propagation delay The time taken for a signal (as opposed to information) to traverse a system.

Public switched telephone network (PSTN)   The complete public telephone system, including telephones, lines and exchanges.

Pulse code modulation (PCM)   Digital transmission technique that entails sampling an analog signal at regular intervals and transmitting the resultant binary information by modulation of a pulsed carrier.

Pulse dial (rotary dial)   Dialling technique where each digit is represented by a coded set of pulses as the dial rotates back to its original position.

Q-SIG   A European standard for inter-PABX signalling based on ITU-T Q.931.

Quality of service (QOS)   A measure of the quality of service based on specified parameters such as delay, residual error rate and blocking probability. Standards for packet switch networks are recommended in ITU-T X.140.

Request to send (RTS)   Modem signal state used to put the local data communications equipment in transmit mode (ITU-T V.24 circuit 105).

Redundancy   (1) The portion of data that can be eliminated without loss of essential information; (2) provision of duplicate components to allow for failure.

Remote procedure call (RPC)   Protocol that allows calls to subroutines located in a remote part of a network.

Repeater   Device that receives a signal, amplifies and retimes it, then retransmits it.

Request for comments (RFC)   Research document on the Internet. Many of these acquire the status of protocol standards.

Response time   The time taken to respond to an input. For message response times it is advisable to distinguish between times based on the first or last bits of the message received or transmitted, for example first-in, last-out or last-in, first-out.

Rlogin   An Internet service for UNIX devices that is slightly more comprehensive than Telnet.

RMON MIB   An extension of SNMP MIB II that contains the objects needed for remote monitoring of a network and provides a standard for protocol analysers.

Router   A device that routes information between LANs based on network-level addresses.

Routing information protocol (RIP) The distance vector routing information protocol used on the Internet with variations for other protocols. Routes are based on minimum hop count.

Scrambler A coding device applied to a digital channel to produce an apparently random bit sequence; an essential component of many modems.

Session layer The fifth layer of the OSI reference model.

Simple mail transfer protocol (SMTP) A service for e-mail on the Internet.

Simple network management protocol (SNMP) A protocol originally recommended for the provision of a basic set of management functions on TCP/IP networks that has since become a widespread open management standard. SNMP version 2 is an enhancement with better security and performance.

Simulation The use of programming techniques to imitate the likely behaviour of a system.

Singlemode fibre Optical fibre with small core diameter that only allows one frequency mode.

Serial line internet protocol (SLIP) Internet datagram protocol that can be presented either synchronously or asynchronously; lacks error correction.

Socket This defines the end-points of a two-way communications channel between processes in the Berkeley model.

Source routing Routing technique where the end-stations are responsible for defining the route.

Source route bridge Bridge supporting IBM's source route bridging between Token Rings.

Spanning tree IEEE 802.1 algorithm to prevent routing loops in transparent bridging.

Spoofing A technique used whereby network devices, such as PADs and routers, respond to pure protocol messages, such as polls, locally on behalf of remote endstations and only send data and control messages across a WAN.

Spray A command implemented on some TCP/IP stacks to send a burst of packets across a network instead of a single packet as in Ping.

Start-stop bits A number of bits used to delineate individual characters in asynchronous transmission.

Subnet   A part of a network physically distinct from others, but sharing the same network address.

Switched multimegabit data service (SMDS)   A cell-based network service definition that uses DQDB technology.

Switched virtual circuit   A virtual circuit between two end-points set up for the duration of a call only.

Synchronous   Having a constant time interval between successive bits, characters or events.

Synchronous data link control (SDLC)   Full-duplex synchronous communication protocol defined by IBM and used in SNA.

Synchronous digital hierarchy (SDH)   European standard for synchronous multiplexer networks, analogous to US SONET.

Synchronous optical network (SONET)   The US standard for synchronous multiplexer networks.

Synchronous transmission modes (STM-N)   The range of signal bandwidths used in SDH, with values N×155.3 Mbps.

Synchronous transmission signal (STS-N)   The range of signal frequencies used in SONET, with values N×51.84 Mbps.

Systems application architecture (SAA)   IBM's common application development environment for programs to run over a wide range of IBM hardware and operating systems.

Systems network architecture (SNA)   IBM's common communication architecture for a wide range of IBM hardware using a range of well defined physical and logical units.

Total access communications system (TACS)   Analog cellular radio standard used in the UK that operates at 900 MHz.

Transmission control protocol (TCP)   This provides end–end flow control and data integrity for IP.

Telnet   The Internet standard service for remote terminal connection.

Terminal server   LAN device that provides connectivity for dumb terminals wishing to connect to a host on the LAN.

Trivial file transfer protocol (TFTP)   A basic Internet file transfer running over UDP and lacking security.

Tag image file format (TIFF)   A method of importing graphics files into desktop publishing programs that incorporates data compression.

Time division multiplexer (TDM)   Device that routes multiple channels down a single path by means of dividing the path into individual timeslots and assigning a slot to each channel.

Token Ring   A ring-shaped LAN operating at 4 or 16 MHz with access controlled by a circulating token, and standardized as IEEE 802.5.

Tone dialling   Use of tones to convey signalling information, such as telephone number, at the start of a call.

Topology   The relative logical or physical arrangement of stations on a network, such as a star or ring.

Trace-route   A command used on many Internet workstations to send a packet to the destination and return with a record of the route taken.

Traffic matrix   A two-dimensional array that shows the quantity of traffic in each direction for each possible source–destination pair.

Transport layer   This is the fourth layer of the OSI Reference Model and provides end–end flow control and integrity for end-stations.

Twisted pair   A pair of insulated wires twisted together but not covered by an outer sheath.

UNIX   An open multi-user operating system standard originally developed by Bell Laboratories.

Value added network (VAN)   Network built from common carrier facilities, but with additional computers to provide enhanced services, such as e-mail.

Very small aperture terminal (VSAT)   An earth station with antenna less than six metres in diameter (normally less than two) to provide access to a satellite network.

Virtual private network (VPN)   Provision of the features normally associated with a private network, especially security and management, by means of software functions on a public network.

Virtual terminal (VT)   An OSI standard for interoperability between heterogeneous terminal types.

Virtual tributary   Term used in SDH and SONET for a structure that enables low-speed lines to be carried and switched through SDH/SONET trunks.

XON/XOFF (transmit-on/transmit-off)   A common form of flow control for terminals, where special characters are sent to indicate the command.

Bibliography

Textbooks

The following list of textbooks contains a mixture of background material as well as some performance matter, particularly mathematical theory.

Black U. (1988) *Physical Level Interfaces and Protocols*, Computer Society Press.

Black U. (1993) *Frame Relay Networks and Implementation,* McGraw-Hill.

Chambers W.C., Fisher B., Lovell C., Powers K. and Reed R. (1995) *OS/2 LAN Server Certification Handbook*, New Riders Publishing.

Coulouris G., Dollimore J. and Kindberg T. (1994) *Distributed Systems: Concepts and Design,* 2nd edn, Addison-Wesley.

Dah Ming Chiu and Sudama Ram (1992) *Network Monitoring Explained*, Ellis Horwood.

Davis R. (1993) *Windows Network Programming*, Addison-Wesley.

Davis R. (1994) *Windows NT Network Programming*, Addison-Wesley.

Day M., Budwick L., Harper E., Homer B., Jeoney J., Krochmal K., Lewis R. and Williams D. (1993) *LAN Operating Systems*, New Riders Publishing.

Elbert B.R. and Martyna B. (1994) *Client/Server Computing: Architecture, Applications and Distributed Systems Management*, Artech House.

Halsall F. (1992) *Data Communications, Computer Networks and Open Systems*, 3rd edn, Addison-Wesley.

Harrison P. and Patel N. (1993*) Performance Modelling of Communication Networks and Computer Architectures*, Addison-Wesley.

Kant K. (1992) *Introduction to Computer System Performance*, McGraw-Hill.

Keiser B.E. and Strange E. (1995) *Digital Telephony and Network Integration*, Van Nostrand Reinhold.

Kershenbaum A. (1993) *Telecommunications Network Design Algorithms*, McGraw-Hill.

Kleinrock L. (1975) *Queueing Systems I: Theory*, John Wiley.

Kleinrock L. (1976) *Queueing Systems II: Computer Applications*, John Wiley.

Leduc J-P. (1994*) Digital Moving Pictures – Coding and Transmission in ATM Networks,* Elsevier.

Loukides M. (1992) *System Performance Tuning*, O'Reilly & Associates Inc.

Martin J. and Chapman K.K. (1987) *SNA, IBM's Networking Solution*, Prentice-Hall.

Martin J. and Leben J. (1992) *DECnet Phase V, an OSI Implementation*, Digital Press.

Miller M.A. (1991) *Troubleshooting Internetworks: Tools, Techniques, Protocols.* M&T Publishing.

Naugle M. (1994) *Network Protocol Handbook*, McGraw-Hill.

Nilausen J. (1994) *APPN Networks* John Wiley.

Nowshadi Farshad (1994) *Managing NetWare*, Addison-Wesley.

Onvural R.O. (1994) *Asynchronous Transfer Mode Networks: Performance Issues*, Artech House.

Partridge C. (1994) *Gigabit Networking*, Addison-Wesley.

Scharwtz M. (1987) *Telecommunications Networks Protocols, Modelling and Analysis*, Addison-Wesley.

Sidhu G., Andrews R. and Oppenheimer A. (1990) *Inside AppleTalk,* 2nd edn, Addison-Wesley.

Smith P. (1993) *Frame Relay*, Addison-Wesley.

Spohn D.L. (1993) *Data Network Design*, McGraw-Hill.

Stallings W. (1995) *ISDN and Broadband ISDN with Frame Relay and ATM*, 3rd edn, Prentice-Hall.

Stevens W.R. (1993) *TCP/IP Illustrated*, Addison-Wesley.

Steenstrup M.E. (1995) *Routing in Communications Networks*, Prentice-Hall.

Tanenbaum A.S. (1988) *Computer Networks*, 2nd edn, Prentice-Hall.

Theakston I. (1995) *NetWare LANs Performance and Troubleshooting*, Addison-Wesley.

Thorpe N.M. and Ross D.E. (1992) *X.25 Made Easy*, PHI UK.

Van Norman H.J. (1992) *LAN/WAN Optimization Techniques*, Artech House.

Technical articles

Cohen D. (1981) A Network Voice Protocol NVP-II, University of Southern California.

Cole R. (1981) A Packet Voice Protocol, University of Southern California.

Lam S. (1980) A carrier sense multiple access protocol for local networks, Computer Networks, Vol 4.

Useful RFCs

A lot of useful background information is also contained in the Requests For Comments (RFCs) of the Internet community.
Some of the more interesting ones are listed below with their main topic.

869	Nagle Algorithm
1001, 2	NetBIOS in TCP and UDP
1004	Type of Service Queuing Algorithm
1055	SLIP
1057	SUN Remote Procedure Call
1072	TCP for Long Delays
1073	Telnet Windows
1075	DVMRP
1094	NFS
1245	OSPF performance issues
1246	Early OSPF experience
1247	OSPF
1323	TCP Options
1356	Encapsulation in X.25 and ISDN
1372	Telnet Remote Flow Control
1434	Data Link Switching (DLSw) – preliminary
1477	IDRP
1478	IDRP Architecture
1479	IDRP Specification
1483	Bridging LAN protocols over ATM
1490	Encapsulation in Frame Relay
1504	AURP
1531	DHCP
1541	OSPF
1553	Compressed IPX Headers
1577	IP over ATM
1583	OSPF
1584	MOSPF
1604	Frame Relay Service MIB
1613	Cisco X.25 over TCP (XOT)
1618, 9	PPP over ISDN and SDH
1634	IPXWAN
1638	Bridging PPP (BCP)
1654	BGP-4
1661	PPP
1663	Reliable PPP
1700	Assigned Numbers (well-known ports, etc.)
1717	MP

1723	RIP-2
1752	IPng
1757	RMON
1793	OSPF Demand Circuits
1795	DLSw
1819	InternetStreams Protocol ST-2+

RFCs are widely available on the Internet. A list of up-to-date sites can be obtained by automatic e-mail from

RFCInfo@indiana.edu

with message text:

getting rfcs

help:ways_to_get_rfcs

ITU-T and IEEE standard recommendations can be obtained from Omnicom in the UK, as well as from the respective issuing organizations. Lists of ITU-T recommendations are listed on the ITU's web site (see below) together with ordering instructions.

Tariffing data for the main industrial countries is available in *Tariffica* from Omnicom in the UK. This consists of an annual with about 500 pages together with bimonthly updates of about 200 pages. In addition, there is a PC-based Pricer module to calculate the actual tariffs for specific locations.

DataPro from McGraw-Hill also contains quite a large amount of tariffing information, particularly for the USA.

World Wide Web sites

Much useful up-to-the-minute information applicable to WAN performance can be obtained by searches on the web, with access via the command;

http://www.sitename

and a selection of useful sitenames are listed below. More generally, most American communications companies have sitename of the form: company name.com.

Sitename	Information
atmforum.com	ATM Forum documents
att.com	AT&T Services
bt.co.uk	British Telecom services
itu.ch	Lists of ITU-T standards
novell.com	NetWare features (USA)

novell.de   NetWare Fault Reports (Europe)
digital.com   DECnet features
cup.hp.com/netperf   HP's Netperf benchmark software
mci.com   MCI services
sprint.com   Sprint Services
uswest.com   US West Services
wiltel.com   LDDS-Wiltel Services

Frame Relay Forum documents can be obtained via

> http://frame-relay.indiana.edu/frame relay

News groups

The following newsgroups on Usenet provide useful sources of information relevant to network performance.

comp.compression   MPEG, JPEG, Lempel-Ziv
comp.dcom.cell-relay   ATM
comp.dcom.frame-relay   Frame Relay
comp.dcom.isdn   ISDN and Cable Modems
comp.dcom.modems   Modems

Index

100 Base 4T, 121
100 Base TX, 121
100 Base VG, 120
3270, 78
5250, 78
802.9A Iso-Ethernet, 224
95th percentile, 289

A

A-bit, 106, 109
AAL, 211
AAL1, 199, 212
AAL2, 212
AAL3/4, 212
AAL5, 199, 212, 216, 219, 296
ACF/VTAM, 246
ACK, 94
acknowledgement, 81
ADD, 252
Add Name Query, 176
Addressing schemes, 143
ADPCM, 44
ADSL, 288
ADSP, 116
advertisements, 85
AEP, 115
AFP, 190
All Routes Broadcast, 129, 132
AMPS, 262
analog lines, 4, 20
APPC, 82, 244
APPC/PC, 183
Apple Transaction Protocol, 190
Appleshare, 190
AppleTalk, 114, 157, 185, 219, 244
AppleTalk timers, 158
Application Programming Interface, 220
APPN, 160

ARQ, 29, 30
arrival rate, 293
AS/400, 82
ASP, 115, 116
asynchronous RPC without reply, 173
asynchronous RPC with reply, 173
AT&T, 266
ATM, 209, 228, 249, 271
ATM cells, 210
ATP, 115
AURP, 168
Automatic Network Routing, 160
availability, 17, 269, 273
avalanche decay, 107

B

B-channel, 51
B node, 178
Bandwidth Balancing, 207
bandwidth managers, 47
bandwidth on demand, 193, 235
bandwidth overhead, 63, 219
bandwidth reservation, 132, 165
baselining, 240
BECN, 106, 108, 217
Bell standards, 20
Bellman-Ford algorithm, 139
bit error rate, 29, 36, 68, 73, 109, 218, 230,
    278, 296
BERT, 250
BGP-3, 142
BGP-4, 142
bit stuffing, 68
block acknowledgements, 188
block size, 36
blocking, 80
Bonding, 51
Border Intermediate System, 155